Gale Storm

Gale Storm
A Biography and Career Record

DAVID C. TUCKER

McFarland & Company, Inc., Publishers
Jefferson, North Carolina

ALSO BY DAVID C. TUCKER
AND FROM MCFARLAND

Martha Raye: Film and Television Clown (2016)

*Joan Davis: America's Queen of Film, Radio
and Television Comedy* (2014)

*Eve Arden: A Chronicle of All Film, Television,
Radio and Stage Performances* (2012)

*Lost Laughs of '50s and '60s Television:
Thirty Sitcoms That Faded Off Screen* (2010)

Shirley Booth: A Biography and Career Record (2008)

*The Women Who Made Television Funny:
Ten Stars of 1950s Sitcoms* (2007)

Frontispiece: Gale Storm in the Universal thriller *Abandoned* (1949).

**ISBN (print) 978-1-4766-7177-2
ISBN (ebook) 978-1-4766-3246-9**

LIBRARY OF CONGRESS CATALOGUING DATA ARE AVAILABLE

BRITISH LIBRARY CATALOGUING DATA ARE AVAILABLE

© 2018 David C. Tucker. All rights reserved

*No part of this book may be reproduced or transmitted in any form
or by any means, electronic or mechanical, including photocopying
or recording, or by any information storage and retrieval system,
without permission in writing from the publisher.*

Front cover image of publicity photograph of Universal-International
contract player Gale Storm, 1950 (author's collection)

Manufactured in the United States of America

*McFarland & Company, Inc., Publishers
Box 611, Jefferson, North Carolina 28640*
www.mcfarlandpub.com

To my nephews, Timothy and Daniel Sassone ...
and the newest member of our family,
Kim Haynes Sassone.

Table of Contents

Acknowledgments ix
Preface 1

I. Biography 5
II. The Films 37
III. Television 114
IV. Radio 211
V. Recordings 226

Appendix A: Soundies and Telescriptions 233
Appendix B: Gale Storm in Comics 236
Appendix C: The Films of Lee Bonnell 238
Chapter Notes 245
Bibliography 249
Index 251

Acknowledgments

Gale Storm passed away in 2009, but her memory still inspires loyalty that was evident to me as people stepped up to help with various aspects of this book.

I appreciate those who granted me interviews, among them Gale's daughter Susanna Harrigan, grandchildren Brendan and Erin Harrigan, and acting colleagues David Frankham and Ken Prescott. Gale's niece, Sharon Divine, went above and beyond, sharing memories passed down through her mother (Gale's sister), as well as a lovely family portrait. Thanks to the Rev. Robert Perry, music minister of the church Gale attended for more than 25 years, I was able to see a DVD of the tribute program her fellow church members gave her in 2005, as well as one of the Christmas cantatas she so enjoyed narrating. Linda Wood, daughter of Gale's late record producer Randy Wood, graciously shared her memories, as did Debora Masterson, daughter of Gale's second husband Paul Masterson.

Ron Baker, co-founder of Gale's fan club, talked at length with me about his longtime friendship with Gale. Only days after we met, he sent me copies of the last two Gale Storm films that had been eluding me, as well as some rare memorabilia. Drawing on his own background as a musician, he has spent considerable time over the years documenting Gale's singing career, and readily shared his knowledge. Jeremy Brunner furnished me with three episodes of *My Little Margie* I could find nowhere else, allowing me to write from the perspective of having viewed the entire series. Researcher Caroline Cubé afforded me access to scripts of episodes of *The Gale Storm Show: Oh! Susanna* from the Special Collections division of UCLA's Charles E. Young Research Library, while Todd Everett shared his notes from his 1990s interview with Gale. Archivist and author Cary O'Dell provided a DVD of Gale's 1993 appearance at the Museum of Broadcast Communications in Chicago. G.D. Hamann's clippings from defunct Los Angeles newspapers of the 1940s were helpful in tracing Gale's film career, as were microfilmed pressbooks from Monogram Pictures, held by the Wisconsin Historical Society.

James Robert Parish, who has long been a supportive friend and mentor, drew on his own vast film collection, furnishing copies of multiple movies that I needed to see to research this book. Lynn Kear is always a fount of wisdom, as well as a terrific friend. Others who have offered encouragement and support in ways both big and small include Markell Dorsey, Stacey Woodall Purdy, Betsy Reedy and Susan Kimmel Wright, just to name a few.

And, as always, I'm grateful for the help and support of the most important people in my life, Ken McCullers and Louise Tucker.

Preface

In the course of more than 40 years as an entertainer, Gale Storm (1922–2009) received little critical attention, and even fewer awards. But she didn't work for critics or film historians; she worked for the audience. She made films, television shows and records that gave people pleasure, and helped them put aside their own worries.

Her innate likability, along with a contagious sense of fun, came across clearly in her performances. In 1957, not long after her sitcom *The Gale Storm Show: Oh! Susanna* had been renewed for a second season, she told a *TV Guide* interviewer, "My theory about why some shows succeed and others don't is that on TV, in contrast to the movies, something about the inside of a person comes over on that little screen. People like you or don't like you not so much by what lines you say or what movements you make but by what you *are*."[1] The reaction she received from audiences lasted throughout her life, as she described in 1993: "They feel they're my friend, and it's just a wonderful relationship. They really feel like you're their friend, because you come into their living room and you're just a part of their family."[2]

Audiences followed her through a successful film career, starring roles in two TV sitcoms, and stage work in the 1960s and 1970s. In time, she was recognized with three stars on the Hollywood Walk of Fame, acknowledging her achievements in television, music and radio. Still, she was often underestimated by critics and industry professionals. After her first six months in Hollywood, as a contract player at RKO, her option was dropped, and she was told she had no future in the motion picture business. Some 30 films later, critics roundly disparaged her TV sitcom *My Little Margie*, predicting a quick and deserved demise. It ran for four seasons. Doom was also predicted, with equal inaccuracy, for her second series *The Gale Storm Show: Oh! Susanna*, which lasted four years.

I first researched and wrote about Gale Storm more than ten years ago, as part of a book about pioneering female sitcom stars of the 1950s. At the time I began working on *The Women Who Made Television Funny* (McFarland, 2007), I had relatively little familiarity with Gale Storm's work, though it quickly became obvious that she merited inclusion in the book. Unlike actresses Lucille Ball and Gracie Allen, whose early television shows I had known and loved for years, I only vaguely remembered long-ago reruns of Gale's show *My Little Margie*. From its opening showing Margie and her father in old-fashioned picture frames, I somehow concluded back then that it was a stuffy show. Going back to it decades later, I soon realized nothing could be further from the truth.

I wrote a letter to Miss Storm, requesting an interview. She responded promptly, and we had two lengthy telephone conversations in January 2006. At the time, my focus was on her 1950s TV series, so they were the main topic of conversation. Even in her mid-eighties, not in the best of health, her hearing diminished, she was charming, and often spontaneously funny. Our first conversation was cut short because she was expecting the arrival of a home health aide; with a girlish giggle that was pure Margie Albright, she added, "But I won't tell you exactly what she's coming here to do."

She plainly enjoyed reminiscing about her Hollywood days. After our first conversation, I sent her a few clippings that I had gathered. One was a *Variety* item saying that, during the shooting of a prizefighting sequence on *My Little Margie*, the assistant director had accidentally struck her, knocking her out cold. She confessed in 2006 that she had no recollection of this whatsoever, although she could vividly remember other mishaps. I also sent her an article quoting Hal Roach, Jr., on why he had offered her the role of Margie Albright. She was delighted to get it, saying she had always wondered why she was chosen.

Although Gale Storm enjoyed film stardom in the 1940s and early 1950s, it was not the type of fame that found her co-starring with Clark Gable or being directed by William Wyler. After a brief stint under contract at RKO, the result of winning a radio talent contest, Gale began freelance movie acting in 1941. From 1942 to 1949, she was a contract player at Monogram, the Poverty Row studio that routinely shot low-budget B films in six days. To fully appreciate much of her movie career calls for the ability to enjoy films made hastily on Hollywood's Poverty Row—often high on entertainment value, if not aesthetic triumphs. In researching this book, I found that I had that capacity, their shortcomings tempered for me by their amiable charm. From there, she went on to briefer stays at Universal and at Columbia, where she starred in three pictures recognized today as vintage *film noir*. Surprisingly, given her later sitcom stardom, she did relatively little comedy in movies, though *G.I. Honeymoon* (1945) was certainly a harbinger of things to come.

In the course of researching and writing seven books, I have done my best to be truthful (which is not to say harsh) about the actors they spotlighted. Occasionally that has involved relating stories that were not entirely flattering to the people involved, and a biographer can easily be dismayed by what he learns about a star he has admired. I am happy to say that spending more than a year, and hundreds of hours, researching Gale Storm resulted in little, if any, disillusionment. If that's a spoiler, then so be it. Perhaps the most controversial aspect of her life was her descent into alcoholism in the 1970s, which she described frankly in her 1981 memoir *I Ain't Down Yet*. Even that she turned into a positive, using her celebrity as an opportunity to bring other women out of secrecy and shame, and encourage them to seek help for their addiction.

This book aims to supplement her own autobiography with a more detailed look at her career, as well as a portrait of her later years. It opens with a biography of Gale, beginning with her birth in a small Texas town as Josephine Cottle and tracing a career as an actress and singer that ultimately lasted nearly 50 years. Research for this section draws on interviews with colleagues and family members, as well as genealogical records, newspaper interviews and coverage in trade publications.

An annotated filmography follows, examining in detail her feature films, with synopses, excerpts from reviews and critical commentary. The "Television" section contains production histories and episode guides for Gale's hit sitcoms *My Little Margie* (1952–55) and *The Gale Storm Show: Oh! Susanna* (1956–60). Detailed descriptions of the episodes are based, whenever possible, on my viewings. Unfortunately, nearly half of the *Oh! Susanna* episodes are not readily available. Having never had an official, complete DVD release, the show exists today mostly on discs shared by collectors, which typically contain about 80 of the series' 143 segments.

Where a first-hand viewing was not feasible, I have filled in details to the extent possible. Writer-producer Lou Derman oversaw the show's fourth and final season, and in his papers at UCLA were scripts from some 16 episodes I had been unable to view. UCLA holds a few episodes on videotape, with additional ones on 16mm film that I hope will be fully preserved when funds permit. Beyond that, I drew on newspaper and *TV Guide* listings from that era, as well as consulting online sources such as IMDb and the Classic TV Archive.

Also covered in this section are Gale's TV guest appearances and her brief stint as hostess of *The NBC Comedy Hour* (1956). Details are provided about three potential Gale Storm series that never came to fruition, including her 1963 Desilu sitcom pilot *The Gale Storm Show: A-OK, O'Shea* and her 1970s effort to bring about a sequel to *My Little Margie*.

Subsequent sections cover her work in radio, notably a series of *My Little Margie* episodes that are largely distinct from the TV series, and her work as a pop singer in the 1950s. She recorded for only about two years in the mid–1950s, yet secured a place as a charting performer, earning a gold record for her recording of "I Hear You Knockin.'"

The book's appendices provide information about Gale's appearances in short musical films of the 1940s and 1950s (Soundies and Telescriptions), as well as the use of her image in comic books. I have included a filmography for her first husband Lee Bonnell, who was also an RKO contract player in the 1940s, and appeared in around 25 films, both for that studio and afterwards as a freelancer.

I

BIOGRAPHY

> "If I have one talent, it's that I am always able to be happy doing what I'm doing."—*Gale Storm in 1957*[1]

On the evening of May 25, 2005, a sleek black limousine pulled slowly into the driveway of the South Shores Church, in the coastal town of Dana Point, California. As a crowd of churchgoers looked on, cheering, a small elderly woman emerged from the back seat. Dressed to the nines, Mrs. Paul Masterson, leaning on the arm of her son Phil, walked carefully down a makeshift red carpet, as flashbulbs popped and fans applauded.

The still-beautiful, slightly frail Mrs. Masterson had recently celebrated her 83rd birthday. Until the age of 17, she had been known as Josephine Cottle (her birth name). For much of her adult life, she had been Mrs. Lee Bonnell, mother to four children. She was widowed twice. But the members of the church she had attended for more than 20 years were honoring her on this day with a tribute to her life as the actress and singer Gale Storm.

It had been 50 years since host Ralph Edwards hosted a similar tribute to Gale on his television show *This Is Your Life*. Like that long-ago occasion, this event was carefully planned as a surprise. Gale had just been out to dinner with her son and daughter-in-law, and thought they were on their way to a tribute program in his honor. Instead, she found herself beaming as a bouquet of flowers was pressed into her arms, and friends called out greetings. She made her way slowly down the church's center aisle, all eyes on her. "I can't believe this!" she exclaimed, smiling widely. Helped into a seat onstage at the front of the large sanctuary, she was teary, saying, "I'm absolutely without words."

After a few introductory remarks, the lights in the church dimmed and a series of images flickered across a large projection screen. Sixty-five years dropped away, and the audience saw a young actress, newly arrived in Hollywood, playing a teenage shop assistant in *Tom Brown's School Days* (1940). The clips continued, mostly in black-and-white, as Gale Storm rode alongside cowboy star Roy Rogers (*Red River Valley*), sang the novelty song "Tahiti Sweetie" (*Lure of the Islands*) and performed in a Gay '90s nightclub (*Sunbonnet Sue*). The films, and the years, rolled by quickly: *It Happened on 5th Avenue*, Westerns with Rod Cameron and Audie Murphy. Then it was time to remember the television star: plotting and scheming against bewildered dad Vern Albright in *My Little Margie*, singing "Heat Wave" on *The Ed Sullivan Show*, and enjoying the sights and sounds of Capri (actually a soundstage facsimile) on *The Gale Storm Show: Oh! Susanna*. On stage after the video presentation, singers performed two of the songs which had been charting hits for Gale in the 1950s, "I Hear You Knockin'" and "Dark Moon."

A member of the South Shores Church for more than 20 years, Gale was well-known to the congregation. Many had attended the memorial service in 1986 for her first husband Lee, and/or her 1988 wedding to her second husband at the church. She recalled that it was Lee who had found the church, saying that throughout their married life it had been his job to scout churches whenever they moved. She had sung in the church choir for some years, and occasionally performed solos. In later years, she was prominently featured every year in the church's Christmas cantata, where she assumed the role of narrator, resplendent in a glittering red gown.

Now, for those who had known her only after her retirement from a long and successful career as an entertainer, they had the opportunity to see how a teenage girl of modest circumstances from Houston, Texas, ended up becoming a star.

⌘

The name was a gift, bestowed upon the first prize winner in a talent contest on a 1930s radio show. And so, on December 31, 1939, Josephine Owaissa Cottle, 17 years old and not yet a high school graduate, was renamed Gale Storm, the first step in a career that would eventually find her a successful film actress, star of two popular TV sitcoms and a charting pop singer.

Josephine was born in Bloomington, Texas, on Wednesday, April 5, 1922, at around 11 a.m. She was the fifth child of Walter William Cottle (1886–1923) and his wife Minnie Lee Greenhaw Cottle (1887–1978), and was named after her paternal grandmother, who had died in 1902. The Cottles were an old Texas family, having been among the earliest non–Native American settlers in the region. According to one account, Walter's grandparents, "Stephen Cottle and Sarah Turner Cottle, came to Texas from Troy, Missouri in 1825, to take original Spanish Landgrants," helping to settle a community in Bastrop County that would be known as Cottletown.[2] Jo's great-great-uncle, W.E. Cottle, was a hero at the Alamo. Minnie was the daughter of Albert Alton Greenhaw (1858–1908) and his first wife, Parlee Huff Greenhaw (1861–1899). Mr. Greenhaw was a farmer in the area near Henderson, Texas.

Jo's unusual middle name, Owaissa, was given to her by her sister. "Owaissa means bluebird in Indian," she later explained. "They let my sister name me and she was going through an Indian period then."[3] Sister Lois may have encountered the name in school; Henry Wadsworth Longfellow's epic poem "The Song of Hiawatha" features a bluebird, the Owaissa, who says, "Teach me tones as wild and wayward / Teach me songs as full of frenzy!"

Jo's father was described on his World War

Walter Cottle, father of the future Gale Storm, was, according to his wife Minnie, "a looker" (courtesy Sharon Divine).

I draft registration card as a man of short height and slender build, with brown hair and eyes. His widow later told her granddaughter Sharon that Walter had been "a looker." Jo resembled both her parents but, as Sharon later said, "That beautiful smile came from her daddy."[4]

At the time of his oldest son's birth in 1912, Walter Cottle was employed as a sheet metal worker at McDade Pottery. Since its establishment in 1893, McDade Pottery had grown to be one of the town's most successful businesses, as well as its largest employer. According to historian David Wharton, McDade Pottery shipped "countless flower pots, charcoal-burning clay furnaces ... and other ceramic goods to markets throughout Texas and surrounding states."[5] Cottle worked there at least as early as 1910, in his early 20s, when the U.S. Census reported that he was a laborer. Cottle was still there in 1917, when he applied for a deferment from war service, being the sole support of his wife and children.

Jo's mother was in her mid-thirties when her fifth and final child arrived. Since their marriage in 1908, Walter and Minnie had already welcomed daughters Lois Miriam (1909) and Minnie Marjorie (1914), as well as sons Wilbur Walter (1912) and Joel Braxton (1917). Daughter Minnie Marjorie would be known in the family as Margie, and, according to her daughter Sharon, later received an autographed photo from Gale, inscribed, "To the *real* My Little Margie!"

Josephine, known in the family as "Baby Jo," spent most of her childhood and young adult life in Houston, after brief periods spent living in Bloomington and McDade. Gale wrote in her memoir that her father was a potter, reflecting his years of employment at McDade Pottery. However, by the time of the 1920 census, he was reported working as a bookkeeper for a lumberyard. When Jo arrived on the scene in 1922, Walter was listed on her birth certificate as manager of that lumberyard.

Her father died at age 36 on September 15, 1923, when she was less than two years old. According to his death certificate, he had been suffering from cancer of the liver and pancreas. An article in the *Cameron Herald* (September 20, 1923) noted that city resident S.A. Cottle, a local hotel proprietor and Walter's younger brother, had attended the funeral. Walter, the article stated, "had been in bad health for some time and had traveled extensively in search of health." The *Herald* reported that Walter had died at the Seaton [sic] Infirmary at Austin, Texas.[6] The Seton Infirmary, which opened its doors in 1902, was operated by the Daughters of Charity of Saint Vincent de Paul and, according to a pamphlet issued at the time of its opening, "belongs to suffering humanity in general, irrespective of creed, color, nationality, financial standing or any other limitation."[7] Jo's father was survived for many years by her grandfather, William Zebulon Cottle, who died in 1944 at the age of 92. He was the only grandparent she could remember from her childhood.

The death of Jo's father left the family hard-pressed for money. Mrs. Cottle, after trying to support her family with a millinery shop in McDade that went under, worked long hours as a seamstress to bring in much-needed money. Older siblings Walter and Lois eventually dropped out of school to go to work, while, as Jo's niece recalled, "My mama, Margie, quit school to take care of the younger two (Braxton and Baby Jo) so that Nana could sew and support the family." Jo entered public school at Henry Wadsworth Longfellow Elementary, and then transferred to Albert Sydney Johnson Junior High.

With money short, Mrs. Cottle and her children moved frequently, renting modest homes and trying to stay one step ahead of the rent. At the time of the 1930 census, Jo

A Cottle family portrait: Jo, also known as Gale, is at top. Others are (clockwise) sister Margie, sister Lois, and their mother Minnie (courtesy Sharon Divine).

and her mother were living on Caroline Street in Houston. Mrs. Cottle was listed as unemployed, probably meaning only that she had no regular employer for her work as a seamstress. Jo's older sister Lois was said to be working as a stenographer, while her brother Wilbur was a bookkeeper.

While Jo was still young, her widowed mother remarried, becoming Mrs. Lewis Z. Skadden. The adult Gale Storm remembered this happening when she was in her early teens, but according to Texas public records Minnie became Mrs. Skadden on October 2, 1931, when Jo was nine. Skadden, who was six years' Minnie's senior, was a widower, his first wife Alma having died in January 1930. They were married at St. John's Methodist Church, where the Cottles were members for many years.

As an adult, Gale would confess that she didn't even remember her stepfather's full name, and her relationship with him and her new stepsister Helen (a year older than she) was rocky. She felt that her new stepfather favored his own child over her, and that Helen was envious of Jo's popularity in school. The marriage was not an entirely happy one, and Minnie would separate from her second husband within a few years. Skadden died in 1962. According to Gale's niece Sharon, Minnie had little to say in later years about her second husband: "When he was spoken of, he was Mr. Skadden…" On the other hand, Minnie, according to her granddaughter, kept in her kitchen for most of her adult life a pot Walter had made for her decades earlier.

As a child, Jo's natural talent for entertaining showed itself. "From the time I was a little kid," she later wrote, "when we put together neighborhood shows, I sang and danced. I had no training. We couldn't afford any kind of lessons. But I went on—and wished."[8] At San Jacinto High School, yearbooks from the late 1930s show that Jo Cottle was a member of the Girls' Booster Club, whose aim was "to build up a loyal, enthusiastic and cheerful student body who will develop into citizens who do things worthwhile." Representing her school in the Interscholastic League, Jo won a prize for an original one-act play she wrote. She also impressed teachers and fellow students when she took roles in school plays. Yet she had no sense that someone like herself could aspire to a career as a professional performer.

Though the Great Depression was in full force during much of Jo's adolescence, she enjoyed her teenage years. Years later, Jo's niece Sharon recalled a family memory passed down by her father, C.C. Divine: "Daddy was a sergeant with the Houston Police Department, and he was teaching a class. A teenage Gale Storm came ditty-bopping into the classroom wanting to get his car keys and go joyriding with some friends. She didn't bring his car back on time, and I remember Jo and Daddy laughing about that."

In the summer of 1939, as Jo was awaiting her senior year in school, producer Jesse L. Lasky was in Texas holding auditions for his *Gateway to Hollywood* radio program, a forum aimed at discovering new talent. As Lasky explained it, contests were held in various cities to identify newcomers who would appear on the program. According to Lasky, "The ambitious young performers would be 'screen-tested' on the network, a boy-girl team *starred* each week in specially written radio playlets, with people like Claudette Colbert, Joan Crawford, Edward G. Robinson and Cary Grant supporting them in secondary roles."[9] The contestants brought out to Hollywood would undergo coaching before being heard on the air, and be judged by industry professionals.

Since its January 1939 debut, *Gateway to Hollywood* had crowned one set of winners in April (including Ralph Bowman, who went on a film career as John Archer), and another in July. It had also helped young Linda Darnell win a studio contract at 20th Century–Fox, even though she had been eliminated in the final competition. In the program's final broadcast, two newcomers would be chosen to adopt the already-publicized stage names "Gale Storm" and "Terry Belmont," chosen by Lasky, with a guarantee of being assigned film roles.

It was Jo Cottle's teachers at San Jacinto High School who recognized her talent and encouraged her to try out for the RKO competition. "They couldn't possibly know that they completely changed my life," she would say years later of Miss Collier and Miss Oatman, who taught her English and Latin.[10] Only 17 years old, she was one of the youngest entrants. (In fact, early announcements of the contest had said that 18 years of age was the minimum for female contestants.) At every step of the contest, Jo fully expected to be eliminated, feeling certain that she could sense the judges hesitating every time they passed over her. Had she not won the contest, as she later said, she almost certainly would not have further pursued a show business career.

At the conclusion of the scheduled events across Texas, newspapers reported that "Miss Josephine Cottle of Houston" was now a finalist. "In his search for screen talent, Jesse Lasky picked a boy and girl each from San Antonio, Houston and Dallas and sent the six to Hollywood where Sunday all were eliminated except Miss Cottle and W.C. (Buster) Bryan, announcer on KTSA in San Antonio."[11]

Somewhat to Josephine's surprise, she continued to advance toward the finals. "I never thought I had a chance," she said years later. "Finally I won out in Houston, and was told I would be brought to Hollywood for the finals. My classmates kept asking when. I didn't know. I nearly died of indigestion, I was so nervous."[12] The only contestant to be chaperoned by her mother, Josephine made the trip west to Hollywood in October 1939. While participating in these weekly CBS broadcasts, she was staying at a women-only hotel. Trying to shield her daughter from possible disappointment, Mrs. Cottle repeatedly told Jo as they traveled, "Remember, this is just a nice trip we're taking, nothing else."[13]

But the contest took on an added significance for Jo in an early rehearsal, when she met a handsome, personable male contestant from Indiana, Lee Bonnell. On short acquaintance, Jo impulsively told her mother this was the man she was going to marry. Some years later, she remembered, "I fell in love with Lee ... instantly (and this sounds silly), before I even said, 'How do you do' to him. And I was not that kind of foolish, romantic girl."[14]

Everett Leroy Bonnell, born November 24, 1918, in Royal Center, Indiana, had entered the previous year's *Gateway to Hollywood* contest, but was eliminated early in the proceedings. Lee, tall, lanky and a few years older than Jo, was friendly, but initially looked upon her as something of a little sister, as she was not even yet of legal age. Her previous dating life confined to high school boys, Jo nonetheless set her sights firmly on Lee. In school, she had developed a foolproof technique for attracting a boy's attention without seeming forward: She would allow herself to be caught glancing at him in a friendly way from time to time, then at a certain point, abruptly stop doing so, without acting angry or perturbed. Almost without exception, the young man would then be intrigued enough to seek her out. She found that it worked just as well on Lee as it had on her previous beaux. Their relationship blossomed into a romance, but for a time her mother declared her too young to consider marrying.

On New Year's Eve, 1939, Josephine Cottle and Lee Bonnell—described in newspaper accounts as "a brown-tressed Texas high school senior and ... a tall, black-haired University of Indiana sophomore"—were pronounced winners of the contest, after playing a young married couple in a romantic skit on the broadcast.[15] They were presented with union cards for the Screen Actors Guild and contracts with RKO-Radio Pictures, co-sponsor of the program.

For the next five decades, Josephine Cottle would be known to her public as Gale Storm. While she adopted the name professionally, it never became her legal name, and Lee would continue to call her Jo in private for the rest of their lives, according to daughter Susanna.

RKO had made prior arrangements for the female winner to play a small role in the film *Tom Brown's School Days*, adapted from the classic novel about life in a British boarding school. Jo, now rechristened Gale, reported for work only days after being chosen

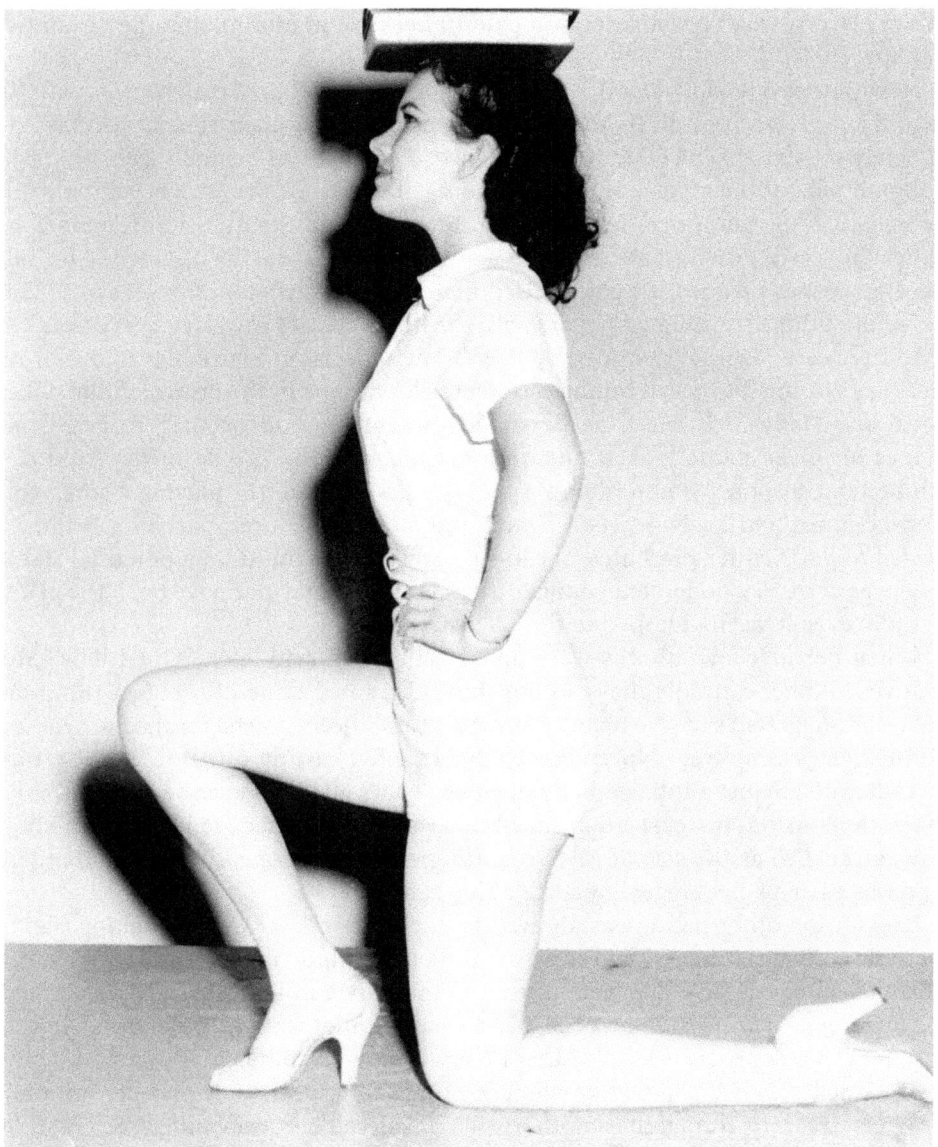

RKO promotes new contract player Gale Storm with a posture lesson.

the contest winner. In a later interview, Gale said that producers Gene Towne and Graham Baker welcomed her to the set with a first day full of mild hazing. As told by interviewer Harry Niemeyer, "Gale's first close-up was a stream of water from the lens of a phony camera. Arc lights suddenly went out and left the stage in total darkness when she had a line to speak."[16] A chair that collapsed underneath her left her mad and frustrated enough to give up the whole idea of being a movie actress, but she determined to be a good sport, and soon won the favor of her jokester colleagues.

Her small role as Effie was not demanding, and she acquitted herself capably. While working at RKO, she was enrolled in the studio school, so that she could finish her interrupted high school education. She also underwent the vocational training given to new contract players, with special attention paid in her case to minimizing the Texan twang of her speech.

Newly arrived in Hollywood, drawn together by their shared experiences with RKO, Gale and Lee grew closer. Both, for different reasons, found their time at RKO less than completely satisfying. The *Gateway to Hollywood* contest had been a successful promotional gimmick for the studio, and the promises of short-term contracts for the winners were upheld. However, once the publicity value wore off, the question remained as to whether these two lucky amateurs could show themselves worthy of keeping on salary. Their *Gateway to Hollywood* wins entitled them to "contracts for 20 weeks at $125.00 a week, with options running to 7 years with greater increases in salary every year."[17]

In Lee's case, he was frustrated by RKO's initial decision to use him in minor roles, sometimes too small to merit billing onscreen. He was lost in the crowd of films like the musical *Too Many Girls*. He soon persuaded executives to drop the "Terry Belmont" name, as his given name looked fine on a marquee, but as Lee Bonnell he didn't fare much better. Gale, on the other hand, spent her first six months playing a small role in a prestige film (*Tom Brown's School Days*) and a larger featured part in a B film, *One Crowded Night*. Neither presented her in such a way as to build up a potential star, and the teenage actress, who looked younger than her years, may not have been the glamour girl studio executives had hoped to find.

When her first few months were up, as Gale often said later, "Out I flew." Studio executives told her candidly they did not think she was destined for bigger things as an actress, and suggested she give up her Hollywood ambitions. As she recalled to syndicated columnist Hal Humphrey (November 28, 1954), RKO casting director Ben Piazza told her, "Gale, you are just a little comedy ingénue. That's all you'll ever be. Take my advice, go back to Houston, or marry that nice boy." More than a decade later, when she was firmly entrenched as the star of *My Little Margie,* Piazza phoned her to say that letting her go was perhaps the biggest mistake of his career.

Lee, on the other hand, was allowed to stick around. RKO was making plenty of films with a wartime theme, and it wasn't difficult to find small speaking roles for the handsome young actor. When not enlisted in the movie military (*Men Against the Sky, The Navy Comes Through*), he was cast as a succession of waiters, hotel desk clerks and reporters. But real progress as a leading man was slow to come.

On January 2, 1941, having known each other for a year, Gale and Lee announced their plans to marry, though her mother still considered her too young. Lee's future was looking especially promising that spring, when RKO gave him a year's extension on his contract and a pay raise, and announced that he would be placed in bigger roles. He was cast in *Look Who's Laughing,* in a sizable role as leading man to Lucille Ball. That summer, he spent two weeks in Denver, where RKO executives had arranged for him to get experience on stage playing a leading role in a play, James Thurber and Elliott Nugent's *The Male Animal.*

Released by RKO, Gale wasn't idle long. Whatever name value she had from that studio, combined with her beauty and work ethic, won her several film roles in 1941. Her fresh-faced beauty was well-suited to playing a heroic cowboy's best girl, as she did for Roy Rogers, and producers just assumed (wrongly, in her case) that a girl from Texas was right at home atop a horse. Just as importantly, she demonstrated in a short time that she could work at the rapid pace that Poverty Row pictures demanded, with few retakes allowed. In her first year as a freelancer, she racked up credits at Monogram, PRC and Republic, among other studios, sometimes making only a few hundred dollars for a week's work. *Variety* reported in May that she was being tested for a role in MGM's next Andy Hardy film, but she wasn't cast. She also found work performing in Soundies, the short musical films that played in specially designed video jukeboxes. On May 23, 1941, syndicated columnist Jimmie Fidler claimed that Gale "is getting more fan mail than many bigtime stars."

In September, Gale was on the cover of *Look* magazine, along with her childhood friend Betty Ann Anderson. The two young ladies were featured in a multi-page photo spread documenting a recent trip to Alaska, with Gale quoted as saying, "As kids in Houston we used to daydream about someday seeing the world together.... Neither of us had ever been up in an airplane before or stayed overnight in a big hotel."[18] *Look* photographer Earl Thiesen captured Gale and her chum as they toured Alaska and parts of Canada, meeting Mounties, fur traders and Blackfoot Indians.

Expecting he would be called up for military service, Lee and his fiancée went forward with plans to be married that fall. Three days after taking out a license, they were married in Houston on September 28, 1941, at St. John's Methodist Church, pastor Dr. B.O. Powers officiating. Overcome with emotion, she said, "I walked down the aisle with my nose running, tears streaming down my face, and Kleenex clutched under my bouquet. The minister was so panicked at the sight of my face that he made it the fastest ceremony on record."[19] After the ceremony, they took a honeymoon that included a trip to South Bend, Indiana, where Gale met her new in-laws for the first time.

Not long after the wedding, Lee underwent his physical, in preparation for his anticipated enlistment in the Army. However, the results showed that Lee's eyesight was too poor to make him useful as a soldier, and for the moment he was turned away. But after the attack on Pearl Harbor on December 7, 1941, Lee felt even more compelled to serve his country, and he soon enlisted in the Coast Guard. He would be stationed close to home, but his movie career was on hiatus for nearly four years.

Impulsive as Gale's initial attraction to Lee may have seemed, time proved that they in fact were a quite compatible couple. Both were serious about their Christian beliefs, and made time for participating in church services and activities. Both wanted children, and valued family life. To her family, Gale was still "Baby Jo," and her mother and siblings continued to be protective of her. Said Gale's niece Sharon, "Lee realized if he wanted the marriage to work, he needed to keep Nana in Houston and Jo in California." The young couple bought her mother a three-bedroom brick house, with a screened-in porch, on what was then the outskirts of Houston. Sharon added, "The neighborhood developer took a liking to Aunt Jo and one of the streets in the subdivision is named Gale." Later, Gale's sister Margie and *her* husband, a policeman, bought a house in the same community, where they raised their daughter Sharon. Sharon grew up with her grandmother (Gale's mother) nearby, and recalled her as "prim and proper," placing importance on social niceties: "how to set a table, proper table manners..."

Having settled her mother into a well-deserved retirement after years of struggle, Gale was free to concentrate on her burgeoning film career. Among the Poverty Row studios where she had happily toiled was Monogram. Studio executives decided it would be useful to have a young ingénue under contract, as cameras were grinding on low-budget films practically every day.

Producer Lindsley Parsons, who had already cast Gale in *Let's Go Collegiate*, *Freckles Comes Home* and *Lure of the Islands*, brought her in for an interview, and she was offered

Lobby card for *Freckles Comes Home* (Monogram, 1942), in which Gale is romanced by Johnny Downs.

a contract at a salary of $300 per week. By Hollywood standards, it was modest pay for an up-and-coming leading lady, and she had no illusions about where Monogram and its low-budget pictures stood in the industry. Still, it offered the promise of steady work, and she decided to accept.

Monogram would keep her under contract for seven years, until 1949. Her versatility made her easy to cast, and the studio kept her busy. She was not only an ideal ingénue, but a talented singer. She could plausibly play teenagers, or college students, in the Monogram films aimed at the youth market. At the same time, she could handle leading-lady roles. She showed herself capable of keeping up with the lightning-fast production schedule at Monogram, where many of her early films were made in six days. An actress who needed frequent retakes, or who wouldn't learn her lines, would have been shown the door in short order. At Monogram, the perks of stardom were few and far between. Gale remembered that she had to plead with producer Lindsley Parsons ("I just nagged at him, nicely, until I wore him down"[20]) to be allowed to view dailies of her scenes. She treated it as a learning experience, noting what did and didn't work well in front of the camera, all the time aware that, whatever she saw, nothing would be reshot.

Happy to be working, Gale made no fuss about the material she was handed, whether it was a jungle melodrama, a zombie horror film, or a crime thriller. Looking back some years later on her Monogram tenure, she said, "One time we rushed a picture so fast we never finished it. Honest. With one reel missing, we just cut it, released it—and never heard a complaint."[21] Still, despite the pressure of intense deadlines on the set, she later said, "The hours weren't so bad. I don't remember feeling overworked."[22] She impressed industry insiders sufficiently that Monogram almost struck a deal with RKO in 1944, which would have shared her services between the two studios, but negotiations fell apart. Still, it was satisfying for Gale to be wanted by RKO, only a few years after the studio had found her unworthy of keeping on a modest salary. The interest from RKO at least won her a pay raise at Monogram.

Gale gave birth to her first child, son Phillip Lee Bonnell, in March 1943. She would have three sons during her years at Monogram. "They were wonderful," she later said of her studio colleagues. "They even had the courtesy to call me and ask whether it was all right to schedule another picture, or was I going to have another baby!"[23] Despite the new arrival, she still managed to appear in five Monogram films that year.

During World War II, she was a popular pinup with soldiers. Monogram provided the men of Camp Haan in Riverside, California, with a picture of her, blown up to six feet in size. She also appeared as a pinup in *Yank* magazine, distributed to servicemen overseas, and took part in rallies to sell war bonds. In May 1944, while negotiations for her shared contract with RKO were underway, she took part in RKO's premiere of *Show Business*, held as a benefit for the hospital care of wounded servicemen. She was one of several dozen actresses, including Lucille Ball and Lana Turner, who served as dates for recuperating soldiers that night.

By the mid–1940s, Gale's name had sufficient drawing value to put on a marquee, and the studio began placing her in more important roles. In 1945, *Forever Yours*, her most ambitious film to date, starred her as a socially prominent young woman whose life is uprooted when she is diagnosed with infantile paralysis. The film, one of her favorites, drew favorable critical notices for her, and was one of Monogram's most successful of the year. Said Dorothy Manners in the *Los Angeles Examiner* (January 22, 1945), "Gale Storm definitely steps into the star brackets in her portrayal.... She is vivid as the social butterfly and surprisingly restrained and moving in the dramatic moments after she is afflicted."

Gale's releases that year went a long way to demonstrate her versatility. Her other films were *Sunbonnet Sue,* a period musical, and *G.I. Honeymoon,* a comedy that afforded her the chance to show a different side of herself, not unlike what audiences would later see in *My Little Margie*. Industry observers were taking notice. Said columnist Harry Niemeyer, "If more of her Hollywood sisters could learn that a motion picture actress should be a lot more than a pretty face attached to a high-powered publicity campaign, there would be less meteoric careers ending as quickly as they began.... Gale has been quietly building the solid groundwork of an accomplished actress, in the only way it can be done—with hard work and lots of patience."[24]

After the war, changes in the movie industry led to a retooling of Monogram's approach to the marketplace. Studio executives saw an opportunity to expand the company beyond B movies and established a separate division, Allied Artists, to make more ambitious films. One of the first was *It Happened on 5th Avenue*. The script arrived while Gale was still in the hospital after the birth of her son Peter. While she was mostly pleased with the completed picture, she was greatly disappointed and hurt by producer-director Roy Del Ruth's insistence that her singing in the film be dubbed. Working alongside

Charlie Ruggles, Don DeFore, Ann Harding and others, Gale held her own, making the ingénue role of Terry appealing and warm, and the film would be one of her best-remembered.

Upon his release from the Coast Guard in early 1946, Lee was invited back to RKO, a studio that made a point of welcoming their actors who had served with distinction in the military. For the second time, he was promoted as a contract player in training. But before the year was out, after again being overlooked for important roles, he would be given his release. In May 1946, Gale and Lee welcomed their second son, Peter Wade. Paul William followed in October 1947.

Seeing his film career winding down, Lee began searching for another career avenue. He enrolled in Chapman College, engaged in Bible studies and considered the possibility of entering the ministry, but he ultimately concluded that this was not his calling. In 1947, Gale and Lee formed a production company, Bonnell Productions, hoping to make inspirational films. They had obtained the rights to the life story of W.H. Alexander, a minister who had won acclaim for his work with juvenile delinquents. Lee and Gale intended to call it *Hand on My Shoulder* and enlisted Frank Tashlin to develop the screen-

In 1947, Gale co-starred with Victor Moore (left) and Charles Ruggles (right) in *It Happened on 5th Avenue*. It was the first release from Monogram's Allied Artists division, created to showcase higher-budgeted films.

play. Commented syndicated columnist Louella O. Parsons (September 24, 1947), "Far be it from me to say that the Reverend Alexander's story is a sort of Protestant *Going My Way,* but it has the same wholesome appeal." But Lee and Gale were unable to realize their goal of producing films. On February 27, 1950, the *Los Angeles Times*' Edwin Schallert reported that Lee had acquired the rights to an original movie scenario, "The Spinning Wheel," as a vehicle for his wife. The story called for her to "play the daughter of a wealthy family who takes a job in a night club to solve the mystery surrounding the murder of her boyfriend." That project also failed to coalesce.

Gale and Lee were determined not to let her film success, and his career disappointments, affect their relationship. In the early 1950s, Lee, troubled by the fact that his wife's income was largely supporting their family, took a job in the insurance industry, which ultimately afforded him the opportunity to have a successful business career. He also continued to apply his business expertise to Gale's career.

Publicity photograph of Monogram/Allied Artists contract player Gale Storm, 1947 (author's collection).

When her seven-year Monogram contract expired in 1949, Gale decided to explore new horizons and accepted a multi-picture deal with Universal. Her first Universal release, *Abandoned,* was a well-made thriller that offered her the starring role (after Ann Blyth rejected it). After completing three Universal pictures, she broke her ties with the studio when executives assigned her to a secondary female role she didn't want. According to *Daily Variety* (September 12, 1949), "She had advised them she wasn't satisfied with her role in *Outside the Wall*.... Marilyn Maxwell–Richard Basehart starrer that was slated to roll today." A brief stint at Columbia followed, but times were tough at movie studios, and Gale found herself mostly cast in average-quality Westerns, not exactly what she'd had in mind.

After completing her role in *Woman of the North Country* at Republic in early 1952, Gale found herself, at the age of 30, seriously considering retirement from the screen. As she later admitted, had she been at the height of demand for her services, she might not have done so. But as film work was slowing for her, she found the idea of having more time at home with her family appealing. Lee's career in insurance was thriving, giving them reassurance that the family would be well provided for.

However, even without film roles, she still found opportunities to perform. In early 1952, she was on stage in St. Louis, co-starring with fellow film actor William Eythe in a production of John Cecil Holm's romantic comedy *Gramercy Ghost*. The play had enjoyed a fairly short Broadway run the previous year.

She also got her feet wet in television. Movie actors were just beginning to accept that TV could be a legitimate source of work, although the best-paid stars of the era still steered clear of it (or were contractually forbidden to appear). With no thought of the long term, Gale took roles in a few TV anthology series, and appeared occasionally as a celebrity guest on shows like *Pantomime Quiz*. Even before *My Little Margie* came along, however, she considered projects that would have placed her in a weekly television show. In September 1950, she teamed with her movie leading man Don DeFore for *Mr. and Mrs. Detective,* a live half-hour. It was broadcast as part of an anthology series, but was in fact a pilot. In 1951, *Daily Variety* (January 5, 1951) reported that James Schwartz Pro-

Rod Cameron was Gale's leading man in *Woman of the North Country* (1952), her final theatrical film.

ductions "has packaged television series starring Gale Storm in a format framed around a mother recounting nursery tales to her tots," but nothing came of this either.

Unexpectedly, she was invited by producer Hal Roach, Jr., to play one of the two starring roles in his new filmed situation comedy *My Little Margie*, co-starring Charles Farrell. She was cast as a headstrong young woman living with her widowed father, as the two waged an unending battle of wills. The pay fell short of what she'd received in recent years as a movie actress; at first, she earned $750 a week for playing Margie Albright. She had not been the first choice to play the role. However, as Roach explained, "I watched her for years, and thought to myself that she had terrific possibilities that had never been exploited."[25] Not overlooked was the fact that she had experience doing low-budget films, making her less likely to be overwhelmed by the demands of shooting a weekly TV show.

My Little Margie made its bow on CBS's Monday night schedule in June 1952. For the next 13 weeks, the show was seen as the summer replacement for TV's hottest program *I Love Lucy*, to which it was often compared. Over the past few months, *I Love Lucy* had become an enormous popular and critical success, and those shoes could not easily be filled, even temporarily. But audiences liked Gale's show, escapist entertainment that

Hal Roach, Jr. (pictured in 1953 with wife Alva) was responsible for Gale's casting in *My Little Margie*.

delivered its share of belly laughs, and its ratings were better than expected. When its summer run wound down, viewer mail demanded its return.

Pleased by the response, Philip Morris executives decided to keep *My Little Margie* going. Network schedules for that fall were pretty much locked up, but NBC found a slot on Saturday nights where the show could air for five weeks that fall. In October, *Margie* was back on the air, and *Variety* was soon reporting that it was TV's fourth most popular show. Within a few weeks, Roach made a deal with CBS and Philip Morris; the result was a *Margie* radio adaptation, which began that December, as well as a regular run for the filmed series, which returned to CBS in January 1953. Critics harrumphed that the show had gotten better since its debut when they had slammed it. When the show began a new season on NBC that fall, *Variety* (September 9, 1953) ate its previous words, describing *Margie* as "network quality programming, and it's proven its value by the way it catapulted Gale Storm back into the public eye.... The scripts may not be the most original in the world, but [Frank] Fox and [George Carleton] Brown always manage to come up with a few extra twists that Miss Storm, [Charles] Farrell and the rest of the cast lend polish to and make them appear bright and original."

Her television work brought acclaim and recognition beyond what she'd enjoyed in the 1940s. "Now every time I go shopping," she said a few months after *Margie*'s premiere, "people stop me on the street to say how much they enjoy the program. That never happened to me when I was in pictures."[26]

"Television's just the answer to everything for me," she told another reporter. "*Margie* has already given me the chance to get away from those sweet little ingénues. I've never had more fun in my life. The better the writers get to know you, the better they can write for you."[27] There was even a renewed interest in Gale for film roles: *Variety* reported (October 15, 1952) that her agent was negotiating with producer Lester Cowan for her to play the female lead in his forthcoming *Main Street to Broadway*. As it turned out, though, television would be keeping her plenty busy for the next few years.

Unlike many actors whose private lives were at odds with their public image, Gale enjoyed a happy home life with her husband and family. Even *Confidential*, in the 1950s, would have had trouble dishing any dirt about the wife and mother who taught Sunday school classes in her spare time. While her life lacked controversy, she was nonetheless good copy, as Gale routinely displayed a lively, impish sense of humor in interviews that charmed listeners. (Asked a few years later to explain why her second sitcom, *The Gale Storm Show: Oh! Susanna* was so popular, she said, "Nobody watches it—so nobody complains. It's very simple."[28]) She was appreciative of her success, but insisted she "couldn't go high hat if it were in my system. After all, I'm the mother of three children and they are one of the best anti-ego devices ever invented."[29] She said that her family was supportive of her TV career, despite the fact that it kept her away from home for long hours. "When I was working in pictures, the boys couldn't understand why I had to be away. I'd make a movie that wouldn't be out for six months or more. But now they understand why I'm gone. They can hear the radio show on Sundays and watch the TV show on Wednesdays. They take a pride in *My Little Margie* themselves."[30]

According to Lee, there was little similarity between Margie Albright and his wife, whom he still called by her given name of Jo. "People wonder about Jo," Bonnell said, "whether she is acting or playing herself. Actually, she is quite different from Margie. Jo is very level-headed and practical."[31]

An unexpected accolade came Gale's way in the spring of 1953, when she was named

Gale and husband Lee Bonnell in the early 1950s, dressed up for an evening out.

honorary mayor of the Sherman Oaks community. Saying her campaign expenditures had been extremely modest—"I bought a new lipstick"—she pledged to "balance the budget as soon as I can find out where they keep it."[32] She was installed in her new office by actor Jim Backus, co-star of the NBC sitcom *I Married Joan*. Since Charles Farrell was already the honorary mayor of Palm Springs, the new office meant that both of *Margie*'s stars were "elected" officials.

During her summer hiatus from *Margie*, Gale was offered, and accepted, lucrative nightclub bookings. In June, she was headlining in San Diego, doing songs and patter. *Variety* (July 1, 1953) called her act "highly successful" and "a strong bet for any nitery," adding, "She has a winning Mary Martin quality of freshness, bountiful talent and exuberance ... [Her] not large but attention-grabbing voice is pleasant, bolstered by singer's clear enunciation. Act itself has continuity and purpose to which she adds sincere flair for being liked...." From there, Gale traveled to Las Vegas, where she had a multi-week run at the Hotel Thunderbird. Her songs included "Blue Skies," "Moulin Rouge" and "Cow Cow Boogie." *Billboard* (July 18, 1953) called her "a versatile and pleasing vocalist. Tiny and cute, and with a winning personality...." Business was strong, justifying her $7,500 weekly salary at the Thunderbird, and demonstrating that TV performers could be a draw in clubs. Though she would play a return engagement in Vegas the following summer, she admitted that she and Lee were not particularly attuned to life in the gambling mecca. The money she earned went toward the construction of their home in Encino, where they would live for the next 20 years.

In the summer of 1954, Gale was onstage in *Wish You Were Here* at the Texas State Fair. The *Dallas Morning News'* John Rosenfield (June 6, 1954) called it

> [A]n enormous, sumptuous show, about as spectacular as anything our summer theater has ever attempted. [Gale] gave the Dallas production a point of strength missed elsewhere.... She presented a wholesome pretty-girl-next-door appearance. She managed a pretentious vocabulary without losing sympathy. She read her lines well and for an encouraging quota of laughs.

While in Dallas, Gale took part in a Fourth of July program at the First Methodist Church. As special guest soloist, she performed Max Reger's "Lullaby" and "Hear Ye, Israel," from Mendelssohn's *Elijah*.

As the 1954–55 season of *My Little Margie* played out, Gale's success continued to bring accolades and recognition. That spring, she served as honorary national chairman for National Sunday School Week, observed in April. While appreciative of being recognized, Gale was nonplussed by some of the awards that came her way. Named "most glamorous business woman of the year" by a professional association in 1955, Gale couldn't help laughing: "I'll remember that when I'm wearing curlers, have cold cream on my face and I'm asking my husband for lunch money because I can't add."[33] Syndicated columnist Louella O. Parsons (September 30, 1955) commented that Gale "continues to amaze me," marking her 14th wedding anniversary looking youthful as ever, and happily mothering "three tall sons."

In 1955, *My Little Margie* was canceled, though with 126 episodes available, it quickly began to play in reruns. Out from under the workload of a weekly TV series, Gale paused to consider where her career might go next. In October 1955, she displayed her acting chops in a one-hour live drama on the prestigious *Robert Montgomery Presents*, "Tomorrow Is Forever," assuming the role originally played in a 1940s film by Claudette Colbert. Gale later called this "the best part I ever had."[34]

Increasingly, music began playing a larger role in her life and career. For some time, she had been taking singing lessons. As she began to be seen more frequently singing on TV variety shows, an eight-year-old girl in Tennessee unexpectedly won her a career break.

"I was a huge fan of Gale Storm as a little girl, and never missed an episode of *My Little Margie*," Linda Wood explained years later.[35] When she saw her favorite star singing on *The Colgate Comedy Hour*, Linda called her father, Randy Wood, into the room. Wood was the president of Dot Records, an up-and-coming company he had founded. "I begged him to contact her and sign her up," said Linda.

Gale and Lee made the trip to Gallatin, Tennessee, where the Wood family lived, to discuss a deal. Linda was deliriously happy to have Gale as a guest in her home. "I vividly remember hovering in the hallway outside her door waiting for her to emerge in the morning," Linda said. "But what I remember most was how kind she was to me, a little girl whom she knew literally idolized her."

Randy Wood, who had already signed young Pat Boone to a recording contract, wanted Gale to record for his label as well. He couldn't afford to entice her with lavish pay, but Gale and Lee agreed to work on a percentage basis (rather than taking stock in the company, which she later admitted she should have done). Wood had a good reputation in the music business. "He certainly was one of the most ethical people I ever met," said Lawrence Welk, who later formed a partnership with Wood. "He really cared about people and seeing them succeed."[36] In the fall of 1955, Gale traveled to Chicago, where she recorded her first songs for Dot under Wood's direction. She bowed to his expertise and allowed him to select the songs, the arrangements and other aspects of her performance. Surely neither of them expected that her first recording for the company, a cover of "I Hear You Knockin'," would become a gold record.

She remembered the anticipation of her family, waiting to hear it played on the radio for the first time. Lee, her kids and even the maid were monitoring the radio in hopes of hearing it. "Finally," said one columnist, "Gale was backing out of her garage and turned on the car radio and there it was. Frantically, she blew her horn. The whole household came tumbling out to listen. The maid tripped and injured her leg. It was quite a debut."[37]

Busy with her singing and television guest appearances, Gale had thought little about the prospect of doing a second weekly series, and in fact was inclined to think she'd rather not do another. For several weeks in early 1956, she hosted *The NBC Comedy Hour*, a trouble-plagued show featuring stand-up comedians. Hal Roach, Jr., liked the idea of putting both of his *Margie* stars into follow-up series of their own, and Gale's contract with him still had several months to run. *The Charles Farrell Show*, a situation comedy, soon turned up as a summer replacement series on CBS. Meanwhile, Lee Karson, a scriptwriter who'd been involved primarily in the radio version of *Margie*, had a story idea about a young woman serving as social director on a cruise ship. Having proved her popularity with TV audiences, Gale was offered a better deal this time: a $3000 weekly salary, plus an ownership stake in the series, which would be called *The Gale Storm Show: Oh! Susanna*. Cast in featured roles were Roy Roberts as her blustery boss, Captain Simon Huxley, and ZaSu Pitts as her best friend and roommate, Elvira "Nugey" Nugent.

The show also offered an ideal opportunity to introduce her records to a large audience as they were released. The chance to sing regularly on her own series was difficult for Gale to resist. Susanna Pomeroy, her TV character, regularly did song-and-dance numbers for the entertainment of passengers, with musical scenes written into every third or fourth episode. While filming of the series pilot was still underway, the Nestlé Company signed on to sponsor the new show. Production of early episodes was complicated by the fact that Gale was unexpectedly pregnant, some nine years after the birth of her last child. Gale's doctor gave her permission to work through mid–September, making it imperative to get as many episodes in the can as possible before she was sent home to await her baby. That fall, her daughter Susanna (named for the sitcom character) arrived, completing Gale and Lee's family.

"We felt it was really the least we could do," Gale said lightly of naming her daughter Susanna. "I discovered I was pregnant about two weeks after we started filming this series

Gale personally recommended Roy Roberts for the role of Captain Simon Huxley in *The Gale Storm Show: Oh! Susanna*. She had been impressed by his fine character portrayals in guest appearances on *My Little Margie*.

and it did come as rather a jolt to the sponsors. I must say, they took the news chivalrously, never faltered. I worked for seven months and by some miracle, we were able to film enough shows, but it was a real race."[38] Gale credited Lee with taking an active role in raising their children. "Lee is the kind of husband who loves babies," she said. "When the three boys were infants, he got up with me every night, and I sometimes felt he got as much out of it from the paternal standpoint as I did maternally—he's not just a 'play' daddy."[39]

The Gale Storm Show: Oh! Susanna debuted on CBS in the fall of 1956. Dropped into a competitive Saturday night time slot, opposite Lawrence Welk on ABC and Sid

Caesar on NBC, the often-underestimated Miss Storm fared better than critics expected. Her show gave Welk a run for its money, outranking it in the ratings more often than not, and left *Caesar's Hour* bringing up the rear. During its second season (1957–58), her show was in Nielsen's Top 20, the third most popular situation comedy series on TV. Guest stars appeared with more frequency than they had on her first sitcom. The series ultimately enjoyed a four-year run, switching to ABC in 1959, and was repeated on ABC's daytime schedule.

Gale's sons Peter (left) and Paul Bonnell were guest players in "The Phantom Valise," a 1957 episode of *The Gale Storm Show: Oh! Susanna.*

Her routine when the series was in production called for her to report to the Roach studios at 6:30 a.m., allowing two hours for hair, makeup and wardrobe before shooting began at 8:30. Filming on most days wound down around 6 p.m., leaving her able to be at the family dinner table half an hour or so later. She was in bed by 8:30 most nights.

Gale's recording career was short-lived, lasting about a year and a half. The amount of time she was spending with Randy Wood sparked jealousy from Lee, although she assured him that his concerns were unfounded. Ultimately, feeling the strain in her marriage, Gale decided that her family and home life took precedence. In 1957, she stopped recording. (In the 1960s, she released one record under the auspices of her own company.)

Even without a recording career, her days were still hectic, combining her job as a sitcom star with her family responsibilities. In the spring of 1958, overwork caught up with Gale, and she was hospitalized for abdominal surgery. She termed her malady "second series-itis," explaining, "When you do a second series, you become so tired you're numb. You say to yourself, 'I can't possibly be tireder than I am now,' so you do more.... Do a guest shot? Why not? Go on a personal appearance tour? Sure! Then all of a sudden—wham! It hits you."[40] More illness followed the next year, when Gale was treated for a ruptured spinal disc. The successful procedure finally put a stop to back pain she had been experiencing for much of the run of her second TV show.

With the dawn of the 1960s, Gale's television career went into an unexpected slump. In part, it was just the trend of the time: Westerns were the most popular fare on TV, and many of her female colleagues, like Ann Sothern (whose second series was canceled in 1961), felt similarly left out. Even if she wasn't working as steadily as she had in the past, there was still plenty of Gale Storm to be had on TV. Five-day-a-week reruns of both her sitcoms were enjoying wide popularity. While this was a testament to her continued appeal, it also meant that there was a risk of overexposure. Gale's friend, actor Ken Prescott, speculated that she was "too nice for her own good" where her career was concerned, more interested in the work itself than in aggressively promoting herself.[41] Another friend, Ron Baker, noted, "She was kind of tired of television, and she wanted to do other things."[42]

According to a fan magazine account, there were also "disquieting rumors about her health." Husband Lee downplayed the seriousness of it, saying her years of working long hours on two TV series had simply caught up with her. He told an interviewer, "After being exhausted for eight years, she's just now [1965] beginning to feel healthy again. She enjoys being home and she has plenty to keep her busy.... We're beginning to enjoy life to the fullest and I wouldn't care if she never worked again."[43]

In the mid–60s, Gale worked only occasionally on television, playing guest roles in two episodes of *Burke's Law*, and doing infrequent talk and game show appearances. With time on her hands, however, and her growing boys not so dependent on having her at home, she began a second career in a medium she'd never before had much time to explore: live theater.

Daily Variety (May 15, 1962) reported that Gale made her summer stock debut starring in *Wildcat*, with bookings in Buffalo, New York, Wallingford, Connecticut, and Framingham, Massachusetts. The musical comedy, written by N. Robert Nash with songs by Cy Coleman and Carolyn Leigh, had been only a modest success on Broadway, fueled largely by Lucille Ball in the lead, but it was extensively revived in the years afterward by Gale, Martha Raye and others. Gale's TV popularity sold tickets in the summer stock arena, and her comedic and singing abilities made her well-suited to musical comedy. The bookings also afforded an opportunity to cast her son Phillip, who was considering a performing career, in a minor role. "I was a little bit frightened at first," Gale said of her *Wildcat* booking, which she described as "a rough engagement—rough because it was done in a tent in the round. It was a huge arena and hotter than a pistol, with ramps we had to run up and down in order to get offstage and onstage. Sometimes it seemed like I was trying out for track! But it was fun."[44]

In September 1962, a crisis reared its head when Phillip, then a junior at the University of California, was badly hurt in a Malibu traffic accident, sustaining injuries to his head and arm. Syndicated columnist Bob Thomas (November 12, 1962) reported, "A hole had to be put in his forehead to repair the damage. Doctors despaired for the sight of one eye. The left arm required an operation to re-set a bone." Gale's son was on the mend by the end of the year, though his college education had to be put on hold for a few months.

While Gale's TV career was uneventful in the early 1960s, Desilu executives still followed her work. In 1962, when negotiations with Vivian Vance to co-star in *The Lucy Show* were bogging down, Gale was reportedly one of the actresses considered to serve as Lucy's sidekick. While that didn't pan out, she made a deal in early 1963 to do a Desilu pilot for what would have been her third network sitcom, *The Gale Storm Show: A-OK, O'Shea*. Gale hoped that the new series would have a regular role for Phillip, now an aspiring actor. "He seems to like it," Gale told Bob Thomas of her son's forays into show business. "I think he's good, too." The proposed new show, casting her as a WAC, ran into production problems, however, and Desilu executives decided against pitching it to sponsors for the fall 1963 schedule.

Having enjoyed her *Wildcat* run, Gale was back on the boards the following summer, headlining *Finian's Rainbow*. With a book by E.Y. Harburg and Fred Saidy, music by Burton Lane, and lyrics by Harburg, the musical comedy had run for more than a year on Broadway in the late 1940s, where Ella Logan originated the role of Sharon.

In early 1964, Gale's older sister Margie died in Houston, the first of her siblings to pass away. The news came as Gale was making a guest appearance on *Burke's Law*, Aaron Spelling's celebrity-studded detective series starring Gene Barry. According to her niece Sharon, the production company hurried through filming the remainder of Gale's scenes so that she could be with her family. "She left California immediately following the shooting," Sharon recalled. "She arrived at my house in complete makeup, threw her mink coat on the couch, and ran to Daddy." When word got out that Gale would attend the funeral, Sharon said, some people went to the service in hopes of seeing the Hollywood star up close. But, as Sharon noted, "She came in and had no makeup on, and a hat with a black veil and no one could see her face. I appreciated the way she comported herself."

Aside from her *Burke's Law* appearances, Gale did little acting on television in the mid-1960s. "I never thought I'd have to hear producers say I was between ages again," Gale lamented in 1969. "When I was younger they told me I was too old to play ingénue roles and too young for leading ladies. Now they tell me I'm too young to play a role as a mother and too old to play somebody's daughter. At least that's what my agents tell me."[45]

The growing popularity of dinner theater gave Gale her best performance venue in the 1960s. The concept had been around since the mid-1950s, as the *New York Times* noted, but reached its zenith nearly a decade later, as suburbanites began to seek light entertainment that didn't require them to venture into a downtown area. According to

John Gruen, "Crime in the cities has risen to an alarming degree, and people are frankly afraid to walk the city streets after dark ... dinner theaters have come along to offer neon-lit safety, convenience, economy—plus the attraction of a night out on the town."[46]

January and February 1967 found her at the Pheasant Run Playhouse in St. Charles, Illinois, starring in *Grand Prize*, a comedy by Ronald Alexander that had a brief Broadway run in 1955. Gale stepped into the lead role originated by June Lockhart, a secretary who turns the tables on her employer, winning the chance to trade places with him for 24 hours thanks to a TV show called *Boss for a Day*. She followed that with a run as Nellie Forbush in *South Pacific* at a dinner theater in New Jersey.

"People come from miles around to see me—it's so satisfying," she said of her stage work. "The feeling people have about you generates things within yourself. It makes you feel good to play to a theater full of people. That's where you find out whether they want to see you."[47]

Her boys were young adults now, and her family began to expand. Peter, who would go on to serve in in Vietnam, was the first of her children to marry, in 1967; Phillip wed in 1971, Paul in '72. She did relatively little professionally in 1968 and 1969. According to Ron Baker, she devoted much of her time to being "just Mom," especially to adolescent daughter Susie, now the last of her children still in the nest. She also kept up with singing and dancing lessons, even if a professional booking wasn't imminent, and appeared on the talk show of her friend and neighbor Steve Allen. In the spring of 1969, Gale traveled to Alabama and served as a judge for the America's Junior Miss pageant, televised on NBC.

When she wanted to work, however, she was still able to keep busy on the stage. She was on the boards in *The Unsinkable Molly Brown* in the summer of 1970, playing an engagement in Kansas. The following spring, she began a lengthy stage run in the Dallas–Fort Worth area, starring in Abe Burrows' *Cactus Flower*. "The thing that has been so satisfying about my appearing in dinner theaters is that I'm not away from home too much. And when I am away, Lee and Susie commute to see me. Sure, that eats up a lot of the profits, but it's worth it."[48]

While appearing in *Cactus Flower*, she explained her continued eagerness for work: "There's a creative energy that I must use up, otherwise I just waste it in other ways—and that's a shame. I like to think that I'm in the position to pick and choose parts, so when something comes along that I want to do, I do it."[49] After that engagement, her theatrical agent Ben Pearson received a letter from Windmill executive Cash Baxter, which was reproduced in a *Daily Variety* ad (July 30, 1971). Saying it had been a "tremendous joy" to host Gale's performance, Baxter added, "She is a delight, personally, as well as an enormous box office draw. Her work is in superb order, her appearance, stunning, her professionalism unquestioned."

In the fall of 1971, Gale was on stage in Lubbock, Texas, starring in Neil Simon's *Plaza Suite*. A reporter present during rehearsals called her "a determined worker. Watching her rehearse on the four-square stage at the Hayloft this week, her script in hand, following director Jack Stillman's direction and blocking, one sees a pro in action."[50]

In 1972, Gale starred at Chicago's Drury Lane Theater in Howard Teichmann's *A Rainy Day in Newark*. Best-known for his comedy *The Solid Gold Cadillac*, Teichmann enjoyed much less success with *Newark*, which ended its 1963 Broadway run after only seven performances. Gale played Elizabeth Lamb, a clock company owner who butts heads with a union boss.

Although she was still working steadily, Gale was largely out of sight and out of mind as far as Hollywood was concerned, causing a magazine interviewer in 1972 to ask bluntly, "Have you retired?" After explaining that she still enjoyed TV work, and was receptive to doing more, Gale added, "A series … is pretty demanding, and I've always felt that unless it's something you just can't resist, you shouldn't do it. I've been approached about a couple of series again recently, and they sounded good, but I haven't seen the complete scripts yet."[51] A year or so later, Gale and Lee teamed with writer Lee Karson to devise a possible sequel to *My Little Margie,* but the project never got off the ground.

Another favorite stage show during those years was Jay Presson Allen's comedy *Forty Carats,* which opened on Broadway in 1968 and ran nearly two years. Popular on the dinner theater circuit in the 1970s, *Carats* offered a strong lead role for a star of a certain age, in a story about a romance with a younger man. Actor-dancer Ken Prescott played the male lead in a mid–1970s production in Atlanta. Some 25 years her junior, he vividly recalled his introduction to Gale, who greeted him with the deadpan statement, "If you tell me you were five years old, sitting on the couch watching *My Little Margie,* I'm going to slap you silly!"

The ice thus broken, the two quickly became friends, and Prescott was impressed by Gale's talent and work ethic. "She was great to work with," he said. "There was no whining and complaining; she was very energetic and focused on her work." Some actors playing the dinner theater circuit were inclined to go through the motions, content to give a lackluster performance of material they'd performed many times previously. Prescott said that Gale was not of this ilk, approaching her work with energy and enthusiasm. "She was a great actor because she always listened and responded."

A new concern had crept into Gale's life, developing so gradually that she wasn't fully aware when it overtook her. By the mid–1970s, her family was worried about her use of alcohol. Looking back, Gale said, "I can't pinpoint any traumatic experience that got me started on alcohol. I had absolutely no excuses—I had a wonderful, supportive husband, a family who cared for me. And that made me feel worse. I was filled with guilt, shame, disgust."[52] For some five years in the mid- to late 1970s, Gale took part in various treatment programs for alcoholism, including Alcoholics Anonymous, but inevitably found herself backsliding after she left rehab. The doctors and counselors who treated her, at Cedars-Sinai and elsewhere, pressed her to identify the stress or trauma behind her need to drink. When she came up empty, they often assumed she was being uncooperative, or refusing to take her treatment seriously.

She was warned by doctors that she had developed a diseased liver that put her health in jeopardy, but even so struggled to curb her drinking. As Lee later wrote, "There was a conspiracy of silence. No one wanted to talk about it. We all knew that Gale was an alcoholic, but we just didn't like to think about it…. I enabled her by catering to her, by doing things for her, by not being up-front with her…"[53] Because she continued to work on stage during this period, she persuaded herself that her alcoholism was manageable. "It was the best acting job I ever did," she said. "During the seven years prior to going into the hospital, I was doing dinner theaters around the country and I would never, ever have a drink before a performance."[54] Indeed, she was so functional as an alcoholic that she could win rave reviews even at the height of her addiction.

Nineteen seventy-four found her in Ohio, starring in Sam Bobrick and Ron Clark's romantic comedy *No Hard Feelings.* As Roberta Bartlett, an attractive woman in her forties who leaves her husband for a relationship with a waiter, Gale recreated the role performed in the show's brief Broadway run by Nanette Fabray.

Two years later, Gale was onstage at Salt Lake City's Gaslight Theatre in *Cactus Flower*, earning the praise of newspaper columnist Dan Valentine. Following in the footsteps of Broadway star Lauren Bacall, whom Valentine remembered as "willowy and blasé" in the role, and Ingrid Bergman in the film ("She played it like she'd never had a toothache"), Gale impressed the columnist, who wrote, "Gale Storm plays the part pert and nervous and with great charm and heart—and with an infectious spirit of fun. It's a great show..."[55]

There was little work for her in television, where she was mostly appreciated for what she had done in the past. In March 1977, Gale was presented with the Pacific Pioneer Broadcasters' "coveted Golden 'Ike' Award for distinguished performance in the medium of television."[56] Among the guests present, aside from her family, were her *My Little Margie* co-star Charles Farrell and *Gale Storm Show* producer Alex Gottlieb, who jokingly reminisced, "Gale always showed up for work at the same time every morning—30 minutes late." Her movie leading men Donald O'Connor and Rod Cameron were in attendance as well.

On February 1, 1978, Gale's mother Minnie, by then living in a nursing home, died of respiratory failure at the age of 90. She was buried in the cemetery at McDade, alongside first husband Walter, who had left her a widow more than 50 years earlier. Gale's sisters Margie and Lois had already passed away.

In early 1979, Gale checked into the Raleigh Hills Hospital in Oxnard, California, for what would be her most successful attempt yet to cure her alcoholism. Her illness was proving increasingly disruptive to her work life as well as her family; she'd recently struggled to complete a *Cactus Flower* engagement because she couldn't remember her lines, though it was a show she'd played multiple times. She'd also been advised by doctors that she was doing serious harm to her body. Previous efforts to curb her drinking, through Alcoholics Anonymous and other programs, had failed. While acknowledging the psychological motives that led patients to drink, the Raleigh Hills program, in which she enrolled for two weeks, dealt with the chemical addiction itself. The form of aversion therapy used in the program proved remarkably effective. "After the fifth day," she recalled in 2006, "you felt like you could smell someone pouring a drink five miles away, and it's revolting! I knew when I finished those treatments that I was done."[57]

That summer, confident that she had overcome her addiction, Gale did her first television commercial for the Raleigh Hills hospital chain. It was her own idea to use her celebrity status to draw attention to the problem of alcoholism and the availability of treatment. At first hospital officials were hesitant, since her sobriety was relatively recent. Her commercials typically used a simple format in which she addressed the audience, saying that the hospital had helped her, and might be able to help them. She was paid very little to do them, usually the minimum amount she had to receive as an AFTRA union member. They were particularly effective in reaching women, for whom excessive drinking was sometimes even more stigmatized than it was for men. Eventually she accepted a position as a paid consultant with the company.

Gale's longtime fans were startled by her candid admission of her addiction and recovery. She had worked in Hollywood, and in theaters and nightclubs, for nearly 40 years, and had a reputation that was lacking in scandal, blemish or controversy. "I guess times have really changed," Gale said. "Ten years ago—even five—if I'd done a commercial about being an alcoholic, people in the industry might have said, 'Oh, oh, better not hire her. She might flip out on us or something.' But now I get nothing but positive reactions."[58]

The release of Gale's commercial provoked a curious reaction from old friend Frank Fox, who had created the character of Margie Albright. Taking out a small ad in *Daily Variety* (November 28, 1979), Fox published an open letter to Gale, expressing dismay that her Raleigh Hills spot dropping the name of her TV persona, "might be taken as [the] endorsement" of his fictitious character. Fox, saying only he was qualified to speak on Margie's behalf, quoted her as saying, "The ONLY help and hope for alcoholics is AA."

Shortly after her release from the hospital, she was booked as a guest star on *The Love Boat,* the popular ABC series often described as a latter-day version of *Oh! Susanna.* Gale admitted that she had "quite a few qualms" about her first stint in front of the camera after a long hiatus. But "everyone in the cast, in the crew, was so terribly, terribly nice."[59] Back in the spotlight, Gale collaborated with author Bill Libby and published her autobiography, *I Ain't Down Yet* (the title taken from a song in *The Unsinkable Molly Brown*) in 1981.

Gale was delighted to be a guest star on *The Love Boat* in 1979.

Susanna's marriage in 1980, to Procter & Gamble executive Joseph Harrigan, meant that all of Gale and Lee's kids were settled. At the time of her book's release, Gale already had five grandchildren. Around the same time, the Bonnells sold their longtime home in Encino and purchased a smaller one in Tarzana. They also bought a house in the seaside community of Monarch Beach, as they were ready to spend more time relaxing. At the time of Lee's retirement in 1982, he had built the Lee Bonnell Massachusetts Mutual Life Insurance Agency, headquartered in Encino, into one of the largest in California.

For the next ten years, she worked sporadically on TV. Completely at ease describing her alcoholism and recovery, knowing it could help others, she turned up on talk shows such as *Over Easy, Hour Magazine* and *The John Davidson Show.* She continued to work as a consultant to the Raleigh Hills hospital chain, until corporate issues put the enterprise out of business in the 1980s.

While Gale was feeling better than she had in years, Lee's health was beginning to falter. After a long stint in which he was her caretaker, the roles were reversed. In the last several years of his life, he suffered both a stroke and a heart attack. He died on May 12, 1986, of another heart attack, at Santa Monica Hospital. Memorial services were held a few days later at the South Shores Church. "It was absolutely a great marriage," she said of her years with Lee. "It was a terrific marriage, and it got better and better, not because we were lucky but because we worked at it ... which makes it pretty devastating when you lose it, by durn."[60] Not long after Lee's death, Gale sold their Monarch Beach home, needing a fresh start, and relocated to Dana Point, California.

In the spring of 1987, still adjusting to life as a widow, Gale was delighted to be teamed with two other veteran actresses, Betty Garrett and Sheree North, in a show called *Breaking up the Act*. Terry Kingsley-Smith's script cast the ladies as members of the Phil Jerome Trio, a 1940s girl group who had made an impression on young soldier Jimmy Carter during World War II, and were reunited years later for an appearance at President Carter's White House. According to publicist Alan Eichler, Ross Hunter had directed a production in 1982 that starred Garrett, Evelyn Keyes and Jan Sterling, That show had played the Burt Reynolds Dinner Theatre in Florida. Nearly five years later, Gale took on Keyes' role in a production directed by actress Marcia Rodd. Said the reviewer for the *Pinellas County Review* (May 22, 1987), "The chemistry among the three women sparkles and fizzles." The show's producers hoped to take it to Broadway, but "it never went beyond the dinner theater circuit," Eichler said.[61]

Two years after she was widowed, Gale married for a second time. The groom was Paul Masterson, a former executive at ABC-TV. Like Gale herself, Masterson, born November 11, 1917, had at one time been a performer, working as a radio announcer and later as host of an afternoon show on Los Angeles' KABC-TV, *Masterson's Madhouse*, "which involved viewers taking part in a scavenger hunt during the showing of a movie."[62] His show was so popular, according to his daughter Debora, that it eventually had to be taken off the air, as the audience grew and the scavenger hunt integral to its format ballooned out of hand with eager participants.

As Paul's family grew (he and his first wife ultimately had three children), he was urged by colleagues like ABC's Elton Rule to consider a more stable career than performing. In the late 1950s, according to Debora, her father made the switch, first going into sales at ABC and ultimately becoming Vice-President, Administration, for the network. By the time of his retirement, he was the network's third-ranking official.

Paul and Gale were introduced in the summer of 1987 at a dinner party at the home of mutual friend Linda Leighton, whom Gale had known since the days of *Gateway to Hollywood*. Masterson had been alone since the death of his first wife five years earlier. "We just hit it off real keen," Gale said shortly before her wedding. "He's intelligent and has a marvelous sense of humor. I love him, but I just like him, too. He's something special."[63] Her second wedding took place at the South Shores Church on April 23, 1988. Her daughter Susanna was matron of honor and son Phillip gave away the bride.

"They were so cute together," recalled Debora of the couple who found love for the second time later in life. "They seemed awfully happy together." Debora said her father "gave me the gift of learning," noting that he was "always learning new things, studying." Paul Masterson spoke French fluently, played classical piano, and happily served as accompanist to his new wife. "Gale loved to sing along with him," Debora said.[64] He and Gale also maintained their interest in several charitable organizations; in the late 1980s, he served as president of the Permanent Charities Committee of the Entertainment Industries, an organization originally founded by Samuel Goldwyn nearly 50 years earlier.

The new Mr. and Mrs. Masterson, when not indulging their love of travel (they took trips to India and China, among other destinations), lived in a home "on a cliff, with a beautiful ocean view," in Laguna Beach, Debora said. Gale's grandson Brendan, looking back on family visits, remembered being impressed as a child that the house in Laguna Beach had its own elevator. "He was always super-nice to us," said Brendan of Paul.[65] Gale and her husband also maintained a Los Angeles apartment on Beverly Boulevard.

In 1989, Gale gave her last professional acting performance, as a guest star in an episode of the hit series *Murder, She Wrote*. She was cast as the new mother-in-law of recurring character Grady, Jessica Fletcher's nephew. According to Ron Baker, there was an opportunity there for Gale's role to recur, but she didn't especially care for the character as written.

Gale and Paul took part in film festivals and other events where fans gathered to meet her. In September 1993, she, Betty White and Jane Wyatt were guests at a Museum of Broadcast Communications event in Chicago, a conference studying the changing roles of women in television. Artwork promoting the event merged Gale's face with that of Candice Bergen's Murphy Brown, symbolizing both the differences, and the similarities, that could be observed over the course of 40 years. In a moderated discussion held during the conference, the three actresses talked openly about their own TV work and their experiences behind the scenes, as well as how the world—and, consequently, the medium—had adapted. Gale confessed to some nostalgia for an earlier age, saying, "I think we could really use some nicer, kinder role models in today's television."[66]

While Gale and her colleagues were rightly acknowledged as pioneers, the women were taken aback to see that the characters they had played so many years earlier were now subject to criticism from a younger generation that thought them too subservient to men. The actresses took part in numerous press interviews during their Chicago stay. Cary O'Dell, who co-curated the conference, recalled one radio interview that was particularly bothersome. The host, who, O'Dell said, "didn't do her homework ... assumed that all female TV images of the 1950s were of put-upon housewives standing forlornly in the kitchen." Gale and Betty White were asked if they had given any thought to "the damage you were doing" by playing such roles. "Betty and Gale did what they could to defend themselves—graciously," O'Dell noted, "but the interviewer's misinformation was so ingrained that she was not receptive to it."[67]

"It was all I could do to contain my anger," said the normally cheerful White afterwards. "It's wrong to look at those early shows with today's values." Betty and Gale pointed out that they played women who at least seemed to adopt the roles expected of them in the 1950s, but were anything but downtrodden. Referencing *Our Miss Brooks, I Married Joan* and Gale's *My Little Margie,* Betty noted, "It was a time when men were in charge of the work force and the home, but these women were finding ways to get their way."[68] Given a chance to address the issue in *TV Guide* (December 4, 1993), Gale said, "I don't think that these roles disparaged women, heavens no. I've had so many letters from women who said they regarded Margie and Susanna as role models. Margie was liberated. She would try anything. Her father didn't always like it, but she made herself free. And Susanna was a career girl."

In 1994, Gale traveled to Charlotte, North Carolina, where she was a guest at the Western Film Fair. Not experienced in the fan convention scene, she had brought along no pictures or other memorabilia to sell, but happily signed anything fans put in front of her. "Whatever anybody brought, she signed," said her longtime admirer Ron Baker, who met her in Charlotte and became a friend. He noted with a laugh that she was inclined to let out a small scream of dismay when asked to autograph pictures from *Revenge of the Zombies,* which she didn't count as a favorite ("not her kind of film," Baker said), but inscribed them nonetheless. Seeing how much she enjoyed the experience, and how pleased she was to realize that there were still many people who liked her work, Baker told her, "You need a fan club!" Not long afterwards, the Gale Storm Appreciation Society was formed. It would remain active for the next 15 years.

Gale quickly became a popular guest at nostalgia events like the meetings of the

Radio Enthusiasts of Puget Sound (1994), SPERDVAC (1995) and others. In 2000, she traveled to Parsons, Kansas, taking part in that town's then-annual tribute to her *Gale Storm Show* co-star ZaSu Pitts.

Though Gale did no acting for films or television in the 1990s, she was receptive to the idea, according to stepdaughter Debora Masterson, who worked as a talent agent during that period and took her on as a client. "She wanted to do some more appearances on television," Debora said, noting that Gale "came close" to booking several roles. "I'd love to work more," Gale noted in 1994, "but sometimes people think that if you're not working, it's because you don't want to be."[69] Debora also worked to get Gale's 1950s shows back on television, but was ultimately advised that the ownership rights were too tangled and uncertain.

One of the roles that got away, as recorded in Gale's datebook, was a guest appearance on *Becker*, a CBS sitcom (1998–2004) starring Ted Danson as a curmudgeonly New York City doctor. In November 1999, Gale read for the dual role of Evelyn and Edith Crane in an episode titled "The Hypocratic Oath." The story involved Becker's nurse, Margaret (Hattie Winston), being summoned to a lawyer's office because she was mentioned in a former patient's will. The late patient, seemingly sweet-natured Evelyn, announces her bequests via a videotaped will. Margaret is joined by Evelyn's twin sister Edith, a sour woman interested only in what she will inherit. The producers ultimately chose character actress Kathleen Freeman for the part. Given that the script as ultimately shot called for the actress to call someone "a colossal pain in the ass," and reminisce about a lover who used to "call me his little whore," it may be just as well as Gale wasn't cast.

If there seemed to be no place for Gale in 1990s Hollywood, her life was satisfying and full nonetheless. However, her second marriage, while happy, was much shorter than her relationship with Lee. "I showed him the best eight years of his life," she later said[70]; Masterson died of cancer on May 10, 1996, in Laguna Beach at age 79.

In the 2000s, Gale's website was established, affording her another venue to keep in contact with fans. While some celebrities merely accommodated their fans, or took advantage of opportunities to make money from them, Gale was different, said daughter Susanna. "She really enjoyed chatting with her fans. She was always very appreciative."[71] Ron Baker recalled that those she knew well could look forward to a personal phone call on their birthday, with Gale singing "Happy Birthday" for an audience of one.

An important aspect of Gale's later years was her membership at the South Shores Church in Dana Point. In 1993, she began serving as narrator of the church's annual Christmas concert, which she termed "a privilege, an honor, and a joy." According to the Rev. Robert Perry, Gale "wore a red dress that everybody loved"[72] for the performance. Under the Reverend Perry's supervision, an original cantata was performed each year, bringing together an array of music, from classical to pop. Gale's narration tied together the various elements. In the 2002 program, she read excerpts from the Bible, introduced a teenage harpist to perform a solo, recited a Christmas poem, and told a funny story about a mischievous child actor who decides to pad his role as the innkeeper in a holiday pageant.

Though she rarely left home in her later years, she made a point of attending rehearsals for the event. "A professional wants to rehearse, and wants to get it right," the Reverend Perry noted. "She would come in days before, work with the microphone, the sound guys..." After the performance, she sat in a custom-built sleigh alongside the church's huge Christmas tree, and posed for photographs with attendees.

She also enjoyed being in touch with her grandchildren. "She would just call them up randomly, and chat," Susanna said. "They had a good rapport." According to her grandson Brendan, they too could look forward to a greeting on their birthdays. "She wouldn't even say hello," he noted. "She'd just start right into the 'Happy Birthday' song." Her granddaughter Erin, who relished Gale's sense of humor, recalled the time her grandmother called and mentioned that she'd overheard Erin's aunt say how she pretty she was. While Erin was taking in the compliment, her grandmother joked, "Well, don't just assume I think the same!"[73]

Brendan remembered annual visits from Gale at Christmastime. She typically held court from a recliner in Susanna's living room. Brendan and his siblings referred to Gale as "the fancy grandma," because "she looked fancy all the time." Even in the evenings, he said, she would be sporting "a nightgown that looked like she should be going out on the town." According to Erin, "fake eyelashes and lipstick" were *de rigueur* as well. As a child, Erin's dress-up box was filled with costumes and costume jewelry passed down from her grandmother.

"We always had nicknames for her and she loved all of them," Brendan said. "Our favorite was [sic] Granny and Grans, and we always did a line from the movie *Happy Gilmore* where Shooter McGavin says, 'Hi Grandma…' and even though she never knew what we were talking about, she laughed along with us." Watching Gale's film *It Happened on 5th Avenue* became a family holiday tradition, and Gale enjoyed the screening as much as anyone. "She loved to watch herself," Erin said. "I think it brought her back to that time."

Aside from visiting with her children and grandchildren, she was an avid University of Southern California football fan. According to son Phillip, she had an accessorized USC sweatshirt she wore every time her team played. "She didn't miss a game," he said. "Even if we weren't together, we would be on the telephone during the game."[74]

More than a quarter-century after she stopped drinking, she said that she never struggled with the temptation again. "I never had 'white-knuckle' sobriety. I never ever needed [liquor] or wanted it again."[75]

Near the end of her life, the members of the South Shores Church honored their famous member with a tribute. The festivities began with Gale going to dinner with her son and daughter-in-law, where they were picked up in a limousine, and then arriving at the church, where members had gathered to honor her. Participants tried to "make it seem like she was on the red carpet," said the Reverend Perry, with flash cameras recording the moment as she arrived on the scene. Stepping inside, she was greeted by a standing ovation; "The church was packed, everybody cheered," he noted. The tribute program featured clips from her movie and television work.

In the mid–2000s, with Gale now in her eighties, her health began to decline. Suffering from chronic neck pain, she eventually underwent surgery; according to Ron Baker, she hoped it would relieve some of the pain. The operation was not a great success. "She never really recovered from that," said Baker, who noted that the aftermath, which included wearing a neck brace, "basically confined her to home."

Until shortly before her death, she continued to live independently at her Dana Point home, with a housekeeper at her service and her sons Paul and Phillip nearby. As she grew frailer, Paul's wife Gail stepped in to provide the caregiving. A few days before Gale passed away, daughter Susanna had her admitted to a convalescent hospital in Danville, California. The location was chosen so as to put her closer to Susanna and other family members, where they could more easily see to her needs. Unfortunately, by the time she was admitted, her health was in rapid decline. Noted Gale's niece Sharon, "The last time I spoke to her, she was old, and tired of enduring the challenges of age."

Still, even at that stage, she retained her flair for spontaneous wit, said Brendan. "What I loved about her most was her sense of humor," he said. "She was always just giving a sarcastic remark, regardless of the situation." If she was being fussed over by family members, asked repeatedly how she felt, or whether she needed anything, Brendan said, she was apt to reply something like, "I need you to just stop talking!"

Gale passed away on June 27, 2009. She was survived by her four children, eight grandchildren and four great-grandchildren. Media coverage of her passing was somewhat overshadowed by the deaths of Michael Jackson and Farrah Fawcett the same week. Her oldest son Phillip passed away in October 2016 after a long illness.

Gale's granddaughter Erin credited her example, going from a modest upbringing to Hollywood stardom, with demonstrating "an infiniteness about what we can do in this life." Gale's son Phillip said, "When I think of Mother, I think of the fact that she had more courage than anyone I've ever known. Just a courageous lady and a class act."[76] Said Susanna, simply, "She was a good lady."

II

THE FILMS

Feature Films

Tom Brown's School Days (1940)

Cast: Sir Cedric Hardwicke (*Dr. Thomas Arnold*), Freddie Bartholomew (*East*), Jimmy Lydon (*Tom Brown*), Josephine Hutchinson (*Mary Arnold*), Billy Halop (*Flashman*), Polly Moran (*Sally Harowell*), Hughie Green (*Walker Brooke*), Ernest Cossart (*Squire Brown*), Alec Craig (*Old Thomas*), Gale Storm (*Effie*), Lionel Belmore (*Tavern Keeper*), Barlowe Borland (*Grimsby*), Dick Chandlee (*Tadpole Martin*), Harry Duff (*Westcott*), Antoinette Rotche (*Tom Brown's Nanny*), Peter Madden (*Jacob*), Frank Mills (*School Porter*), Rita Carlyle (*Maid*), Ian Fulton (*Old Brodie*), Forrester Harvey (*Sam*), Paul Mathews (*Lexton*), Leonard Willey (*Farmer Jenkins*), Harold Entwistle (*Dustman*), Harry Duff (*Westcott*), Alexander Pollard (*Butler*)

Director: Robert Stevenson. *Producers*: Gene Towne, Graham Baker. *Adaptation and Screenplay*: Walter Ferris, Frank Cavett, Gene Towne, Graham Baker. *Additional Dialogue*: Robert Stevenson. *Based on the novel by* Thomas Hughes. *Associate Producer*: Donald J. Ehlers. *Photography*: Nicholas Musuraca. *Musical Score*: Anthony Collins. *Special Effects*: Vernon L. Walker. *Art Director*: Van Nest Polglase. *Associate*: L.P. Williams. *Costumes*: Edward Stevenson. *Set Decorator*: Darrell Silvera. *Editor*: William Hamilton. *Assistant Director*: Sam Ruman. *Montage*: Douglas Travers. *Recording*: Richard Van Hessen, James G. Stewart. *Technical Director*: Ian Fulton.

RKO Radio Pictures; released July 19, 1940; B&W; 86 minutes.

Dr. Thomas Arnold, a renowned private tutor, is offered a position as headmaster of the respected boys' school, Rugby. Welcoming the opportunity to put some of his educational theories into practice with 300 students, he sets out to make the school, traditionally "a nursery of soldiers and statesmen, athletes and scholars," into a place where boys are taught the virtues of responsibility and honesty. His ways make him controversial with school faculty whose approach is described by one as "Feed him one end, beat the other—that's education!" Willing to expel any student found to be dishonest or unworthy, Dr. Arnold wins over the Board of Trustees with the help of one member in particular, Squire Brown.

As a show of support for Dr. Arnold, Squire Brown enrolls his own son Tom at Rugby. Wanting to fit into his new environment, Tom learns the ways that have taken hold at the school—that upperclassmen routinely bully the younger boys, who are expected to

Lobby card from *Tom Brown's School Days* (RKO, 1940), in which Gale made her film debut. Pictured (left to right) are Polly Moran, Gale, Jimmy Lydon, and Alec Craig.

do any task or chore demanded, including coming on the fly when their older housemates yell, "Fag!" With the help of fellow student East, his first friend at Rugby, Tom inspires the other boys to revolt against the cruel practices. Courageous even when pitted against bigger, stronger boys, or subjected to physical tortures, Tom earns the respect of his classmates as well as his headmaster, who decries the rampant bullying at the school. After a fistfight between Tom and the worst of the bullies, Flashman, the upperclassman is expelled. But when Tom's classmates mistakenly believe he did the unthinkable and "told tales" to the headmaster, they turn against him. With the encouragement of Dr. Arnold's kindly wife Mary, Tom decides against leaving the school. His worst offense comes when he borrows the cart and horse of the local tavern keeper, a deed for which East is wrongly blamed. Wanting to show East what it is like to be blamed for something one didn't do, Tom instead causes his mentor Dr. Arnold to lose faith in his integrity, and believe that his tenure at Rugby has been a failure.

Not yet 18 years old, Gale made her film debut in the minor role of Effie, niece of the local tavern keeper, Sally Harowell. Making her first entrance past the film's halfway point, Gale has only a few minutes of screen time, but acquits herself ably. Her most notable scene comes when Effie provides a critical bit of help to Tom Brown in a moment of need, earning her a grateful kiss on the forehead.

Tom Brown's School Days' cast was rich with experience. Gale shares scenes with character actress Polly Moran (1883–1952), whose film credits dated back to the silent era, with Moran providing comic relief as the local tavern keeper. Furnishing more fine character support are Alec Craig (1884–1945) and Barlowe Borland (1877–1948) as members of the Rugby faculty and staff, the latter unbilled. The always watchable Sir Cedric Hardwicke (1893–1964) exudes dignity and integrity as Dr. Arnold, ably supported by Josephine Hutchinson (1903–1998) as his ever-loyal wife. Moviegoers in 1940 may have not expected to find one of the Dead End Kids in a British boys' school, but indeed Billy Halop (1920–1976) appears as Flashman, the upperclassman who takes delight in lording it over the younger boys.

Playing the title character, Jimmy Lydon (born 1923) was recruited from the Broadway stage. He was cast in his first important film role, Tom Brown, at age 16. Originally given more serious roles such as this one, for which he won wide acclaim, he would be almost fatally typecast in 1941, when Paramount executives assigned him to play the comic character of Henry Aldrich. That B-movie series ran for several years, until his boyhood was far behind him. Lydon and Gale later worked together in television, as he made several appearances in her second sitcom. During production of *Tom Brown*, he was one of her fellow students at the RKO Studio's school.

Like Thomas Hughes' 1857 novel on which it was based, *Tom Brown's School Days* uses a fictional form to tell the story of a real English school and its renowned headmaster. Author Hughes (1822–1896) was a student there in the 1830s, during the period when the real Dr. Thomas Arnold presided over the institution. Hughes' novel was first adapted to motion pictures during the silent era and continued to be remade at periodic intervals, most recently as a 2005 made-for-TV film in England. The subject matter of the film is still topical more than 75 years after its completion, with its emphasis on bullying among young people. As Dr. Arnold says, "There have been bullies in every school, in every community, in every nation. Sooner or later humble men will rise and throw them down."

Studio publicity called it "A Picture as BIG as the Famous Book!" and "gripping, vivid, and exciting entertainment for all, young and old." Producers Gene Towne and Graham Baker, working under an independent deal with RKO, adapted other classic literary works to film in the early 1940s, making *Little Men* (which also starred Lydon) and *Swiss Family Robinson*. Director Robert Stevenson (1905–1986) was a Britisher himself, making his debut in America after successfully helming films in his native country. He was Oscar-nominated for his direction of *Mary Poppins* (1964), and was in his later years a house director for Disney. Production of *Tom Brown's School Days* commenced in late 1939. Crew member Ian Fulton was himself an alumnus of the real Rugby School (class of 1936), as denoted in the film's opening titles.

Assigned reading for many students in the first half of the 20th century, *Tom Brown's School Days* was thought by some reviewers to be a title moviegoers would not care to revisit. However, *Film Daily* (June 24, 1940) called it "finely made, roundly acted, and certain to score wherever it is shown." Said *Motion Picture Daily* (June 24, 1940), "It is a sound and solid piece of entertainment based on a memorable book.... Full of incidents alternately amusing and grave, the film slips smoothly along its way with its thoughtful side effectively brought forward at agreeable intervals, never over-emphasized but always gratifyingly present." Although few reviewers took note of Gale's film debut, *Daily Variety* (June 10, 1940) listed her as one of the players who "all make their parts count." The film was not a box office success, reportedly losing RKO upwards of $100,000.

One Crowded Night (1940)

Cast: Billie Seward (*Gladys*), William Haade (*Joe Miller*), Anne Revere (*Mae Andrews*), Paul Guilfoyle (*Jim Andrews*), Emma Dunn (*Ma Mathews*), George Watts (*Pa Mathews*), Dick Hogan (*Vince Sanders*), Gale Storm (*Annie Mathews*), J.M. Kerrigan (*"Doc" Joseph*), Don Costello (*Lefty*), Gaylord Pendleton (*Mat*), Charles Lang (*Fred Matson*), Adele Pearce (*Ruth Matson*), Casey Johnson (*Bobby Andrews*), Harry Shannon (*McDermot*), Ferris Taylor (*Lansing*), Francis Sayles (*Jasper*), Sammy Stein (*Mike*)

Director: Irving Reis. *Executive Producer*: Lee Marcus. *Producer*: Cliff Reid. *Screenplay*: Richard Collins, Arnaud D'Usseau. *Story*: Ben Holmes. *Photography*: J. Roy Hunt. *Art Director*: Van Nest Polglase. *Associate*: Lucius Croxton. *Wardrobe*: Renié. *Recording*: John L. Cass. *Editor*: Theron Warth.

RKO Radio Pictures; released August 9, 1940; B&W; 67 minutes.

The Mathews family—Ma and Pa, their daughters Mae and Annie, and Mae's little boy, Bobby—eke out a living operating an auto camp and lunch counter in the midst of the hot, dreary Southwestern desert. The family was forced to leave their home and business in Duluth when Mae's husband Jim, a bank clerk, was convicted of being an accomplice in a robbery. Far away from friends, family and cruel gossip, they have waited four years for an appeal or parole that might clear Jim. Younger daughter Annie, bored and frustrated by her drab lunch counter existence, can't appreciate Vince, the nice young man who's interested in her. Waitress Gladys is on the verge of marrying her good-hearted boyfriend, truck driver Joe.

The arrival of guests shakes up the Mathews' lives. There's slick-talking Brother Joseph, whose sales of "Mahatma Indian Nerve Tonic" are too infrequent to allow him to pay his bill when his truck breaks down outside. Ruth Matson, a pregnant woman on her way to San Diego to see her husband who's in the Navy, collapses in the heat, and has to be put to bed. And just when the Mathewses receive a letter from their lawyer, advising that Jim has an impending parole hearing that may free him from prison, the convict himself shows up, on the lam after breaking out, wounded, but determined to clear his own name. Nervously watching every new arrival after her husband persuades her to hide him temporarily, Mae isn't sure what to make of several other men who appear and book lodgings. Meanwhile, ready to elope with Joe, Gladys proves to have a past of her own, which threatens her plans for a happy new life. On the "crowded night" of the film's title, everything comes to a head as the destinies of the staff and guests of the Autopia Court play out in a climax that finds guns blazing in the normally quiet establishment.

After her debut in *Tom Brown's School Days*, RKO executives gave Gale her second and last assignment as a contract player with this B movie, filmed in May 1940. This modest but entertaining drama gives her better scenes to play than her first film.

When we first see Annie, she's perspiring as she cooks on a hot grill, pausing to stare resentfully at an advertising poster that shows a beautiful model enjoying a cool soft drink. "All you need's a bottle of Tropicola," she says scornfully to Gladys, reading the ad copy as the smoke from the grill swirls around her. "And some sand, and an ocean, and a four-weeks vacation," she adds. Unhappy with her lot, Annie brightens momentarily when Joe brings her a movie magazine, and she's told she bears a resemblance to Ginger Rogers. The immature teenager courts danger by accepting the sleazy attentions of visitor Mat, who offers her a way out of her present circumstances that is fraught with risk.

One Crowded Night was an apt title for Gale's second RKO film, as this publicity still demonstrates. Cast members pictured are (left to right) Charles Lang, Ferris Taylor, Anne Revere, Paul Guilfoyle, Harry Shannon, Dick Hogan, and Gale, with Gaylord Pendleton stretched out below.

While *One Crowded Night* gives Gale an interesting role, it's not the type of film that would necessarily boost the stock of a young leading lady. Gale's beauty is still apparent, but is deemphasized here in the interests of verisimilitude. The cast is dressed believably to play blue-collar people living on a modest income, and the makeup artist's chief duty seems to have been keeping the actors looking appropriately sweaty for the desert setting. The screenwriters nicely delineate a sizable number of characters, giving almost every performer at least one or two meaty scenes to play, although the sheer amount of exposition needed to unearth everyone's backstory eats up quite a bit of screen time. In the interests of appreciating the film, it may be better not to dwell on the substantial role that coincidence plays in bringing together all the characters who descend upon the auto court simultaneously, and prove to have multiple connections.

Studio publicity claimed that, because "each role ... was so equally vital to the plot's complications, the producer deliberately avoided signing a star for the picture."[1] This is an early film role for Anne Revere (1903–1990), previously better known as a stage actress. She went on to win a Best Supporting Actress Academy Award for *National Velvet*. Top-billed Billie Seward (1912–1982), playing troubled heroine Gladys, had amassed a number of film credits in the 1930s without breaking through to top stardom. Dick Hogan (1917–1995), cast as Gale's love interest Vince, played mostly bit roles prior to this, and continued to do so for some time afterwards, wrapping up his film career with a small part as the murder victim in Alfred Hitchcock's *Rope*. Hogan and Storm were teamed again in *Uncle Joe*.

Director Irving Reis (1906–1953), previously a playwright and a radio producer, went on to direct *All My Sons*. Screenwriter Arnaud D'Usseau (1916–1990) later achieved success on Broadway with his play *Tomorrow the World*, which ran for 500 performances in 1943–44.

Film Daily (August 16, 1940) predicted, "Lots of filmgoers are going to like this offering ... it is life and it's lively." Also praised were its "sincere and moving characterizations." *Motion Picture Daily* (August 16, 1940) dubbed this "the *Grand Hotel* of the tourist camps," praised the film as "replete with action and suspense," and credited the cast for "making the most of their material...." *Motion Picture Herald* (August 24, 1940) called it an "unpretentious but suspenseful wayside thriller.... [I]t is all done excitingly and happily." Said *Variety* (August 21, 1940), "It's competently made, but the story is commonplace and there isn't a trace of boxoffice draw in the cast."

After the completion of this film, RKO executives opted not to pick up Gale's option.

Uncle Joe (1941)

Cast: Slim Summerville (*Joe Butterfield*), ZaSu Pitts (*Julia Jordan*), Gale Storm (*Clare Day*), William Davidson (*J.K. Day*), Dorothy Peterson (*Margaret Day*), Dick Hogan (*Bill Jones*), Frank Coghlan, Jr. (*Dick*), James Butler (*Bob*), Maynard Holmes (*Skinny*), Brenda Henderson (*Ann*), Howard Hickman (*Banker Jones*), John Holland (*Paul Darcey*), Marvin Hatley and His Orchestra (*Themselves*), John Maxwell (*Radio Announcer*), Lynton Brent, Frank O'Connor (*Limerick Judges*)

Directors-Supervisors: Raymond E. Swartley, Howard M. Railsback. *Screenplay*: Al Weeks. *Story*: Glenn Rohrbach. *Songs* "Woogie Hula," "The Land of Nod," "Inspirational You": Marvin Hatley.

Wilding Picture Productions; completed in 1941; never released theatrically; B&W; 51 minutes.

Young Clare Day's parents don't approve of her budding relationship with a pretentious painter, and decide to cool it off by sending her to visit her Uncle Joe in the country town of Baysville, Iowa. Joe lives alone and occupies himself inventing household gadgets and tending to his simple farm. Initially unable to see the attractions of rural life, Clare gradually begins to appreciate the fresh air, good food and peaceful quiet that she finds there.

Clare makes quite an impression on the young men of the community, who still remember her as the gawky, skinny kid she used to be. Uncle Joe reminds them, "You made life miserable for her when she was here eight or nine years ago," but now Bill Jones and his pals are eager to make a good impression on the lovely young woman she's become. They also conspire to make sure that Clare sees her snobbish boyfriend Paul (whom her father describes as "that crackpot artist") in a new light when he pays a visit to Baysville.

Clare is distressed to learn that good-hearted local widow Julia Jordan, who was her mother's best friend as a girl, and at one time Uncle Joe's sweetheart, is about to default on her mortgage and lose her home. With the help of Uncle Joe, Bill and their friends,

Clare sets out to help Julia by winning the $1000 prize being offered by her father's radio program. The Dainty Soap Company, of which Mr. Day is president, has a weekly contest to complete a limerick promoting the firm's products. Clare and Uncle Joe submit an entry in Julia's name, not knowing that the lady herself is also entering the contest. Despite his daughter's plea, Mr. Day refuses to award the prize to Mrs. Jordan even after liking her entry. But before the evening is through, it looks as if Mrs. Jordan may not only save her home, but rekindle an old flame with Uncle Joe.

According to *Business Screen* magazine #7 (1941), *Uncle Joe* was produced at the Hal Roach studios, made for the industrial market by the John Deere Company. This source credited Jean Yarbrough as the director and said the picture would be shot in color. Indeed, there is an unsubtle bit of product placement, as viewers are given a good look at Uncle Joe's John Deere tractor. The film was screened in small towns, often as part of a "John Deere Day" event sponsored by a local dealer, to which farmers were given free admission. Similar to the "Streamliners" films Roach was making at the time, this is shorter than a normal feature film, running just over 50 minutes. Press releases sent to local newspapers described it: "Packed with laughs, sentiment and catchy music, this very human story will long be remembered by those who see it." Those who did turn up saw not only this, but more educational co-features like *A Line on Combines* and *Tractor Fuels and Tractors*.

Although two mediocre songs and an instrumental melody are heard during this film's brief running time, Gale is not called upon to sing, and studio musicians for the Dainty Soap radio show get the dubious privilege of performing the "Woogie Hula." Her character does, however, demonstrate her ability to play the accordion.

Perhaps the most noteworthy aspect of *Uncle Joe* is that Gale is teamed for the first time with actress ZaSu Pitts (1894–1963), later her co-star on TV's *The Gale Storm Show*. Pitts' best line comes when she observes of Clare's artist boyfriend, "That young man is all choked up with big words that don't say anything." Slim Summerville (1892–1946), with whom Pitts was teamed in multiple movies, plays Gale's loving uncle with ease and warmth, and has fun with the scenes involving his wacky kitchen gadgets. This was one of his last films.

Gale's association with the Hal Roach Studios would prove to be important to her television career.

City of Missing Girls (1941)

H.B. Warner (*Captain McVeigh*), Astrid Allwyn (*Nora Page*), John Archer (*James J. Horton*), Sarah Padden (*Mrs. Randolph*), Philip Van Zandt (*King Peterson*), George Rosener (*Officer Dugan*), Katherine Crawford (*Helen Whitney*), Patricia Knox (*Kate Nelson*), Walter Long (*Officer Larkin*), Gail [Gale] Storm (*Mary Phillips*), Boyd Irwin (*Joseph Thompson*), Danny Webb (*William Short*), Herb Vigran (*Danny Mason*), Jack Chefe (*Apartment House Manager*), Lloyd Ingraham (*D.A. William Fowler*), Donald Curtis, Ralph Peters (*Reporters*)

Director: Elmer Clifton. *Producers*: Max Alexander, George M. Merrick. *Screenplay*: Oliver Drake. *Story*: Elmer Clifton, George Rosener. *Additional Dialogue*: George Rosener. *Photography*: Edward Linden. *Settings*: Fred Preble, James Altweis. *Sound Engineer*: Clifford Ruberg. *Editor*: Charles Henkel. *Assistant Director*: Arthur Alexander.

Select Attractions, Inc.; released March 27, 1941; B&W; 73 minutes.

Police Captain McVeigh and Assistant District Attorney James Horton are tasked with investigating the disappearances of several young women who worked as showgirls. Complicating things is *Times-Record* newspaper reporter Nora Page, who despite her attraction to Horton continues to publish sensationalized stories about the investigation.

McVeigh and Horton suspect shady King Peterson, whose lucrative activities include gambling houses and sleazy nightclubs, of being involved in the disappearances and in the death of Thalia Arnold. Peterson is recruiting new talent through the Crescent School of Fine Arts, which promises naïve young women "big money earned while waiting" for their breaks in show business. Offered a $10,000 bribe to take the heat off Peterson, Horton refuses it and digs deeper.

Elderly Mrs. Randolph reports her granddaughter Pauline missing. The young lady surfaces long enough to reassure her grandmother that she's landed a new job that will help her attain her performing ambitions. Pauline also recruits pretty young Mary Phillips, who is impressed by her visit to the Crescent School.

Peterson is warned that Pauline "learned a lot about your rackets, and she's beginning to blab," and soon she turns up dead. The police raid the Crescent School, where Mary Phillips is taken into custody and questioned about what she saw. Mary is unable to pick out of a police lineup the "actress" who took her and Pauline there, though Horton hauls in various young ladies who perform in Peterson's nightclubs. The lady in question, Kate Nelson, accepts a bribe from Peterson to lure the young assistant D.A. to her apartment and set him up to take a compromising photograph. Soon Nelson is also dead, and Horton considers resigning from the D.A.'s office, considering himself a failure.

Nora, determined to get to the bottom of things, infiltrates the Crescent School and catches the eye of Peterson. But when she's identified by his cohort as a newspaper reporter, Peterson brings matters to a head by showing Nora the involvement of someone near and dear to her in the nefarious racket.

Freelancing after her release from RKO, Gale landed a small role in this cheaply made film. Billed tenth in the cast list, she also has her professional name misspelled. Much of her limited dialogue consists of "Yes, sir" and "No, sir," as she answers questions from the police, and looks at suspects in a lineup. Still a teenager during production, she brings a believable touch of innocence and charm to her role as a naïve girl who aspires to be a professional dancer (though she knows her mother wouldn't approve), and is all too ready to be taken in by the staff of the Crescent School, saying, "It's just like a dream!"

Director Elmer Clifton (1890–1949), who also worked on the original story for *City of Missing Girls,* entered the film industry as an actor during the silent era, appearing in D.W. Griffith's classics *The Birth of a Nation* (1915) and *Intolerance* (1916). He made the switch to directing in the late 1910s, and is credited with discovering a young Clara Bow. By the sound era, however, he was directing low-budget Westerns, melodramas and exploitation films, including *Assassin of Youth* and *Youth Aflame.* It was Clifton's illness on the set of *Not Wanted* (1949) that led actress Ida Lupino to direct for the first time.

Top-billed H.B. Warner (1875–1958) was another veteran of the silent era, perhaps best-remembered for playing Jesus Christ in Cecil B. DeMille's *The King of Kings* (1927), or for being one of Norma Desmond's "waxworks" in *Sunset Blvd.* (1950). According to a less-than-reliable source, the film's pressbook, he said *City of Missing Girls* gave him "the most emotionally satisfying role I ever enacted in my long movie career." He and Gale had crossed paths earlier, when he took part in the *Gateway to Hollywood* contest, as leading man John Archer had also done. Astrid Allwyn (1905–1978) is cast as the clichéd girl reporter, Nora Page. Nora impulsively prints rumors and half-truths without scruple, saying to Jimmy Horton, "If I can't get my news from you, I have to make it myself. That's my job!" Allwyn, who retired from films in 1943, is the mother of actress Melinda O. Fee.

Philip Van Zandt (1904–1958), here slightly resembling William Powell, gives a professional performance as slimy bad guy Peterson, who explains that some of the girls he hires just happen to take bookings out of town, from which they don't return, having decided they "like the climate" elsewhere. He will turn up again in Gale's film *Between Midnight and Dawn* and an episode of *My Little Margie*. Distinctive character actor Herb Vigran (1910–1986) is unbilled for his featured role as Danny, managing director of the Crescent School.

George Rosener is credited with "additional dialogue" for the film, which hopefully didn't include such exchanges as bad guy Peterson, visiting the D.A.'s office, asking if he can smoke, to which Jimmy Horton retorts, "I don't care if you burn!" Rosener also contributes one of the worst performances in the film, as a policeman whose wavering accent seems to be trying for some combination of stereotypical Irish and "Noo Yawk."

Although correctly classed as an exploitation film and released by an independent company, *City of Missing Girls* is pretty tame stuff by the standards of that genre. There's no nudity or titillating scenes played in lingerie, as had begun to turn up in some other exploitation products of the day, and the screenplay is too covert to specify exactly what misfortune befalls the young ladies who fall in with King Peterson. Nonetheless, the National League of Decency awarded the film a B rating ("Objectionable in part") for its "sordid background."

At the time *City of Missing Girls* (1941) was released, Gale wasn't yet famous enough to be featured in ads. In fact, her name was misspelled (as "Gail") in the opening credits.

If the film itself was relatively tame, the pressbook had a few suggestive "catch lines" to make it sound lurid:

- "Filched from the intimate blood-smeared diary of a veteran homicide dick!"
- "They were pretty feminine blossoms, doomed to wilt in the underworld of vice!"
- "When they did their masters' bidding, they lived—when they rebelled, they died!"

- "Death mocks ambition as beauty rides fame's roller coaster to an unmarked grave!"

Showman's Trade Review (July 5, 1941) reported a "simple but effective" display an Idaho theater owner used to promote the film: "On a table were articles of feminine wearing apparel," accompanied by a sign that read, "Whose clothes are these? If you have information concerning the whereabouts of this Missing Girl, please contact the manager of this theatre."

Film Daily (April 9, 1941), noting that the "missing girls" story "is always with us," found *City of Missing Girls* an adequate example of the genre: "[I]ts sob-sister sensationalism ... is certain to fill its function handsomely..." *Motion Picture Herald* (April 5, 1941) thought it "lacks the qualities of dialogue and direction to put it above run-of-the-mill exposes..." *Variety* (April 2, 1941) found the film "wearisome," saying, "Premise upon which yarn is based is both vague and unconvincing."

Saddlemates (1941)

Cast: Robert Livingston (*"Stony" Brooke*), Bob Steele (*"Tucson" Smith*), Rufe Davis (*"Lullaby" Joslin*), Gale Storm (*Susan Langley*), Forbes Murray (*Colonel Langley*), Cornelius Keefe (*Lt. Bob Manning*), Peter George Lynn (*LeRoque/Wanechee*), Marin Sais (*Mrs. Langley*), Marty Faust (*Chief Thunder Bird*), Glenn Strange (*Little Bear*), Ellen Lowe (*Amanda Langley*), Iron Eyes Cody (*Black Eagle*), Ed Cassidy (*Captain Miller*), Yakima Canutt (*Wagon Driver*), Spade Cooley (*Fiddle Player*), Henry Wills (*Bobtail Horse*), Philip Kieffer (*Army Sergeant*), Curley Dresden (*Blacksmith*), Slim Whitaker (*Huggins*), Chief Many Treaties (*Talking Bull*), Chick Hannan (*Card Player*), Art Dillard (*Cavalry Trooper*)

Director: Les Orlebeck. *Associate Producer*: Louis Gray. *Screenplay*: Albert DeMond, Herbert Dalmas. *Original Story*: Bernard McConville, Karen DeWolf, based on characters created by William Colt MacDonald. *Production Manager*: Al Wilson. *Photography*: William Nobles. *Editor*: Tony Martinelli. *Musical Score*: Cy Feuer.

Republic Pictures; released May 16, 1941; B&W; 56 minutes.

Texas Rangers Stony, Tucson and Lullaby have been trying to track the elusive Comanche Indian Chief Wanechee, who strikes fear in the white settlers of the region. When a Congressional ruling establishes that the territory is no longer part of the state of Texas, the Rangers move on to another post, leaving behind the three scouts to assist the incoming U.S. Cavalry. Impressed with Susan, the pretty daughter of Colonel Langley, leader of the Army command, Stony and his buddies agree to enlist in the Army and help the cause.

Colonel Langley wants to try peaceable solutions with the Indians, despite the warnings of the Mesquiteers. The former Texas Rangers have trouble adapting to Army discipline and are suspicious of the post's translator LeRoque, who is in fact Wanechee in disguise. They warn Langley that the Indians held up a stagecoach and are in possession of rifles, endangering the safety of the Army wives and family members expected to arrive shortly. Though Susan encourages her father to accept the Mesquiteers' advice, he finds them unsuitable soldiers, and soon all three have been discharged from their Army duties.

Acting independently, Stony and his pals take two Indians captive and learn the secret of Wanechee's identity. Wanechee, in his guise as LeRoque, informs Langley of the Mesquiteers' skirmish with the Indians. Langley sends his second-in-command, Lt. Manning, to arrest the trio, and upon his arrival the Mesquiteers' captives are found to be dead (thanks to the conniving Wanechee). Accused of the murders, the Mesquiteers are on their way to jail until Susan intervenes. Colonel Langley and his men, naively believing they are to sign a peace treaty with the Comanches, are instead taken captive, leaving it to Stony, Tucson, and Lullaby to protect the approaching wagon train of civilians—including Langley's wife and son—from the marauding Indians.

Saddlemates marks Gale's debut in the Western genre, one to which she returned with some frequency throughout her motion picture career. This standard B Western is one of more than 50 "Three Mesquiteers" features released by Republic between 1936 and 1943. Competently shot on a tight budget, it benefits from the use of some stock action footage from earlier films to flesh out the action scenes, but these elements are capably melded into the new movie. It is a remake of the Gene Autry vehicle *Ride, Ranger, Ride,* released five years earlier. Typical of the era, the screenplay presents the Comanches as violent and bloodthirsty, though there are indications that a rival faction within the tribe would be willing to work peaceably with the white settlers.

Gale's Susan Langley is smart, a better judge of character than her father, and a beauty who catches the eye of both Stony and Tucson. Her father, in charge of the Army unit, makes practically every wrong decision possible, causing her to say worriedly after he makes one harebrained announcement, "I hope it comes out all right, Dad." Later, she does a bit of impromptu playacting that frees the Three Mesquiteers to ride to the rescue of her father and the members of the imperiled wagon train. Romance in the film goes largely unfulfilled, though two of the Mesquiteers earn a grateful kiss from Gale's character.

The film's heroics are mostly in the hands of Robert Livingston (1904–1988) and Bob Steele (1907–1988). Rufe Davis (1908–1974), better known to a later generation as Floyd Smoot on TV's *Petticoat Junction,* provides the comic relief here as Lullaby as well as a novelty song, "Just Imagine That." He's assisted by Ellen Lowe (1898–1984), cast as Susan's Aunt Amanda, a man-hungry spinster whose interest in him is not reciprocated. Marin Sais (1890–1971) shows up late in the film as Mrs. Langley, who proves to be surprisingly handy with a rifle, and considerably more helpful than her ineffectual husband. Forbes Murray (1884–1982), experienced at playing executive types, makes Captain Langley look more competent than he ultimately proves to be.

Motion Picture Herald (June 14, 1941) praised *Saddlemates* for "providing excellent western entertainment..." According to *Showmen's Trade Review* (June 14, 1941), "Lots of Indians, plenty of action, riding and gunplay, not to mention a bit of comedy ... make *Saddlemates* a readily acceptable outdoor contribution for the western fans." Gale, said *Variety* (June 18, 1941), "is most prominent in support and extremely attractive," while *Motion Picture Daily* (June 10, 1941) noted that she and featured actor Peter George Lynn "lend able support."

Before the year was out, Gale was signed for another Republic Western, *Jesse James at Bay.* Around the time of *Saddlemates'* release, *Variety* reported that she was being tested for a role in an upcoming MGM Andy Hardy film, but she was not chosen.

Gambling Daughters (1941)

Cast: Cecilia Parker (*Diana Cameron*), Roger Pryor (*Chance Landon*), Robert Baldwin (*Jimmy Parker*), Sigi [Sig] Arno (*Professor Bedoin*), Gale Storm (*Lillian Harding*), Charles Miller (*Walter Cameron*), Al Hall (*Dean*), Eddie Foster (*Nick*), Janet Shaw

(*Katherine Thompsen*), Marvelle Andre (*Dorothy*), Roberta Smith (*Mary*), Judy Kilgore (*Gloria*), Gertrude Messinger (*Jane*)

Director: Max Nosseck. *Producer*: T.H. Richmond. *Screenplay*: Joel Kay, Arnold Phillips. *Original Story*: Sidney Sheldon, Ben Roberts. *Additional Dialogue*: Genevieve Hogan. *Associate Producer*: Melville Shyer. *Music Directors*: Dick Russom, Joe Ortiz. *Photography*: Mack Stengler. *Editor*: Guy V. Thayer, Jr. *Art Director*: Frank Sylos. *Sound Engineer*: Ben Winkler. *Assistant Director*: Joe Dill.

Producers Releasing Corporation; released August 1, 1941; B&W; 63 minutes.

Diana Cameron, a student at the Lakeside School for Girls, is upset because her father Walter repeatedly cancels plans for her to visit him, claiming he's too busy with his work as a financier. Meanwhile, curious about where their French professor spends his off hours, Diana's roommates Lillian and Katherine follow him one evening to a roadhouse, the Angel's Roost, which has a gambling den beneath the main club. Walter Cameron is on the scene that evening, although his daughters' friends fail to notice him. Chance Landon, who manages the club for his mysterious, never-seen boss, determines that the young ladies from well-to-do families are worth cultivating. He befriends them and encourages them to try their hand at gambling. Lillian, who's attracted to Chance, unwisely takes advantage of the club's credit line over the new few days until she runs up a $13,000 gambling debt. Katherine, who also lost money at the club, is forced to stage a phony robbery at her parents' house, making off with jewels that she can use to pay what she owes.

Lillian, who's written some indiscreet letters to Chance, is horrified when he tells her that his boss expects repayment of her debt in short order. With her parents away, Lillian goes home to New York, accompanied by Diana. While Diana learns that her father has been trying to hide financial difficulties from her (admitting that he's the type of banker who "loses millions"), Lillian steals some jewelry from her family home. The gems she pockets aren't sufficient to meet the crooks' demands. Desperate, she almost overdoses on a sleeping potion, and is sent to the school infirmary to recuperate.

Insurance investigator Jimmy Parker notices the similarity between the two recent jewel robberies and the fact that the daughters of both families are enrolled at Lakeside. With the reluctant consent of the school's dean, Parker poses as a gymnastics instructor in order to investigate what's going on at the school. Befriended by Diana, Jimmy confesses his true mission, and she pledges her help. The girls of the school take Landon's henchman Nick captive, trying to recover Lillian's letters and jewels. But further investigation into the Angel's Roost threatens to expose someone well-known to Diana as the real culprit behind the gamblers' den.

Although *Variety* reported that Gale made this film on loanout from RKO during her stint there as a contract player, other sources confirm that she was already freelancing by May 1941, when the picture was filmed. This was Gale's only film for Producers Releasing Corporation, a Poverty Row studio that occasionally made even Monogram seem slightly extravagant. *Gambling Daughters* reflects its low budget and hasty shooting schedule. The camera pans nonchalantly by the bare ends of set walls in a scene set in the dormitory, with no one taking the trouble in post-production to perform an edit to avoid pointing up how shoddy the sets are. Music Directors Dick Russom and Joe Ortiz appear on-camera as piano players working at the Angel's Roost, using those instruments to provide most of the film's threadbare musical score.

As Lillian, Gale has a few dramatic opportunities here, including her teary plea to the unseen gambling boss, who fails to take pity on her, and her condemnation of the "filthy beast" Chance Landon when he betrays her. The film opens with a scene showing Gale's character Lillian, identified in dialogue as "the best swimmer of the Lakeside School," taking first place in a school swim meet. However, this scene serves no particular purpose except to put Gale and a few other starlets into swimsuits for a few minutes, and has nothing to do with the rest of the film.

Top-billed Cecilia Parker (1914–1993) was an MGM contract player best-known for playing Andy Hardy's sister Marian in the popular Hardy series. Cast as her leading man, though he doesn't become a prominent character until the latter half of the film, is her real-life husband, actor Robert Baldwin (1904–1996). Baldwin, as Jimmy Parker, is given some mild comedy to play, as the not-very-convincing instructor who's flipped on his back by a girl demonstrating judo, and endures an unwanted cold shower when he hides in the girls' dormitory room. Roger Pryor (1901–1974), cast here as the slick gambler who preys on Lillian, was at this time the real-life husband of actress Ann Sothern. He and Parker are billed above the film's title, though his role is somewhat subordinate.

Credited as co-author of the original story is a young Sidney Sheldon (1917–2007), earning one of his first screen credits. The finished screenplay, such as it is, meanders a bit, making it difficult for a time to tell whether Diana or Lillian is supposed to be the focal character. The film was edited by Guy V. Thayer, Jr., who later served as associate producer of *My Little Margie*. It subsequently played on television as *The Professor's Gamble*.

Motion Picture Daily (September 8, 1941) thought the film "suitable as a secondary feature" and credited it with having "exploitation possibilities." *Showmen's Trade Review* (September 13, 1941) said, "Mechanical and uninspired direction plus a slow-moving and obvious plot relegate this picture to the second half of dual bills... [It's] slow and draggy." *Film Daily* (September 16, 1941) thought Max Nosseck's direction "manages to generate some suspense..."

Let's Go Collegiate (1941)

Cast: Frankie Darro (*Frankie Monahan*), Marcia Mae Jones (*Bess Martin*), Jackie Moran (*Tad*), Keye Luke (*Buck Wing*), Mantan Moreland (*Jeff*), Frank Sully (*Herk Bevans*), Gale Storm (*Midge Lawrence*), Billy Griffith (*Professor Whitaker*), Barton Yarborough (*Coach Walsh*), Frank Faylen (*Speed Dorman*), Marguerite Whitten (*Malvina*), Paul Maxey (*Bill Miller*), Tristram Coffin (*Slugger Wilson*), Gene O'Donnell (*Announcer*)

Director: Jean Yarbrough. *Producer*: Lindsley Parsons. *Screenplay*: Edmond Kelso. *Music Director*: Edward Kay. *Lyrics*: Harry Tobias. *Photography*: Mack Stengler. *Editor*: Arthur E. Roberts. *Assistant Director*: William Strohbach. *Sound Director*: Glen Glenn. *Settings*: Dave Milton. *Art Director*: Charles Clague.

Monogram Pictures; released September 12, 1941; B&W; 61 minutes.

The boys of Rawley University's Kappa Psi Delta fraternity, led by Frankie, Tad and Buck, eagerly await the arrival of newcomer Bob Terry, whose athletic abilities are expected to be a boon to the school's rowing team. Their girlfriends, including Bess and Midge, have arranged for their sorority to host a welcoming reception for Terry. Only hours before the party, the boys learn that Bob Terry was drafted and won't be coming to Rawley, making the boys fear that the sorority sisters will be angry.

Lobby card for *Let's Go Collegiate* (1941), Gale's first film at Monogram. At left, she holds hands with star Frankie Darro.

When Frankie spots a strong, if seemingly dimwitted, lunkhead named Hercules ("Herk"), they offer him ten dollars to pose as Bob Terry on the night of the party, in order to postpone giving the girls the bad news. Rough around the edges, Herk is none too convincing as a prep school graduate, but the girls enjoy the attention and admiration he lavishes on them. The next day, Herk decides to stick around and continue the impersonation. His fear of the water makes it a challenge to pass him off as a rowing crew member, and his lack of education is all too apparent in Professor Whitaker's biology class. Much to the boys' disappointment, their girlfriends have become infatuated with the phony Terry, and return the boys' fraternity pins.

With coaching, Herk proves to be a more successful crew member (with a "brilliant stroke") than the other boys anticipated, and quickly becomes the team's best hope of winning the championship. On the day of the race, Herk is recognized as a bank robber on the lam, while it comes to the attention of Bess and Midge that he has promised himself to both of them.

Billed by studio publicists as an "uproarious musical comedy of campus life," this was Gale's first film for Monogram and for producer Lindsley Parsons (1905–1992). Though *Let's Go Collegiate* offers Gale only a smallish featured role, she is given the opportunity to sing two solo numbers, "Since You Came Along" and "Sweet Sixteen." She and Marcia Mae Jones, as Bess, do their best with the implausible situation that finds them awed and impressed by Herk, for reasons that the script and Frank Sully's performance make elusive. Aside from Gale, practically all the major participants here, including actors Darro, Moreland, Jones, Moran and Luke, along with screenwriter Kelso and director Jean Yarbrough, had recently finished making *The Gang's All Here* for producer Parsons. Yarbrough (1900–1975) directed Gale again in *Freckles Comes Home* and *Lure of the Islands*.

Fraternity life is depicted as thoroughly innocuous here, with Frankie and his buddies taken aback when Herk suggests livening up the punch at the party with a little liquor. Only one line of dialogue hints at hazing activity: A pledge ventures an unsolicited opinion in one scene, to which Darro's Frankie snaps, "Quiet, frosh! You're lucky you still got your underwear." It's a bit surprising that the vigilant censors of the era didn't object to the gag concerning seasick medicine given to Herk, which is called "Aunty Upchuck's Seasick Pills."

Top-billed Frankie Darro (1917–1976) made a series of comedies for Monogram in the 1940s, often paired with Mantan Moreland as his sidekick. Even Gale, at 5'4" and in heels, towers over the diminutive Darro, whose size helped him play boyish roles well into his twenties. Moreland, once again playing Jeff, is cast here as a man-of-all-work employed at the fraternity house. Not surprisingly, given the period, ethnic and cultural sensitivity toward the African-American and Chinese-American characters is scant. Moreland, whose character is used by the fraternity boys to play piggyback, and winds up in a garbage can, is given lines like, "Honest, gentlemen! I'm the stupidest man I ever saw." Although Keye Luke (1904–1991) makes a rather mature fraternity boy, he plays the role with his usual dignity and competence, despite a few too many lines that begin, "Old Chinese proverb say…" It was probably meant as inclusive for the time that Kappa Psi Delta has an Asian brother, but it's noteworthy that he's the only one who's seen attending the fraternity and sorority parties stag, and is not permitted to exhibit any interest in the pretty Caucasian girls. He walks away in dignified silence when a boorish alumnus sees him at the dance and says, "What tong do you belong to?" Two actors who would enjoy featured roles in 1950s sitcoms turn up here as fraternity alumni, Paul Maxey (*The People's Choice*) and Frank Faylen (*The Many Loves of Dobie Gillis*).

Let's Go Collegiate received generally respectful reviews upon its release, at least with those who understood the audience for which it had been made. *Showmen's Trade Review* (September 20, 1941) was impressed by Gale: "She has looks, sings quite well and has enough acting ability to handle regulation ingénue roles with credit and charm." *Film Daily* (September 16, 1941) predicted that *Let's Go Collegiate* "should catch the 'back to school,' and the seasonal 'college sport' interest, and should find a welcoming spot as a filler for twin billings, with satisfactory box office response from the juve trade…" Gale was among the cast members credited with turning in "fine performances…" *Motion Picture Herald* (September 20, 1941) credited the modestly budgeted picture with "freshness, spirit, liveliness, humor and the essentials of entertainment generally."

Jesse James at Bay (1941)

Cast: Roy Rogers (*Jesse James/Clint Burns*), George "Gabby" Hayes (*Sheriff Gabby Whitaker*), Sally Payne (*Polly Morgan*), Pierre Watkin (*Phineas Krager*), Ivan Miller (*Judge Rutherford*), Hal Taliaferro (*Paul Sloan*), Gale Storm (*Jane Fillmore*), Roy Barcroft

(*Vern Stone*), Jack Kirk (*Rufe Balder*), Hank Bell (*Charlie Davis*), Chester Conklin (*Town Drunk*), Rex Lease (*Gregg*), Edward Peil, Sr. (*U.S. Marshal*), Fern Emmett (*Emmy Davis*), Charles R. Moore (*Mose*), Luke Cosgrave (*Cartwright*), John Dilson (*Collins*), Kit Guard (*Bartender*), Chuck Morrison (*Cole Younger*), Billy Benedict (*Young Davis*), Rick Anderson, Foxy Callahan, Lloyd Ingraham (*Card Players*)

Director-Associate Producer: Joseph Kane. *Screenplay*: James R. Webb. *Original Story*: Harrison Jacobs. *Production Manager*: Al Wilson. *Photography*: William Nobles. *Editor*: Tony Martinelli. *Music Director*: Cy Feuer.

Republic Pictures; released October 18, 1941; B&W; 59 minutes.

History books tell us that notorious outlaw Jesse James (1847–1882) was killed at the age of 34, by a member of his own gang. As this film claims in an opening title card, "But there is another legend—vouched for by many old-timers of Missouri—which goes like this…"

Unscrupulous Phineas Krager, on behalf of the Midland and Western Railroad, offers "free land" to Missouri newcomers willing to farm and develop it. The farmers undertake the backbreaking work with the understanding that they will subsequently be able to purchase clear title to the land for no more than $3 an acre. But once the area has been improved to the railroad company's satisfaction, it is put up for sale at $100 an acre, and the original settlers told they have no valid claim on it. With the help of lawyer Paul Sloan, who says his own family was similarly victimized, the farmers press their case in court. Judge Rutherford acknowledges the settlers' moral rights, but is forced to concede that the railroad owns the property.

Sheriff Whitaker, seeing that the farmers need "a fighting leader," writes a letter to "George W. Jessup" in Nebraska, who's really his old friend Jesse James. While Jesse is a wanted man, Whitaker hopes he can surreptitiously aid the farmers in retaining their land. Soon after, one of Midland and Western's trains is robbed, and suddenly the farmers have ready cash on hand to buy their deeds. Meanwhile, James' lookalike, gambler Clint Burns, "the best poker player in Missouri," arrives in town and is mistaken for the wanted outlaw. Furious that land claims are being purchased with money he's sure was stolen from the railroad, Krager hires Burns to commit crimes in the community, hoping they will be attributed to Jesse James and turn public sentiment against the man many now regard as a "Robin Hood" hero.

Polly Morgan and Jane Fillmore, reporters for the *St. Louis Journal,* arrive in town and are on the scene when Sheriff Whitaker's house is set on fire by Clint Burns. Moments later, a man who looks almost like Burns shows up and rescues the sheriff from the blaze Burns himself set. The newcomer confesses to the reporters that he is Jesse James but asks them to withhold the story, with the promise that he will lead them to an even better one.

A raid on James' purported hideout results in Burns being killed, but being identified as James. Assuming his lookalike's identity, James thwarts Krager's efforts to bribe him into leaving town, but the ruse is exposed when Jesse is forced to defend himself in a gunfight over a card game. With the help of Sheriff Whitaker, sympathetic Judge Rutherford and the *St. Louis Journal* ladies, James rides into action to expose the bad guys and restore peace.

Clocking in at just under an hour, this fast-paced and lively shoot-'em-up, filmed in the fall of 1941, gives Roy Rogers (1911–1998) the chance to play a dual role, with a screenplay that whitewashes Jesse James and makes him a folk hero. This is the first of three Rogers films in which Gale appeared in short order. In his memoir, Rogers said of his pre–Dale Evans leading ladies, "None of them lasted long for the simple reason that playing opposite me wasn't much of a plum part."[2]

Seventh-billed Gale joins Sally Payne (1912–1999) in playing what *Leonard Maltin's Classic Movie Guide* has described as "two of the dumbest Eastern newspaper reporters ever seen." Without wishing to go overboard refuting that statement, it's fair to say that Payne, who has the larger and more comedic role, portrays the dumber, more foolhardy of the two. Taking a statement in which villain Krager tells her the land deeds are being bought with stolen money, she scribbles notes in her copy pad and asks cheerfully, "Can you prove it, or do I use the word 'alleged'?" Later in the film, she shows herself to be reckless with the gun someone foolishly gave her.

Not wasting much time ordering sarsaparillas in the local saloon, Polly and Jane jump full-fledged into the action, trying to rescue the sheriff from a blazing house, barging into the house where Jesse James is believed to be hiding, and watching enthralled as the good guys shoot it out with the bad guys in the climax. "I never thought we'd get a story like this when we left St. Louis," Jane gushes. Gale also functions as Rogers' leading lady in this outing, as Jane is let in on the true identity of the visitor from Nebraska and comes to his aid on several occasions. Gale, who would later say that movie producers overestimated her horsemanship skills (based on her Texas upbringing), rides competently here, and is the recipient of Rogers' only song in the film.

Reviewer Leyendecker of *Film Bulletin* (December 29, 1941) rated *Jesse James at Bay* "another lively Roy Rogers outdoor vehicle with the usual high quota of riding action and shooting thrills." Gale and Sally Payne were described as "attractive, although scarcely credible as newspaper reporters of the '90s." *Showmen's Trade Review* (October 18, 1941) found Rogers' bad guy character unconvincing, as "it is hard to mask his good nature and congeniality with a black hat and a two-day growth of whiskers." Gale, said the review, made "a most attractive heroine." *Motion Picture Daily* (October 13, 1941) predicted that Western fans "should find the presentation wholly satisfactory." Said *Variety* (October 15, 1941), "Joseph Kane, director-producer, has paced his yarn with the skill usually found in better programmers, and James R. Webb's scripting is above par." This was an early credit for screenwriter Webb (1910–1974), who went on to win a Best Original Screenplay Oscar for *How the West Was Won* (1962).

Jesse James was previously played by Tyrone Power in a much higher-budgeted Fox film, released in 1939. Actor Alan Baxter offered another take on the outlaw in *Bad Men of Missouri,* released earlier in 1941.

Red River Valley (1941)

Cast: Roy Rogers (*Roy Rogers*), George "Gabby" Hayes (*Gabby Whittaker*), Sally Payne (*Sally Whittaker*), Trevor Bardette (*Allison*), Gale Storm (*Kay Sutherland*), Robert Homans (*Sheriff Sutherland*), Hal Taliaferro (*Murdock*), Lynton Brent (*Feld*), Jack Kirk (*Sheep Rancher*), Edward Peil, Sr. (*Cattle Rancher*), Dick Wessel (*Truck Driver*), Monte Montague (*Mechanic*), The Sons of the Pioneers

Director–Associate Producer: Joseph Kane. *Original Screenplay*: Malcolm Stuart Boylan. *Photography*: Jack Marta. *Editor*: William Thompson. *Music Director*: Cy Feuer.

Republic Pictures; released December 12, 1941; B&W; 62 minutes.

Back home for a visit, radio star Roy Rogers (accompanied by the Sons of the Pioneers) is being given a homecoming party when an explosion goes off, signifying that the town bank is being robbed. Unidentified crooks make off with $182,000, money earmarked for expenses and payroll on the White Mountain Dam, which is currently under construction. With the dam construction already plagued by accidents and other problems, it seems that someone doesn't want it completed.

Rather than stop the project for lack of funds, Roy suggests that the local ranchers raise money by selling their cattle, though they'll have to do so at a loss. Rancher Allison instead proposes that the residents sell their stockholders' rights in the Red River Land and Water Company to him and his business partners, with the promise that they'll be able to buy back in later. Gabby, the local barber, and his daughter Sally believe Roy is right, but most of the cattlemen prefer Allison's proposal. Suspicious, Roy warns the local sheriff, "When you fellows turn over the controlling interest to the water company to Allison, he'll own the whole valley." Unable to make his point by persuasion, Roy pretends to leave town in order to do a radio performance in El Paso, but actually postpones the stockholders' meeting by kidnapping the sheriff. Also taken along is the sheriff's pretty daughter Kay, whom Roy has been romancing. After Kay's unsuccessful escape attempt, Sally Whittaker warns Roy that his enemies suspect he's not really in El Paso, so he does his radio broadcast by remote telephone hookup as a cover.

Tracked down at their hideout, a sheepherder's shack in the hills, Roy's men are captured and jailed, but Roy soon masterminds a jailbreak. Sure that Allison knows more than he's saying about the missing bank funds, Roy and his men descend upon the Casa Rio, a gambling den operated by Allison's cohorts, to force the crooks out into the open.

This 20th century Western presents Roy as a celebrity, an amalgam of his screen character and his own persona. The story incorporates the usual gunplay and horsemanship, but also automobiles used for a quick getaway, tire tracks that may provide evidence, and the use of 1940s telephone and radio technology to advance the story. Along with the comic relief of Gabby Hayes, music is prominently featured here, with the Sons of the Pioneers singing tunes like "When Payday Rolls Around." *Red River Valley* is a remake of a Gene Autry Western released only five years previously, though with some notable changes to the story and characters.

Gale once again plays Roy's love interest in her second Rogers film, released only a few weeks after their first teaming. Here, they are already a couple when the story opens, but have their relationship endangered by a disagreement that finds her being loyal to her father, the sheriff. Given less screen time than in her other films with Rogers, Gale gets into the action when she's kidnapped along with her father. Not one to take this lying down, she escapes the first chance she gets, trying to sound the warning alarm, and banters with Roy about how much he will "enjoy" a stay in jail.

Sally Payne, who appeared with Gale in all three of her Roy Rogers Westerns, here plays Gabby's daughter, as she will again in *Man from Cheyenne*. Though Payne and Hayes are given the bulk of the comedic chores, Robert Homans, as the irritated sheriff with whom Roy argues, gets the funniest line when he snaps, "I don't mind you so much on the radio, 'cause I can always turn you off [*snapping fingers*] ... just like that."

Variety (December 31, 1941) considered this one of Rogers' stronger films from a musical standpoint, reuniting him with the Sons of the Pioneers after a gap of several years. Regarding Payne and Storm, the reviewer added, "Both girls, lightly considered by the writing department, are okay." Said *Motion Picture Daily* (December 15, 1941), "Splendid photography, a good job of direction, especially the staging of the action scenes, standard performances and nicely handled musical numbers combine to make *Red River*

Valley effective entertainment for Western audiences." *Motion Picture Herald* (December 20, 1941) termed it "an entertaining, tuneful and action-packed story photographed against the hill-and-plain background familiar to most western fans."

Freckles Comes Home (1942)

Cast: Johnny Downs (*Freckles Winslow*), Gale Storm (*Jane Potter*), Mantan Moreland (*Jeff*), Irving Bacon (*Constable Caleb Weaver*), Bradley Page (*Nate Quigley*), Marvin Stephens (*Danny Doyle*), Betty Blythe (*Minerva Potter*), Walter Sande (*Jack Leach, aka "Muggsie" Dolan*), Max Hoffman, Jr. (*Hymie*), John Ince (*Hiram Potter*), Lawrence Criner (*Roxbury B. Brown III*), Irving Mitchell (*Mr. Winslow*), Gene O'Donnell (*Monk*), Si Jenks (*Lem Perkins*)

Director: Jean Yarbrough. *Producer*: Lindsley Parsons. *Screenplay*: Edmond Kelso. *Suggested by the Novel by* Jeannette Stratton Porter. *Music Director*: Edward Kay. *Songs*: Edward Cherkose, Edward Kay. *Photography*: Mack Stengler. *Production Manager*: William Strohbach. *Editor*: Jack Ogilvie. *Sound Director*: Glen Glenn. *Technical Director*: Dave Milton.

Monogram Pictures; released January 2, 1942; B&W; 60 minutes.

Recent college graduate Freckles Winslow is going home to Fairfield, Indiana (population 500), for a visit. En route, he tells a fellow bus passenger what a peaceful and relaxing place the town is, unaware that he's talking to a gangster on the lam. "Muggsie" Dolan, who's adopted the new name Jack Leach, decides a stay in Fairfield is just the place to lay low after a recent bank heist.

Freckles' best friend Danny, who operates the Argonaut Hotel in Fairfield, desperately needs his help with a problem. Danny spent the money his uncle sent him to buy a 60-day option on some local property, believing it could be profitably developed. Now grouchy Mr. Potter at the bank is ready to foreclose, putting Danny in financial jeopardy. Meanwhile, Jeff, who works as a porter at the hotel, is doing his best to unload a worthless "gold-divining" machine for which he paid far too much.

Freckles thinks Danny's investment could be saved, and the sleepy town revitalized, if he could persuade members of the road commission to build a spur from the main highway that would run through Fairfield. One of the commissioners casting a vote is Freckles' dad;

Johnny Downs and Gale make an appealing young couple in *Freckles Comes Home* **(Monogram, 1942).**

unfortunately, another is Mr. Potter, and the two family patriarchs have been feuding for years. Danny suggests that Freckles ask his childhood sweetheart, Potter's daughter Jane, for help obtaining her dad's vote. Jane, a very pretty young lady, is delighted to see Freckles again when they both attend the annual Loyal Order of Corn Huskers dance, but sends him away in anger after realizing the ulterior motive behind his attentions to her.

Seeing the simple townspeople as victims ripe to be rooked, Jack Leach sends for his "associate," Mr. Quigley, who organizes a bond drive for the new road that's designed to fleece the locals of their money. Mr. Potter, seeing visions of dollar signs, falls for Quigley's slick campaign, and even Jane, still on the outs with Danny, finds the newcomer personable.

With the bond campaign in full swing, inept local constable Caleb Weaver is startled to find the body of Jack Leach in his hotel room, a knife in his back. Two G-men arrive on the scene in a bit of fortuitous timing, but Freckles correctly suspects they are just two more crooks in cahoots with Quigley. Unable to get much help from the local law, Freckles, Danny, Jeff and even Jane hope to prevent the crooks from robbing Potter's bank on their way out of town.

Once again, as in *Uncle Joe*, Gale plays a young woman who's grown up quite a bit since a boy from her childhood last saw her; Freckles remembers Jane as "that gawky, pigtailed Potter brat." Gale sings a duet, "Where We Dream Tonight," with Johnny Downs. Second-billed, she not only makes a beautiful love interest, but even provides a handy firearm in a moment of crisis.

The film's pressbook continued to play up the contest win that brought Gale to California, but jazzed up the story with a few details that were pure invention. The publicity boys claimed she chose her own movie star name: "She was passing a United States weather observatory when she glanced at a weather report that ... read, 'Storm—Beware of Gale.' 'And,' said Gale Storm after hectic weeks trying to find a name, 'what's good enough for Uncle Sam to tell the world is good enough for me.'" Also crediting her with an artistic bent, another item said that she had spent her downtime on set "working on a clay model of Johnny Downs' head, which she completed before the picture was finished."

Mantan Moreland (1902–1973), whose comic skills perked up many a mediocre B movie, can't do much to help here, given the material screenwriter Edmond Kelso gave him. For much of the movie, he's stranded in a subordinate story that finds him feuding pointlessly with the chauffeur who drove Mr. Quigley to town. Much of his dialogue references razors, dice and other stereotypical accouterments with which African-American characters of the era were often saddled.

According to studio publicity for *Freckles Comes Home*, "It's a homebody sort of picture about smalltown [sic] folks who outwit a pack of big city wiseacres and there's enough action to please everyone." The ad campaign described Downs and Storm's characters: "He's fresh from college and she's just plain fresh ... two delightful puppy lovers who hardly stop fighting long enough for a kiss!" Though the pressbook bragged about exterior sets that were meticulously created to mirror the town as the Porters wrote about it, the shots of Fairfield look suspiciously like a leftover set from a Monogram Western.

Freckles Come Home was a 1929 novel by Jeannette Stratton Porter, a follow-up to her mother's *Freckles,* published in 1904. As the "Suggested by" credit given the younger novelist implies, this is at best a loose adaptation.

Variety (April 8, 1942) predicted good box office returns, "for this one has all the ingredients of a successful small-town story ... [T]here's enough action in it to please everyone." Gale, said the same reviewer, sang well, and "scores heavily with her most important screen assignment to date...." *Harrison's Reports* (February 1, 1942) was less impressed, calling it "just a fair program picture," but noted, "Gale Storm has a pleasing personality."

Man from Cheyenne (1942)

Cast: Roy Rogers (*Roy Rogers*), George "Gabby" Hayes (*Gabby Whittaker*), Sally Payne (*Sally Whittaker*), Lynne Carver (*Marian Hardy*), William Haade (*Ed*), James Seay (*Sheriff Jim*), Gale Storm (*Judy Evans*), Jack Ingram (*Chuck*), Bob Nolan (*Bob*), Guy Usher (*Cattlemen's Association Chief*), Monte Montague (*Cattlemen's Association Officer*), Ivan Miller (*Edwards*), Jack Kirk (*Bill Burroughs*), Bob Burns, Edward Peil, Sr. (*Ranchers*), Spade Cooley (*Cowhand*), Eddie Lee (*Houseboy*), Lynton Brent (*Clerk*), Al Taylor (*Messenger*), Frank Brownlee (*Man Carrying Packages*), Ted Mapes (*Cowhand at Dance*), The Sons of the Pioneers

Director–Associate Producer: Joseph Kane. *Original Screenplay*: Winston Miller. *Photography*: Reggie Lanning. *Editor*: William Thompson. *Music Director*: Cy Feuer. Republic Pictures, released January 16, 1942; B&W; 60 minutes.

Judy Evans, niece of cattle rancher Gabby Whittaker, visits the Wyoming Cattlemen's Association office in Cheyenne to enlist more help in fighting rustlers plaguing the region. From the office window, Judy and the men watch in admiration as Roy Rogers, a quick and careful shot, foils a robbery. A representative of the U.S. Department of Commerce, noting that the theft of "beef earmarked for government" is a federal crime, offers Roy a job investigating the case.

Having been raised on Gabby's ranch "like a son," Roy is able to show up for a visit without attracting suspicion. While there, he renews his acquaintance with his childhood pal Judy, now a very pretty young woman, and with Gabby's daughter Sally and another rancher, Marian Hardy. Marian, who inherited the Hardy ranch after the death of her father, is the mastermind behind the rustling operation, though the young woman, educated in an Eastern school, uses her glamour and her femininity to divert suspicion from herself.

When the rustling operation finally culminates in a murder, Roy

Before signing a long-term contract with Monogram, Gale made three films with Roy Rogers, including *Man from Cheyenne* (1942).

uncovers the secret tunnel where the bad guys prepare stolen cattle for shipment by truck, and heads to the Hardy ranch to confront Marian's foreman and his henchmen. While Gabby and the other men still believe Marian is innocent, Judy and Sally aren't convinced, and take on the task of preventing her from making a hasty escape once the jig is up.

Gale's third picture with Roy Rogers, shot in the fall of 1941, was released only about a month after *Red River Valley*. Using several of the same cast members and crew as *Jesse James at Bay*, this film once again finds Gale playing the star's love interest. In what was becoming a running theme in her films, Gale's character attracts the attention of a man who knew her as a child, when she had "pigtails and freckles," and is quick to notice how much she has grown. While the men of the community are largely fooled by Marian's superficial charms, which she often uses to gather useful information about efforts to foil the rustlers, Judy and Sally (who calls her "Poison Puss") are not so easily blinkered. Scarcely civil to one another, Judy and Marian trade barbs when they meet:

> MARIAN: You always look so healthy. I wish my skin weren't so sensitive. I'd love to be able to get sunburned.
> JUDY: I'd like to see you sunburned.

Judy is visibly annoyed when Marian flirts with Roy, offering to host a party in his honor. Though he doesn't think he was anything but polite and friendly, she snaps, "If you'd leaned any closer to her, you'd have fallen out of your saddle."

Containing many of the stock elements fans expect in a B Western, *Man from Cheyenne* also deviates from the norm in ways that broaden its appeal. It seems to be consciously appealing to adult viewers, especially women, without unduly alienating the young boys who made up a big part of his audience. Aside from the incipient love triangle of Roy, Judy and Marian, which receives ample screen time, and the novelty of a female crook, there's what one character disgustedly calls "a heap of kissin'," and even a beefcake glimpse of Roy in the shower. Though it doesn't make much difference for a time after the action shifts from Cheyenne, this is another modern-day Western, set in 1941, and the screenwriter incorporates a car chase into the finale, along with the expected gun battles and fisticuffs.

Lynne Carver (1916–1955) capably exudes venom as the villainess who says, "You think I want to stick around this God-forsaken country for the rest of my life?" The three female principals memorably settle their differences in a lively scene where Judy and Sally successfully accost the fleeing Marian. Payne's character gets the funniest line in the scene: Sizing up Marian, she says, "Look, sister, if I'm gonna have trouble with you, I'll have to slap you bowlegged—or am I too late?" But it's Gale, as Judy, who delivers an even more satisfying—and final–resolution. Squaring off with her citified rival, Judy takes on Marian in a tussle, finally telling her, "While you were learning the conga, I was learning this!" as she punches her lights out.

Showmen's Trade Review (January 17, 1942), noting the deviations from normal Western fare, said, "Winston Miller deserves credit for an original script that *is* original in many respects ... [I]ts innovations may inspire other producers to forsake usual western film clichés, partly at least, and inject new and refreshing entertainment angles." *Motion Picture Herald* (January 17, 1942) thought Gale and other cast members "aid the swift progression of the story." In March 1942, syndicated columnist Jimmie Fidler wrote, "Attention, Rogers fans! His best yet..."

Though Gale had teamed successfully with Roy Rogers in three Republic Westerns, displaying a nice chemistry with her leading man, the contract she signed with Monogram Pictures in the spring of 1942 would keep her too busy to meet up with the singing cowboy again.

Lure of the Islands (1942)

Cast: Margie Hart (*Tana O'Shaughnessy*), Robert Lowery (*Wally*), Guinn "Big Boy" Williams (*Jinx*), Gale Storm (*Maui*), Ivan Lebedeff (*The Commandant*), Warren Hymer (*Albert*), The Bray Sisters (*Dancers*), John Bleifer (*Lt. Lavar*), Satini Puailoa (*Matu*), Namure Nordman, Maito Mayo (*Native Girls*), Kam Tong (*Lt. Kono*), Tristram Coffin (*Skipper*), John Casey (*Chief*), Jerome Sheldon (*Paul Mollett*), Angel Cruz (*Japanese Pilot*)

Director: Jean Yarbrough. *Producer*: Lindsley Parsons. *Screenplay*: Edmond Kelso, George Bricker, Scott Littleton. *Music Director*: Edward Kay. *Songs* "Lure of the Islands," "Tahiti Sweetie": Edward Cherkose, Edward Kay. *Tahitian Songs Arranged by* Namure Nordman. *Dance Director*: Maita Mayo. *Photography*: Mack Stengler. *Editor*: Jack Ogilvie. *Production Manager*: William Strohbach. *Sound Director*: Glen Glenn. *Technical Director*: Dave Milton. *Wardrobe*: Lou Brown.

Monogram Pictures; released July 3, 1942; B&W; 61 minutes.

American government agents Wally and Jinx are assigned to infiltrate a South Seas island, Tanukai, where there is believed to be "fifth column activity," seemingly involving Nazi and Japanese collaboration. Dropped off nearby, the men swim to shore, claiming to be sailors whose ship was torpedoed by the enemy. The Commandant of the island, not impressed by Jinx's claim that they are "unconscious objectors," tells them they may stay for two days, when a ship will be leaving for the mainland. Suspicious of their motives, the Commandant arranges for them to be followed by guards at all times.

Wally and Jinx's assignment becomes more enticing when they meet some of the beautiful ladies who live on the island. While most of them speak no English, Tana, who had an American father, greets them pleasantly. She explains that she is taboo on the island, because she refused to take part in an arranged marriage. The mutual attraction between Wally and Tana leads him to hope she will tell him the island's secrets. She promptly agrees to do so, but in turn, she wants to marry him and leave the island. In order to be alone with Wally, Tana enlists the help of her cousin Maui to entertain Jinx.

Wally and Jinx discover the location of a powerful radio transmitter, which they disable. The Commandant demands that the natives clear a grove of trees so that a landing field can be constructed, as an incoming flight bearing Japanese soldiers is expected within 24 hours. The native chief is taken into custody when he refuses the Commandant's instructions. Wally and Jinx liberate the chief, but when Wally hems and haws on his promise to marry Tana, she betrays them to the Commandant. With only hours left before the Japanese fighter plane arrives, the American agents must escape from custody, take control of the radio transmitter and prevent a takeover of the island.

Billed above the title is well-known burlesque dancer Margie Hart (1913–2000). Monogram signed Hart to a one-picture deal in the spring of 1942. Studio publicity described Hart as "a shining light of the burlesque stage for the past seven years, [who] has far exceeded any erstwhile rivals in drawing power and earning capacity." Newspaper ads advised ticket buyers, "Now you can see her CLOSE-UP ... dancing, fighting, LOVING ... as a tropical Mata Hari whose torrid allure teases secrets from men of all nations!" The film, moviegoers were promised, "is filled with the romantic color of the South

Seas—with stalwart native musicians, swaying dancing girls, grass skirts and sarongs, and especially singing and dancing numbers..."

Given the state of motion picture censorship in 1942, it was a cinch that Monogram couldn't show as much of Hart on screen as burlesque patrons were accustomed to seeing. Still, in her memoir, Gale recalled that Hart astounded cast and crew when, told that her costume needed reworking, she nonchalantly took off her top in the middle of a busy soundstage and handed it over. During the film's spring 1942 production, Hart told journalist Frederick C. Othman she wasn't much enjoying her new life as a movie star, between the long hours, the itchy costumes and the constant critique she was given: "Keep my chin up and my stomach in, and not slouch and not sway and hold my head back and my chest out and keep my hair curled and my legs straight and I don't know what all else until I just had to sit down and cry."[3] She claimed that only the fear of a lawsuit prevented her from walking out on the production midstream. For all the coaching, Hart's delivery of dialogue such as, "Well, I see you got out of the clink all right. Have any trouble?" is monotonously flat, and imbued with more than a touch of nasality. Not surprisingly, Hart's stint as a Hollywood star proved to be short-lived.

Even in a grass skirt, with flowers in her hair, Gale doesn't look much like anything but the all–American girl she is. Her character thinks Robert Lowery's Wally is "pretty," but curls her lip in disdain when asked to cozy up to Jinx. Only after being told he is a wealthy American hog farmer does she consent to keep company with him. Gale contributes one lighthearted song number, "Tahiti Sweetie," which tells the story of a girl whose fellow prefers dance to romance. True to the era in which it was made, the film's script is replete with references to "heinies" and "Japs." It's difficult to see why concocting this film called for the efforts of three screenwriters.

This is the first of three pictures in which Gale worked with Robert Lowery (1913–1971), to be followed in short order by *Campus Rhythm* and *Revenge of the Zombies*. He also turned up in guest roles on *My Little Margie*. Lithuanian-born Ivan Lebedeff (1894–1953) gives a competent, relatively understated performance as the Nazi commandant. This was Gale's first film with Guinn "Big Boy" Williams (1899–1962), whose numerous movie credits ran largely to Westerns; they will appear together once more, in *Al Jennings of Oklahoma*.

Theaters showing *Lure of the Islands* received a pressbook that was perfectly frank about the film's chief selling points, urging managers to play up the girl-watching angle. "A midnight premiere is a natural for this kind of attraction," publicists suggested. "Hire some flesh acts—girl performers who can strut their stuff and give out with torchy songs—and announce the most sizzling after-hours show ever to hit the town! If you are located near a defense plant with a 'swing shift,' aim plenty of ballyhoo at the workers who'll just be getting out in time for the show." In Indiana, according to *Showmen's Trade Review* (January 30, 1943), an enterprising theater manager double-booked *Lure* with PRC's *Jungle Siren*, starring Ann Corio, for a "Battle of the Burlesque Queens" promotion.

Film Daily (October 8, 1942), while acknowledging that Hart might well draw some men to the theater, called *Lure of the Islands* "a painfully inept film.... [Characters] are thoroughly unbelievable, as is most of the action.... The cast gives a poor account of itself." *Motion Picture Herald* (November 28, 1942) reported a Mississippi exhibitor's exasperated reaction: "Of all the stupid junk to come out of the American film capital this reaches a new high. It is amateurish, short, and above all, not worth a one-day stand with a strong filler for a double bill."

Not everyone was displeased. According to the *Hollywood Citizen-News'* James Francis Crow (June 3, 1942), it was "on the basis of her work in *Lure of the Islands*" that Monogram decided to offer Gale a seven-year contract.

Smart Alecks (1942)

Cast: Leo Gorcey (*Mugs*), Bobby Jordan (*Danny Stevens*), Huntz Hall (*Glimpy*), Gabriel Dell (*Hank Salko*), Stanley Clements (*Stash*), Bobby Stone (*Skinny*), Sunshine Sammy [Morrison] (*Scruno*), David Gorcey (*Peewee*), Maxie Rosenbloom (*Butch Brocalli*), Roger Pryor (*Joe Reagan*), Gale Storm (*Ruth Stevens*), Walter Woolf King (*Dr. Ormsby*), Herbert Rawlinson (*Captain Bronson*), Joe Kirk (*Mike*), Sam Bernard (*Dr. Thomas*), Dick Ryan (*Warden*), Marie Windsor (*Nurse*), Betty Sinclair (*Receptionist*)
Director: Wallace Fox. *Producers*: Sam Katzman, Jack Dietz. *Original Story and Screenplay*: Harvey H. Gates. *Associate Producer*: Barney A. Sarecky. *Photography*: Mack Stengler. *Editor*: Robert Golden. *Art Director*: David Milton. *Sound Engineer*: Glen Glenn.
Monogram Pictures; released August 7, 1942; B&W; 66 minutes.

Mugs and his gang take note when their pal Hank begins dressing to the nines and flashing a fat billfold. Hank thinks he's found a good "racket," with "easy money," until his new friends Mike and Butch make him an accomplice in a bank robbery during which a teller is wounded. Hank ends up in jail, thanks largely to the eyewitness testimony of patrolman Joe Reagan and his girlfriend Ruth Stevens. Ruth, a nurse at the Bowery Receiving Hospital, is the older sister of gang member Danny, who's blamed by his friends for Hank's conviction.

Ruth and Danny's annoying new neighbor, who introduces himself as Mr. Blake, is none other than Butch, one of the bank robbers. When Butch confiscates the boys' baseball after his apartment window is broken during a game, Danny pursues him. Recognized by Joe as a wanted man, Butch is arrested. Danny, who tackled him, receives a $200 reward.

Danny's friends think the reward should be shared equally among the seven of them, not knowing that Danny intended to spend it on baseball uniforms the gang had been wanting. Tossed into jail overnight after breaking into Danny and Ruth's apartment to snatch the cash, Mugs and company disavow Danny. But when Hank turns up, having escaped from the penitentiary, and tips them off that his former cohorts are also on the loose, looking to avenge themselves against Danny for his testimony, the boys rush to their pal's defense. Captured by the bad guys, Danny is given a beating that leaves him needing a delicate brain operation. Dr. Ormsby, from the hospital where Ruth works, seems to be just the man, but his $1000 minimum fee well is beyond what Danny and his friends can afford.

This was Gale's only film with the East Side Kids, who cranked out 21 entries in their popular series during a five-year stay at Monogram in the early 1940s. An offshoot of the Warners films of the late 1930s featuring the "Dead End Kids," this series originated by producer Sam Katzman would eventually evolve into "The Bowery Boys."

Her role more prominent than her eleventh-place billing in the opening credits would suggest, she plays an upright, attractive professional woman who doesn't entirely approve of the gang with which her brother hangs out. Serving as the film's moral compass, her character doesn't hesitate to help the police track Hank after the bank robbery, despite his friendship with her brother; as Danny remarks, "She's got some mighty definite ideas about telling the truth." However, when policeman Joe Reagan seems to be viewing Mugs and his friends too harshly, thinking they belong in reform school, her character, Ruth, reminds him that these kids grew up with none of the usual advantages: "Most of them never even had a new pair of shoes in their lives. The only playground they know

The pressbook cover for *Smart Alecks* (Monogram, 1942) illustrated such key scenes as (bottom left) Gale's character falling into the clutches of bad guy Maxie Rosenbloom.

is the street. They've had to fight for every inch of elbow room. Sure, they're tough—but not half as tough as they appear."

The film's climax finds Gale as the damsel in distress when she falls into the clutches of the bad guys. Not content to stand by and be rescued, she gives one of them a solid conk on the head with a vase.

Playing Gale's love interest is Roger Pryor, with whom she previously worked in *Gambling Daughters*. Although she's playing the older sister of an East Side Kid, at 20 she's younger than most of the actors cast as gang members, including stars Leo Gorcey (1917–1969) and Huntz Hall (1919–1999). Walter Woolf King (1899–1984), perhaps best remembered for his role in the Marx Brothers' *A Night at the Opera* (1935), has a couple of amusing moments as the erudite Dr. Orsmby, who can barely understand a word of the boys' fractured English. Bringing up the rear, in terms of the billed cast, is Marie Windsor (1919–2000), in one of her first film appearances. She turns up near the end of the film as a beautiful hospital nurse who is the object of some artless flirting from Huntz Hall's Glimpy, as well as a fervent kiss from Mugs.

In the film's pressbook, theater managers were advised:

> It's easy to give your lobby and marquee an East Side atmosphere. Hang a line of wash around the marquee, and be sure to include patched drawers, socks with big holes in the feet, torn shirts, etc. Have a couple of urchins playing marbles in the lobby. Get a record of "The Sidewalks of New York" and keep it blaring out over the p.a. system.... All these gags will help put over the rough-house fun their fans expect from the rambunctious East Side Kids.

By the time of this film's release, audiences and critics alike knew pretty much what to expect from the East Side Kids. Still, *Film Daily* (June 25, 1942) was somewhat impressed by *Smart Alecks*, saying, "No other film these boys have made has as much human interest as is packed into these six reels ... [I]t will really please any audience you sell it to." Gale was one of the players the reviewer felt "deserve mention for their fine performances." *Motion Picture Daily* (June 23, 1942) concurred that a better-than-normal story had the film "averaging out on the plus side as compared to their earlier pictures." A Boston exhibitor reported to *Motion Picture Herald*'s "What The Picture Did for Me" column (May 29, 1943) that *Smart Alecks* "was enjoyed by the kids especially; although several men and women got a few good laughs out of it."

Foreign Agent (1942)

Cast: John Shelton (*Jimmy*), Gale Storm (*Mitzi Mayo*), Ivan Lebedeff (*Okura*), George Travell (*Nick Dancy*), Patsy Moran (*Joan Collins*), Lyle Latell (*Eddie McGurk*), Hans Schumm (*Dr. Warner*), William Halligan (*Bob Davis*), Herbert Rawlinson (*Stevens*), Boyd Irwin (*Jennings*), Kenneth Harlan (*George McCall*), David Clarke (*Beck*), Fay Wall (*Anna*), Edward Peil (*Nelson*), Paul Bryar (*Bartender*), Jack Mulhall (*Editor*), Anna Hope (*Flo*), Jack Raymond (*Little Fellow*), Vince Barnett (*Drunk*), Rita Douglas (*Girl at Bar*), Jean King (*Maid*), Kenne Duncan (*Tom*), Pat McKee (*Spike*)

Director: William Beaudine. *Producers*: Martin Mooney, Max M. King. *Screenplay*: Martin Mooney, John Krafft. *Original Story*: Martin Mooney. *Photography*: Mack Stengler. *Music Director*: Edward Kay. *Song "Down Deep in My Heart"*: Bill Mellette. *Song "Taps for the Japs"*: Bill Anderson. *Editor*: Fred Baine. *Sound Engineer*: Glen Glenn. *Art Director*: Dave Milton. *Production Supervisor*: George Moskov. *Assistant Director*: Gerd Oswald.

Monogram Pictures; released October 9, 1942; B&W; 64 minutes.

The death of a movie studio electrician, Mr. Mayo, found hanging in his apartment and deemed a suicide by police, was actually a murder. Mayo was perfecting plans for a studio searchlight filter "which should provide maximum defense against enemy bombers"; it's the object of hot pursuit by foreign agents. Unbeknownst to the enemy, Mayo entrusted the blueprints to his actress daughter Mitzi, who also works as a singer at the Harbor Club.

Thwarted in their initial attempt, the agents ransack the apartment of Mitzi and her roommate, stuntwoman Joan, hold up Joan and her beau Eddie at gunpoint, and steal Mitzi's car, all to no avail. The blueprints are safely in the hands of Mitzi's boyfriend Jimmy, a sometime actor who's eager to join the war effort. Jimmy is assigned to aid radio commentator Bob Davis in his efforts to track down the traitors conspiring against U.S. interests through subversive groups like the National American Peace Association, which uses a pacifist front to influence citizens against the campaigns of World War II. Davis has identified a couple of the small fry criminals, Nelson and Jennings, and Jimmy follows them to track down ringleader Dr. Warner. With the help of another studio electrician, Jimmy arranges to get a working model of Mayo's searchlight, which proves valuable to U.S. military forces. Engaging in mutual wiretapping, Jimmy and Mitzi learn more about the Nazis' plan to bomb Los Angeles (a "demoralizing catastrophe" for Americans), while Dr. Warner and his secretary-mistress realize that the jig is up and hurriedly set their plans in motion.

An entertaining film for those who don't place great importance on believability, *Foreign Agent* provides Gale with one of her first fully adult roles at Monogram. She sings two songs at the Harbor Club, notably the unforgettable "Taps for the Japs" (to the accompaniment of an accordion, no less). The gimcrack script gives her the chance for no more than fleeting regrets at the violent death of Mitzi's father, as only a short time afterwards she's gaily planning for an evening out with Jimmy and chatting with her pal Joan about their men friends. Billed above the title as her leading man is actor John Shelton (1915–1972), whose character "Jimmy" doesn't even rate a last name. Shelton was at this time the husband of singer-actress Kathryn Grayson. Both Shelton and Storm show off their purported ability to mimic "foreign" accents, which becomes a story point near the end of the film.

Character actress Patsy Moran (1903–1968) is featured as Mitzi's friend and roommate Joan Collins (*sic*!), a plainspoken, plain-featured woman who earns $35 a day as a movie stuntwoman. (Coming home from a rough day at work, she complains that she "fell off a horse 11 times before the director was satisfied"). Actor Ivan Lebedeff, who capably played a foreign agent in *Lure of the Islands,* is, not surprisingly, less successful here, miscast as an "Oriental" bad guy.

Very much a product of its time, and fascinating as a time capsule as much as a well-made motion picture, *Foreign Agent* assures us that all good Americans support the war effort, and that anyone who does not is a dupe, or worse. Alluding to the wartime rubber shortage, Mitzi tells Joan to be careful with her car, saying, "Look, honey, you can always get a new boyfriend, but just try and get a new tire!" As for the dearth of young men not already in military service, Mitzi cracks, "If this war lasts much longer, we'll be making pictures with all-women casts," a prospect her friend Jimmy doesn't find altogether unappealing. The script cautions moviegoers to "Shut Your Trap and Beat the Jap," instructions a young patron of the Harbor Club fails to take to heart: She blabs the whereabouts of her sailor boyfriend to a sympathetic bartender.

Although director William Beaudine has been nicknamed "One-Shot" for his alleged aversion to second takes on his films, recent apologists have argued that the moniker is undeserved. However, there's certainly some evidence of hasty shooting in this film, as when actor Herbert Rawlinson, in his only scene, noticeably muffs a line, saying, "He has a room in an old off ... in an old factory building downtown." Economy is the order of the day, which is nothing unusual for six-day Monogram films, but here the seams are showing a bit more obviously than usual. The small amount of wartime action seen is depicted entirely through grainy, dirt-flecked stock footage, while the milieu of a busy urban newspaper office is depicted by cutting in a stock shot lifted from another film, followed by footage of actor Jack Mulhall sitting at a desk barking into a phone. After two chairs are used to decorate the foyer of Mayo's apartment building, one of them inexplicably turns up a few scenes later atop a file cabinet in Dr. Warner's office, where it remains for the rest of the film. Beaudine was assisted by a young Gerd Oswald (1919–1989), who would go on to direct films like *A Kiss Before Dying* (1956) and the ill-fated Bette Davis vehicle *Bunny O'Hare* (1971).

Campy moments abound. The wiretapping of the bad guys' headquarters is accomplished by the running of a heavy black cord down the front wall of the building, a few feet from the entrance, which not surprisingly attracts the attention of the men it's intended to entrap. An enemy agent receives secret military instructions by installing a small device on the needle of his record player, which serves to decode a top-secret message imbedded in Eddie Kay's otherwise innocuous piano solo "To a Water Lily." When good guy Jimmy reports to his new boss for an assignment, he's intercepted by three mugs who each try in turn to beat him up, Bob Davis' way of seeing if he's tough enough for the assignment. Since the puny sound effects accentuating the punches sound more like bitch slaps than heavyweight pugilism, the intended effect is somewhat negated. If the film, with its parsimony, pompous speeches and pretentious self-importance, lets off a faint whiff of the legendary writer-director Edward D. Wood, Jr., that impression is only solidified by the presence of two bona fide Wood players: Rawlinson as Jimmy's boss and an unbilled Kenne Duncan, seen briefly as an FBI agent.

Ann Lewis of *Showmen's Trade Review* (August 1, 1942) reported on a set visit during production, where she witnessed co-star Lyle Latell "being patched up by the makeup man" after a fight scene that got out of hand. "That must have been some scene," Lewis commented, "for in spite of the bleeding and dizziness, Lyle finished it. This is one time when the blood in the recorded scene will be real, not just realistic."

According to *Variety* (October 28, 1942), *Foreign Agent* was "moderately good melodrama," but complained that the story, "while very plotty, has a tendency to drag toward the end." The reviewer liked the songs Gale sang, but felt she "sells them weakly, her voice being lightweight." On the other hand, he thought Lebedeff was "excellent as a Jap." *Motion Picture Daily* (September 15, 1942) rated the film a "well-made melodrama ... an excitingly and tersely told story..." *Motion Picture Herald* (September 19, 1942) also gave it a nod of approval: "[T]he film is a meaty offering taking advantage of recent news developments as items in the plot..."

Rhythm Parade (1942)

Cast: Nils T. Granlund and the Florentine Gardens Revue, Gale Storm (*Sally Benson*), Robert Lowery (*Jimmy Trent*), Margaret Dumont (*Ophelia MacDougal*), Chick Chandler (*Speed Merrill*), Cliff Nazarro (*Cecil "Rocks" MacDougal*), Jan Wiley (*Connie*), Sugar

Geise (*Patsy*), Julie Milton (*Sparky*), Ted Fio Rito and His Orchestra with "Candy" Candido, The Mills Brothers, Jean Foreman, Sylvia McKay, The Theodores (*Revue Members*)

Directors: Howard Bretherton, Dave Gould. *Producer*: Sydney M. Williams. *Original Screenplay*: Charles R. Marion, Carl Foreman. *Photography*: Mack Stengler. *Lyrics and Music*: Dave Oppenheim, Roy Ingraham. *Song "Tootin' My Own Horn"*: Edward Kay, Edward Cherkose. *Production Manager*: William Strohbach. *Technical Director*: Dave Milton. *Costumes*: Mme. Houda. *Recording*: Jack Noyes. *Editor*: Carl Pierson.

Monogram Pictures; released December 11, 1942; B&W; 68 minutes.

Showgirl Sally Benson, appearing in Nils T. Granlund's revue at the Florentine Gardens club, is thrilled by the chance to win her big break, a starring role in producer "Rocks" MacDougal's new musical in New York. Temporarily entrusted with the care of her sister's infant son Sparky, Sally accepts her agent Speed's advice to keep the baby a secret until the show opens. Attracted to her leading man Jimmy Trent, Sally tells him about Sparky, and he promises to go along.

With the exception of Sally's jealous rival Connie, her friends and colleagues do their best to corroborate her story. But the ruse falls apart when Rocks finds the baby backstage, and a few too many of them try to cover for Sally, claiming Sparky as their own. Busted, Sally admits the truth, costing her the Broadway gig and throwing a monkey wrench into her developing romance with Jimmy. While Sally reluctantly enters into Speed's latest brainstorm, donning a blonde wig to audition for Rocks a second time under an assumed name, Jimmy, who's regretting his breakup with her, receives some unexpected help in patching things up from the producer's seemingly hardnosed sister Ophelia.

Impresario Nils T. Granlund (1890–1957), often billed simply as NTG, was in the early 1940s the producer of a popular Hollywood-based floor show chock-full of songs and pretty girls. Monogram made a deal with Granlund to adapt his show to the movies, with the title originally announced as *Bye, Bye, Baby*. Filmed in September 1942, *Rhythm Parade* devotes much of its running time to presenting some of the prime acts from Granlund's then-current revue—or, as *Billboard* (September 12, 1942) put it, "Monogram is bodily lifting the NTG revue from the Florentine Gardens." A slender thread of story concerning Sally's career aspirations, and her romance with Jimmy, takes a back seat to musical performances by the Mills Brothers, Ted Fio Rito's orchestra and a parade of chorus girls. Granlund, known to his showgirls as "Granny," also plays himself onscreen, and is given a few dialogue exchanges, including several pertaining to a particularly dimwitted chorus girl known to her friends as "Unconscious." Of that character, he says, "This kid is so dumb, she thinks a Jeep is female Jap."

With its brief running time and multiple revue acts, *Rhythm Parade* does a decent job of spotlighting Gale's singing voice, featured in songs including "Mimi from Tahiti" and the finale, "Petticoat Army," but there are better showcases in her future at Monogram. Her second film with Robert Lowery, this finds them paired as a romantic duo, more so than their other outings. More memorable solo numbers here include one by novelty singer Candy Candido (1913–1999), a voice artist with an unusual ability to bridge vocal registers seamlessly, going instantaneously from soprano to bass, with a few stops in the middle. In his number "Seven Beers with the Wrong Kind of Man," he alternately voices both a flighty female and her burly, baritone boyfriend.

Among the supporting performances is a welcome appearance by the great Margaret Dumont (1882–1965), veteran of multiple films with the Marx Brothers, here playing a slightly atypical role as a businesslike bookie who proves to have a softer side. The always-reliable Chick Chandler (1905–1988) makes the most of his limited screen time as Sally's less-than-capable agent, doing schtick with a baby bottle filled with bourbon.

Seen as one of the chorus girls is newcomer Yvonne De Carlo (1922–2007), who in real life was given an early career break by her casting in Granlund's show. Choreographer Dave Gould (1899–1969) was deemed to be sufficiently critical to *Rhythm Parade* to merit his crediting as co-director, alongside Howard Bretherton. This was Gale's only film for Bretherton, whose credits ran largely to B Westerns.

Variety (June 23, 1943) predicted that *Rhythm Parade* "should do satisfactorily in face of the present demands for more escapist entertainment," noting that it had "been ably directed ... moves at a snappy pace, and has been given good production..." According to *Motion Picture Herald* (December 19, 1942), the filmmakers' efforts "reflect determination and ability in stretching a budget over distance and area challenging their virtuosity." *Motion Picture Daily* (December 18, 1942) noted the film's "extremely slight narrative and little motivation to connect the series of musical numbers." In the *Herald*'s "What the Picture Did for Me" column (October 16, 1943), a small-town theater owner from North Dakota called it a "very good musical in the low price bracket; better than some top price musicals."

The Crime Smasher (1943)

Cast: Edgar Kennedy (*Captain Murphy*), Richard Cromwell (*Sgt. Patrick Flanagan*), Gale Storm (*Susan Fleming*), Mantan Moreland (*Eustace Smith*), Frank Graham (*"Professor" Cosmo Jones*), Gwen Kenyon (*Phyllis Blake*), Herbert Rawlinson (*James J. Blake*), Tristram Coffin (*Jake Pelotti*), Charles Jordan (*Biff Garr*), Vince Barnett (*"Gimp"*), Emmett Vogan (*Police Commissioner Gould*), Maxine Leslie (*Mrs. Jake Pelotti*), Mauritz Hugo (*Tony Sandol*), Sam Bernard (*Gangster*)

Director: James Tinling. *Producer*: Lindsley Parsons. *Screenplay*: Michael L. Simmons, Walter Gering. *Original Story*: Walter Gering. *Photography*: Mack Stengler. *Editor*: Carl Pierson. *Production Manager*: William Strohbach. *Sound Director*: Glen Glenn. *Technical Director*: Dave Milton. *Music Director*: Edward Kay.

Monogram Pictures; released January 29, 1943; B&W; 61 minutes.

With a crime wave in full swing, Police Captain Murphy and his squad are under criticism from the commissioner, newspapers and the public. Most of the crime can be attributed to two warring factions that, between them, control the city: the gangs led by Jake Pellotti and Biff Garr. Though they supposedly have an understanding in which each controls a designated part of town, tensions arise when Pellotti is kidnapped and held for $20,000 ransom.

Refusing the police's help, Pellotti takes matters into his own hands, and soon the body of one of Garr's men is pushed out of a moving car outside police headquarters. Found hovering over the corpse is a slight, nattily dressed man who introduces himself as "Professor Cosmo Jones," expert in "psychological criminology." Under questioning, he admits that he recently earned a diploma in detection from a correspondence course, and wants to volunteer his services as a special investigator, saying that he can "crush this cavalcade of crime..." Unimpressed, grouchy Captain Murphy threatens to clap the newcomer into jail, until young Sergeant Patrick Flanagan intercedes.

Amused by the little amateur detective, Sgt. Flanagan is giving him a ride home

Captain Murphy (Edgar Kennedy, right) looks askance at lovebirds Richard Cromwell and Gale Storm in this lobby card from *The Crime Smasher* (Monogram, 1943).

when they both witness the attempted kidnapping of heiress Phyllis Blake. Flanagan comes to her rescue, but is taken aback when Phyllis and her boyfriend downplay the incident, asking that it be kept out of the papers. Staying behind at the scene, Cosmo meets janitor's assistant Eustace Smith, and they discover the body of a man, Mike Andrews, who was apparently shot during the melee. Since no one else was seen firing a gun, Sgt. Flanagan is held accountable, and the police commissioner insists that he be busted to a patrolman's pay and status while the incident is investigated. The demotion, which threatens to become a dismissal if Andrews dies, disrupts the young sergeant's plans to marry girlfriend Susan Fleming, the police commissioner's secretary.

Cosmo, who appoints Eustace as his assistant, persuades Phyllis to recant her story and save Sgt. Flanagan's career. Phyllis agrees to do so, but seems to want the handsome sergeant for herself, which doesn't sit well with Susan. Before she can clear the policeman's name, Phyllis is kidnapped again, and her oil tycoon father turns up the pressure on the police to solve the case. Against his better judgment, Sgt. Flanagan aligns himself with the amiable Cosmo Jones, who promises that, with the sergeant's help, he can "not only recover your stripes but, if I may transgress in the vernacular, square it with Susan!" Jones outlines a plan to force the kidnappers to show themselves, a risky one since it puts the warring gangs at odds once again.

The film represented Monogram's attempt at developing a series based on the popular radio show *The Adventures of Cosmo Jones*, which had begun in 1940. *Motion Picture Herald* (September 19, 1942) reported the studio's acquisition of film rights, which included the services of star Frank Graham (1914–1950) and writer Walter Gering. The deal called for two films, with options for additional entries.

The radio show found Graham voicing all the characters in each week's drama. According to the film's pressbook, "[F]or the past three years Graham's unusual ability as a protean actor has had full scope in weekly broadcast playlets.... Graham has played not only the title part, but every other role in the entire series, sometimes totaling as many as twelve distinct parts in a single play." Although Graham plays only the lead character here, the script establishes the idea that, as Cosmo puts it, "I combine the talents of voice mimicry and ventriloquism." Gering's story called for Cosmo to vocally impersonate Captain Murphy, Sergeant Flanagan and Phyllis' father. Graham's other motion picture credits mostly found him working as a voice artist. He died by suicide in 1950.

Monogram originally intended to call this film *The Adventures of Cosmo Jones*, matching the radio program title. The film's opening credits give the title as *Cosmo Jones in "Crime Smasher,"* leaving it unclear whether or not the character name was to be regarded as part of the title. Meanwhile, poster art showed it as *Cosmo Jones in "The Crime Smasher."* The publicity campaign played up the supposed name recognition of the radio show and the film's blend of suspense and comedy ("a cyclone of crime and chuckles"); one advertisement read, "He's the dippiest detective you've ever seen!" By whatever title you call it, this is a zippy hour of lightweight fun, though it apparently didn't go over so well with audiences in 1943. Director James Tinling, thoroughly experienced in the art of the B movie, keeps the story moving.

Gale goes blonde for her featured role as Pat Flanagan's loyal girlfriend Susan, who bemoans the many dates with her that he breaks in order to carry out his police work. She's supportive when it appears that he's been demoted, assuring him that they can survive on a patrolman's salary. But when she walks into Pat's apartment to find Phyllis Blake planting a kiss on the surprised officer, she erupts in anger, handing him the sandwich she made for him and saying, "Here, you big flatfoot, and I hope you choke on it!"

Film Daily (February 18, 1943) thought *Crime Smasher* "should find favor with audiences as filler-fare on a twin-biller." Though Graham's makeup as Cosmo Jones was called "unsuitable," his performance was deemed satisfactory, and Gale, along with Kennedy, Cromwell, and Moreland, "handled well their assigned portions of screen footage..." According to *Motion Picture Herald* (February 20, 1943), the intended series "starts off without distinction." Reviewer Vance King added that at the preview, "the audience was not enthusiastic." Response apparently led Monogram executives to forego making a second Cosmo Jones film.

Revenge of the Zombies (1943)

Cast: John Carradine (*Dr. Max Heinrich Von Altermann*), Gale Storm (*Jennifer Rand*), Robert Lowery (*Larry Adams*), Bob Steele (*Agent*), Mantan Moreland (*Jeff*), Veda Ann Borg (*Lila Von Altermann*), Barry McCollum (*Dr. Harvey Keating*), Mauritz Hugo (*Scott Warrington*), Madame Sul-Te-Wan (*Mammy Beulah*), James Baskett (*Lazarus*), Sybil Lewis (*Rosella*), Robert Cherry (*Pete*), Franklyn Farnum (*Zombie*)

Director: Steve Sekely. *Producer*: Lindsley Parsons. *Screenplay*: Edmond Kelso, Van Norcross. *Photography*: Mack Stengler. *Production Manager*: Richard L'Estrange. *Editor*:

Richard Currier. *Technical Director*: Dave Milton. *Sound Director*: Glen Glenn. *Music Director*: Edward Kay. *Dialogue Director*: Jack Linder.

Monogram Pictures; released September 17, 1943; B&W; 61 minutes.

Scott Warrington arrives in Louisiana bayou country upon being notified of his sister Lila's sudden death. He's accompanied by his driver, Jeff, and private detective Larry Adams. The longtime family doctor, Harvey Keating, tells Scott that Lila, a young and healthy woman, died under mysterious circumstances on the estate of her husband, Dr. Max Von Altermann. Scott and Larry decide to switch identities, with the detective posing as the grieving brother, so that Scott can have a better opportunity to investigate.

Unbeknownst to Scott and his party, Dr. Von Altermann is the midst of carrying out a nefarious plan. As he explains to a sympathetic visitor, "I am prepared to supply my country with a new army, numbering as many thousands as are required … an army that will not need to be fed, that cannot be stopped by bullets, that is in fact invincible … an army of the living dead." The latest recruit to that army is the doctor's late wife, who lies awaiting burial in an open casket. At his command, she comes to reanimated life, with Von Altermann demonstrating her invincibility by firing a bullet directly at her without effect. The mad doctor believes he has total control of the zombies—his wife, his servant Lazarus and several others—but Lila shows signs of displaying a will of her own.

Although Larry and Scott are suspicious of Von Altermann, his loyal secretary Jennifer Rand tells them that they have misjudged him, and that he adored his late wife. The zombie Mrs. Von Altermann is seen ambulatory by the men, but after an alarm is raised she's found back in her bier again. When Lila's body vanishes from her casket, Scott insists that the police be summoned. The man who comes to the house in response is a crony of the mad doctor, posing as the sheriff. Taking matters into his own hands after Dr. Keating mysteriously disappears, Larry gathers some useful information from the elderly house servant Mammy Beulah. While Dr. Von Altermann plans an escape to his home country, Larry seeks assistance from an unexpected source in defeating the deranged doctor.

Revenge of the Zombies was no doubt gobbled up by young audiences at Saturday matinees in 1943 and in frequent television reruns from the 1950s on. It's the kind of movie that practically demands viewing with a bag of hot buttered popcorn. Story-wise, it bears more than a passing resemblance to an earlier Monogram film, *King of the Zombies* (1941), which had in common with this picture screenwriter Edmond Kelso and co-stars Mantan Moreland and Madame Sul-Te-Wan. Under the direction of Steve Sekely (1899–1979), there are some genuinely striking and eerie moments; unfortunately, the comedy relief of the undeniably talented Moreland has the perhaps-unintended effect of undermining the chills. Too often, it seems like a standard horror film and a horror comedy spliced together, each element fighting the other for supremacy.

Despite her second billing, Gale's role as Von Altermann's live-in secretary is relatively unimportant to the story. (Apparently the doctor's zombies have yet to master typing and shorthand.) Jennifer is not the typical horror film scream queen, since she spends most of the running time seemingly oblivious to much of what goes on around her. Her character is quite content with her employment at the gloomy, secluded mansion, where she has worked for the past six months. Evidently secretarial jobs were not easy to come by, especially for one who freely admits, "You see, I'm not very competent, really," and adds, "In fact, I had a hard time getting a place before I came here." Her most dramatic line comes when she announces, "Madame Von Altermann's body is gone!" After that, she has little of importance to do until the film's closing moments, when she receives an unexpected—and unwelcome—offer to become "the most envied woman in the new world."

This was Gale's only film with John Carradine (1906–1988), who regarded himself first and foremost as a Shakespearean actor, but accepted roles in hundreds of films of varying quality over a long career, both to support his theatrical endeavors and to pay alimony and child support. He gives an unusually restrained performance as the mad doctor, even when called upon to recite lines like, "My wife does not answer your greeting because she is dead!" Moreland, playing virtually the same character he did in *King of the Zombies*, gets his share of laughs here, as when he sees Larry carrying a skeleton and observes, "You sure do find the strangest people to hang out with!" He rushes into the house to tell Larry and Scott there's a zombie in their car, only to find when they investigate that the vehicle is pulling away, causing Jeff to say, "Well, he was in no condition to drive!" Veda Ann Borg (1915–1973), who utters only a few words in the entire film, manages to make herself a striking presence in her scenes as the doctor's late, largely impassive but not inactive wife. James Baskett (1904–1948), seen here as the head zombie, was only a few years away from winning an honorary Oscar for his performance in Disney's *Song of the South* (1946).

A June report in *Motion Picture Herald* noted that *Zombies* filming had begun in late May, with this update indicating that not only Carradine and Storm but Lyle Talbot would have roles in the film. By the time cameras rolled, Talbot was no longer attached to the project. According to *Daily Variety* (May 28, 1943), the film was scheduled to be completed in fourteen days' time, with some 50 extras employed.

Monogram publicity described *Revenge of the Zombies* as "the type of picture which literally keeps the spectator on the edge of his seat," promising "a hair-raising film which conveys the impression of recording a story of actual events." *Motion Picture Herald* (August 7, 1943) wasn't overwhelmed, but conceded that the film had "exploitation possibilities in neighborhoods where the horror picture is favored.... The direction is coherent, the acting competent considering the roles, the sets convincing." According to *Variety* (September 1, 1943), "Robert Lowery and Gale Storm lend adequate assistance," but thought the story "borders on the ludicrous..." After attending a preview, syndicated columnist Jimmie Fidler (October 13, 1943) indicated that *Revenge of the Zombies* lived up to its title: "Just what you'd expect—if you don't expect much..."

Nearly Eighteen (1943)

Cast: Gale Storm (*Jane Stanton*), Rick Vallin (*Tony Morgan*), Bill Henry (*Jack Leonard*), Luis Alberni (*Gus*), George O'Hanlon (*Eddie*), Ralph Hodges (*Tom*), Jerry Rush (*Dick*), Bebe Fox (*Harriet*), Robert Homans (*Judge*), Sarah Edwards (*Miss Perkins*), Kenneth Harlan (*Sammy Klein*), Donald Kerr (*Harry*), Jack Lomas (*Piano Player*), Buster Brodie (*Bald Man*)

Director: Arthur Dreifuss. *Producer*: Lindsley Parsons. *Screenplay*: George Sayre. *Original Story*: Margaret Englander. *Music Director*: Edward Kay. *Choreographer*: Jack Boyle. *Photography*: Mack Stengler. *Production Manager*: William Strohbach. *Technical Director*: Dave Milton. *Sound Recording*: Tom Lambert. *Editor*: Richard Currier.

Monogram Pictures; released November 12, 1943; B&W; 61 minutes.

Seventeen-year-old aspiring singer Jane Stanton almost wins a job at a dive called Gus' Grotto, until the owner realizes she's not of legal age. Aware she's short on money, Gus sends her to apply for an office job with his buddy Tony Morgan. Jane doesn't know that Tony's Acme Brokerage Company is a front for a gambling operation, and on her first day at work she's left holding the bag during a police raid.

After paying a $50 fine, Jane is released from police custody and angrily confronts the duplicitous Tony. Wanting her out of circulation, Tony suggests she enroll in Jack Leonard's School of Voice, Dancing, and Drama, so that she can further her training. Taken aback to learn on her arrival that Leonard's school accepts only students between the ages of eight and 14, Jane takes advantage of a suitcase left behind by another prospective student and transforms herself into girlish "Janie" in order to earn a scholarship. Jack, impressed by her singing ability, thinks she might be just the ticket to improve the fortunes of the school, which is struggling financially. Trying to deny his growing feelings toward the student he believes is only 14, Jack gives her the vocal training she needs. He's on the verge of getting her a contract as a soloist on a radio show when the charade begins to unravel. On the outs with Jack once her deception is revealed, Jane takes up with womanizing Tony, until fatherly Gus takes steps to set things right.

As the young leading lady of *Nearly Eighteen* (1943), Gale wins the romantic attentions of Bill Henry (left) and Rick Vallin (right).

Since signing on with Monogram, one of Gale's assets had been her ability to play both teenagers and adults, depending on what a script required; here, billed above the title for the first time, she does a little of both. *Nearly Eighteen* is an entertaining if lightweight film that provides one of the best showcases yet for Gale's singing, culminating in her production number centered around the song "Smiles for Sale" in the final moments.

As for the story, it depends largely on our willingness to believe that, as one character puts it, "All a girl has to do is wear the right clothes and the right makeup, and she can look as much as ten years younger." At times, credibility is stretched almost to the breaking point, as when Jack's assistant Miss Perkins doesn't recognize "Janie" as the adult woman she met only a short while earlier, because Jane has tied her hair in pigtails, plopped a bow on her head, and donned a more girlish outfit. Jack's obvious interest in his new student borders on bad taste considering that he believes her to be in her early teens. "What a Lot of Things a Girl Can Learn When She's ... *Nearly Eighteen*," read one tagline for the film.

For the most part, Gale isn't asked to play "Janie" as childlike, missing out on some possible comic moments. However, there is a certain charm to her enforced soda shop "date" with two young boys from the school, one of whom declares her "a hep Jill" and adds, "She really burns my leather but good!" Gale does get a funny line describing one of the slightly shopworn women with whom Tony typically keeps company. When he comments, "Girls are like books—sometimes you get a good one, sometimes you get a bad one," she coos, "Why don't you try a first edition, instead of using the circulating library?"

Production was slated for late June 1943. Early blurbs indicated that *Nearly Eighteen* would be adapted from a story by Louis Apple. However, the finished product retained little, if anything, of Apple's work but his title, and credits writer Margaret Englander, author of a story called "This Is Mary Clayton," as the source of the basic plot. The result, according to Monogram publicity, was "a story which is filled with fast-moving incidents, and which gives her ample opportunity to sing the catchy songs which she does so well." Other observers noted a similarity to Billy Wilder's *The Major and the Minor*, released the previous year.

In *Motion Picture Daily* (October 18, 1943), reviewer Helen McNamara wrote, "George Sayre's entertaining and original screenplay is well directed by Arthur Dreifuss and good performances are turned in by Miss Storm, Bill Henry, [Rick] Vallin, Luis Alberni and George O'Hanlon.... Lindsley Parsons has produced a neat little film which will appeal especially to young audiences." Said *Motion Picture Herald* (October 30, 1943), "The musical portion of this film stands up well as songstress Gale Storm pleases with renditions of 'The Little Bell Rang,' 'Let Him Whistle' and 'Walking on Air.'" But overall, according to reviewer L.B., it was "a rather trite production."

Harrison's Reports (September 18, 1943) praised Gale: "She has a pleasant personality and sings popular songs in nice style." *Variety* (October 20, 1943) also took notice of Gale's contributions: "Gale Storm, Texas gal who won the *Gateway to Hollywood* contest several years ago, shows promise as a singer, potentialities as an actress and, what's more, is a looker. In her first featured role for Monogram, she figures in several snappy dance sequences."

Campus Rhythm (1943)

Cast: Johnny Downs (*"Scoop" Davis*), Gale Storm (*Joan Abbott, aka Susie Smith*), Robert Lowery (*Buzz O'Hara*), Candy Candido (*Harold*), Gee Gee Pearson (*Babs Marlow*),

Doug Leavitt (*William Aloysius Smith*), Herbert Hayes [Heyes] (*J.P. Hartman*), Tom Kennedy (*Police Sergeant*), Marie Blake (*Susie Smith*), Johnny Duncan (*Freshie*), Claudia Drake (*Cynthia Walker*), Donald Kerr (*Radio Station Announcer*), Cyril Ring (*Trigonometry Teacher*), Crane Whitley (*Mr. Abernathy*), Wheeler Oakman (*Sponsor*), Jack Rice (*Man with Flowers*)

Director: Arthur Dreifuss. *Producer*: Lindsley Parsons. *Screenplay*: Charles R. Marion, Albert Beich, Frank Tarloff. *Original Story*: Ewart Adamson, Jack White. *Music Director*: Edward Kay. *Songs "You Character," "It's Mutiny," "But Not You"*: Edward Cherkose, Edward Kay. *Songs "It's Great to Be a College Girl," "Walking the Chalkline," "Swing Your Way Through College"*: Lou Hirscher. *Photography*: Mack Stengler. *Production Manager*: Dick L'Estrange. *Technical Director*: Dave Milton. *Sound Recording*: Tom Lambert. *Editor*: Richard Currier.

Monogram Pictures; released November 19, 1943; B&W; 60 minutes.

Young radio singer Joan Abbott, whose popular program is sponsored by Crunchy-Wunchy Breakfast Foods, has been promised a break after concluding the current season, so that she can attend college. When her guardian Uncle Willy signs her up for another stint without her permission, an angry Joan goes AWOL. "I've always dreamed of living at one of the big campuses—sororities, proms—like other kids," she says. "And I'm going to do it—now."

Borrowing the name of an advertising agency receptionist, Joan enrolls at Rawley College as Susie Smith and quickly attracts the attention of the Kappa Psi Delta fraternity boys. In particular, Buzz O'Hara, leader of the fraternity's band, is smitten with her, but Joan is intrigued by shy, brainy young journalist "Scoop" Davis, editor of the *Rawley Sentinel*. Scoop agrees to take her on as a cub reporter, while she pledges the Theta Nu sorority.

Faced with the loss of the "Crunchy-Wunchy Thrush," advertising agency executive J.P. Hartman issues a press release announcing that Joan Abbott is attending college under an assumed name. Scoop, receiving the item at the *Sentinel*, deems the news item phony, a stunt to help Joan Abbott "get some cheap publicity which might attract a few more moronic listeners to her broken-down program." He assigns Susie to write an editorial denouncing it, which she does reluctantly. Theta Nu member Cynthia, jealous of the attention Susie gets from boys, sees the news and figures out the truth. Uncle Willy turns up at Rawley in response to Cynthia's tip, but his cunning niece outsmarts him, forcing him to go back to New York without her. Happy in her new life, she realizes that she and Scoop share feelings for each other and she takes matters into her own hands—and lips—when he's too timid to pursue her.

In New York, having passed off the search for Joan as a successful publicity stunt, Hartman and his colleagues dream up another one for a client looking to hire a youthful band for a radio program. Buzz enters his combo in the nationwide competition, and Joan, while claiming to suffer too badly from mike fright to sing on the radio, gladly coaches her friend Babs to be their soloist. When Babs strains her voice and develops laryngitis, Joan is pressured into taking her place and her true identity is revealed.

Gale Storm movies were coming fast and furious from Monogram in the fall of 1943, with this one released only seven days after *Nearly Eighteen,* and another one right on its heels. Two years after *Let's Go Collegiate,* we pay a return visit here to Rawley University, setting of that film, and to its fraternity Kappa Psi Delta, though none of the characters recur, and Gale is not playing the same person. Perhaps there were some leftover props in the Monogram warehouse.

Campus Rhythm (originally announced under the title *College Sweetheart*) focuses on Gale's singing from the opening scene, providing the best vehicle yet for her musical talent and considerable charm. She's reunited with two of her previous leading men, Johnny Downs (*Freckles Comes Home*) and Robert Lowery, with whom she recently completed *Revenge of the Zombies*. Candy Candido, introduced to movie audiences in *Rhythm Parade*, turns up again here, cast as a fraternity boy. Given that this is a musical comedy, logic occasionally goes out the window. Joan seems not to realize that, hoping to fly under the radar at college, it would probably be better if she didn't impulsively sing a solo to her date at a crowded college dance, or give impromptu vocal training lessons to a classmate. This is an early credit for screenwriter Frank Tarloff (1916–1999), who was blacklisted for several years during the McCarthy era and went on to become an Oscar winner for *Father Goose* (1964).

Studio publicity, recounting Gale's start with the *Gateway to Hollywood* contest, said that, three years later, she was "recognized generally in the film capital as one of the coming stars of American films..."[4] The pressbook suggested various gimmicks exhibitors could use to drum up business:

> The jalopies the school kids used to drive around in have practically disappeared from the American scene because of gas rationing. However, a good gag would be to get the most decrepit one available, plaster it with signs, load it with noisy kids and harness a horse to it for a tour around town. It'll get lots of laughs and comment and folks will know your film is that riotous type of show.

Newspaper ads played up Gale's charms, calling her "a 4-WHISTLE GIRL with a voice that's mello as a cello and a kiss that's pure bliss!" A suggested radio spot from the film's pressbook promised, "Collegiate hi-jinks! Campus romance! Fraternity fun! Don't miss the musical riot of college life ... featuring Gale Storm, Johnny Downs, Robert Lowery—and armfuls of sweater girls!" Exhibitors were encouraged to buy radio time in proximity to musically oriented shows, like those of Kay Kyser and Harry James, that were popular with teenagers.

While reviewers didn't fail to recognize this as a low-budget B movie, they generally gave it, and its leading lady, higher praise than Monogram products typically received. *Film Daily* (October 6, 1943) called *Campus Rhythm* "an excellent musical number with plenty of laughs, songs and college chatter," praised the songs, and added that Gale and Johnny Downs "turn in first-rate performances..." *Motion Picture Herald* (October 8, 1943) called Gale "a performer of ability and charm..." *Motion Picture Daily* (October 6, 1943) concurred: "The film reveals Gale Storm as a young actress and singer of manifest promise."

Where Are Your Children? (1943)

Cast: Jackie Cooper (*Danny Cheston*), Gale Storm (*Judy Wilson*), Patricia Morison (*Linda Woodford*), John Litel (*Judge Edmonds*), Gertrude Michael (*Nell Wilson*), Addison Richards (*Chief of Detectives*), Herbert Rawlinson (*Brooks*), Betty Blythe (*Mrs. Cheston*), Anthony Warde (*Jim Wilson*), Charles Williams (*Mack*), Evelyn Eaton (*Opal Becker*), Jimmy Zahner (*Jerry Doane*), Sarah Edwards (*Matron*), John Laurenz (*Petty Officer Jones*), Neyle Marx (*Herb Walsh*), Horace B. Carpenter (*Gas Station Attendant*), Blanche Payson (*Juvenile Court Matron*), Cyril Ring (*Juvenile Court Officer*), Gary Gray (*Boy in Nursery*), Eilene Janssen (*Girl in Nursery*), Ethelreda Leopold (*Girl in Juvenile Hall*), Johnny Duncan (*Jitterbug*), Jack Gardner (*Sailor*)

Director: William Nigh. *Executive Director*: Trem Carr. *Producer*: Jeffrey Bernerd. *Photography*: Mack Stengler, Ira Morgan. *Screenplay*: William Nigh, George Wallace Sayre. *Original Story*: William Nigh, Neil Rau, George William Sayre. *Production Manager*: William Strohbach. *Technical Director*: Dave Milton. *Sound Recording*: Tom Lambert. *Editor*: Duncan Mansfield. *Set Decorator*: Al Greenwood. *Music Director*: Edward Kay.

Monogram Pictures; released November 26, 1943; B&W; 73 minutes.

Young Judy Wilson, new to the town of Riverdale, works at a lunch counter while living with her brother and sister-in-law, who toil long hours at a shipyard. Danny Cheston is charmed by her as soon as they meet, and talks her into going dancing with him. Judy, not knowing the club to which he escorts her is one that illegally serves liquor to minors, has her drink spiked by Danny's friends. Before Danny can get her safely home, a tipsy Judy is spotted by Juvenile Court officer Linda Woodford, who takes Judy under her wing and urges her family not to judge her harshly. Recognizing the growing problem of juvenile delinquency in Riverdale, Linda appeals in vain for funding from civic leaders, including Danny's mother, who think her ideas of a youth center frivolous during wartime.

Caseworker Linda Woodford (Patricia Morison, left) is concerned about naïve Judy Wilson (Gale Storm, center) in Monogram's juvenile delinquent drama *Where Are Your Children?* (1943). Also pictured: Gale's leading man Jackie Cooper (right).

Unhappy at home with her resentful sister-in-law Nell, Judy is interested in Danny, but he doesn't want to get serious about her, as he expects to be called to Navy duty any day. Unbeknownst to Judy, Danny comes from a well-to-do family, and his domineering mother wants to arrange an appointment for him as an officer. But Danny wants to be "a plain, everyday enlisted man" and make good on his own. Though he misses Judy, he writes a letter telling her it's better for her not to wait, that he's not positioned to give her the life she deserves.

After an argument with Nell, Judy decides to head for San Diego where Danny is stationed. She accepts a ride with Danny's friends Herb, Opal and Jerry, not knowing they have stolen Danny's car. Too late, Judy realizes the others are thrill seekers out for a joy ride, and is horrified when Herb assaults a gas station attendant who later dies.

Hitchhiking the rest of the way to San Diego, Judy meets up with Danny just as his company is preparing to ship out. She's recognized and taken into custody by police, and she looks to be on her way to a stretch in juvenile detention as an accomplice in what had become a murder case. Linda Woodford, who recognizes that Judy is a typical example of the basically good kid gone wrong, appeals to Judge Edmonds of the Juvenile Court to give her another chance, while Danny learns of her troubles and rushes to her side.

As Judy in *Where Are Your Children?* (1943), Gale (left) learns the hard way to choose her friends more carefully. Also pictured are (left to right) Neyle Marx, Jimmy Zahner and Evelyn Eaton.

Where Are Your Children? is a textbook example of the juvenile delinquency drama popular in the 1940s. The underlying theme, lest a viewer miss it, is made perfectly explicit by Linda, who tells local civic leaders, "With their homes broken and disorganized, and their parents too busy to supervise their activities and look after them, then they're bound to get into trouble." The prominent citizens, including Danny's mother, believe the incidents of vagrancy, drunkenness, etc., being reported in town can be attributed to "the transient population," and think this "undesirable element" just needs to be locked up. But tenacious Linda says, "It's my job to keep minors out of the courts, not to bring them in."

Though Jackie Cooper (1922–2011) is top-billed, above the film's title, he's really playing the second lead here, as Judy's love interest. Instead, the dramatic chores mainly fall to Gale, 21 at the time of the film's release. She isn't asked to portray a hardened juvenile delinquent, just a nice girl looking for a little fun and falling in with the wrong crowd. She convincingly sheds tears in her dramatic moments, and plays a drunk scene adequately. "Everything's so *dreamy!*" trills Judy as she gets plastered within moments of taking her first drink, the room fading into a blur. (As one critic cracked, she accomplishes this feat "on approximately one ounce of liquor.") She and fresh-faced Cooper make an endearing couple.

Prominently billed John Litel (1892–1972), one of the most reliable featured players in B movies, doesn't turn up until an hour into the film. Upon arrival, however, he demonstrates his calm competence playing authority figures, as his judge character reels off a few gallons of exposition and scarcely concealed lecture: "Our big problem is not delinquent children—it's delinquent parents, and guardians, and communities." His assured performance is impressive given the amount of dialogue and the rapid pace at which the film was shot. Patricia Morison (born 1915) gets few opportunities to shine, as her character is mostly there to serve a function. Evelyn Eaton (1924–1964) has fun with the role of Opal Becker, a nasty piece of work who arranges for Judy's drink to be spiked, looks on in fascination as Herb commits assault, and is completely unrepentant when finally called to justice, starting tussles with the other girls in juvie and telling the judge she'd prefer to be sentenced to the boys' camp for her punishment.

Producer Jeffrey Bernerd and director William Nigh mostly succeed in concealing the film's modest budget; sets are adequate, if unexceptional, and a number of settings, both indoor and outdoor, are seen. The prop newspaper announcing Judy's criminal case has only a few sentences about the crime under the headline, the filmmakers obviously expecting in the pre-freeze frame world that no one would notice that it turns into an entirely different story with the second paragraph. By contemporary standards, the film is tame, not as openly exploitative as many later films in this genre would be. Jitterbugging, drinking, and a girl fight liven things up.

Studio publicists played up the film as the "First Frank Story of Juvenile Delinquency!" and called it "A Picture Every Mother and Father Should See!" Stories to be planted by theaters in local newspapers promised that the drama unfolded "in startling fashion," before offering "the solution of a question which is becoming increasingly serious, and constitutes an ominous threat to future generations." Gale and co-star Patricia Morison were dispatched to Detroit for the film's premiere in November 1943, but Gale had to face the press alone when Morison fell ill shortly before her scheduled appearances. After making the rounds in Detroit, Gale went on to New York for further publicity efforts.

Film Daily (November 26, 1943) applauded the film, calling it "one that parents and others concerned with the problems of youth will want to see ... [E]ntertainment with a purpose that will prove a powerful magnet for the family trade.... Jackie Cooper and Gale Storm play the boy and girl nicely." *Variety* (December 1, 1943) said, "Miss Storm, very youthful and refreshing, gives a fine performance" in a film that "not only delivers a strong message against juve waywardness and parental neglect but carries rather strong romantic appeal.... Boxoffice prospects are promising."

William R. Weaver, reviewer for the *Motion Picture Herald* (November 27, 1943), attended a preview staged in Hollywood for both press and civic leaders. He predicted that exhibitors playing up the exploitation angle "can sell a vast quantity of tickets," and reported of the preview, "Audience response and comment generally favorable."

The film's success prompted Monogram to release a follow-up, *Are These Our Parents?*, in which Gale did not appear.

Forever Yours (1945)

Cast: Gale Storm (*Joan Randall*), C. Aubrey Smith (*"Gramps" Randall*), Johnny Mack Brown (*Major Tex O'Connor*), Frank Craven (*Uncle Charlie*), Mary Boland (*Aunt Mary*), Conrad Nagel (*Dr. John Randall*), Johnny Downs (*Ricky*), Catherine McLeod (*Martha*), Selmer Jackson (*Williams*), Matt Willis (*Alabam*), Leo Diamond and the Harmonaires (*Themselves*), Maurice St. Clair (*Moving Man*), William Hall (*Pianist*), Russ Whiteman, Billy Wilkerson (*Soldiers*)

Director: William Nigh. *Executive Director*: Trem Carr. *Producer*: Jeffrey Bernerd. *Screenplay*: William Nigh, George Wallace Sayre. *Original Story*: William Nigh, Neil Rau, George Wallace Sayre. *Music Director*: Dimitri Tiomkin. *Photography*: Harry Neumann. *Supervising Editor*: Richard Currier. *Technical Director*: Dave Milton. *Recording*: Tom Lambert. *Wardrobe*: Harry Bourne. *Production Manager*: William Strohbach. *Assistant Director*: Richard Harlan. *Miss Storm's Gowns*: Athena. *Makeup*: Fred T. Walker. *Hair Stylist*: Lorraine MacLean. *Song: "Close Your Eyes and Just Pretend"*: Alan Jaxon, Neil Rau. *Song: "You're the Answer"*: Harry Brown, Robert Watson.

Monogram Pictures; released January 26, 1945; B&W; 83 minutes.

The socialite daughter of a prominent family of physicians, Joan Randall excels at outdoor sports and activities, but also spends much of her time taking part in benefits for servicemen and sick children. Her Aunt Mary disapproves of her hosting parties at the family estate for children suffering from polio, but Joan assures her that they are no longer contagious.

Joan's doctor father welcomes a houseguest, his former student Major Tex O'Connor. Tex wants Dr. Randall's help in testing an innovative treatment he's developed for nerve damage. He has been successfully treating soldiers injured during the war, but believes the same methods could be used in peacetime for other patients, saying, "It's obvious there's no difference in the treatment of a paralyzed muscle whether caused by machine gun bullets or polio." With Dr. Randall's help, his laboratory is set up at the local hospital so that experimentation can continue. When Tex wants to try his procedure on Jimmy, a young polio patient, the hospital board decides it's too risky and declines.

Although she's felt some symptoms of illness, Joan tries to keep them to herself, and is annoyed when Tex takes note of the pain she's trying to minimize. After a busy day of charitable activities, she collapses while singing and dancing at a benefit and is rushed to the hospital. She's soon diagnosed with infantile paralysis.

Miserable, bedridden and cut off from her friends and activities, Joan rapidly loses the will to live. She refuses the marriage proposal of her childhood sweetheart Ricky, fearing that he would be marrying her out of pity. Joan suffers recurring nightmares which, in the opinion of her father and grandfather, are caused by muscle spasms. Gramps thinks it's time to treat her condition with splints. Her father is reluctant, saying, "So it's six weeks of splints, then physical therapy treatments, and the best we can hope for is that one day she'll walk—with the aid of crutches and braces." As this is the best that conventional medicine has to offer, Joan tries to adjust to the idea of a different kind of life than what she had previously enjoyed. Her Uncle Charlie tries to show her that people with disabilities can still function, introducing her to a young blind girl who plays the piano and a disabled ex-serviceman who holds down a job as a moving man. Ricky and Charlie ask Tex to help Joan, but he doesn't feel he should interfere. When Tex visits her, he is displeased to find her coming to accept her gloomy diagnosis. "I've conquered my fear of living," she says heatedly, "and you call me a quitter." Joan insists on being "Tex's guinea pig," the first polio patient to undergo his surgical procedure. As family and friends wait anxiously, Tex prepares to perform the delicate operation that, one way or another, will determine Joan's future.

For the first few minutes, as we follow playgirl Joan and learn that she's an excellent horsewoman and fox hunt champion, this film seems to be threatening to turn into *Dark Victory* (1939) on a Monogram budget, with Gale standing in for Bette Davis. Instead, it ultimately shows itself to be a timely depiction of the threat posed by the polio epidemic. A "Special Note" at the film's conclusion says: "The treatment demonstrated in this film has been used on about 500 persons in the Los Angeles Area, but has not previously been available at any other place." Dr. Jonas Salk's polio vaccine would not be available for several more years.

Audiences expecting songs and music from Gale found them mostly in this film's early scenes, as she spends much of the second half flat on her back in bed. Unfortunately, the script doesn't give her the words to depict her plight in the most dramatic fashion, counting instead on tears glistening on her face and cries of pain to elicit audience sympathy for the heroine. Dimitri Tiomkin's music score is serviceable, though the thunderous surge on the soundtrack when Joan collapses is a little over-the-top.

She and Conrad Nagel, as her physician father, have a warm rapport that comes across effectively. Johnny Mack Brown, best-known as a Western star, is some 18 years Gale's senior, but he gives a calm, competent performance that makes their coming together as a couple credible. Mary Boland, in demand as a character actress for much of the 1930s, gets little opportunity to practice the type of comedy for which she was known.

Monogram originally announced the picture under the title *They Shall Have Faith,* subsequently shortening that to *Have Faith,* but then rechristened it *Forever Yours. Film Bulletin* (February 5, 1945) editorialized that the change was ill-advised, though it was apparently a reaction to sluggish ticket sales at its premieres. They complained on behalf of exhibitors that Monogram had discarded "an intriguing title, imparting an appropriate and provocative tone" in favor of one that "has all the sound of some innocuous, trite romantic yarn."

Forever Yours represented a greater than usual commitment of production resources for Monogram: *Showmen's Trade Review* (August 26, 1944) reported that the film's ballroom scenes were shot on the largest set ever constructed at the studio. Gale is also supported by a higher caliber cast than many of her films for the studio offered. Journalist Robbin

Coons reported that it required some effort on the part of producer Jeffrey Bernerd to assemble the group. He wanted to cast Herbert Marshall as Gale's dad, but the actor's agent flatly refused to let him work in a Monogram film. Mary Boland was reluctant as well. Ultimately C. Aubrey Smith broke the logjam, Coons wrote: "Sir Aubrey took the practical view that Monogram's money was as good as anybody's, and it was a good part for him beside."[5] Once Smith was on board, the rest of the cast gradually began to fall into place.

According to studio publicity, "How richly Gale Storm deserves stardom is shown by her mastery of the difficult portrayal which this elaborate Monogram production required." Shortly before its release, Gale served as hostess for a preview at the Monogram studios, to which 50 servicemen were invited.

Trade paper reviews were mixed, though they seemed to be in agreement that Gale was a good choice for the lead. *Film Daily* (December 18, 1944) was impressed by the star's performance: "This offering marks an important step forward in film career of Gale Storm, who, in addition to doing splendid acting, displays unsuspected talents as a dancer and singer." Added the *Los Angeles Times* (December 12, 1944, reviewing the film under its original title), "Characters are naturally drawn, the all-star cast acquitting itself well.... Especially effective photographically are nightmare sequences..." *Variety* (September 26, 1945) liked Gale's singing, but complained, "What starts out as a musical romance winds up as a psychological drama and tear-jerker."

In *Motion Picture Herald*'s "What the Picture Did for Me" column (February 25, 1945), an exhibitor from New Hampshire said that Gale was "better than her material. The picture opens with promise of nice entertainment but drifts into monotonously slow pace." She added that playing the picture during a March of Dimes drive seemed to help business. Gale's *Forever Yours* performance earned her an invitation to President Franklin D. Roosevelt's January 1945 birthday ball, which highlighted a fundraising campaign to fight infantile paralysis.

G.I. Honeymoon (1945)

Cast: Gale Storm (*Ann Gordon*), Peter Cookson (*Lt. Robert Gordon*), Arline Judge (*Flo LaVerne*), Frank Jenks (*Horace P. Malloy*), Jerome Cowan (*Ace Renaldo*), Jonathan Hale (*Col. Hammerhead Smith*), Andrew Tombes (*Rev. Horace*), Virginia Brissac (*Lavinia Thorndyke*), Ruth Lee (*Mrs. Barton*), Ralph Lewis (*Lt. Randall*), Earle Hodgins (*Jonas*), Lois Austin (*Mrs. Smith*), John Valentine (*Major Brown*), Claire Whitney (*Mrs. Brown*), Frank Stephens (*Captain Stein*), Jack Overman (*Sergeant Harrigan*), Jimmy Conlin (*Telegram Messenger*)

Director: Phil Karlstein [Karlson]. *Executive Director*: Trem Carr. *Producer*: Lindsley Parsons. *Screenplay*: Richard Weil, Jr., based on a play by A.J. Rubien, Marion Page Johnson, Robert Chapin. *Additional Dialogue*: Tim Ryan. *Photography*: Harry Neumann. *Art Director*: Dave Milton. *Editor*: Richard Currier. *Music Score*: Edward J. Kay.

Monogram Pictures; released April 6, 1945; B&W; 69 minutes.

Lt. Robert Gordon is in the midst of a hasty wedding to Ann Barton when he receives orders to report for duty at a Nevada military base. Ann and Bob complete the ceremony, with only moments to spare before he's due on a cross-country train. Hoping there will be an opportunity for a honeymoon, Ann hurriedly boards the locomotive, but is unable to secure a berth for herself. Crossing paths with lecherous passenger Ace Renaldo, quick-witted Ann puts one over on him, forcing him to relinquish his drawing room to her. Armed with dinner, champagne and her new negligee, Ann is ready for romance, but the Gordons' connubial bliss is delayed when he's summoned by his commanding officer.

In Faber, Nevada, where Robert will be stationed at Fort Dixon, there's a housing shortage; even the local hotel is renting out access to chairs in the lobby and stretch-outs on its pool tables. Meanwhile, gambling boss Renaldo (the man Ann tricked on the train) warns his good-natured assistant Horace P. Malloy, better known as Blubber, that the police are about to crack down on their illegal operation. Their gambling den is abruptly transformed into an apartment for rent, and when Blubber takes a shine to Ann, she becomes their tenant.

Relishing the opportunity to settle his score with Ann, Renaldo sees his chance when the building is declared off limits to military personnel. Just as Ann is putting the finishing touches on a cocktail party for Robert's fellow officers, Renaldo manages to spread the word that the gambling den is again open for business and tips off the police to raid her afternoon soiree. The disastrous party that ensues leaves Robert afraid his wife has been unfaithful, the other military wives convinced she's pregnant, and Ann in tears just as her aunt arrives unexpectedly.

An opening title announces, "This is the story of a soldier who was late for the wedding ... absent from his honeymoon ... and then discovered that his bride's boudoir had been declared 'Out of Bounds.' As General Sherman once said, 'War is [expletive suggested by symbols]!!!'"

Although by modern standards the film may no longer seem "fairly lusty," as a *Variety* review termed it, *G.I. Honeymoon* does contain an adult element not always seen in '40s romantic comedies, as this is for much of its running time a story about a frustrated bride and groom perpetually stymied at consummating their marriage. (The National League of Decency gave it a B rating, citing its "suggestive dialogue and situations.") The likable, if low-budget, programmer not only showcases Gale's beauty and charm as a gorgeous young bride—as dopey Blubber assesses her, "She's got a lovely profile all the way down!"—but also affords her the opportunity to demonstrate the comedic skills that made her a top television star in the 1950s. There's more than a touch of Margie Albright's scheming in the scenes that find Ann Gordon thinking fast and acting impulsively to get the better of men susceptible to her charms. In reality, Gale's own 1941 marriage to Lee Bonnell was not unlike the situation depicted here, though without the strict deadline. Bonnell reported for military service in August 1941 only a short time before he wed Gale. Ultimately he was rejected for poor eyesight, though he would later serve in the Coast Guard.

Gale's leading man Peter Cookson (1913–1990) had a brief motion picture career (1943 to 1946), including two appearances as leading man to Jean Parker in Monogram's Kitty O'Day series. (On the marquee of the theater across the street from Ann and Robert's apartment is DETECTIVE KITTY O'DAY.) After the war, he had a honeymoon of his own with actress Beatrice Straight, who would go on to win a Best Supporting Actress Oscar for *Network* (1976).

The film is populated with a generous supply of experienced supporting players who help things along, among them Jerome Cowan (1897–1972) as shifty Renaldo, Frank Jenks (1902–1962) as his slightly dimwitted cohort, Virginia Brissac (1883–1979) as Ann's no-nonsense aunt and Arline Judge (1912–1974) as brassy neighbor Flo, floor show headliner at a nearby nightclub of questionable distinction.

Director Phil Karlstein (1908–1985), who would subsequently adopt Karlson as his professional name, ultimately directed Gale in three films. He won acclaim from *noir* fans for his gritty crime thrillers, which included *Kansas City Confidential* and *Tight Spot*. Edward Kay's musical score won Monogram a rare Academy Award nomination.

Production began in the fall of 1944. Ann Lewis of *Showmen's Trade Review* (October 21, 1944), visiting the set, reported on the "whistle dress" Gale donned—"a snugly fitted watermelon color crepe ... trimmed with bands of royal blue material, and has a half bustle in the back that swings as Gale walks." Lewis watched as one of the buildings on the Monogram lot stood in for the site of the apartment Ann rents, with director Karlstein giving Gale a personal demonstration of the proper way to faint into the arms of a military policeman.

G.I. Honeymoon nicely demonstrates Gale's versatility, moving from the somber drama of *Forever Yours* to lightweight romantic comedy. As columnist Erskine Johnson (October 25, 1945) put it, "She has been starred in everything but a remake of *The Birth of a Nation*." He quoted her as saying, "I'll play anything. It's good experience." Studio publicity described *G.I. Honeymoon* as "one of the funniest comedies of the season," adding that Gale "is revealed as an accomplished comedienne..." *Showmen's Trade Review* (March 16, 1946) reported that a Miami theater manager drummed up business for *G.I. Honeymoon* by hiring two young ladies to call area residents and pretend to be Gale Storm, saying, "I'm getting married you know, so be sure to come see me in *G.I. Honeymoon*, at the Rosetta Theatre, Saturday."

Variety (March 21, 1945) commented, "A fairly lusty comedy, skillfully kept from verging on the risqué, this low-budgeter is acceptable fare as a minor dualler." *Showmen's Trade Review* (March 3, 1945) said, "The screenplay is surprising in its excellence, and, but for the weakness of direction, would have been the foundation for a hit sleeper and the big moment for Gale Storm.... Miss Storm looks and acts like she is ready for the big time: she has beauty, wears clothes well and gets everything possible from her dialogue."

Sunbonnet Sue (1945)

Cast: Gale Storm (*Sue Casey*), Phil Regan (*Danny Dooley*), George Cleveland (*Matt Casey*), Alan Mowbray (*Jonathan*), Minna Gombell (*Mrs. Fitzgerald*), Edna M. Holland (*Julia Ross*), Raymond Hatton (*Joe Feeney*), Gerald Oliver Smith (*Masters*), Charles D. Brown (*Father Hurley*), Charles Judels (*Milano*), Jerome Franks, Jr. (*Burke*), Michael Raffetto (*Commentator*)

Director: Ralph Murphy. *Executive Director*: Trem Carr. *Producer*: Scott R. Dunlap. *Screen Adaptation*: Ralph Murphy, Richard A. Carroll. *Original Story*: Paul Gerard Smith, Bradford Ropes. *Prologue*: Sidney Sutherland. *Music Director*: Edward Kay. *Choreographer*: Jack Boyle. *Miss Storm's Costumes*: Fritzi Ehrens. *Wardrobe*: Harry Bourne. *Hair Stylist*: Lorraine MacLean. *Photography*: Harry Neumann. *Editor*: Richard Currier. *Assistant Directors*: Robert Ray, Eddie Davis. *Set Decorator*: Charles Thompson. *Sound Recording*: Tom Lambert. *Production Manager*: William Strohbach. *Art Director*: Ernest R. Hickson. *Songs*: "Sunbonnet Sue" (Gus Edwards, Will D. Cobb), "School Days" (Cobb, Edwards), "On the Old See-Saw" (Edwards), "By the Light of the Silvery Moon" (Ed Madden, Edwards, "Donegal" (Steve Graham), "If I Had My Way" (Lou Klein, James Kendis), "Look for the Rainbow" (Ralph Murphy, C. Harold Lewis), "The Bowery" (Charles H. Hoyt, Percy Gaunt), "While Strolling Through the Park One Day" (Ed Haley), "Yoo Hoo, Ain't You Comin' Out Tonight" (Carson Robison)

Monogram Pictures; released October 6, 1945; B&W; 89 minutes.

In 1890s New York, young Sue Casey enjoys performing musical numbers at her father's saloon in the Bowery. Sue's Aunt Julia, sister of her late mother, witnesses a performance and is appalled. Wealthy and socially prominent Julia, who lives on Fifth Avenue, pulls some political strings to have Matt Casey's beer garden shut down. In doing so, she also sabotages the election campaign of Sue's boyfriend Danny Dooley, a young lawyer running for the post of alderman.

As Christmas approaches, Matt is despondent over the loss of his business, and the Caseys are facing financial trouble. Although Danny has just proposed to Sue, her aunt wants her to come live on Fifth Avenue, where she can be refined into the sort of niece who will be socially acceptable. Sue decides to give in to her aunt's offer, temporarily, when Julia promises to help Matt reopen his saloon in exchange.

Without explaining herself to her father or her beau, Sue allows herself to be introduced to New York society as a debutante at a New Year's Eve ball, an event due to be attended by the governor and his wife. Before Sue can sneak away from the ball, as she had planned to do, her father and Danny crash the event, resulting in a brawl that humiliates Julia. Unexpectedly, Sue's father recognizes an old friend among Julia's high-toned guests, someone who offers a ray of hope to set things right again for the Caseys.

Gale's period musical *Sunbonnet Sue* (1945) teamed her for the first time with handsome tenor Phil Regan (left) Playing featured roles were Charles D. Brown (standing), and George Cleveland (seated).

Monogram publicity described *Sunbonnet Sue* as "The romance of a famous Cabaret Queen and a Playboy Politician in the lush, plush days of New York's wildest era" and "a charming story of a past generation." Before settling on the film's title, others considered were *Belle of the Bowery, The Gay Nineties* and *Old New York*. *Showmen's Trade Review* (June 2, 1945) noted, "Maurice Costello, Stuart Holmes and Eva Novak, stars of the silent era, were engaged for minor roles…" The film's budget was reportedly $400,000, in line with A releases from other studios.

Although the film is brimming with music, not all of it was allocated to Gale. This is the first of two pictures Gale made with Irish-American tenor Phil Regan (1906–1966) as her leading man; he serenades Gale's character with the title song. She solos on "Look for the Rainbow," a number written for the film, and performs "School Days" to a lusty saloon audience in the finale.

Supporting roles are competently played by George Cleveland (1885–1957) as Sue's dad, Edna M. Holland (1895–1982) as her snooty aunt and Minna Gombell (1892–1973), who despite her prominent billing turns up fairly late in the film, as the governor's wife. Alan Mowbray (1896–1969), smoothly capable as ever, plays the somewhat ill-defined role of Jonathan. Although most synopses of the film refer to him as Julia's friend, rather than a family member, he describes Sue as "my niece" in one scene. By Monogram's usual standards, this film has a huge cast, with numerous denizens of Sue and Matt's neighborhood given speaking (or singing) parts to play.

Director Ralph Murphy (1895–1967) had recently completed a lengthy stint at Paramount, where his films included *Mrs. Wiggs of the Cabbage Patch* (1942). In addition to helming the film, he co-authored the screenplay and contributed two songs.

Nash and Ross' *Motion Picture Guide* called this "a pleasant farce that supplies a good many musical numbers aimed at tugging memories of the good old days," while *Motion Picture Daily* (September 25, 1945) gave it a compliment rarely heard at Monogram, calling its production values "high grade in every particular." *Showmen's Trade Review* (September 29, 1945) predicted success for the film: "What nostalgia and entertainment this fine musical from Monogram holds for the average audience…. Gale Storm is her usual, splendid self; charming, attractive and capable in every department, be it dancing, singing or acting." Syndicated columnist Jimmie Fidler (September 30, 1945) noted, "A weak plot is more than balanced by the appeal of old-time songs."

In the summer of 1945, with the film completed and awaiting release, trade papers noted that Monogram had exercised its option to keep Gale as a contract player for another year. Certainly her three releases for the year—a somber drama, a light-hearted comedy and this musical entry—had demonstrated her versatility and her value to the studio.

Swing Parade of 1946 (1946)

Cast: Gale Storm (*Carol Lawrence*), Phil Regan (*Danny Warren*), The Three Stooges [Moe Howard, Larry Fine, Curly Howard], Connee Boswell, Louis Jordan and His Tympany Five, Will Osborne and His Orchestra (*Specialties*), Edward Brophy (*Moose*), Mary Treen (*Marie Finch*), Russell Hicks (*Daniel Warren, Sr.*), Windy Cook (*Specialty*), John Eldredge (*Bascomb*), Leon Belasco (*Pete*), Jack Boyle (*Dancing Partner*), Dewey Robinson (*Process Server*), Edna Holland (*Mrs. Greene*), Robert Homans (*Policeman*), Wilbur Mack (*Businessman*), Edward Earle, Emmett Vogan (*Club Customers*), Nell Craig (*Matron*)

Director: Phil Karlson. *Executive Director*: Trem Carr. *Producers*: Harry A. Romm, Lindsley Parsons. *Screenplay*: Tim Ryan. *Original Story*: Edmond Kelso. *Additional Dialogue*: Nicholas Ray. *Music Director*: Edward Kay. *Choreography*: Jack Boyle. *Photography*: Harry Neumann. *Supervising Editor*: Richard Currier. *Production Manager*: Glenn Cook. *Art Director*: Ernest R. Hickson. *Technical Director*: Dave Milton. *Chief Set Electrician*: John M. Lee. *Set Decorators*: Charles Thompson, Vin Taylor. *Recording*: Tom Lambert. *Hair Stylist*: Lorraine MacLean. *Miss Boswell's Gowns*: Kathryn Kuhn. *Wardrobe*: Harry Bourne. *Makeup*: Harry Ross.

Monogram Pictures; released March 16, 1946; B&W; 73 minutes.

Aspiring singer Carol Lawrence is pounding the pavements looking for a job, knowing she is already behind on her rent. She visits the soon-to-open Embassy Club, hoping for an audition, but is shown the gate, mistaken for a process server. Club owner Danny Warren is leery of being served legal papers before the opening, knowing his snobbish father disapproves of his career aspirations. Indeed, Daniel Warren, Sr., has bought the building where the club is housed and is in the process of trying to deliver eviction papers to his son.

Carol applies for a receptionist job at the National Utilities Company, not knowing that the elder Warren is president of the firm. He offers her a $50 reward if she can serve the papers on his son. Having been kicked out of her apartment, unable even to retrieve her clothes, Carol agrees. When she finally finagles her way into the Embassy Club with the help of hapless dishwashers Larry, Curly and Moe, she mistakenly hands Danny her own eviction notice instead of the legal documents from his father. Feeling sorry for her, Danny has Carol brought back to the club, and after an audition offers her a singing job and gives her a makeshift place to stay backstage. A grateful Carol tears up the eviction notice from Danny's father without serving it.

Disgusted that his employees can't serve the legal papers, the senior Warren decides to do so himself, on opening night at his son's club. Accompanied by Danny's pal Marie, Mr. Warren sees that the club is a big success, but he is recognized by Larry, Curly and Moe, filling in as waiters. With the help of bouncer Moose, they give him the bum's rush. In the ensuing fracas, Mr. Warren is hauled into jail on charges of disturbing the peace and resisting arrest. Before Marie can get him to Danny's club a second time, his lawyer Bascomb shows up finally serves the eviction papers, revealing in the process that Carol was originally hired to do so. Seen as a traitor by her friends at the club, Carol is on the verge of bailing out altogether when Danny steps in.

Story takes a back seat to music and dance numbers in *Swing Parade of 1946,* which devotes most of its running time to the Embassy Club revue. Production values are higher than some of her previous musicals, such as *Rhythm Parade,* making it clear that Monogram executives opened the purse a little wider than in the past. Among the attractions showcased are singer Connee Boswell and the infectiously energetic Louis Jordan and his band, who perform two lively numbers. Once again cast as a newcomer trying to make her way in show business, Gale solos on songs like "Oh, Brother" and Jimmy McHugh and Dorothy Fields' "On the Sunny Side of the Street," as duets with Phil Regan on "Small World." Newspaper ads dubbed the film "That slick pic with the song clicks and the chic chicks!"

Production began in the summer of 1945, with initial reports indicating that Mantan Moreland and Ben Carter would have featured roles and that Del Lord would direct, none of which came true. Studio publicity called it "a veritable kaleidoscope of fast-moving entertainment.... The beauty of the versatile Miss Storm has never before been photographed to such good advantage, and she handles her assignment delightfully, singing alone and with Regan..." Gale is again directed by Phil Karlson, who helmed *G.I. Honeymoon*. Her leading man, for the second time, is Phil Regan, who co-starred with her in *Sunbonnet Sue*. Credited with additional dialogue is Nicholas Ray (1911–1979), who gained far greater fame directing such films as *Johnny Guitar* (1954) and *Rebel Without a Cause* (1955).

Gale's character is named Carol Lawrence, some 15 years before another singer-actress made that name famous with her role in Broadway's *West Side Story*. This is her last film to be released under the Monogram banner, as well as her last for producer Lindsley Parsons, who had been instrumental in signing her as a contract player. The primary character roles are entrusted to Edward Brophy (1895–1960), cast as Moose, and Mary Treen (1907–1989), who plays "plain Jane" Marie. Treen's far more famous film of the same year was *It's a Wonderful Life*. Brophy turned up the following year in Gale's *It Happened on 5th Avenue*.

Said *Showmen's Trade Review* (January 26, 1946), "This top-flight musical will entertain average audiences everywhere.... Miss Storm is her usual able, attractive self..." According to *Independent Exhibitors' Film Bulletin* (September 2, 1946), "One of Monogram's higher-budget offerings, this has an impressive array of songs and some clever dance routines.... Gale Storm ... again demonstrates that she has charm and acting ability worthy of better things..."

While the imminent arrival of Gale's second son would keep her off-screen for much of 1946, an important picture lay just around the corner for her.

It Happened on 5th Avenue (1947)

Cast: Don DeFore (*Jim Bullock*), Ann Harding (*Mary O'Connor*), Charles Ruggles (*Michael J. O'Connor*), Victor Moore (*Aloysius T. McKeever*), Gale Storm (*Trudy O'Connor*), Grant Mitchell (*Farrow*), Edward Brophy (*Patrolman Cecil Felton*), Alan Hale, Jr. (*Whitey Temple*), Dorothea Kent (*Margie Temple*), Edward Ryan, Jr. (*Hank*), Cathy Carter (*Alice*), Johnny Arthur (*Apartment Manager*), Dudley Dickerson (*Joe*), Charles Lane (*Landlord*), George Meader (*Music Store Manager*), Arthur Hohl (*Patrolman Brady*), Abe Reynolds (*Finkelhoff*), Pat Goldin (*Waiter*), Chester Clute (*Phillips*), Edward Gargan (*Policeman in Park*), John Hamilton (*Harper*), George Lloyd (*Moving Foreman*), Linda Lee Solomon (*Young Girl*), Anthony Sydes (*Jackie Temple*)

Producer-Director: Roy Del Ruth. *Screenplay*: Everett Freeman. *Original Story*: Herbert Clyde Lewis, Frederick Stephani. *Additional Dialogue*: Vick Knight. *Associate Producer*: Joe Kaufman. *Songs*: "It's a Wonderful Wonderful Feeling," "That's What Christmas Means to Me," "Speak—My Heart" (lyrics and music, Harry Revel); "You're Everywhere" (lyrics, Paul Webster, music, Harry Revel, vocals, The King's Men). *Music Score*: Edward Ward. *Photography*: Henry Sharp. *Production Manager*: Glenn Cook. *Assistant to Producer*: Clarence Bricker. *Assistant Director*: Frank Fox. *Editor*: Richard Heermance. *Music Editor*: J.K. Wood. *Art Director*: Lewis Creber. *Set Decorator*: Ray Boltz. *Recording Engineer*: Corson Jowett. *Chief Electrician*: John Lee. *Makeup*: Harry Ross. *Furs*: Willard George. *Fashion Supervisor*: Lorraine MacLean.

Allied Artists; released April 19, 1947; B&W; 115 minutes.

Aloysius T. McKeever, known to his friends as Mac, is a carefree type (some call him a hobo) who for the past three years has been riding out the cold New York winters by taking up unauthorized residence in the boarded-up Fifth Avenue mansion of Michael J. O'Connor. O'Connor routinely winters in Virginia, leaving his New York abode free (except for a nightly check by patrolmen on the local beat) for Mac and his dog Sam to enjoy the good life from November until early March. In the park, McKeever meets young World War II veteran Jim Bullock, who is at loose ends after being evicted from his apartment, coincidentally because the same Michael J. O'Connor, in one of his many real estate deals, bought the building. Jim, stymied by the postwar housing shortage and his meager income, accepts Mac's invitation to stay at the O'Connor mansion, not realizing they're actually trespassing.

O'Connor is almost entirely preoccupied with his business affairs, a situation which resulted in a divorce from his disillusioned wife Mary. His latest venture is a deal to purchase an unused Army barracks, Camp Kilson, which he means to transform into a huge freight transport operation. He's distracted from his dealings when he's notified that his teenage daughter Trudy has run away from her finishing school.

Trying to keep her location a secret, Trudy goes to the Fifth Avenue house to retrieve clothes to wear to a job interview. She's caught by Mac and Jim, who initially assume she's a thief; eventually, Mac confesses to his new friends that he has no legal right to occupy the mansion. Attracted to Jim, Trudy decides to play along for the time being, so that she can stay without attracting her family's attention. She lands a job at a music shop,

Good-hearted hobo Aloysius McKeever (Victor Moore, left) helps along the romance of Trudy (Gale Storm) and Jim (Don DeFore) in *It Happened on 5th Avenue* (1947).

but Jim's search for work is less successful. The mansion becomes even more crowded when Jim runs into two old Army buddies who are living with their wives and children in a car. McKeever reluctantly agrees to take them in as well. Inspired by Mac, Jim and his buddies dream up a plan to purchase Camp Kilson, with dozens of military men investing a small share each to transform the barracks into housing for young families.

Tracking his daughter to New York, O'Connor is frustrated when Trudy refuses to return to school, saying she has been unhappy for some time. He reluctantly agrees to pose as yet another squatter, "Mike," at his own mansion, so that he can meet Jim, with whom Trudy has fallen in love, and get acquainted without Jim learning of the family wealth. Used to barking out orders, O'Connor is furious when Mac lords it over him, while wearing O'Connor's clothes and smoking his cigars. When her dad threatens to bust the whole scheme, Trudy sends an emergency telegram to her mother Mary, who flies up from Palm Beach to help. Talking her own way into the household as a cook, Mary bickers lightly with Mike, but it is clear they still have strong feelings for each other. Still conducting business as best he can while incognito, O'Connor bids higher and higher on the Camp Kilson property, and tests Jim's mettle by arranging for him to be offered a lucrative job thousands of miles away from Trudy. Mary concludes that her ex-husband's priorities and values have not really changed, and she turns away from him.

On Christmas Eve, in the middle of their holiday celebration, the squatters are caught by two patrolmen, who take pity on them and tell them to vacate the house no later than January. As the deadline approaches, Jim and Trudy's relationship is imperiled, while her parents also seem to be at loggerheads.

Today *It Happened on Fifth Avenue* is a favorite with many viewers as a Christmastime treat, and remains one of Gale's best-known films. However, its original release was in springtime. The picture's originally announced budget was $1,000,000, an immense sum by Monogram standards. Gale's casting was announced in the summer of 1946. The film was Roy Del Ruth's first venture as an independent producer, with release to be arranged through Monogram. Monogram formed a division called Allied Artists Pictures, aimed at producing and distributing higher-budget films than what they normally made, with *It Happened on 5th Avenue* to be the first project.

Gale told the *Los Angeles Times*' Edwin Schallert that she received the script while recuperating in the hospital from the birth of her son Peter. "It seemed all too wonderful, as I read the scenario page by page.... It was just as if everything good had happened all at once—the new baby, the marvelous picture, the fine role I was to play in the production."[6] Gale is delightful as Trudy, and arguably merited better than fifth billing. Though she's playing a rich heiress, she embodies the girl-next-door charm that many prized after the war. Her presence is one of the few clues to this film's connection with Monogram. It is jarring to hear her singing dubbed with a voice quite different from her own, and one that doesn't particularly match her appearance or speaking voice.

Charles Ruggles (1886–1970) takes the seemingly hardhearted and stubborn character of Michael O'Connor and makes him not only watchable but sometimes sympathetic. Ann Harding (1902–1981), given second billing though she doesn't show up until nearly an hour into the film, is matched well with him as they trade barbs. This is Gale's first film with Alan Hale, Jr., later to be known as the Skipper on TV's *Gilligan's Island*. They shared the screen again in *The Underworld Story*.

Producer-director Del Ruth (1893–1961) achieved a distinction of sorts by being one of the few colleagues about whom Gale was not complimentary in her memoir. According to Gale, he insisted that her singing in the film be dubbed, refusing to consider allowing her to use her own voice, despite her previous success with musical films and in Soundies. (In the mid–1950s, she would further demonstrate her singing skills by becoming a recording artist with Dot Records.)

Although the film has been criticized for being overlong (nearly two hours), it packs quite a bit of story into that time and nicely showcases its ensemble cast. The film's publicity campaign included endorsements attributed to various celebrities. One ad quoted Cary Grant as saying, "Enjoyed it immensely. The picture is beautifully mounted, well cast and the direction is of highest calibre." Gale and co-star Don DeFore made personal appearances in Texas in April 1947 for what was described as "a four-way prerelease run in Dallas, Houston, San Antonio and Fort Worth."[7]

Film Daily (February 4, 1947) called it "a delightfully amusing offering," praising Gale as one of "the other featured players who do excellent work." According to *Independent Exhibitors' Film Bulletin* (May 26, 1947), the result was "a first-rate comedy on the whimsey [sic] side," performed by "a cast of competent players, not powerful magnets, perhaps, but who look interesting up on a marquee." Said *Variety* (February 5, 1947), "it offers excellent entertainment and boxoffice values" and "should be a solid pleaser for general audiences."

The Dude Goes West (1948)

Cast: Eddie Albert (*Daniel Bone*), Gale Storm (*Liza Crockett*), James Gleason (*Sam Briggs*), Gilbert Roland (*Pecos Kid*), Binnie Barnes (*Kiki Kelly*), Barton MacLane (*Texas Jack Barton*), Harry Hayden (*Horace Hotchkiss*), Catherine Doucet (*Grandma Crockett*), Sarah Padden (*Mrs. Hallahan*), Douglas Fowley (*Beetle*), Olin Howlin (*Finnegan*), Francis Pierlot (*Mr. Brittle*), Tom Tyler (*Spiggoty*), Chief Yowlachie (*Running Wolf*), Edward Gargan (*Train Conductor*), Paul Bryar (*Smith*), Tom Fadden (*Hines*), Si Jenks (*Horse Trader*), George Meeker (*Gambler*), Anthony Warde (*Barney*), Charles Williams (*Harris*), Milton Kibbee (*Hotel Clerk*)

Director: Kurt Neumann. *Producers*: Maurice King, Frank King. *Original Screenplay*: Mary Loos, Richard Sale. *Music Score*: Dimitri Tiomkin. *Assistant to Producers*: Arthur Gardner. *Photography*: Karl Struss. *Production Manager*: Herman E. Webber. *Set Decorator*: Sidney Moore. *Editor*: Richard Heermance. *Dialogue Director*: Jo Graham. *Special Effects*: Ray Mercer. *Sound Engineer*: Tom Lambert. *Assistant Director*: Frank S. Heath. *Technical Advisor*: Herman King.

Allied Artists; released May 30, 1948; B&W; 86 minutes.

Eastern dude Daniel Bone has inherited his family business as a gunsmith, but finds work scarce in his native Brooklyn. He decides to relocate to Arsenic City, Nevada, even though all he knows about the West is what he's read in books. Working in his favor is his familiarity with guns, which, despite his reluctance to use them, will later cause an admiring bandit to observe, "I ain't never seen no honest man could shoot that good."

During his train trip, he meets a sheltered young woman, Liza Crockett, tightly guarding a map showing where her late father discovered a gold mine. Brought up by her grandmother to deeply distrust men, Liza regards Daniel's attempts to get acquainted with suspicion, and when he prevents a robber, the Pecos Kid, from stealing her purse, Liza wrongly assumes he's the guilty party. In Carson City, Daniel purchases a horse and wagon and offers Liza a ride to Arsenic City, which she haughtily refuses. Crossing the

Eddie Albert plays the title character in *The Dude Goes West* **(Allied Artists, 1948), with Gale as prim and proper Liza.**

desert, Daniel makes the tenderfoot mistake of trusting another bad guy, Texas Jack Barton, who robs him and leaves him unconscious. When he runs into Liza, traveling alone with a team of horses, they form an uneasy alliance to make it safely to Arsenic City. Ambushed by Indians, Daniel, using his book knowledge of Native American Indian customs and sign language, manages to win the respect of Chief Running Wolf and his tribe. Liza takes offense when he claims her as his "squaw" for her own protection, and insists they go their separate ways upon arrival in town.

Arsenic City proves to be a lawless place: As one resident tells Daniel shortly after his arrival, "We're fresh out of sheriffs. Last one held office only an hour. 'Tain't a permanent job." Unbeknownst to Liza, lawyer Hotchkiss, who claims to be her late father's best friend, is in cahoots with Kiki Kelly and her gang, including the Pecos Kid, who plot to steal her map to Harry Crockett's gold cache. Daniel commits the map to memory and then burns it, enlisting the help of his prospector pal Sam to find the mine on Liza's behalf. Led into a confrontation with Kiki and her cohorts, Daniel finds that he has made some friends along the way when they come to his aid in an hour of need.

Like *It Happened on 5th Avenue*, Gale's first picture released through Allied Artists, *The Dude Goes West* is a co-production of Monogram and an independent producer, in this case the King Brothers. During pre-production, the film was known as *The Tenderfoot*. Monogram was no longer pushing her into cheap films made in six days. After being the leading lady in several serious Westerns, here she has the opportunity to take part in a film that gently parodies the genre.

Mary Loos and Richard Sale's screenplay subjects Western tropes to a much milder satire than later films such as *Blazing Saddles* (1974). Unlike comedies like Don Knotts' *The Shakiest Gun in the West,* our hero here is not a comical coward, just a principled man whose methods seem a little out of place in the lawless West. The screenwriters have some mild fun with their hero's name—"It's Bone, not Boone!" he gripes when people get it wrong, as well as settings such as the inscription on Harry Crockett's grave marker: "A Good Friend But a Bad Shot."

This was Gale's only film with Eddie Albert (1906–2005). His character here is faintly reminiscent of *Green Acres*' Oliver Douglas, a man venturing into unfamiliar territory armed largely with erudition. During one scene in which he lectures an angry lynch mob about the Bill of Rights, Hooterville aficionados may be waiting to hear the strains of patriotic music in the background. But Daniel doesn't possess the perennial frustration that was so characteristic of Albert's TV character.

British-born Binnie Barnes (1903–1998), making her entrance nearly an hour into the film, has a strong character role as hard-edged, cigar-smoking Kiki Kelly, proprietress of the Last Chance Saloon and the brains and the nerve behind most of the local crime wave. Handy with a pistol, she growls, "I never ask any quarter as a woman," and has no trouble standing up to Gilbert Roland's Pecos Kid. Barton MacLane (1902–1969), who'd glowered his way through plenty of serious Westerns, is fun as Texas Jack, who's more than a little taken aback by Daniel's good-hearted sincerity. Receiving a note supposedly written by his erudite friend, in which he urges Jack to "come with alacrity, but come alone," the grizzled gunman can't quite figure how he can be alone if Al comes along. Harry Hayden (1882–1955), seen as lawyer Hotchkiss, was the father of actor Don Hayden, who played Gale's boyfriend on *My Little Margie*.

The film was released during a period when box office returns were sagging, threatened by the growing popularity of television. Several reviewers thought *The Dude Goes West* a promising vehicle to draw moviegoers back into theaters. *Independent Exhibitors' Bulletin* (June 21, 1948) called it "a Western that is different ... by virtue of a generous fund of 'Grade A' comedy ... [A]dult audiences everywhere will heartily enjoy its tongue-in-cheek merriment." Said *Showmen's Trade Review* (May 1, 1948), "This is delightful entertainment from start to finish" that could prove to be "one of the sleepers of the season..." According to the *Chicago Tribune*'s Mae Tinée (August 4, 1948), "This unassuming comedy ... has more validity as entertainment than a good many of the expensive horse operas it ribs." *Film Daily* (April 27, 1948) concurred: "This zany laugh piler-upper, properly exploited, should play a merry tune at the box office.... The acting is excellent."

Stampede (1949)

Cast: Rod Cameron (*Mike McCall*), Gale Storm (*Connie Dawson*), Johnny Mack Brown (*Sheriff Aaron Ball*), Don Castle (*Tim McCall*), Donald Curtis (*Stanton*), John Miljan (*T.J. Furman*), Jonathan Hale (*Varick*), John Eldredge (*Cox*), Adrian Wood (*Whiskey*), Wes C. Christensen (*Slim*), James Harrison (*Roper*), Duke York (*Maxie*), Steve Clark (*John Dawson*), I. Stanford Jolley (*Link Spain*), Marshall Reed (*Shives*),

Philo McCollough [McCullough] (*Charlie*), Kenne Duncan (*Steve*), Henry Hall (*Judge*), Tim Ryan (*Drunk*), Kermit Maynard (*Wagon Driver*), Earle Hodgins (*Square Dance Caller*), Ted Elliott (*Pete*), Chris Allen (*Barfly*)

Director: Lesley Selander. *Producers-Screenwriters*: John C. Champion, Blake Edwards. Based on the book by Edward Beverly Mann. *Photography*: Harry Neumann. *Production Manager*: Gene Anderson. *Supervising Editor*: Otho Lovering. *Editor*: Richard Heermance. *Assistant Directors*: Rex Bailey, Harry Jones. *Art Director*: Ernest Hickson. *Set Decorator*: Vin Taylor. *Recordist*: L. John Myers. *Makeup*: Fred Phillips. *Wardrobe*: Courtney Haslam.

Allied Artists; released May 1, 1949; B&W; 77 minutes.

In late 19th century Arizona, a war is brewing between cattlemen, who have long controlled the land, and settlers from Indiana and Illinois ("nesters"), moving in with deeds obtained under land-grant laws. Longtime resident Mike McCall regards the North Valley as grazing territory and crosses swords with the newcomers. On his property is a lake that furnishes the only water in the vicinity. Banker T.J. Furman and his associates, who stand to profit considerably from the land sales, want Mike to share water rights with the nesters but the cattleman refuses, even after Furman tries to call in the $30,000 in notes he owes the bank. Though they are on opposite sides of the war between cattlemen and nesters, Mike and beautiful newcomer Connie Dawson discover a mutual attraction neither will admit.

Unable to settle the dispute by peaceful means, Furman's cohorts put a plan into place: dynamiting the dam that keeps the lake contained, and causing a stampede that will send Mike's cattle hurtling toward a cliff. Along the way, the battle becomes more personal for Mike, whose fun-loving younger brother Tim stumbles on the scene of the crime, and pays with his life. While Mike's friend, Sheriff Aaron Ball, struggles to keep the peace, the simmering tensions quickly come to a boil, causing Mike and Connie to realize they may have been waging war with the wrong people.

A more adult-oriented Western than the ones Gale made with Roy Rogers and others in the early 1940s, *Stampede* depicts a conflict commonplace in the genre: cattlemen vs. ranchers. But the thoughtful screenplay doesn't make it a matter of merely white hats against black hats. Still, there's plenty here to satisfy the action fan, who gets more than his money's worth in gunplay, fistfights, explosions and scenes that justify the film's title.

Gale's entrance, about seven minutes into the film, finds her shot beautifully in medium close-up, by the light of a campfire, her hair hanging long and loose. Rod Cameron's Mike McCall takes an admiring look, and no wonder. Later, he flirts mildly with Connie, remarking, "Man gets a little tired of looking at nothing but cattle," to which she retorts, "I'm surprised you know the difference, McCall." Though she's feisty and spunky, at one point holding Mike at the point of a rifle, he calls her bluff, snatching away her gun. His brother Tim, whom Connie gives a good kick in the shins, retaliates by turning her over on her backside for a spanking.

At 6'5", Rod Cameron (1910–1983) dwarfs the diminutive Storm, and director Lesley Selander uses the disparity to his advantage, twice having Mike lift Connie off her feet so they can speak face to face. Her beauty is emphasized even more by the fact that she is the only actress who has a speaking role in a film otherwise populated exclusively by men. According to studio publicity, Gale received her 17th screen kiss from Cameron in *Stampede*. "But what girl can enjoy a kiss," she supposedly asked, "when she knows the man is more concerned about whether the cameras will do his profile justice, or whether the girl will benefit most from the scene?"[8] Johnny Mack Brown, Gale's leading man in *Forever Yours,* returns to his Western roots here, cast as the sheriff who provides a voice of reason as tensions escalate.

Stampede is the last film Gale shot as a Monogram contract player. During production, it was known as *Fighting Mike McCall.* Like most of her later Monogram pictures, it was released under the Allied Artists banner, a name the company adopted altogether in 1952. Production began in the fall of 1948, when they spent several days on location in Bridgeport, California. Studio publicists claimed that a babysitter had to be put on the payroll, as Gale refused to go on the location shoot unless she could take her sons along.

This is the second of two Westerns produced and written by the team of Blake Edwards and John C. Champion, following *Panhandle* (1948). Edwards (1922–2010) was near the beginning of his producer-director career, which in years to come encompassed the Pink Panther films, *Breakfast at Tiffany's* and several vehicles for his wife Julie Andrews. Champion subsequently produced the Western TV series *Laramie* (NBC, 1959–63), on which Rod Cameron made multiple guest appearances. Lesley Selander (1900–1979) directed more than 100 Western films in the course of his Hollywood career, and his experience with the genre is evident here.

Said *Showmen's Trade Review* (April 30, 1949), "A big-scale Western, jammed with action, good box-office names and some deft performances, *Stampede* should prove rewarding at the box office.... Gale Storm is a saucy settler..." *Variety* (April 27, 1949) thought a slow start hurt the film, but credited the screenwriters for "supplying some rough, tough sequences that will hit the mark with the outdoor fan." Although multiple reviews mentioned that it played theaters in sepia tone, the print released by the Warner Archive is in unenhanced black-and-white. Edward Beverly Mann, whose Western stories originally appeared in pulp magazines, had *Stampede* published in book form by William Morrow in 1934.

In early 1949, Allied Artists' Steve Broidy announced in trade papers that he had acquired the rights to Walter Enderly's "My First Husband," described as "a sophisticated drawing room comedy," as a follow-up vehicle for the team of Cameron and Storm. However, her decision not to renew her contract put the kibosh on the plans. A few years later, she and Cameron co-starred in Republic's *Woman of the North Country.*

Abandoned (1949)

Cast: Dennis O'Keefe (*Mark Sitko*), Gale Storm (*Paula Considine*), Jeff Chandler (*Chief MacRae*), Meg Randall (*Dottie Jensen*), Raymond Burr (*Kerric*), Marjorie Rambeau (*Mrs. Leona Donner*), Jeanette Nolan (*Major Ross*), Mike Mazurki (*Hoppe*), Will Kuluva (*Decola*), David Clarke (*Harry*), William Page (*Scoop*), Sid Tomack (*Mr. Humes*), Perc Launders (*Dowd*), Steve Darrell (*Brenn*), Clifton Young (*Eddie*), Ruth Sanderson (*Mrs. Spence*), Frank Cady (*Nolan*), Edwin Max (*Morrie*), Virginia Mullen (*Nurse Sully*), Jerry Hausner (*Orderly*), Sally Corner (*Nurse Tripp*), Edward Clark (*Coroner's Clerk*), Maudie Prickett (*Nurse Ferris*), Felice Richmond (*Hotel Operator*), Bruce Hamilton (*Doc Tilson*), Billy Gray (*Kid in Park*), Earl Smith (*Shoeshine Sammy*), Isabel Withers (*Mrs. Humes*), Bert Conway (*Delaney*), William Tannen (*Taxi Driver*), Franklin Parker, Dick Ryan, Stuart Wilson (*Plainclothesmen*)

Director: Joe Newman. *Producer*: Jerry Bresler. *Story and Screenplay*: Irwin Gielgud. *Additional Dialogue*: William Bowers. *Photography*: William Daniels. *Art Directors*: Bernard Herzbrun, Robert Boyle. *Set Decorators*: Russell A. Gausman, Ruby R. Levitt.

Sound: Leslie I. Carey, Joe Lapis. *Editor*: Edward Curtiss. *Dialogue Director*: Jack Daniels. *Miss Storm's Wardrobe*: Yvonne Wood. *Makeup*: Bud Westmore. *Hair Stylist*: Joan St. Oegger. *Special Photography*: David S. Horsley.

Universal-International Pictures; released October 6, 1949; B&W; 78 minutes.

Paula Considine, a young woman from a small town, shows up at the Missing Persons Bureau of a large city in search of her sister Mary. The clerk is businesslike and noncommittal, but newspaper reporter Mark Sitko takes an interest in Paula and her plight. Sure he's just in search of a good story, Paula is leery of Mark, but he quickly proves to be helpful, especially when he informs her she's being followed. Mark collars Paula's shadow and identifies him as Kerric, "cheapest private detective in town—specializes in framing divorces, and frightening little children." After some persuasion, Kerric admits that he was hired by Paula's father to find Mary, but claims he has been unable to do so. Once out of Mark's clutches, Kerric visits Mrs. Donner, a well-to-do older woman, and warns her that they are under scrutiny.

At the morgue, an emotional Paula identifies one of the victims in the "Jane Doe book" as her sister. Mary was supposedly found dead in a stolen car, having committed

Mark and Paula (Dennis O'Keefe and Gale Storm, background) pose as a married couple looking to adopt in *Abandoned* (Universal, 1949). Baby broker Mrs. Donner (Marjorie Rambeau, foreground) finds them plausible—at first.

suicide by carbon monoxide poisoning, and upon being autopsied was found to have recently given birth. Paula refuses to believe that her sister killed herself.

Her trust in Mark growing, Paula admits that her last letter from Mary disclosed that she was an unwed mother. The hospital on whose stationery the letter was written has no record of her as a patient, and the maternity ward nurses fail to identify her from her photo. Mark recognizes the pattern of an illegal adoption scheme and speculates that Mary became involved with a baby broker. A visit to the Salvation Army home for unwed mothers reveals that Mary was a patient there until shortly before she gave birth. Another patient, Dottie Jensen, provides further evidence that Mary fell victim to a convincing scam promising her a private adoption. The matron of the home, Major Ross, willingly goes to the police to denounce the scheme that Mark describes and offer her assistance. Kerric, who has been following their progress, updates his cohorts.

Paula hopes that she can recover her sister's baby daughter. Dottie agrees to act as a potential client for Mrs. Donner and her cohorts, while Mark and Paula will assume the roles of a married couple looking to adopt. Although their visit to Mrs. Donner is initially a success, Kerric spots them and blows their cover. Seeing that time is running out, Kerric tries to work the best deal he can, contacting the adoptive mother of Mary's baby and Paula herself, leading her into danger with the promise of uniting her with her niece in return for a cash payout.

Gale's first picture under contract to Universal-International commenced production in May 1949. It's a taut, absorbing thriller that benefits from her strong, understated performance. *Abandoned* creates considerable suspense while tackling a significant social problem of the day; as Mark tells a police buddy, "It's the worst kind of slavery, Mac. For a price, anyone can buy a human being." The film has a semi-documentary feel, aided by location shooting and a pace that maintains viewer attention.

Syndicated columnist Louella O. Parsons reported that Gale was a last-minute choice for the role. Universal executives initially assigned Ann Blyth to play Paula, but the young actress went on suspension rather than accept the part.

According to columnist Earl Wilson (October 9, 1949), Gale's toughest critic may have been on the home front. Told by his mother that she was on her way to the studio to make another film, six-year-old Phillip reportedly asked, "Do you sing in this one?" When she replied in the negative, her little boy said, "Good!" Although Wilson explained that Phillip was just "in the ornery stage," he quoted Gale as saying "hopefully but doubtfully," "I like to think he's jealous of sharing his mother's singing with others."

A fine supporting cast gives strength and color to the film. Raymond Burr (1917–1993), a favorite bad guy of '40s noir films, skillfully plays the sleazy detective who, while menacing, is uneasy about the extent to which he's becoming involved with Mrs. Donner's business. Inherently a bottom feeder, he's accurately summed up by Dennis O'Keefe's Mark, who tells him, "You going legitimate is like a vulture turning vegetarian." Marjorie Rambeau (1889–1970), who would rack up two Oscar nominations in the course of her career, ably portrays the cold-hearted Mrs. Donner, who can at one time ingratiate herself with an unwed mother who could prove profitable to her, while assuring prospective parents she'll help them "avoid the bothersome details of a legal adoption," and just as easily display a spine of steel when she's threatened. Jeff Chandler (1918–1961), being given the star buildup by Universal, is prominently billed for his secondary role as the police chief, which he performs capably. Chandler also narrates the film, using the voice he'd cultivated in radio appearances, his voiceover telling us, "But whatever the time, or wherever the place, this did happen, in a city which may be your home." Other familiar faces—Frank Cady, Jerry Hausner, Sid Tomack—are seen in minor roles, while Jeanette Nolan is solid if low-key in the role of the Salvation Army worker.

Universal publicity assured moviegoers, "*Abandoned* has a story to tell, a vitally important story, but the film is no lecture; rather, it is entertainment of such intensity that it will keep you at the edge of your seat." It also provides an interesting glimpse into the social circumstances and the stigma surrounding what were then called "illegitimate" babies, although the word doesn't appear in this script. The film was shot under the title *Abandoned Woman*, with the second word dropped just prior to release. According to one publicity story, director Joe Newman put his cast through the paces nine times for the climactic scene in which O'Keefe rescues Gale from carbon monoxide fumes. "Miss Storm was covered from head to foot with dirt and the $250 studio-designed outfit she was wearing was ruined beyond recognition. But she came up smiling after each take and was rewarded by the director with an 'Oscar' when the scene was finished. The Oscar was a bar of soap."[9]

In August 1949, Sheilah Graham reported that *Abandoned* would receive Universal's biggest publicity buildup for the year. According to *Showmen's Trade Review* (October 8, 1949), *Abandoned* world-premiered in Detroit that fall, with Gale and featured player Meg Randall in attendance. The event, which benefited a Salvation Army hospital, was spotlighted in a half-hour radio program about black market adoptions, aired throughout the state of Michigan. Noting that stories of illegal adoptions had been prominent in newspapers at the time of the film's release, *Motion Picture Daily* (October 5, 1949) commented, "*Abandoned* will rack up substantial grosses in every situation where intelligent showmanship is put to work." *Variety* (October 5, 1949) called it "a punchy [melodrama] with plenty of exploitation angles ... [T]he plot drives speedily to the finish line without any detours for unnecessary romantic by-play." Less impressed, the *Los Angeles Times*' Edwin Schallert (October 29, 1949) praised the performances but concluded, "Add up all the values in this picture, and they do not reach a sufficient total for anything like an outright recommendation. The technical style is good, and the players show capability, but the subject itself is less than enticing for a major melodrama."

The Kid from Texas (1950)

Cast: Audie Murphy (*William Bonney*), Gale Storm (*Irene Kain*), Albert Dekker (*Alexander Kain*), Shepperd Strudwick (*Roger Jameson*), Will Geer (*O'Fallon*), William Talman (*Minninger*), Martin Garralaga (*Morales*), Robert H. Barrat (*General Lew Wallace*), Walter Sande (*Crowe*), Frank Wilcox (*Sheriff Pat Garrett*), Dennis Hoey (*Major Harper*), Ray Teal (*Sheriff Rand*), Don Haggerty (*Morgan*), Paul Ford (*Sheriff Copeland*), John Phillips (*Sid Curtis*), Harold Goodwin (*Matt Curtis*), Zon Murray (*Lucas*), Tom Trout (*Denby*), Rosa Turich (*Maria*), Dorita Pallais (*Lupita*), Pilar Del Rey (*Marguarita*), Jack Ingram (*Wagon Driver*), Dick Wessel (*Bart, the Jailer*), William Fawcett (*Cook*), Edmund Cobb (*Hale*), Beulah Parkington (*Mrs. Hale*), Jack Shutta (*Deputy*), Watson Downs (*Bookkeeper*), Pierce Lyden (*Hagen*), James Burke, William Gargan (*Blacksmiths*)

Director: Kurt Neumann. *Producer*: Paul Short. *Screenplay*: Robert Hardy Andrews, Karl Kamb. *Story*: Robert Hardy Andrews. *Photography*: Charles Van Enger. *Technicolor Color Consultant*: William Fritzsche. *Art Directors*: Bernard Herzbrun, Emrich Nicholson. *Set Decorators*: Russell A. Gausman, Oliver Emert. *Sound*: Leslie I. Carey, Robert

Pritchard. *Editor*: Frank Gross. *Music*: Milton Schwarzwald. *Gowns*: Rosemary Odell. *Hair Stylist*: Joan St. Oegger. *Makeup*: Bud Westmore.

Universal-International Pictures; released March 1, 1950; Color; 78 minutes.

In 1879 New Mexico, ranchers are warring with over property rights. Lawyer Alexander Kain and his business partner, Roger Jameson, are confronted in their office by armed men trying to serve an arrest warrant on behalf of their rival, Major Harper. Young William Bonney comes to their aid, showing off his impressive marksmanship, and earns himself a job as a ranchhand, thanks to a grateful Jameson.

Though Jameson knows Billy has had a violent past, starting with killing his own stepfather for mistreating his mother, he gives the young man a fair chance, and is rewarded with Billy's loyalty. Showing his respect for Jameson, "the only man that ever treated me like I was good enough to shake hands with," Billy agrees to put his guns away until they are needed. Kain, who's more dubious about Billy, arrives at the ranch with his beautiful young bride Irene in tow. Both Billy and Irene clearly take note of each other, enjoying a pleasant chat under the moonlight. Kain remonstrates with his bride for being friendly with the help.

The governor of the New Mexico Territory calls on Kain and Harper to end their violent feud, and both men agree. When several of Harper's henchmen turn up at the

Audie Murphy (left) played the title role in *The Kid from Texas*, with Gale as his love interest.

Kain ranch, wanting revenge for being shot by Billy, Jameson tries to handle the situation with nonviolent means, and is promptly shot dead. Strapping on his gun belt once more, Billy vows to avenge his friend and mentor's death, however long it takes.

Taking over ranch operations, Kain professes to decry Billy's violent ways, but finds him useful to carry out the war with Harper, which continues despite the governor's demands. With newly appointed Sheriff Pat Garrett vowing to end the violence, Kain and Harper profess a truce. With no loyalty to Billy, Kain contributes to a $10,000 reward on his head. While everyone else involved in the violence is given a pardon, Billy refuses to stop his vendetta against the remaining men responsible for Jameson's death, notably the malevolent Minninger. Captured by Minninger, charged with murder and sentenced to hang, Billy breaks jail and heads to the Kain ranch, where a final, bloody resolution awaits.

Once again, a Western outlaw proves unable to resist Gale's charms. This is just one of many screen adaptations of the life of Henry McCarty (1859–1881), also known as William Bonney and as Billy the Kid. The incipient romance between Billy and Mrs. Kain remains unrequited, though she proves to be a loyal friend to him, coming to his defense when he's facing a murder charge. Her character, stuck in a presumably arranged marriage with an older man, is angered by her husband's tactics with Billy and his other ranch hands. Though she says she was brought up to respect her husband, her big speech finds her saying heatedly: "When you send men out to risk their lives over a few head of cattle, yes, I doubt you…. All you're interested in is the safety of your property. I think it's shameful of you to take advantage of a boy like that, to use him. A boy of my own age." Her defense of Billy earns her a slap in the face from her jealous spouse. Billy's love for Irene ultimately leads to the outlaw's downfall.

Though she has few dramatic opportunities in this film, Gale is beautifully photographed by Charles Van Enger and costumed in a variety of becoming gowns in her role as a wealthy man's pampered wife. Her deal with Universal also provided audiences with their first opportunity to see her in Technicolor.

This was an early starring role for real-life war hero turned actor Audie Murphy (1925–1971). A Texan like Gale, Murphy went on to play the lead in MGM's adaptation of *The Red Badge of Courage* (1951), star as himself in the 1955 movie version of his memoir *To Hell and Back,* and become a reliable leading man of Western movies for much of the 1950s. The 25-year-old Murphy and Gale share billing above the title. Though still a noticeably inexperienced actor, his boyish looks and slight build (he is just barely taller than Gale) make him a good choice to play the outlaw who died at the age of 21, and this film helped establish him as an action hero. He and Gale were each paid $10,000 for *The Kid from Texas,* filmed between late May and late June 1949. One set visitor watched as the two shot a brief scene set on a moonlit patio. The finished scene would run less than one minute onscreen, "yet before Director Kurt Neumann was satisfied with the action and proper inflection from the actors, the cameras rolled 16 times!"[10]

Studio publicity claimed *The Kid from Texas* set a new record for the number of deaths depicted onscreen: "More than Hoot Gibson, Art Acord and Tom Mix ever knocked off in any three pictures, [Audie] Murphy kills 21, all but three of the people who start with him in the Technicolor film." Under those circumstances, the film necessarily has a sizable cast, with some fine character actors livening things up. William Talman (1915–1968), several years before attaining his well-remembered role as Hamilton Burger on TV's *Perry Mason,* is effectively slimy as Billy's most formidable adversary, armed with both brains and nerve. Another future TV star, *The Waltons*' Will Geer (1902–1978), has some funny moments as Billy's sidekick O'Fallon, more loyal than brave, who says frankly, "Guns make me nervous." Geer was blacklisted a short time later, and was largely absent from movie screens until the mid-1960s. The smooth, capable performance of Shepperd Strudwick (1907–1983) as Jameson makes it a pity that he succumbs to gunfire before the film is half over. Another always-busy character player, Parley Baer (1914–2002), narrates the film. Kurt Neumann (1908–1958) had previously directed Gale in *The Dude Goes West*.

Modern Screen (April 1950) was doubtful as to the accuracy of this account of Billy the Kid, but said, "It's absorbing, and the Technicolor is gorgeous." The *Chicago Tribune*'s Mae Tinée (April 29, 1950) thought Gale "fresh and wholesome in appearance, altho [sic] an ineffectual actress."

Curtain Call at Cactus Creek (1950)

Cast: Donald O'Connor (*Edward Timmons*), Gale Storm (*Julie Martin*), Walter Brennan (*Rimrock Thomas*), Vincent Price (*Tracy Holland*), Eve Arden (*Lily Martin*), Chick Chandler (*Ralph*), Joe Sawyer (*Jake*), Harry Shannon (*U.S. Marshal Clay*), Rex Lease (*Yellowstone*), I. Stanford Jolley (*Pecos*), Ferris Taylor (*Maxwell*), Paul Maxey (*Smith*), Eddy Waller (*Jailer*), Lane Bradford, Edmund Cobb, Terry Frost (*Henchmen*), Al Haskell, Hank Worden (*Townsmen*)

Director: Charles Lamont. *Producer*: Robert Arthur. *Screenplay*: Howard Dimsdale. *Story*: Stanley Roberts, Howard Dimsdale. *Photography*: Russell Metty. *Technicolor Color Consultant*: Robert Brower. *Art Directors*: Bernard Herzbrun, John F. DeCuir. *Set Decorators*: Russell A. Gausman, Ruby A. Levitt. *Sound*: Leslie I. Carey, Richard DeWeese. *Editor*: Frank Gross. *Dance Director*: Louis Da Pron. *Costumes*: Rosemary Odell. *Hair Stylist*: Joan St. Oegger. *Makeup*: Bud Westmore.

Universal-International Pictures; released May 25, 1950; Color; 86 minutes.

The Tracy Holland Repertory Company, a theatrical troupe touring the Old West, arrives in the small town of Cactus Creek, Arizona, just as bank robber Rimrock Thomas and his gang are plotting their latest crime. The troupe's performance, attended by most of the townspeople, offers the perfect distraction for the bank robbery. But even while plans for the caper are underway, Rimrock finds himself distracted by his infatuation with leading lady Lily Martin.

Doing all of the troupe's work behind the scenes is meek Edward Timmons, who runs himself ragged providing sound effects, props, stage management and virtually every other element required to put on the show. Enamored of the theater, and promised a chance to realize his own performing dreams, Edward has devoted three years to this thankless job. But thanks to egotistical Holland, who finds him more useful as a stagehand than as a performer, and denigrates his talent, Eddie seems destined never to get his break.

Edward is in love with ingénue Julie Martin, and she with him, but she is growing impatient with his devotion to Holland and his company. Finally taking matters into her own hands, she interrupts a performance to tell her diffident beau, "I've made up our minds. We're getting married." But Edward is reluctant, later confiding, "I love her too much to let her be tied up to a failure for the rest of her life."

After the bank robbery, Rimrock Thomas stows away on the Holland company show wagon. He saves Edward from being robbed, and the grateful young man offers him a job, unaware that "Mr. Johnson" is the bank robber being hotly pursued. When the troupe arrives at its next stand, Powder River, the banker is warned by a marshal that Rimrock Thomas may once again use the performance as a distraction. Thomas' gang members learn that the marshal is in town, and they urge their boss to choose another bank, but he can't resist the temptation to pull off a job under the nose of his longtime nemesis. Undercover with the theatrical troupe, Thomas enjoys the opportunity to get better acquainted with Lily, and takes an interest in seeing Eddie realize his dreams. With Tracy Holland and another troupe member tied up during the show, Eddie takes the stage and demonstrates his talent as a comic performer and dancer. Unfortunately, the timing of the bank robbery leads the law in Powder River to conclude that Eddie was an accomplice.

Donald O'Connor is Gale's leading man in *Curtain Call at Cactus Creek* (Universal, 1950).

Rimrock busts the young man out of jail, saving him from the hangman's noose, but leaving Eddie convinced he's hopelessly branded as a criminal.

Returning to the genre of Western comedy after *The Dude Goes West*, Gale is second-billed in this amiable film aimed at family audiences. Like much of Universal's product for the year, it used the draw of Technicolor in hopes of competing with the growing popularity of television. Syndicated columnist Bob Thomas (February 8, 1949) predicted good things for Gale at her new studio, saying, "She's a talented girl; watch for her career to zoom."

As love interest to leading man Donald O'Connor (1925–2003), Gale acquits herself well, keeping pace with him as a dance partner and offering a few songs. Her musical numbers include "Home! Sweet Home!," with specially written lyrics to accompany the plot of a temperance melodrama, "The Curse of Drink," as well as a minstrel routine, "Are You from Dixie?" which left her with an indelible memory. Many years later, Gale recalled, "We had one musical number in blackface. The makeup man put this grease on us—and I don't know how a makeup man could make such a mistake—but we couldn't get it off for two days!"[11]

This is Gale's only film with Eve Arden (1908–1990), whose own TV stardom (in *Our Miss Brooks*) came at roughly the same time as Gale's. Arden and Vincent Price have fun with the juicy roles of Tracy Holland and his leading lady; Holland is an unmitigated ham who quotes Shakespeare at every opportunity, while his leading lady Lily is unimpressed by his egotism, and bemused by the clumsy romantic attentions of rough-hewn career crook Rimrock Thomas. Walter Brennan (1894–1974) ably presents both the menace and the surprising softer side of Rimrock.

Screenwriter Howard Dimsdale (1914–1991) also wrote *The Traveling Saleswoman* with Joan Davis, another Old West comedy which saw release during the same year. Paul

Maxey, seen in a small role here, turned up frequently as a character player on *My Little Margie*.

In the *Chicago Tribune* (July 29, 1950), Mae Tinée said that *Cactus Creek* "manages to provide quite a few chuckles…. It's a happy sort of hokum which most audiences will find fine for escape purposes." In the July 20, 1950, *Oakland Tribune*, Wood Soanes described the film as "pretty contrived, but it is also very funny…" Praising Dimsdale's script and Charles Lamont's direction, Soanes also gave plaudits to the cast, including Gale: "Miss Storm handles both solos and a blackface double with O'Connor efficiently." *Daily Variety* (May 24, 1950) said Gale "adds charm to her role in addition to lending neat support to O'Connor in several musical interludes."

The Underworld Story (1950)

Cast: Dan Duryea (*Mike Reese*), Herbert Marshall (*E.J. Stanton*), Gale Storm (*Cathy Harris*), Howard da Silva (*Carl Durham*), Michael O'Shea (*Ralph Munsey*), Mary Anderson (*Molly Rankin*), Gar Moore (*Clark Stanton*), Melville Cooper (*Major Redford*), Frieda Inescort (*Mrs. Eldridge*), Art Baker (*Lt. Tilton*), Harry Shannon (*George "Parky" Parker*), Alan Hale, Jr. (*Shaeffer*), Stephen Dunne (*Chuck Lee*), Roland Winters (*Stanley Becker*), Sue England (*Helen*), Lewis L. Russell (*Calvin*), Frances Chaney (*Grace*), Phil Arnold (*Gus*), Charles Evans (*Harvey Eldridge*), Harry Harvey (*Mr. Lister*), Teddy Infuhr (*Johnny*), Eddie Parks (*Mr. Mullins*), Harry Strang (*Police Sergeant*), Sam Balter, Douglas Evans (*Newscasters*), Paul Bryar (*Helen's Father*), Carl Sklover (*Turk Meyers*), Don McGuire (*Reporter in Bar*), Ned Glass (*Editor, Atlas News Service*), Edward Van Sloan (*Minister at Funeral*), Jack Mower (*Mr. Stewart*), Jean Dean (*Stanton's Secretary*), Jay Adler (*Munsey's Assistant*)

Director: Cyril Endfield. *Producer*: Hal E. Chester. *Screenplay*: Henry Blankfort. *Adaptation*: Cyril Endfield. *Story*: Craig Rice. *Associate Producer*: Bernard W. Burton. *Photography*: Stanley Cortez. *Production Manager*: Allen K. Wood. *Assistant Director*: William Calihan. *Art Director*: Gordon Wiles. *Editor*: Richard Heermance. *Set Decorator*: Ray Boltz. *Dialogue Director*: G. Joseph Dell. *Technical Adviser*: Ben F. Melzer. *Sound*: Tom Lambert. *Set Continuity*: Bobbie Sierks. *Hair Stylist*: Stephanie Garland. *Makeup*: Tom Tuttle. *Wardrobe*: Esther Krebs, Leonard Harris. *Set Supervisor*: Dave Milton. *Music Director*: Irving Friedman. *Music*: David Rose.

United Artists; released July 26, 1950; B&W; 90 minutes.

When reporter Mike Reese prints a story revealing that an underling will testify against crime boss Carl Durham before a grand jury, the result is an early morning drive-by shooting in which the prospective witness, Turk Meyers, is killed and District Attorney Ralph Munsey injured. At Munsey's urging, Reese is fired, and soon realizes he's been blacklisted by other newspapers.

Seeing an ad seeking a partner to invest in a small-town newspaper, the *Lakeville Sentinel,* Mike extracts $5000 from Durham, whose life he saved. Although young Cathy Harris, left to assume leadership of the *Sentinel* after the death of her father, its publisher, badly needs the money Mike offers to invest, she is leery of his slick ways and overarching interest in money. Shortly after his arrival in town, Diane Stanton, daughter of a big-city newspaper publisher who makes his home in Lakeville, is found murdered. While Cathy mourns her school friend Diane, Mike jumps on the story. Behind closed doors, Diane's husband, the ne'er-do-well son of the prominent Stanton family, admits to his father that he killed her. Torn between his loyalty to his daughter-in-law and the potential smear

The staff of the *Lakeville Sentinel* preps another issue in *The Underworld Story* (1950). Pictured (left to right) are Harry Shannon, Gale Storm, and Dan Duryea.

on the family name, E.J. Stanton realizes there is a possible way out when it develops that Diane's maid has gone missing, as has the lady's jewelry.

The maid, young African-American Molly Rankin, turns to Cathy for help, admitting that she pawned the gems on Diane's instructions but insisting that she did not kill her. As the situation plays out, Mike seems to work every angle. He convinces Molly to turn herself over the police, and is angry when D.A. Durham refuses to pay him the $25,000 reward offered for the capture of the killer. Furious, Cathy wants to dissolve their partnership, but Mike persuades her that Molly's best chance lies in using the *Sentinel* to win public opinion to her side. While the urban newspapers paint Molly as guilty, the *Sentinel* campaigns on her behalf, and Mike persuades socially prominent resident Mrs. Eldridge to mount a defense committee to raise funds for her attorney—not disclosing that he expects to earn a 50 percent cut of lawyer Stanley Becker's fee.

With public sentiment growing in Molly's favor, the Stantons decide they must deal with Mike. Father E.J. favors a subtler approach, using his connections to insure that advertising and subscriptions for the *Sentinel* begin to dry up, and the work of her defense committee is brought to a halt. Learning that Mike claims to have new evidence that will absolve Molly, Clark Stanton panics and enlists the help of Carl Dunham, too foolish to realize that he will be unable to maintain control of the situation once the strong-willed crime boss gets involved. Mike tells Cathy, "The truth's the truth, and we're going to shove it down their ivy-covered throats."

Gale's postwar films reflect a growing trend toward realistic, grittier stories. *The Underworld Story*, billed by studio publicists as "a fast-paced drama of murder and intrigue, played against a newspaper background," is not the gangster film its title implies. It gives us a morally ambiguous lead character in Mike Reese, whose true nature remains elusive through much of the film's running time. Although Dan Duryea's character is clearly attracted to Cathy, telling her in a distinctly un-businesslike manner, "You're the kind of a partner I've always wanted," he doesn't handle her with kid gloves, strong-arming his way into a position as editor of the *Sentinel* and showing little evidence of being a man she might admire. Duryea has a strong chemistry with Gale Storm; they teamed again soon afterwards in *Al Jennings of Oklahoma*.

Once again, Gale is playing a newspaperwoman, as she will another time in *The Texas Rangers*. Here she subtly delineates a character who, like the audience, isn't certain what to make of her new partner. At times she is firmly in his corner, as he devises a canny scheme to work on Molly's behalf; just as quickly, she can find herself saying angrily to him, "Did you ever rob graves, Mr. Reese?" Throughout, there are moments where she watches Duryea, doubt flitting across her face as she puzzles out this man who, as she puts it, speaks a different language.

In addition to Gale's performance, a gallery of strong supporting players enrich the film. An old hand at playing wealth and poise, Herbert Marshall (1890–1966) makes E.J. Stanton a layered, unpredictable character who may have more in common with crime boss Durham than he cares to admit. Howard da Silva (1909–1986), chillingly effective as the misleadingly genial, smiling Durham, would make only a few more pictures before his 1951 testimony to the House Un-American Activities Committee got him blacklisted for the rest of the 1950s. Michael O'Shea (1906–1973) plays the district attorney who sizes up Mike Reese's avarice, telling him in mock sympathy, "Things are tough all over. Pretty soon, a man won't be able to sell his own mother." In smaller roles, Frieda Inescort (1901–1976) attracts notice as strong-willed Mrs. Eldridge, of whom another character says, "At moments like these, I'm glad I'm a bachelor." Mary Anderson (1918–2014), who lacks the most obvious qualification for playing Molly—the actress is Caucasian—nonetheless lends a quiet dignity to the character; realizing Mike tried to sell her out for a $25,000 reward, she observes, "That's a high price for a human being. I had a great-grandfather who was sold for much less." This is one of only a handful of films for Gar Moore (1920–1985), who registers strongly as the spoiled rich boy.

The film's working title was *The Whip*. Principal photography took place in the late summer of 1949. According to syndicated columnist Hedda Hopper (August 2, 1949), star Duryea entered into a partnership with producer Hal E. Chester (and Mitch Hamilburg) to form Rambler Productions, with this film to be the first output from the venture.

Director Cy Endfield (1914–1995) was making a bold personal statement with *The Underworld Story*, one that made him somewhat controversial at the time. Like da Silva, Endfield attracted the interest of anti–Communist forces and chose to relocate to England, where he made films such as *Zulu* (1964). Like Gale, he had made low-budget films in the 1940s at Monogram. The crisp, striking cinematography of the acclaimed Stanley Cortez (1908–1997) adds to the film's mood, one that fits neatly with what would later be labeled *film noir*. Hard-boiled mystery writer Craig Rice (1908–1957), in reality one Georgiana Ann Craig, provided the film's original story.

Although the subject of Communism doesn't arise in *The Underworld Story*, much of its biting commentary on American society can be taken as a reaction to blacklisting. The unreliable nature of public opinion, and how it can be manipulated, emerges as a central theme. At one point, when Mike is being hounded, Cathy's employee Parky comments, "Looks like they're burning witches again."

The makers of *The Underworld Story* found reviewers working for daily newspapers not sympathetic to the film's viewpoint, and reviews were harsh. The *Los Angeles Times'* Philip K. Scheuer (August 4, 1950) found the rampant amorality among key characters off-putting, but concluded, "In its crude way—and despite unevenness in the quality of writing, direction and performances—the film does exert a repellent kind of fascination." A brief notice in the *Chicago Tribune* (August 12, 1950) called the film "exceedingly inept," adding, "The story is complicated and unconvincing, and the script utterly corny."

Between Midnight and Dawn (1950)

Cast: Mark Stevens (*Officer Rocky Barnes*), Edmond O'Brien (*Officer Dan Purvis*), Gale Storm (*Katherine "Kate" Mallory*), Donald Buka (*Ritchie Garris*), Gale Robbins (*Terry Romaine*), Anthony Ross (*Lt. Masterson*), Roland Winters (*Leo Cusick*), Tito Vuolo (*Romano*), Grazia Narciso (*Mrs. Romano*), Madge Blake (*Mrs. Mallory*), Lora Lee Michel (*Kathy Blake*), Jack Del Rio (*Louis Franissi*), Philip Van Zandt (*Joe Quist*), Peter Mamakos (*Adams*), Wheaton Chambers (*Blake*), Frances Morris (*Mrs. Blake*), Douglas Evans (*Detective Captain*), Alex Gerry (*Oliver*), Mary Alan Hokanson, Louise Kane (*Police Dispatchers*), Richard Karlan (*Officer Charlie Nichols*), Billy Gray (*Petey Conklin*), William E. Green (*Judge*), Nolan Leary (*Jury Foreman*), Charles Marsh (*Henpecked Husband*), Maudie Prickett (*Nagging Wife*), Tony Taylor (*Thurlow Conklin*), Steve Pendleton (*Eddie*), Eric Mack (*Booking Officer*), Marc Krah (*Rocco*), Myron Healey (*Officer Davis*), Harry Harvey (*Driver*), Tom Daly (*Deputy*)

Director: Gordon Douglas. *Producer*: Hunt Stromberg. *Screenplay*: Eugene Ling. *Story*: Gerald Drayson Adams, Leo Katcher. *Photography*: George E. Diskant. *Art Director*: George Brooks. *Editor*: Gene Havlick. *Set Decorator*: Frank Tuttle. *Assistant Director*: James Nicholson. *Gowns*: Jean Louis. *Makeup*: Clay Campbell. *Hair Stylist*: Helen Hunt. *Sound Engineer*: Russell Malmgren. *Musical Score*: George Duning. *Music Director*: Morris Stoloff.

Columbia Pictures; released October 1, 1950; B&W; 89 minutes.

Police officers Rocky Barnes and his partner Dan Purvis, friends since they served together in the Marines, share a "prowl car" that patrols the city streets on the night shift, tackling everything from an attempted robbery in progress to a restaurant owner whose building is bombed after he refused to pay protection money. Throughout the night, they receive dispatches from the station's Communications Center, and impulsive Rocky becomes intrigued with "those cream and honey tones of that new girl." He bets his fellow officers $5 that the woman will turn out to be as beautiful as her speaking voice.

Recognizing the voice when he hears it again in his lieutenant's office, Rocky learns that it belongs to Kate Mallory, a new employee. Responding to the playful flirting of both men, she agrees to an evening out with the two of them. Unable to leave work at work, Dan takes his friends to the Starlight Club, owned by gangster Ritchie Garris. At the club, Dan recognizes Leo Cusick, a mob boss from the East who has just arrived in town. Soon it becomes clear that a war is brewing between Garris and Cusick.

At the end of the evening, Rocky and Dan both want to see Kate again, but she tells them she has a strict rule: never more than one date with a policeman. The daughter of an officer who died in the line of duty, Kate tells her mother, "A policeman's still going to have no part in Katherine's romantic life.... The man I marry is going to work in a nice, safe office." She's angered when her mother rents the apartment next door to Rocky and Dan, but finds herself warming up to them as they get better acquainted. Ultimately, love blooms between Rocky and Kate and she accepts his marriage proposal.

When gangster Cusick is murdered in an execution-style shooting, the police put out a dragnet for Ritchie Garris, and it's ultimately Dan and Rocky who bring him in. Sentenced to death, Garris escapes from jail a few days before Rocky's wedding and exacts his murderous revenge against the policeman. In the aftermath of her fiancé's death, Kate worries that Dan's vengeful fury is turning him into "a brutal policeman," which drives a wedge between them. Undeterred, Dan continues to follow Garris' girlfriend, nightclub singer Terry Romaine, sure that she will lead them to the violent mobster.

According to a studio publicity release,

> In taking the audience behind the wheel and behind the guns of a police prowl car, Columbia Pictures obtained a shot-in-the-streets realism by photographing the downtown business area of Los Angeles.... Careful attention was paid to the police detail and routine with police headquarters scenes filmed at the Los Angeles Police Station. Police officers acted as advisers.[12]

Referred to in early trade announcements as *Prowl Car,* the film ultimately released as *Between Midnight and Dawn* offers plenty to satisfy the action fans, but also gives Gale one of her stronger dramatic film roles as Kate Mallory. In a scene crackling with activity at the Communications Center, listening to radio calls as Dan and Rocky go in pursuit of Garris, she says not a word but conveys her fright with her face, knowing her friends are in danger. Later, she delivers a moving performance at Dan's bedside after he's shot, trying to keep up a brave front as she banters with him.

Mark Stevens plays one of two cops who love Kate (Gale Storm) in *Between Midnight and Dawn* (Columbia, 1950).

Looking back, Gale would remember leading man Edmond O'Brien as "an exceptionally strong actor."[13] Her hairstyle here makes her resemble Margie Albright, the TV character she began playing in early 1952. Leading man Mark Stevens (1916–1994) enjoyed considerable TV success in the 1950s with starring roles in *Martin Kane* and *Big Town*. O'Brien (1915–1985) was only a few years away from his Oscar-winning performance in *The Barefoot Contessa*. There's another "Gale" in the cast, actress Gale Robbins (1921–1980), who plays Garris' lady friend. Robbins later turned up as a guest player on *My Little Margie*.

The *New York Times*' Bosley Crowther (October 2, 1950) commented, "[A] fast cops-and-robbers show.... Gale

Storm is conventionally lightweight as the orphan of a hero of the force..." *Harrison's Reports* (September 30, 1950) panned it as "a routine cops-and-robbers melodrama, handicapped by a creaky plot and by stilted dialogue," but acknowledged that "it generates a fair share of suspense and excitement." Performances were described as "adequate." *Daily Variety* (September 27, 1950) said, "Gale Storm gives her role charm in spite of its poor development," and opined that the film "might have gone completely off the deep end" without Gale and her leading men.

Al Jennings of Oklahoma (1951)

Cast: Dan Duryea (*Al Jennings*), Gale Storm (*Margo St. Claire*), Dick Foran (*Frank Jennings*), Gloria Henry (*Alice Calhoun*), Guinn "Big Boy" Williams (*Lon Tuttle*), Raymond Greenleaf (*Judge Jennings*), Stanley Andrews (*Marshal Ken Slattery*), John Ridgely (*Dan Hanes*), James Millican (*Ed Jennings*), Harry Shannon (*Fred Salter*), Helen Brown (*Mrs. Salter*), Robert Bice (*Pete Kincaid*), George J. Lewis (*Sammy Page*), Jimmie Dodd (*Buck Botkin*), Eddie Parker (*"Doc" Wrightmire*), James Griffith (*Slim Harris*), Bill Phillips (*Bill Mertz*), John Dehner (*Thomas Marsden*), William Norton Bailey (*Robert Kyle*), Charles Meredith (*Judge Evans*), Louis Jean Heydt (*John Jennings*), Harry Cording (*Mike Bridges*), Theresa Harris (*Terese*), Jimmy Bates (*Young John Jennings*), Ann Codee (*Mme. Le Cler*), John Hamilton (*Schyler*), Mary Alan Hokanson (*Mrs. Jennings*), Hank Patterson (*Jeff*), Tommy Ivo (*Young Ed Jennings*), Rudy Lee (*Young Frank Jennings*), Libby Taylor (*Martha*), Harry Tyler (*Train Clerk*), Guy Beach (*Jury Foreman*), Bob Burns (*Bank Clerk*), Kernan Cripps (*Tim*), Myron Healey (*Confederate Corporal*), Donald Kerr (*Saloon Waiter*), George Lloyd (*Train Engineer*), Charles Marsh (*Bailiff*), Blackie Whiteford (*Stagecoach Guard*), Leroy Johnson (*Outlaw*)

Director: Ray Nazarro. *Producer*: Rudolph C. Flothow. *Screenplay*: George Bricker. From a book by Al Jennings, Will Irwin. *Photography*: W. Howard Greene. *Art Director*: Victor Greene. *Technicolor Color Consultant*: Francis Cugat. *Editor*: Richard Fantl. *Set Decorator*: Louis Diage. *Music Director*: Mischa Bakaleinikoff.

Columbia Pictures; released January 17, 1951; Color; 78 minutes.

Al Jennings, a hot-headed young lawyer from a family of lawyers, has a regrettable tendency to settle arguments, even in courtrooms, with his fists. After quarreling with his father, a judge, Al is accompanied by his brother Frank to start a new life in the Oklahoma Territory. Upon arrival, Al rescues a citified young woman, Margo St. Claire, from a runaway team of horses. Al is attracted to the beautiful visitor from New Orleans, but she rebuffs him initially, finding him brash and forward.

Al and Frank's plans to open a law practice in Oklahoma go awry when he comes to the defense of his brother Ed, also a practicing attorney. After defeating Tom Marsden in a legal case involving Margo's uncle, Ed is shot and killed by his opponent. Taking the law into his own hands, Al demands that Marsden sign a confession. In the ensuing argument, Al kills Marsden in self-defense. Sure that they will not receive justice, Al and Frank go on the lam. Staying temporarily at a cattle ranch that is a cover for cattle rustlers, the Jennings brothers first pretend to join the gang, then become members in earnest. Al becomes the ringleader in a series of bank and stagecoach robberies, eluding arrest until the bounty on his head reaches $25,000.

When it gets too hot to stay in Oklahoma, Al persuades Frank to accompany him to New Orleans, from which they can't be extradited, and where Al can renew his acquaintance with Margo. Assuming a new identity, Al establishes a legitimate business and

The title character in *Al Jennings of Oklahoma* (Columbia, 1951), played by Dan Duryea, pitches woo to refined Margo (Gale Storm).

makes plans to marry Margo, but a railroad detective recognizes him and is determined to capture him for the reward. With Margo's help, Al emerges victorious over the detective and returns to Oklahoma, where he intends to pull one last job before retiring. With some underhanded tactics, the marshal captures the Jennings boys, and they stand trial. Margo waits to see if she and Al can ever be reunited.

Based (perhaps loosely) on a real story, *Al Jennings of Oklahoma* tells the story of a man who, as the narrator puts it, "abandoned the practice of law to break the law." The real Jennings (1863–1961) became a Western star in silent films and unsuccessfully ran for governor of Oklahoma.

Once again, as in *Jesse James at Bay,* Gale plays a refined young woman irresistibly attracted to an outlaw. As Al tells her, "You're the only woman I've ever remembered more than a day or two." Technicolor photography shows off her delicate beauty and makes the most of her vivid gowns. Not just a pretty face, she proves her mettle during a New Orleans dustup when, dressed in a frilly outfit for tea in the garden, she coolly pulls a gun on the railroad agent and defends her man. This is her second picture with Dan Duryea, with whom she was previously teamed in *The Underworld Story.* Duryea evidently numbered some women moviegoers among his fans, even if they didn't especially care for Westerns. Gale later said, "Dan Duryea was very gentle and likable, a direct contrast to the despicable characters he frequently played, and very professional."[14] It also reunited her with Guinn "Big Boy" Williams, her co-star from *Lure of the Islands* nearly ten years earlier.

Gloria Henry (born 1923), later to play loving mom Alice Mitchell on TV's *Dennis the Menace,* receives higher billing than her brief role as silly flibbertigibbet Alice Calhoun merits. Stanley Andrews, seen as the marshal, would soon be known as "The Old Ranger," host of the syndicated Western series *Death Valley Days.*

Variety (January 17, 1951) credited director Ray Nazarro with "an excellent feeling of pace and action," and said the cast was "generally satisfactory." Gale, said the reviewer, "is beautifully costumed and looks fine in color." According to the *Los Angeles Times'* John L. Scott (April 11, 1951), "Ray Nazarro directed with a vigorous hand.... The dialogue could be improved, but that's true of nine out of 10 westerns.... Performances are routine..." Said Howard H. Thompson in the *New York Times* (May 18, 1951), "The dialogue is natural and gets a free-and-easy delivery from the cast ... [A] climax which whitewashes [the heroes] almost beyond recognition is plain ridiculous."

The Texas Rangers (1951)

Cast: George Montgomery (*Johnny Carver*), Gale Storm (*Helen Fenton*), Jerome Courtland (*Danny Carver, aka Danny Bonner*), Noah Beery, Jr. (*Buff Smith*), William Bishop (*Sam Bass*), John Litel (*Major John B. Jones*), Douglas Kennedy (*Dave Rudabaugh*), John Dehner (*John Wesley Hardin*), Ian MacDonald (*The Sundance Kid*), John Doucette (*Butch Cassidy*), Jock O'Mahoney [Mahoney] (*Duke Fisher*), Stanley Andrews (*Marshal Gorey*), Edward Earle (*Lowden*), Myron Healey (*Captain Peak*), Joe Fallon (*Jimmy*), Edward Peil, Sr. (*Pinkerton Man*), Charles Trowbridge (*Governor*), Dick Wessel (*Arkansas*), Paul E. Burns (*Pete*), Dick Curtis (*Prison Guard*), John L. Cason (*Train Guard*)

Director: Phil Karlson. *Producer*: Bernard Small. *Screenplay*: Richard Schayer. *Story*: Frank Gruber. *Photography*: Ellis Carter. *Art Director*: Harold MacArthur. *Editor*: Al Clark. *Set Decorator*: Howard Bristol. *Assistant Director*: Emmett Emerson. *Sound Engineer*: George Cooper. *Music Director*: Mischa Bakaleinikoff. *Gowns*: Jean Louis.

Columbia Pictures; released June 3, 1951; Color; 73 minutes.

In post–Civil War Texas, after Union occupation of the state ends, lawlessness runs rampant. The Texas Rangers, demobilized during the war, are called to active duty under the leadership of Major John B. Jones. As the Rangers' efforts begin to bring peace to the area, outlaw Sam Bass calls a meeting of the state's best-known thieves, stagecoach robbers and bank robbers, including Butch Cassidy, the Sundance Kid and John Wesley Hardin. Bass proposes that the men work in unison to pull off bigger jobs and keep the Rangers at bay.

With strength in numbers, the "Long Riders Protective Association," as one member dubs them, mounts new attacks against the people of Texas. The governor warns Major Jones that the bad men must be apprehended before the legislature goes into session or the Rangers will be deemed a failure and their appropriations cut off.

Knowing he needs help, Major Jones visits the state penitentiary and offers convict Johnny Carver ("one of the best platoon sergeants I ever had") a probationary appointment to the Rangers. Carver, who turned to crime after his family was killed by Union forces, is promised a full pardon if he uses his inside knowledge of the outlaws to bring them to justice. Carver accepts and negotiates the release of his buddy Buff Smith. The two are sworn into service.

Helen Fenton, publisher of the *Waco Star,* is appalled by the plan to allow convicts to join the ranks of the Rangers and prints a scathing editorial ("Convict Killers Become Rangers"). But when Bass and his men arrive in Waco, she recognizes the imminent danger.

Johnny and Buff seek the hideout of Bass and his cohorts, but Johnny is most interested in avenging himself against the Sundance Kid, who betrayed him during a robbery a few years earlier—one in which Helen's father was killed. They are met on the trail by Johnny's younger brother Danny, who joined the Rangers under an assumed name, causing Johnny to suspect that Major Jones doesn't trust him. Together, they track down the Sundance Kid, and Johnny kills him in a gun battle. At first, Johnny says avenging himself against the Kid has completed his personal mission, and he tells Buff and Danny he'll be leaving Texas. Danny, loyal to the Rangers, takes his own brother into custody, intending to escort him to prison. But when the three men are ambushed by more of Bass' men, Danny is forced to give his brother his gun back. In the gunfight, Danny is shot and killed, causing Johnny to once again assume his duties as a loyal Ranger.

Learning that Bass and his men plan a bank robbery in the town of Benton, Johnny gets there first, taking the loot into his possession and letting it be assumed that he's gone rogue again. Major Jones reluctantly puts out orders to bring him in, dead or alive, not knowing that Johnny is using the staged robbery to infiltrate Bass' gang. Tipping off Bass to a $1 million cash cargo being carried by train, Johnny talks the greedy outlaws into collaborating on the job, in reality hoping to set them up so that the Rangers can finally capture them.

Production of *The Texas Rangers* began in August 1950. It was photographed using the SuperCinecolor process. The cast is populated with faces familiar to Western fans. Once again cast as a newspaperwoman of the Old West, Gale plays a considerably feistier and more capable one here than she did in *Jesse James at Bay.* Told that the dangerous Sam Bass and his men are staying at a hotel in town, Helen calmly walks into the place and confronts him face to face, even trying to snatch a gun and shoot the Sundance Kid when an opportunity arises. Watching her storm out of Major Jones' office after learning he enlisted convicts, Johnny's sidekick Buff observes, "Whew! That filly leaves a trail like a prairie fire!" Unlike Gale's characters in some previous Westerns, Helen has no sympathy for outlaws and no wish to be one's girlfriend. It is not until the final act that she and Johnny have more than a passing conversation. When she angrily confronts him in Waco, believing that he has violated his oath to the Rangers, Johnny

Gale co-starred with George Montgomery in *The Texas Rangers* (1951).

looks her over and says, "Sister, you wouldn't be a bad looker if you'd wash some of that printer's ink off your face and hands." The remark earns him a slap in the face, but before the story is over she sees Johnny in a new light. Gale was costumed by Jean Louis.

Leading man George Montgomery (1916–2000) was already a veteran of quite a few Westerns; he went on to have his own Western TV series, *Cimarron City* (NBC, 1958–59). He was the real-life husband of singer Dinah Shore from 1943 to 1963. William Bishop (1918–1959), who co-starred in the NBC sitcom *It's a Great Life*, died of cancer at age 41. John Litel, who previously supported Gale in *Where Are Your Children?*, has a strong supporting role as the head of the Rangers, which he essays with his usual competence. Jerome Courtland (1926–2012), seen as boyish Danny, had more success as a director than an actor, going on to helm multiple episodes of *Dynasty, Knots Landing, The Love Boat* and other popular shows of the 1970s and 1980s.

The often-acerbic Bosley Crowther, in the *New York Times* (July 14, 1951), wrote, "We cannot suggest that you are likely to encounter an element of surprise ... unless, that is, you have never before seen a Western film.... But there are a couple of gunfights that Phil Karlson has crisply and gingerly staged and ... the action is as good as, or maybe better than, any of the sort you're likely to see on TV." *Harrison's Reports* (June 2, 1951) deemed it "an exciting western melodrama.... The directing and acting are skillful, and the color photography fine."

Woman of the North Country (1952)

Cast: Ruth Hussey (*Christine Powell*), Rod Cameron (*Kyle Ramlo*), John Agar (*David Powell*), Gale Storm (*Cathy Nordlund*), J. Carrol Naish (*John Mulholland*), Jim Davis (*Steve Powell*), Jay C. Flippen (*Axel Nordlund*), Taylor Holmes (*Andrew Dawson*), Barry Kelley (*O'Hara*), Grant Withers (*Henry Chapman*), Stephen Bekassy (*Andre Duclos*), Howard Petrie (*Rick Barton*), Hank Worden (*Tom Gordon*), Virginia Brissac (*Mrs. Dawson*), Leo Cleary (*Sheriff*), Hal K. Dawson (*Dispatcher*), George Chandler (*Harris*), Thurston Hall (*Mayor Spencer*), Lucien Littlefield (*Parvin*), Sandra Spence (*Millie*), Sid Tomack (*Hotel Clerk*), Ken Christy (*Drummer*), John Maxwell (*Doctor*), Dub Taylor (*Bob*), Fred Essler, John Halloran (*Gunsmiths*)

Director–Associate Producer: Joseph Kane. *Screenplay*: Norman Reilly Raine. *Story*: Charles Marquis Warren, Prescott Chaplin. *Photography*: Jack Marta. *Art Director*: Frank Arrigo. *Music*: R. Dale Butts. *Editor*: Richard L. Van Enger. *Sound*: Dick Tyler, Howard Wilson. *Costume Designer*: Adele Palmer. *Set Decorators*: John McCarthy, Jr., Charles Thompson. *Special Effects*: Howard Lydecker, Theodore Lydecker. *Makeup Supervisor*: Bob Mark. *Hair Stylist*: Peggy Gray.

Republic Pictures; released September 5, 1952; Color; 90 minutes.

In the largely undeveloped Minnesota of the early 1890s, the wealthy Powell family controls most of the lucrative iron ore trade, and seeks new deposits. Steely, beautiful but tough Christine Powell, in charge of the business, is interested in a possible mine at Mesabi, but it is currently leased to Kyle Ramlo. Kyle's late father, a geologist, traced iron ore on the property, but lacked the money to develop it. With his lease due to expire shortly, Kyle approaches the Powells with an interest in establishing a partnership, but the greedy Powells aren't interested in sharing the wealth. Shrewd Christine immediately recognizes that Kyle has unearthed "the greatest iron ore strike this country's ever seen..."

Though Christine finds Kyle attractive—somewhat to the dismay of his loyal girlfriend Cathy—that doesn't stop her from enlisting her brother Steve to rob him of the money he needs to pay his lease. Finding Steve's distinctive gun on the premises after he's held up, Ramlo vows to get even. Learning that Steve is friendly with the members of a gang who robbed a train and killed the conductor, Ramlo corrals them, collecting a $25,000 reward. Now flush with funds, Kyle forms the New Era Iron Mine Company to work the mine. Kyle's company succeeds in crowding the Powells out of the market. Busy with work, Kyle neglects Cathy, who's looking forward to a future with him, while Christine refuses to adjust to a life of reduced circumstances.

Despite Kyle's clear victory, it's Cathy who realizes that her man still has an unhealthy obsession with the Powells. As she tells her beau, "You fought the Powells and you won. You're the iron master now. But you're not sure of yourself. You could be generous if you felt safe." Instead, Kyle revels in bankrupting his former rivals. But Christine, knowing Kyle is attracted to her despite himself, seduces him into marriage. Upon return from his European honeymoon, Kyle learns who his true friends are—and who he should never have trusted.

Top-billed Ruth Hussey (1911–2005) plays the title character in this "North-Western" adventure story, originally announced under the title *Minnesota*. Compared to Gale's role, Hussey's is by far the showier and meatier of the two. The film reunites Gale with Rod Cameron, her leading man from *Stampede*. Unfortunately, much of the relationship between Kyle and Cathy takes place off-screen, requiring Gale to invest her character with enough depth and sincerity to win the audience's approval. Cameron, meanwhile, is capable as ever in his heroics, despite a script that makes his character too foolish to know when a woman is playing him. Despite his billing as one of the stars, John Agar (1921–2002) has a smallish, mostly thankless role as Christine's weakling brother.

Many of the cast members are veterans of more standard Western films; Dub Taylor's distinctive face and voice make him very noticeable in a bit part. Screenwriter Charles Marquis Warren (1912–1990) went on to work as writer and producer on the popular television Westerns *Gunsmoke* and *Rawhide*. Gale is directed, for the fourth and final time, by Joseph Kane, who helmed three of her Western films earlier in her career. In real life, the Mesabi Range's valuable ore was discovered in the 1860s.

Motion Picture Daily (July 30, 1952) said, "*Woman of the North Country* has several favorable qualities, not the last of which are the beauteous Minnesota country ... [A] fairly interesting, although at times slow-moving, melodramatic story, and a cast containing some pretty marketable names..." In the *New York Times* (August 30, 1952), reviewer O.A.G. noted, "Gale Storm, is quite appealing, and gives promise of being a first-rate actress."

As her swan song in motion pictures, *Woman of the North Country* is less than impressive. But by the time of its release, she was already the star of *My Little Margie*, and from this point forward left her movie career behind, focusing instead on television and music recording for the remainder of the 1950s.

Short Subjects

Rim of the Wheel (1951)

Cast: Gale Storm (*Virginia Sutton*), Lee Bonnell (*Ken Sutton*), Francis Ford (*"Dad" Dickerson*), Nan Boardman (*Mrs. Hammond*), Phillip Bonnell (*Billy Sutton*), Roger Broddus (*Johnny Sutton*), Marta Mitrovich (*Rosalie*)

Director: William F. Claxton. *Executive Producer*: S.M. Hershey. *Screenplay*: Charles F. Royal. *Original Story*: Elsie Williams. *Photography*: Benjamin H. Kline. *Assistant Directors*: Maurice Vaccarino, Lou Perlof. *Sound*: Glen Glenn. *Art Director*: Fred Preble. *Music Director*: Alberto Columbo. *Casting Director*: Vance Carroll. *Set Dressings*: Harry Reif.

Family Films; released 1951; B&W; 23 minutes.

Housewife and mother Virginia Sutton is trying to balance domestic demands, child care and her charitable and social activities. After firing the family maid, Rosalie, for incompetence, Virginia's stress level increases. "I never have a minute to myself!" she complains. Elderly "Dad" Dickerson, father of the Suttons' neighbor Mrs. Hammond, chides Virginia for her "gallivantin'." Helping to babysit the Sutton boys one night while their parents attend a country club function, Dad teaches the boys about the proper way to pray.

The next day, he challenges Virginia to reassess her priorities in life, saying she's "always running after something not worth running after, always on edge, always on the go.... Get off the rim, and get closer to the axle. You'll be close to God, and at peace." Dubious, Virginia responds, "How could anybody be at peace nowadays? This is a troubled world." But as Virginia ponders the old man's advice, she begins thinking about making some changes to the way she and her family live.

Made under the auspices of Family Films, formed to produce inspirational stories for the church rental market, this short offers an opportunity for Gale to play opposite her real-life husband Lee Bonnell, with their son Phillip seen as one of their offspring. Family Films was able to retain several Hollywood professionals to contribute to their film output; director William F. Claxton (1914–1996) enjoyed a lengthy career spent primarily in television, with an occasional feature such as *Night of the Lepus* (1972) among his credits. Actor Francis Ford (1881–1953), cast as the moral conscience of the film, was an experienced character actor who sometimes appeared in the pictures of director John Ford, his younger brother. A separate Family Films short, *Missionary to Walker's Garage* (1954) featured Gale's *My Little Margie* co-star Don Hayden as a non-believer who sneers at the proselytizing hero, "Don't you ever get tired of prayin'?"

Educational Screen (January 1952) gave *Rim of the Wheel* an approving review: "The casting and the acting are very satisfactory. The story moves along and holds the interest. The message of the film is clear and has wide application." The 16mm short was named "most timely Christian film of the year" by the organization Christian Youth Cinema, Inc.

How to Go Places (1954)

Gale "and her family, the Lee Bonnells" are featured in this short promotional film produced for Chevrolet. Running just over ten minutes, it shows the Bonnells preparing for a vacation trip by automobile. Viewers are given tips for packing, safety, getting better gas mileage, and car games to keep children entertained during a long drive. The film was made available to civic groups, and later aired as a filler on television.

Note: See Appendix A for information on her 16mm Soundies.

III

Television

My Little Margie

 Producer: Hal Roach, Jr. *Associate Producer*: Guy V. Thayer, Jr. *Production Manager*: Dick L'Estrange. *Photography*: Walter Strenge. *Supervising Editor*: Roy Luby. *Editors*: Bert Jordan. Guy Scarpitta. *Sound*: Charles Althouse, Joel Moss. *Photographic Effects*: Jack R. Glass. *Art Director*: McClure Capps. *Set Decorator*: Rudy Butler. *Assistant Directors*: Dick Moder, Wilbur McGaugh, Nate Watt. *Set Continuity*: Connie Earle, Hazel W. Hall. *Film Coordinator*: James Cairncross. *Music Editor*: Ted Cain. *Sound Editor*: Jim Bullock. *Special Effects*: Ira Anderson. *Miss Storm's Wardrobe*: Terri-Styles of California, DeDe Johnson. *Miss Storm's Hats*: Caspar-Davis of California. Roland Reed TV Productions.

In the early days of television, Gale achieved perhaps the height of her career prominence when she accepted the starring role in the situation comedy *My Little Margie*. It was the second successful TV sitcom produced by the Hal Roach Studios, following *The Stu Erwin Show* (aka *The Trouble with Father*).

 Just as most established movie stars eschewed TV in 1952, film studios were, for the most part, equally hands-off, reluctant to collaborate with the rival medium that was hurting attendance at theaters nationwide. Not so the Roach Studios, entering the TV arena at a time when the movie business was struggling. "In 1948 we had to decide what the future would be for us," the younger Roach explained. "We'd done just about everything in our studio, from the $6,000,000 *Joan of Arc* to *Our Gang* comedies.... The Roach Studio cut its teeth on shorts, so we were in a good position to make movies cheaply and quickly for television."[1] With major studios unwilling to go into TV production, Roach took advantage of the opportunity. Although his father supported his efforts, some observers were anticipating a fall for Roach Jr. "They all thought I was an idiot," Roach later said of his film industry colleagues, "and it actually helped. Left me with nothing very serious to live up to."[2]

 "We had to try to convince television people of the possibility of using film," Roach said in another interview. "They were mostly ex–radio people, and they didn't know much about pictures. We didn't know much about radio. It took some doing for us all to get together."[3]

 After several false starts, Roach Jr. proved his detractors wrong when he sold the family-oriented sitcom *The Stu Erwin Show* to ABC. Debuting in the fall of 1950, it lasted 128 episodes and ran until 1955, then enjoyed a healthy afterlife in reruns.

With that success under their belts, Roach and his colleagues began to develop other television properties. According to Roach Jr. it was a situation from his own family life that provided the basic inspiration for *My Little Margie*. When Roach's teenage daughter Shari quarreled with her parents about attending a movie on a school night, the argument ended with the young lady stomping off to her room. Roach said to his wife, "My Lord, she's hard enough to handle now. What'll happen when she's over 21 and we have no legal control over her?"[4] The basic concept was turned over to writer Frank Fox, who developed the characters of Margie, Vern and their associates. "Frank Fox ... had a secretary named Margie," Gale later explained. "That's where the name came from. But I guess the character just came out of his imagination."[5]

The premise of the series found Vern Albright, a middle-aged New York City investment counselor, living in a luxurious high-rise apartment, the Carlton Arms, with his irrepressible 21-year-old daughter Margie. A widower, Vern tried (largely in vain) to exert a steadying influence on Margie, who was prone to wild schemes. Margie, on the other hand, thought her father's busy social life too strenuous for a man of his age and wanted to see him settle down. Other regularly seen characters included Margie's boyfriend Freddie Wilson, Vern's frequent date Roberta Townsend (who lived down the hall) and his irascible, elderly boss George Honeywell. Also featured was Charlie, the Carlton Arms' elevator operator, who often found himself roped into a scheme by one or the other of the Albrights. Across the hall from the Albrights was elderly Florence Odetts, a fun-loving, much-married widow who quickly became Margie's best friend.

Several of the early scripts focused on Margie and Vern's attempts to interfere in each other's love life. Both were attractive people who enjoyed the company of the opposite sex, but were in no great hurry to make a permanent commitment. Margie wanted to end her father's relationship with Roberta Townsend. Though Margie professes to like Roberta, she explains, "But she's not right for you, Dad. Always keeping you out dancing half the night like a college boy ... much too wearing for a man of your age." Likewise, Vern looks disdainfully on Margie's weak-willed, usually unemployed boyfriend Freddie, whom he describes as "that drooling droop," a "beady-eyed pipsqueak" or simply "Muttonhead." Margie has a great fondness for Freddie, who is unceasingly devoted to her, but is easily distracted by the more attractive, personable prospects who come along in almost every episode.

Like *The Stu Erwin Show*, *My Little Margie* was produced in a partnership between Roach and Roland Reed TV Productions, Inc. Reed broke into show business as a movie extra in the 1920s, went on to become an editor, a director and, since 1938, the proprietor of a production company that specialized in making industrial films.[6] He provided the production expertise. The series was filmed on the Roach lot in Culver City.

The role of father Vern Albright proved the easier of the two leads to cast. Roach was a friend of retired actor Charles Farrell, best-remembered for his romantic leads some 25 years earlier, often opposite Janet Gaynor. Some years earlier, Farrell's decision to buy some land in Palm Springs, before it became a fashionable resort, proved lucrative for him. The tennis club he and actor Ralph Bellamy founded there grew by leaps and bounds. From a financial standpoint, he had no need to take up acting again, but he agreed to give *Margie* a try. Farrell later said, "TV movies are informal and fun.... I decided to try the show because it couldn't do me any harm. A bad program could hurt some actors, but I was out of the business, so what could I lose?"[7]

Although it's now difficult to imagine anyone but Gale as Margie Albright, the role wasn't locked in for her from the beginning. On February 23, 1952, *Broadcasting* reported that Hal Roach Productions was beginning production the following week on *My Little Margie*: "Charles Farrell and Mona Freeman will star as father and daughter in the domestic comedy format." However, Freeman (1926–2014) dropped out of the project on short notice, leaving Roach in search of a star.

Audie Murphy's actress wife Wanda Hendrix (1928–1981) was also offered the role, according to *Daily Variety* (June 1, 1954), but "nixed it because she didn't like the script." Gale told authors Boyd Magers and Michael G. Fitzgerald that Marjorie Reynolds, later to play William Bendix's wife on *The Life of Riley,* was another candidate to play Margie. Gale later said with characteristic modesty, "I know they were scraping the bottom of the barrel when they offered me the job—they'd offered the part to actresses who were hotter."[8] But she too was hesitant to accept the role. "I read the script for the pilot," she recalled some years later, "and didn't like it, because I thought it smacked just a tiny little bit of incest. So I took it back and explained what I felt about it. I said I was probably wrong, but that it bothered me, and that I didn't want to do it."[9] Roach agreed to make script revisions, and the results pleased her enough that she signed on. *Variety* announced her casting as Margie in May. Roach soon succeeded in locking down a deal for *My Little Margie* to be sponsored by Philip Morris, as the summer replacement for *I Love Lucy.*

Margie clearly showed the influence of the Roach studio's slapstick approach to comedy. Not filmed in front of a studio audience, as *I Love Lucy* was, the show could stage comedy segments that were almost cartoon-like in their approach. If elderly Mr. Honeywell had a vase crashed over his head, an act that would surely have killed or seriously injured a man of his age in real life, he simply passed out cold for a few minutes, no more seriously hurt than Wile E. Coyote suffering his umpteenth fall from a high cliff. When Vern was thrown out of someone's apartment, a dummy was shown sailing across the hallway, followed by a shot of Charlie Farrell sprawled in the floor looking dazed. Geared strictly as light entertainment, the show had no pretensions to deeper meaning or cultural significance. It just made viewers laugh and relax.

My Little Margie's regular director, former vaudevillian Hal Yates (1899–1969), brought to the show experience writing and directing comedy shorts for funnymen Leon Errol and Edgar Kennedy. Gale would recall him as a difficult director to please, inclined to blow his stack under pressure, but acknowledged that she honed her comedic skills under his tutelage. "I thought comedy was something you had a flair for, or you happened to have good timing," she later said. "I had no idea that there were definite rules."[10] Gale's niece Sharon also had reason to remember Yates' temper. As a child, Sharon visited the

My Little Mona? Actress Mona Freeman, pictured in a publicity still for Fox's *Junior Miss* (1945), was originally chosen to play Margie Albright.

Margie set during the shooting of an episode. Giggling at the scene playing out, Sharon was admonished by Yates who, she remembered years later, "scared the crap out of me."

Five more actors were chosen to play recurring characters, not all of whom appeared in any given episode. Gertrude W. Hoffmann (1871–1968) was cast as Mrs. Odetts, the Albrights' apartment house neighbor who loved being a part of Margie's schemes. Born Eliza Gertrude Wesselhoeft, she first began acting in her native Germany in the 1910s. Giving up her career to raise a family, she made a comeback at the age of 60, after the death of her husband Ralph Hoffmann, an ornithologist who served as the director of the Santa Barbara Museum of Natural History. Originally joining a local little theater group, Gertrude got her motion picture break when its director arranged for her to play a part in the RKO film *Before Dawn* (1933). Mrs. Odetts became Gertrude's best-known role. She appeared in a number of motion pictures, playing minor roles in *Foreign Correspondent* (1940), *The File on Thelma Jordon* (1949), *The War of the Worlds* (1953) and others. One correspondent wrote,

> The rough schedule of a weekly television show doesn't faze Mrs. Hoffmann in the least. As you can see on your screen, she is as agile as a kid of 70. She drives the 20 miles from her Los Angeles home to the studio in her own car, and makes the 2½-hour trip to visit her daughter in Santa Barbara several times a year.[11]

Veteran movie character actor Clarence Kolb (1874–1964) was chosen to play crotchety George Honeywell, Vern's boss at the investment firm of Honeywell and Todd. Prior to his movie work, Kolb was well-known as half of the vaudeville team of Kolb and Dill, which initially did a Dutch-accent routine. Later they starred in musical comedies; according to Kolb's *Variety* obituary (December 2, 1964), "Their [West] Coast versions of New York musical hits usually were fully plotted shows ... with a full chorus line." Kolb's film credits, where he perfected his blustery persona, included such classics as *His Girl Friday* and *Adam's Rib*. Honeywell frequently decries Margie's efforts to involve herself in company affairs, describing her in one episode as "110 pounds of human TNT who could blow up this whole deal quicker than you can say Margie Albright!"

Cast as elegant Roberta Townsend, Vern's steady, Hillary Brooke (1914–1999) was an actress whose résumé—like Gale's—was rich in B movies of the 1940s. A native of Astoria, New York, Brooke parlayed an elegant wardrobe and a speaking style that sounded faintly British into steady work. While making frequent appearances on *My Little Margie*, she also played a recurring role on the syndicated *Abbott and Costello Show* (1952–54).

Don Hayden (1926–1998) won the role of Margie's loyal, none-too-bright boyfriend Freddie Wilson. He was the son of Lela Bliss and Harry Hayden, who ran an acting school that Gale briefly attended. Don had previously played small roles in films such as (coincidentally) *Margie* (1946), as well as Samuel Goldwyn's *I Want You* (1951), where he can be glimpsed as one of the nervous young men waiting in the anteroom of the local draft board.

Mostly ignored by the press, Hayden attracted newspaper ink primarily for his off-screen marriages. In April 1954, after divorcing actress Gay Nelson, he married Wallace Beery's 22-year-old daughter Carol Ann, but separated from her after about six months. In November, syndicated columnist Louella O. Parsons (November 8, 1954) reported that, according to Carol Ann, "Don walked into his beach house and told Carol Ann he was definitely through with marriage and that he wanted her to leave." She filed for divorce in December 1954 and was granted her decree the following February. Though she had told Parsons in November that "there had been no hint of trouble in their marriage [and] no quarrels," she later testified, "He was very rude to me. He shouted at me and screamed at me and used profane language. On several occasions he slapped me."[12] Before the year was out, Hayden married Melinda Markey, daughter of Joan Bennett and producer Gene Markey; they had a son, Kevin Markey Hayden, but were divorced in the late 1950s.

African-American actor Willie Best (1916–1962) played the recurring role of Charlie, elevator operator in the Albrights' apartment building. Busy Best worked almost constantly at the Roach studios in the early 1950s, juggling his *Margie* duties alongside a role as handyman Willie on *The Stu Erwin Show* and the part of Willie Slocum in the syndicated adventure series *Waterfront* (1954–55). He had enjoyed a successful career as a movie featured player dating back to the early 1930s, but roles began to dry up for him in the late 1940s, when activist groups put pressure on producers and studios to phase out the type of stereotypical characters he was usually assigned to play. Best's private life hit the newspapers in May 1951, when he and a female companion were jailed in connection with narcotics charges, further limiting his film opportunities. However, he continued to work at the Roach studios through the mid–50s.

Through the Milton Biow advertising agency, Roach sold *My Little Margie* to sponsor Philip Morris for a 13-week run in the summer of 1952. Originally intended to serve only as *I Love Lucy*'s off-season replacement, *Margie*, as one journalist noted, "failed to achieve the fantastic ratings of *Lucy* but its score was impressive by ordinary standards." Critics were almost uniformly dismissive. Syndicated columnist John Crosby (June 29, 1952) blasted the show with both barrels: "[A]n amazingly complete illustration of how not to make a television show ... an awful lot of plot, tons of it ... the direction, and especially the writing, are still plain bloody awful." *Time* magazine (November 9, 1953) described it as "badly written [and] ineptly acted..."

The viewing audience begged to differ. After its summer run, the show "was duly dropped by [Philip Morris]. Then began the mail deluge. It was so impressive that the same sponsor had taken extra TV time to bring back Margie ... and already has inaugurated a radio adaptation."[13] Asked to explain the show's appeal, Gale said, "I think it's because *Margie* tries to give something to everyone.... Kids love the show, teenagers go for Margie, women still think of Charlie Farrell as their matinee idol, the girls go gaga over the clothes worn by me, and I get all sorts of love notes from the fellows." She added that many older viewers took inspiration from the still-active characters played by Clarence Kolb and Gertrude W. Hoffmann.[14]

While Gale was not involved in the scriptwriting process, and her feedback was seldom sought, she noted that, over the course of a successful show's run, writers gradually began to pick up on the star's behavior and incorporate aspects of it into the character she played. Early on, Gale inadvertently contributed an element that would stick in viewers' memories for years to come. Some have referred to it as a "trill"; she herself termed it "the Margie gurgle." It was a sound Margie used to express dismay, usually at the point where her current predicament seemed to be at its most hopeless. Gale would turn to the camera and emit a noise that served roughly the same purpose as Lucy Ricardo's teeth-baring grimace, which her writers termed "the spider." It originated as an impromptu gesture by Gale while shooting an episode. "I don't recall ever doing that [noise] at home, and one day on the set, for some reason, something went wrong..." Her spontaneous reaction struck those around her as funny, and soon it would be written into the show's scripts. Years later, she recalled, "Some very sophisticated people will come up to me, and wait until nobody's looking, and they'll say, 'Would you make that noise?'"[15]

Philip Morris sponsored another five-week run on NBC's Saturday night schedule beginning in October 1952, while a more permanent berth was sought. The series acted as a placeholder for Bob Cummings' new show *My Hero,* set for a November debut. In early 1953, the show returned to CBS, this time airing Thursdays at 10 p.m., replacing *Racket Squad* (another Hal Roach show). Syndicated columnist Bob Foster (December 23, 1952) grouchily reported the show's imminent return in December. Reminding readers of the show's beginnings as a summer replacement, Foster noted, "Despite the fact that most of us [critics] couldn't see the thing at all—considering it so much junk—it clicked and in four weeks was fourth on the Hooper and Neilson [sic] ratings."

According to associate producer Guy V. Thayer, Jr., each *Margie* was produced on a budget of $18,500. The three-camera format pioneered for sitcoms by *I Love Lucy,* which entailed filming a show with a live studio audience, was not used. Staff at the Roach studios had devised several ways to lower costs for the multiple shows being produced on the lot. Thayer explained,

> With less than an hour's work the sets of *My Little Margie* … are converted into the sets for the syndicated *Rocky Jones, Space Ranger*…. The *My Little Margie* unit makes three or four pictures in succession. Then we give the players a needed rest and go ahead with three or four *Rocky Jones* films, using the same crew, changing only the director.[16]

The closing credits for the crew of *My Little Margie* are virtually indistinguishable from other Roach shows of the period, and many of the same actors turn up in different series. The *Margie* cast and crew often worked six-day weeks, completing two episodes in that time span.

The 10 p.m. time slot was not ideal for a show with Margie's family appeal. That summer, Philip Morris opted not to sponsor the show for the 1953–54 season. *Motion Picture Daily* reported, "Scant hours after Philip Morris failed to pick up the option … producers Hal Roach Jr. and Roland Reed sold the package to NBC who already has 3 sponsors bidding."[17] That fall, *Margie* began a two-year run on NBC, paired with Joan Davis' *I Married Joan* in an early-Wednesday-evening slot, with the Scott Paper Company ultimately signing on to sponsor Gale's show. For the remainder of its prime time run, *Margie* was used to promote Scott's line of paper towels, tissue and wax paper. The Wednesday slot was a competitive one, with Arthur Godfrey's CBS show a Top Ten favorite. A few months after Gale's show bowed on NBC, however, *Variety* (February 24, 1954) reported, "It's no secret that the NBC boys have been silently rejoicing over the inroads that the Joan Davis and *My Little Margie* competition has been making on the Godfrey Wednesday hour."

The show's popularity took Gale to a new level of stardom, and even resulted in new attention being paid to her low-budget films of the 1940s. "In fact," she cracked, "I may use some of my *Margie* profits to buy them back—so I can keep them off TV."[18] In early 1954, *Billboard* (January 16, 1954) reported that the Roach studio finalized a deal to license *My Little Margie* merchandise, with "cartoon books, comic books and dresses featuring Miss Storm and Farrell." A *My Little Margie* comic book introduced later that year proved highly popular, its run far outlasting that of the TV show in prime time.

According to Thayer, *Margie* now had so many episodes in the can that the company was looking forward to its network demise. "Right now," he told syndicated columnist Erskine Johnson (February 14, 1954), "we're sorry that *My Little Margie* is sold to a national

Broad comedy, often including outlandish costumes, was a hallmark of Gale's hit TV series *My Little Margie.*

sponsor.... Our films on the shelf could be making more money than we make from turning out a new show each week." The producers knew they had a gold mine waiting to be unleashed.

Nonetheless, going into the show's fourth season in the fall of 1954, producers planned to spruce the show up a bit. They decided to open up its horizons in search of new story ideas, doing more episodes out of the confines of the Albright apartment and the Honeywell and Todd offices. Subsequent installments found the Albrights traveling to Las Vegas, Hawaii, Bermuda and England, though the series never in fact left the company soundstages. The popularity of a new competing series, ABC's *Disneyland,* cut deep into the family audience of *Margie,* and ratings declined as the season progressed.

In the spring of 1955, the Scott Paper Company declined to sponsor *My Little Margie* for the fall season, choosing to pick up *Father Knows Best* instead. The move puzzled some industry observers, as Robert Young's CBS family sitcom had struggled in the ratings during its first season. Nevertheless, Gale's show came to an end after 126 episodes. Roach and Reed didn't actively seek another sponsor. As Gale explained to a visitor during production of one of the final episodes, "Vern's Butterflies," "The present producer, Roland Reed, says he won't make any more [*Margie*] films. He wants to cash in on the reruns."[19]

That fall, *My Little Margie* began daily reruns in dozens of TV markets, handled by Official Films. At that point in TV history, there were few off-network sitcoms available for five-day-a-week "stripping," and *Margie* proved quite popular. By late summer, *Variety* (August 31, 1955) reported that the show was sold in Chicago, Boston, Detroit, Nashville and many other key markets. In the summer of 1956, columnist James Bacon noted that Gale was offered $400,000 for her rights in perpetuity to the *My Little Margie* films, but said no. Instead of an outright sale, Gale and her manager-husband Lee opted to let the residuals trickle in for however the reruns might be popular, anticipating a far greater payoff that way. That proved to be the right choice.

By 1960, Official Films advertised in *Broadcasting* (February 1, 1960) that the *Margie* films—"Now in 6th, 7th and even 8th run" in some markets—remained a ratings draw. Solid ratings scores were reported in Chicago, Minneapolis, Washington, D.C., Boston and more, as well as smaller cities. An ad in *Sponsor* (February 13, 1961) announced that reruns outpaced those of other off-network sitcoms like *I Married Joan, The George Burns and Gracie Allen Show* and *Our Miss Brooks.*

The show was discovered by a new generation of viewers in the 1980s, when daily reruns were seen on the Christian Broadcasting Network, but it has never had an official DVD release.

Looking back on *Margie,* Gale told syndicated columnist Erskine Johnson (August 24, 1957), "It made me not only grateful but humble. I had a feeling about the show that not even the early critics could discourage. It was a feeling that *My Little Margie* was something special, like God had said, 'This is it!' It was."

Season One

Contemporary sources disagree on the order and/or air date that the first season episodes aired. The listings presented below represent the most reliable information currently available. *Daily Variety* (June 17, 1952) reviewed the premiere, making it clear that "Reverse Psychology" aired on June 16, 1952. On June 3, 1952, *Daily Variety* reported that "prints of first *My Little Margie* show will be on way to CBS-TV stations throughout the country Friday [June 6, 1952]." Since the early episodes were not being disseminated via the nationwide coaxial cable, it is possible that some stations aired them in a different order than others.

"Reverse Psychology" (June 16, 1952)

Writers: Frank Fox, G. Carleton Brown. *Director*: Hal Yates.

Cast: Hillary Brooke (*Roberta Townsend*), Don Hayden (*Freddie Wilson*), Clarence Kolb (*George Honeywell*), Willie Best (*Charlie*), Eileen Stevens (*Mildred*)

Summary: Using a newly published book, *Reverse Psychology* by Professor D.J. Windsail, Margie tries to convince Vern to stop seeing Roberta, unaware that Vern is using the same technique to discourage her relationship with Freddie. Seeing Roberta carrying a wedding dress (which she's delivering on behalf of her boss), Margie assumes her father is eloping. There's chaos when both couples, along with Mr. Honeywell, board a train to Greenwich, Connecticut.

Notes: This episode establishes Mr. Honeywell as a dog lover who trains his pets for shows. Thanks to Philip Morris' sponsorship, everyone who attends Vern's impromptu party smokes. This episode introduces all but one of the show's recurring characters, with Mrs. Odetts yet to appear.

Quote: VERN (telling Margie she can do better than Freddie): When the right boy comes along, I'll know.
MARGIE: Swell, and I hope the two of you will be very happy together.

"A Friend for Roberta" (June 23, 1952)

Writers: Frank Fox, G. Carleton Brown. *Director*: Hal Yates.

Cast: Hillary Brooke (*Roberta Townsend*), Don Hayden (*Freddie Wilson*), Douglas [Douglass] Dumbrille (*Angio Piazza*), Gertrude Hoffmann (*Miss Odetts*), William E. Green (*Warnock*), Willie Best (*Charlie*), John M. Kennedy (*Announcer*)

Summary: Coming home from a night at the theater, Vern and Roberta argue over her infatuation with opera singer Angio Piazza. Seeing an opportunity to break up her father's romance, Margie plots to bring Roberta and the singer together. Her plan backfires when Piazza thinks it's Margie herself who wants to meet him.

Notes: Gertrude Hoffmann makes her first appearance as the Albrights' neighbor, introduced here as *Miss* Odetts.

"Radioactive Margie" (June 30, 1952)

Writers: Frank Fox, G. Carleton Brown. *Director*: Hal Yates.

Cast: Don Hayden (*Freddie Wilson*), Clarence Kolb (*Mr. Honeywell*), Gertrude Hoffmann (*Mrs. Odetts*), George Pembroke, Peter Leeds, Bob Carraher

Summary: Thinking Freddie needs gumption to get ahead in the business world, Margie convinces him that the Arizona land he inherited is rich with uranium. At first offering Freddie a job so as to get in on the deal, Mr. Honeywell and Vern soon learn of Margie's trick and play one of their own, making her believe that exposure to the soil has made her radioactive. Mrs. Odetts intervenes just in time to let Margie turn the tables.

Notes: This is the first aired episode to follow what will become the show's most common plot construction: Vern tries to "teach Margie a lesson," but she ends up outsmarting him. It also features Margie's famed "gurgle," which she employs when Vern tells her Honeywell and Todd are investing $200,000 in Freddie's worthless land. Gertrude Hoffmann returns as Margie's buddy across the hall, who's now called Mrs., rather than Miss, Odetts. Actor Bob Carraher made multiple appearances in the series, usually cast as a policeman.

Quote: MRS. ODETTS (to Freddie, who called her a sweet old lady): I'm not sweet and I'm not old. I'm so young, I help Boy Scouts across the street.

"Margie Sings Opera" (July 7, 1952)

Writers: Frank Fox, G. Carleton Brown. *Director*: Hal Yates.

Cast: Clarence Kolb (*George Honeywell*), Florence Bates (*Mrs. Stegmuller*), Fortunio Bonanova (*Mr. Branchetti*), Gertrude Hoffmann (*Mrs. Odetts*), Gloria Eaton (*Ginny Clark*), Marshall Bradford (*Tom Clark*)

Summary: Doing a favor for a friend, Margie poses as her pal Ginny for a meeting with a noted Italian opera singer. Taking advantage of her new friendship, Margie invites Mr. Branchetti to a party, which Vern hopes will impress his client Mrs. Stegmuller. But when Margie's deception is uncovered, Mr. Branchetti is a no-show at the party. Now Margie must transform herself into a bald, 200-pound opera singer.

Notes: Mrs. Odetts, now in full swing as Margie's buddy and co-conspirator, thinks her latest wild scheme "sounds like fun." The great character actress Florence Bates (1888–1954), whose film credits included classics like *Rebecca* (1940) and *I Remember Mama* (1948), began a transition to television in the early 1950s, appearing on popular shows like *I Love Lucy* and *Our Miss Brooks*. Her new livelihood was cut short by her death at age 65.

"Margie's Sister Sally" (July 14, 1952)

Writers: Frank Fox, G. Carleton Brown. *Director*: Hal Yates.

Cast: Ron Randell (*Westley Charlton, Jr.*), Don Hayden (*Freddie Wilson*), Gertrude Hoffmann (*Miss Odetts*), Sheila James (*Norma Jean Odetts*), Willie Best (*Charlie*), Tom Mann (*Boy*)

Summary: Vern wants Margie to entertain the visiting son of his old British pal, but Margie, based on an old photo, balks, expecting Westley Charlton, Jr., to be "a prize goon." Dressing up as an 11-year-old girl to discourage Westley, Margie is shocked when he proves to be suave and handsome. In hopes of getting invited to a ball Westley is attending, Margie invents her "sister" Sally, who looks more like her usual self. But when Miss Odetts' visiting granddaughter busts Margie's cover, Westley and Vern decide to have some fun making her keep up the pretense of two separate identities.

Notes: An inside joke finds Charles Farrell's character, Vern, bubbling with enthusiasm over "an old Charlie Farrell picture running on television…. I wouldn't miss it for anything." Sheila James (born 1941), seen as visiting Norma Jean Odetts, was a regular cast member of another Roach sitcom, *The Stu Erwin Show*.

"Costume Party" (July 21, 1952)

Writer: Nathaniel Curtis. *Director*: Hal Yates.

Cast: Hillary Brooke (*Roberta Townsend*), Don Hayden (*Freddie Wilson*), Clarence Kolb (*George Honeywell*), Roy Roberts (*Frank Cragg*), William Newell (*Jimmy Potts*), Willie Best (*Charlie*)

Summary: Disliking Mr. Honeywell's propensity for mixing business with social occasions, Vern declines an invitation to the masquerade party his boss is throwing. Margie and Mr. Honeywell conspire to make Vern change his mind by encouraging Roberta to attend the party in the company of her other steady date, stuffy game hunter Frank Cragg. Opting to attend at the last minute, Vern decides to be Roberta's knight in shining armor, while a prowler who dons a costume creates havoc in the Albright apartment.

Notes: As the show continued to develop its style, this episode built to the type of slapstick climax *Margie* fans came to expect from it. According to this script, Mr. Honeywell is retired, though he still holds the title of president and founder of the company, and comes to the office nearly every day. Guest star Roy Roberts went on to be Gale's co-star in her second sitcom, *The Gale Storm Show: Oh! Susanna*.

Gale and co-star Charles Farrell, reviewing a *My Little Margie* script.

"Margie Plays Detective" (July 28, 1952)

    Writers: Frank Fox, G. Carleton Brown. *Director*: Hal Yates.

    Cast: Hillary Brooke (*Roberta Townsend*), Clarence Kolb (*Mr. Honeywell*), Don Hayden (*Freddie Wilson*), Fortunio Bonanova (*Mr. Maderra*), Poppy Delvando (*Mrs. Maderra*), Gloria Talbott (*Maurine*), Malcolm Mealey (*David*), Gertrude Hoffmann (*Mrs. Odetts*), Willie Best (*Charlie*)

Summary: When Mrs. Odetts' adult grandchildren sneak into the Albrights' apartment to retrieve a power of attorney she hid there, Vern thinks Margie has been entertaining Freddie on the sly, and Roberta thinks Vern has another girlfriend. Before the night is over, punches have been thrown, Vern's client has been tied up, and Margie's trip to Havana is in serious jeopardy.

    Notes: Actress Gloria Talbott (1931–2000), seen here as Mrs. Odetts' granddaughter, would become a cult figure with her starring roles in *I Married a Monster from Outer Space* and *Daughter of Dr. Jekyll*. *Variety* (July 30, 1952) still wasn't liking the show much, complaining about "weak scripting and ludicrous slapstick," and opining that for the sake of the network and the sponsor, "it's probably a good thing that *Lucy* comes back into the time slot soon."

"Insurance" (August 4, 1952)

    Writers: Jesse Goldstein, G. Carleton Brown, Frank Fox. *Director*: Hal Yates.

    Cast: Clarence Kolb (*George Honeywell*), Don Hayden (*Freddie Wilson*), Gertrude Hoffmann (*Mrs. Odetts*), George Givot (*Luscious Lou*), Valerie Vernon (*Mrs. Lou*), Charles Evans (*Mr. Hartford*), Florence Lake (*Mrs. Hartford*), Byron Foulger (*Professor Nelson*)

Summary: When Vern resolves to get into better physical condition, walking home from work and refusing food and drink, Margie thinks they're in the poorhouse. Mrs. Odetts' story about the 1929 stock crash leads her to fear a despondent Vern may be a danger to himself. Freddie's college professor, recruited to help Margie's dad, advises complete agreement with anything Vern says, even when he mistakes two prospective tenants for the apartment for the clients he's supposed to be cultivating.

    Notes: Mrs. Odetts makes a joking reference to then-popular singer Johnnie Ray (1927–1990), known for his emotional singing style, and claims to have a copy of his newest "platter," "A Barrel Full of Teardrops."

"Margie's Mink" (August 11, 1952)

    Writers: Nathaniel Curtis, G. Carleton Brown. *Director*: Hal Yates.

    Cast: Clarence Kolb (*George Honeywell*), Don Hayden (*Freddie Wilson*), Victor Milan (*Sir Saiyid Nasif*), Saul Gorss (*Kalif Whadi*), Willie Best (*Charlie*)

Summary: When Margie mistakenly receives a mink ordered by Sir Saiyid Nasif, the United Nations delegate from Barabia, she tells her father it was sent to her by a suitor. Nasif meets Margie and decides she would be the perfect choice to serve as his first wife. Desperate to prevent Margie from marrying Nasif, Vern enlists the help of Freddie to give his daughter a good scare.

"Efficiency Expert" (August 18, 1952)

    Writers: Frank Fox, G. Carleton Brown. *Director*: Hal Yates.

    Cast: Hillary Brooke (*Roberta Townsend*), Don Hayden (*Freddie Wilson*), Alvy Moore (*Dillard Crumbly III*), Charmienne Harker (*Betty Fuller*)

Summary: Insisting that Freddie is not good enough for Margie, Vern wants her to have a man who's "ambitious, aggressive and affirmative." When she meets annoying dullard Dillard Crumbly III, the new efficiency expert at Honeywell and Todd, Margie decides he'll make Freddie look good by comparison. Tipped off by Roberta that Margie is tricking him, Vern pretends to like her new beau, and neither father nor daughter will back down until there's a wedding in the works.

Notes: Character actor Alvy Moore (1921–1997), who's nicely spotlighted here as the tiresome Dillard, achieved his greatest fame as dotty Hank Kimball on *Green Acres*. This episode's very funny final act is unusual in that, for once, Margie and Vern are conspiring together against an outsider, rather than butting heads.

"Hooded Vern" (August 25, 1952)

Writers: Frank Fox, G. Carleton Brown. *Director*: Hal Yates.

Cast: Richard Simmons (*Norman Masterson*), Otto Waldis (*Seven*), Teresa Tudor (*Countess*), Paul McGuire (*Bradley*), Dian Fauntelle (*Waitress*)

Summary: Margie likes the looks of FBI man Norman Masterson, but can't find a socially proper way to express her interest. With Mrs. Odetts' help, she tries to attract his attention by transforming herself into a slinky, foreign-accented Mata Hari. Aware he's being played, Mr. Masterson conspires with Vern to make Margie believe she's going undercover into a dangerous espionage encounter.

Notes: At the close of the program, sponsor Philip Morris presented a clip from the *I Love Lucy* episode "Lucy Fakes Illness," originally aired on January 28, 1952, with the announcement that TV's #1 show was returning for a second season in three weeks. According to this script, Mrs. Odetts' first name is Florence. Dian Fauntelle, seen here as a waitress, settled into the recurring role of Betty, secretary in the office of Honeywell and Todd.

"The Contract" (September 1, 1952)

Writers: Frank Fox, G. Carleton Brown. *Director*: Hal Yates.

Cast: Hillary Brooke (*Roberta*), Don Hayden (*Freddie*), Alix Talton (*Helen Chaney*), Cliff Ferré (*Bill Watson*), Eileen Stevens (*Mildred*), Clarence Kolb (*Mr. Honeywell*), Gertrude Hoffmann (*Miss Odetts*), Sandy Sanders (*Cowboy*), Willie Best (*Charlie*)

Summary: Margie and Vern's plans for a quiet dinner together rapidly spin out of control when Mr. Honeywell presses Vern to sweet-talk client Helen Chaney into signing a new contract, and Bill Watson reminds Margie they have a date for that evening. Mix in a jealous Freddie, and Roberta's unexpected return home from a trip, and the ingredients are all present for a nice evening with Margie, Vern and their four dates.

Notes: Miss Odetts returns, and is again a willing conspirator in one of Margie's schemes, as she will so often be in the future. Actress Alix Talton's last name is misspelled "Tolton" in the closing credits.

"Vern's Chums" (September 8, 1952)

Writers: Frank Fox, G. Carleton Brown. *Director*: Hal Yates.

Cast: Clarence Kolb (*George Honeywell*), Hillary Brooke (*Roberta Townsend*), Don Hayden (*Freddie Wilson*), Harry Tyler (*Chauncey*), Harry Brown (*The Dodger*), Harry Hayden (*Stephen Wilson*), Lela Bliss (*Mrs. Wilson*), Willie Best (*Charlie*)

Summary: Wanting Vern to like Freddie better, Margie invites his parents to dinner, knowing that Mr. Wilson has just been named chair of a foundation that could give Honeywell and Todd a lucrative account. Mistakenly thinking Margie is laying the groundwork for marrying Freddie, Vern calls on two old vaudevillian friends to help him make the worst possible impression on the staid Wilsons.

Notes: Actor Don Hayden's real-life parents, Harry Hayden (1882–1955) and Lela Bliss (1886–1980), appear here as his father and mother. Active as film actors for many years, they also operated a Hollywood acting school. This was the final aired episode of the show's original summer season on CBS.

Season Two

"Conservative Margie" (October 4, 1952)

Writers: Frank Fox, G. Carleton Brown. *Director*: Hal Yates.
Cast: Hillary Brooke (*Roberta Townsend*), Kathryn Card (*Priscilla Cromwell*), Bob Nichols (*Cabot Cromwell*), Kathleen Mulqueen (*Woman Guest*)

Summary: Wanting to impress Vern's stuffy Bostonian client Mrs. Cromwell, Margie fills the Albrights' apartment with rented Early American furniture and adopts the guise of "Margaret," Vern's strait-laced daughter. The plan succeeds too well when Mrs. Cromwell decides Margie would make a suitable wife for her repressed grandson Cabot. A surprise visit from Cabot finds Margie dressed normally, causing her to adopt yet another role, that of Roberta's daughter Clarice.

Notes: Actress Kathryn Card (1892–1964), seen here as Mrs. Cromwell, went on to play the recurring role of Lucy Ricardo's scatterbrained mother on *I Love Lucy*, and turned up again on *Margie*. For the purposes of this plot, Willie Best's Charlie is nowhere in sight, so that Cabot and Margie can be trapped together on the stalled elevator. Actor Bob Nichols (1924–2013) made multiple *Margie* appearances, whenever a plot called for a slightly weak-willed, nerdy man.

"Margie's Career" (October 11, 1952)

Writers: Frank Fox, G. Carleton Brown. *Director*: Hal Yates.
Cast: Don Hayden (*Freddie Wilson*), Edwin Max (*Danny*), Ben Weldon [Welden] (*Harry*), Ben Cameron (*Mitch*), Jack Lomas (*Notes*), Doris Fulton (*Dancer*)

Summary: Convinced she's "star material," Margie launches a singing career, landing her first job in a dive called the Big Dipper Club. Vern and Freddie conspire to give her a scare by hiring Freddie's actor friend Harry to impersonate a gangster. When Vern shows up to save the day, he unwittingly tangles with the real hoodlum who owns the club.

Notes: This is the first episode to make notable use of Gale's singing voice, which earned her a recording contract during the show's run. Here she sings "Ballin' the Jack."

"Vern Needs a Rest" (October 18, 1952)

Writers: Frank Fox, G. Carleton Brown. *Director*: Hal Yates.
Cast: Clarence Kolb (*George Honeywell*), Don Hayden (*Freddie Wilson*), Lucien Littlefield (*Harry, the Janitor*), Emory Parnell (*Trimble*), Franz Roehm (*Cobbler*), Sydney Mason (*Doctor*), Bobby Watson (*Brannigan*), Willie Best (*Charlie*)

Summary: Wanting a Florida vacation, Margie sets out to convince her father he's exhausted from overwork. Thanks to the shoes she has weighted down with lead, the fluctuating temperatures she arranges in the Albright apartment, and a ventriloquist with a talking dog act, Vern soon begins to believe her. But then he wises up to her tricks and decides to convince her she's driven him over the edge for real.

Note: Character actor Emory Parnell (1892–1979) became one of the show's more frequently used guest players, ultimately racking up five appearances.

"Missing Link" (October 25, 1952)

Writers: Frank Fox, G. Carleton Brown. *Director*: Hal Yates.

Cast: George Givot (*Willie Walker*), Don Hayden (*Freddie Wilson*), Frank Jares (*Sir MacGregor*), Dick Elliott (*Edward Kinka*), Herb Vigran (*Toomey*), Frank Scannell (*First Reporter*), Ralph Brooke (*Second Reporter*)

Summary: Margie has $400 to invest, but finds her father's financial advice too conservative. Wanting a quick return, she allows herself to be talked into buying controlling interest in wrestler Willie Walker. Advised that wrestlers need a promotional gimmick, Margie bills him as "The Missing Link," straight from the wilds of the jungle. Exploiting Willie's one known weak spot, Vern conspires to make Margie's scheme a losing proposition.

Notes: Actor George Givot, seen previously in "Insurance," makes his second *Margie* appearance as a dopey wrestler. According to *Daily Variety* (October 9, 1952), Gale was hurt while filming this episode "when assistant director Nate Watt, indicating to audience of extras the ref's count, accidentally brought his fist down on her, scoring a kayo." Allowed to rest for a couple of hours, and treated by a doctor, she was able to resume work.

"Blonde Margie" (November 1, 1952)

Writers: Rik Vollaerts, George Carleton Brown. *Director*: Hal Yates.

Cast: Clarence Kolb (*George Honeywell*), Hillary Brooke (*Roberta Townsend*), Don Hayden (*Freddie Wilson*), Gertrude Hoffmann (*Mrs. Odetts*), Angela Stevens (*Nancy*), Brad Johnson (*Rocky*), Rodney Bell (*Waiter*)

Summary: When Vern refuses to take Margie on a business trip, she threatens to marry Freddie while he's gone. Mr. Honeywell recruits his niece, an aspiring actress, to pose as a showgirl who can come between Freddie and Margie. Learning of the plot against her, Margie dons a blonde wig and takes the place of the interloper.

Notes: This episode is completely outlandish—and quite funny. It asks us to believe that Freddie can't recognize his own girlfriend once she puts on a wig, even with his face inches from hers. The episode, which features all the cast regulars except for Willie Best's Charlie, is an especially good showcase for Don Hayden.

"Who's Married?" (January 1, 1953)

Writers: Frank Fox, G. Carleton Brown. *Director*: Hal Yates.

Cast: Hillary Brooke (*Roberta Townsend*), Don Hayden (*Freddie Wilson*), Gertrude Hoffmann (*Mrs. Odetts*), Jack Rice (*Personnel Man*), Paul Maxey (*Peterson*), Fred Sherman (*Clerk*), Ralph Brooke (*Investigator*), Willie Best (*Charlie*)

Summary: Angry that Freddie has once again lost his job (in a pickle factory), Vern decrees that he can no longer see Margie until he's been steadily employed for three months. Vern's new client Mr. Peterson is hiring, and prefers to employ married men. As a result of some misunderstandings, Vern thinks Margie and Freddie are secretly married and expecting their first child. Margie, on the other hand, thinks it's her dad and Roberta who deserve the congratulations.

Notes: Character actor Paul Maxey, seen here as Mr. Peterson, had a recurring role on another popular sitcom of the 1950s, *The People's Choice*. He quickly became a favorite of the *Margie* producers, appearing in three more episodes before the year was out, and another in the final season. He also played a minor role in Gale's film *Let's Go Collegiate*. The series returned to CBS with this installment.

"New Neighbor" (January 8, 1953)

Writers: Frank Fox, G. Carleton Brown. Director: Hal Yates.
Cast: Clarence Kolb (*George Honeywell*), Gertrude Hoffmann (*Mrs. Odetts*), John Hubbard (*Harvey Lane*), George Meader (*Mr. Todd*), Barbara Hill (*Betty*), Willie Best (*Charlie*)

Summary: While Vern is out of town, Mr. Honeywell arranges for their new client, Harvey Lane, to rent the apartment above the Albrights. Coming home early, Vern shares Margie's irritation over their noisy new neighbor, and they launch into a war of retaliatory noise. When Margie and Mr. Lane meet at the Honeywell and Todd office, she's horrified to realize he's the "ignorant ignoramus" upstairs that she and her father have been tormenting.

Notes: This episode features a rare appearance by the "Todd" half of Honeywell and Todd. Actor John Hubbard (1914–1988), who was directed by Hal Roach, Sr., in the film comedy *Turnabout* (1940), became a favorite *Margie* player, usually cast as a debonair, slightly older love interest for Gale.

"The Motorcycle Cop" (January 15, 1953)

Writers: Frank Fox, G. Carleton Brown. Director: Hal Yates.
Cast: Richard Martin (*Sgt. Albert Tyrell*), Jack Rutherford (*Chief Carlin*), Jack Wilson (*Barney*), James Parnell (*Motor Cop*)

Summary: Appointed to head a citizens' commission on crime control, Vern warns Margie to stay out of any trouble that might cause embarrassing publicity. When a handsome young motorcycle officer gives her a speeding ticket, and asks Margie for a date, she accepts in hopes he'll dismiss the ticket. Margie's determination to prove Sgt. Tyrell's speedometer is inaccurate lands her in the Police Academy locker room, where she's drafted to take part in a judo demonstration for a visiting Vern.

"The Indians" (January 22, 1953)

Writers: Frank Gill, Jr., G. Carleton Brown. Director: Hal Yates.
Cast: Hillary Brooke (*Roberta Townsend*), Alf Kjellin (*Will Solensten*), Clarence Kolb (*George Honeywell*), El Brendell [Brendel] (*Olaf Lundstrom*), Gertrude Hoffmann (*Mrs. Odetts*), Don Hayden (*Freddie Wilson*), Charles Cane (*Desk Sergeant*)

Summary: Vern and Mr. Honeywell court a dignified Swedish businessman, Olaf Lundstrom, as a prospective client, and want to keep him far away from Margie. Against

Roberta's advice, they hire a young actor to impersonate Mr. Lundstrom, to trick Margie, leading the real client to wonder why this impostor is posing as him. When the fake client tells Margie he wants to meet some American Indians, she promises to introduce him to a tribe that lives in Central Park, whose members happen to resemble her father, her friends and even the real Mr. Lundstrom, incognito.

Note: Dialect comedian El Brendel (1890–1964) was a vaudeville veteran who played comic Swedish-accented roles in numerous films of the 1930s and 1940s. Alf Kjellin (1920–1988), seen as the phony Mr. Lundstrom, is better known as a busy film and television director whose credits include *Ice Station Zebra,* as well as multiple episodes of *Hawaii Five-O, The Waltons* and other popular series.

"The Two Lieutenants" (January 29, 1953)

> *Writers*: Frank Fox, G. Carleton Brown. *Director*: Hal Yates.
> *Cast*: Gertrude Hoffmann (*Mrs. Odetts*), Chris Drake (*Lt. Howard Allen*), George Nader (*Lt. Ralph Brooks*), Don Hayden (*Freddie Wilson*)

Summary: Mrs. Odetts confesses to Margie that she's been corresponding with a serviceman, using Margie's name and picture. Margie reluctantly agrees to meet with Lt. Brooks during his visit to New York, unaware that another of Mrs. Odetts' military pen pals will turn up at the same time. Faced with two men wanting to marry her, Margie decides to invite them both to dinner, where she will convince them she is the last woman they'd want as a wife.

Note: Actor George Nader (1921–2002) would be a Universal contract player during the 1950s, and also starred in the low-budget cult film *Robot Monster*.

> *Quote:* FREDDIE: We're going steady, aren't we?
> MARGIE: You may be going steady. I'm dating at least five other fellows!

"Hollywood Trip" (February 5, 1953)

> *Writers*: Frank Fox, G. Carleton Brown. *Director*: Hal Yates.
> *Cast*: Gertrude Hoffmann (*Mrs. Odetts*), Fritz Feld (*Andre Duprez*), Walter Wolf [Woolf] King (*Van Ness*), Larry Carr (*Jack Winslow*), Jim Bannon (*Dead Eye*), John Close (*Assistant Director*), Helene Hayden (*Trapeze Girl*)

Summary: Planning a trip to Hollywood, where he is closing a lucrative deal involving a movie studio, Vern reluctantly agrees to take Margie along, with Mrs. Odetts as her chaperone. At the Rovan Pictures studios, Margie manages to get tour guide Jack Winslow fired, and disrupts the production of temperamental director Andre Duprez's film. Conspiring with the studio boss and Jack, Vern arranges for Margie to be "discovered" and cast in a role she'll never forget.

Notes: Character actor Fritz Feld (1900–1993) brings his usual brio (and his trademark "pop") to the role of the flamboyant director. The use of a stunt person, and a clown costume, allows 81-year-old Gertrude Hoffmann's character to do some lively bouncing on a trampoline.

> *Quote:* MRS. ODETTS (to Margie, as they prepare to hop onto a borrowed scooter): Can you drive one of these things?
> MARGIE: We'll know in a minute.

"Hillbilly Margie" (February 12, 1953)

Writers: Elwood Ullman, Edward Bernds. *Director*: Hal Yates.

Cast: Clarence Kolb (*George Honeywell*), Charles Halton (*Carruthers*), Bob Easton (*Luke Tolliver*), John Dierkes (*Paw Tolliver*), Virginia Rose (*Ellie Mae*), Roscoe Ates (*Zeke*), Nora Busch (*Grammaw*), William McCormick (*McGrew*)

Summary: Some crucial shares of stock are in the possession of the Tollivers, a hillbilly family from the remote town of Squirrel Gap. Sent by Mr. Honeywell to close the deal, Vern goes along with Margie's suggestion that they dress and talk like the locals in order to fit in. The Tollivers take a liking to the Albrights and pay them a return visit in New York, where Margie revamps the apartment to make them feel at home.

Notes: Actor Robert Easton (1930–2011), seen here as the Tollivers' hayseed son, parlayed his gift for accents into a successful career as a dialect coach. Note that, nearly ten years before *The Beverly Hillbillies*, the daughter of the family is known as Ellie Mae.

"Hypochondriac" (February 19, 1953)

Writers: Frank Fox, G. Carleton Brown. *Director*: Hal Yates.

Cast: Robert Nichols (*William Apperson*), Gertrude Hoffmann (*Mrs. Odetts*), Mira McKinney (*Mrs. Apperson*), Lyle Latell (*Lee Bradford*), Joanne Jordan (*Miss Sherman*)

Summary: Honeywell and Todd's prospective client is a young man who's been turned into a hypochondriac by his grandmother, and convinced he's too sickly to manage a business career. To persuade Mr. Apperson his fears are exaggerated, Margie casts herself as Mrs. Odetts' granddaughter Clarice, who has a whole laundry list of ailments and symptoms. When he realizes Margie has tricked him, Apperson enlists Vern's help in giving her a taste of her own medicine.

"Cry Wolf" (February 26, 1953)

Writers: Alan Woods, John Kohn. *Director*: Hal Yates.

Cast: Gordon Jones (*Tex Mulloy*), Herb Vigran (*E. Thomas Grant*), Don Hayden (*Freddie Wilson*), John War Eagle (*Indian*), Bill Hale (*Cowboy*)

Summary: When Vern refuses to take Margie along on his trip to Mexico, she hires a publicity agent to spread the word that she's dating playboy Tex Mulloy, a Texas oil millionaire. The constant stream of flowers and gifts arriving the next day convinces Vern that his daughter had a raucous night on the town, but a cash bribe elicits the truth from her publicist. Calling Margie's bluff, Vern arranges for an actor to impersonate her suitor and arrive at the apartment to claim his "filly."

"Homely Margie" (March 5, 1953)

Writers: Jack Krutcher, G. Carleton Brown. *Director*: Hal Yates.

Cast: Clarence Kolb (*George Honeywell*), Don Hayden (*Freddie Wilson*), William Ching (*Joe Sparks*), Anne O'Neal (*Miss Michaels*), Paul Wexler (*Bill Houseman*)

Summary: To prevent Margie from meeting the handsome son of a client, Vern shows the young man a retouched photo that makes his daughter look quite unappealing. When he expresses a willingness to meet her anyway, Vern is forced to enlist Margie's help in carrying out the gag. Inventing her "cousin Carolyn from Philadelphia" so that she can ditch the disguise and date him, Margie is trapped when her new beau decides to help Vern's "ugly daughter" by finding her an equally drab guy through a dating service.

Notes: Don Hayden's Freddie has an active role in this episode, including a brief stint in drag. This episode features two uses of "the Margie gurgle."

"Trapped Freddie" (March 12, 1953)

Writers: Frank Fox, G. Carleton Brown. *Director*: Hal Yates.

Cast: Don Hayden (*Freddie Wilson*), Hillary Brooke (*Roberta Townsend*), Willie Best (*Charlie*)

Summary: After Freddie keeps Margie out past her curfew, Vern tells his daughter she won't get her new convertible unless she stays away from her boyfriend for one month. Then Vern comes home early from work, sick with the flu, on the afternoon Freddie is paying an unauthorized visit. With the help of some sedatives, Margie tries to keep her dad from discovering Freddie hidden in the apartment.

Note: This episode features only the recurring cast, no guest players.

"Vern, the Failure" (March 19, 1953)

Writers: Frank Fox, G. Carleton Brown. *Director*: Hal Yates.

Cast: George Meader (*Mr. Todd*), Emory Parnell (*Mr. Staub*), Leo Britt (*Doctor*), Don Hayden (*Freddie Wilson*), Helene Hayden (*Waitress*), Claudette Thornton (*Secretary*)

Summary: Attending his class reunion makes Vern feel unsuccessful, because he has not attained the presidency of his company. Margie tries to make Vern assert himself by arranging for him to receive a phony job offer from a rival firm, Conway and Staub. When the gag backfires, costing Vern his job, Margie must impersonate Vern's elderly British client in order to show how valuable he is to Honeywell and Todd.

Note: This episode finds George Meader playing a substantial role as the seldom-seen Mr. Todd, while Clarence Kolb's Mr. Honeywell is nowhere in sight.

"Stock Control" (March 26, 1953)

Writers: Frank Gill, Jr., G. Carleton Brown. *Director*: Hal Yates.

Cast: Don Hayden (*Freddie Wilson*), Clarence Kolb (*George Honeywell*), Thurston Hall (*Jack Reynolds*), William E. Green (*Mr. Perrott*), Willie Best (*Charlie*)

Summary: Vern lives to regret placing Margie in charge of their household finances, when she slips up on a few details—like paying the phone bill. While Margie struggles to demonstrate that she has a head for business, Freddie proudly announces his new job with Reynolds and Perrott, a rival firm to Honeywell and Todd. The reason for Mr. Reynolds' hiring Freddie becomes clear when Margie realizes that both companies are competing for stock in Amalgamated Chemical—and she happens to own 100 shares.

Note: Not unlike Lucy Ricardo, Margie has an unusual accounting system, which includes a box labeled PMBCA ("Possible Mistake—Better Check Again").

"Buried Treasure" (April 2, 1953)

Writers: Alan Woods, John Kohn. *Director*: Hal Yates.

Cast: George Meader (*Mr. Todd*), Ric Roman (*Lefty*), Paul E. Burns (*Mailman*), Joe Devlin (*Joe*)

Summary: Vern is looking forward to a relaxing two-week vacation on Long Island, but after a few days Margie is bored and wants to go home. Vern's phony treasure map, and rented Spanish doubloon, convince Margie there is buried treasure to be found. Margie ropes in Mr. Todd, who does find a cache of jewels on the property. Two gangsters show up unexpectedly and want it for themselves.

Notes: According to Gale Storm, her stunt double was seriously injured filming this episode's climactic scene. The script called for Margie to drop from a skylight and throw a net around the two bad guys, but the stuntwoman broke her back in the fall. Once again, George Meader appears as Mr. Todd in the absence of Clarence Kolb's Mr. Honeywell.

"The Golf Game" (April 9, 1953)

Writers: Frank Gill, Jr., G. Carleton Brown. *Director*: Hal Yates.
Cast: Don Hayden (*Freddie Wilson*), Clarence Kolb (*George Honeywell*), Herbert Heyes (*Burl Konkle*), Carlo Tricoli (*Harrison*)

Summary: Margie schemes to get Freddie a job at Honeywell and Todd by showing he can bring in a prospective client who's a renowned golfer. By hiring a performer and his trained dog, who retrieves and places balls on command, Margie helps Freddie impress Mr. Honeywell. But when Vern's boss decides that what the firm needs is "young blood," Margie sets out to make her discouraged father an even better golfer than her boyfriend.

"They Also Serve" (April 16, 1953)

Writer: Nathaniel Curtis. *Director*: Nate Watt.
Cast: Ray Montgomery (*Tom Chandler*), Clarence Kolb (*George Honeywell*), John Eldredge (*Charles Chandler*), Queenie Smith (*Emily Chandler*), Douglas Wood (*J.R. Johnson*), Freddie Sherman (*Hotel Clerk*)

Summary: Sent out of town for meetings with important client J.R. Johnson, Vern is dismayed to learn that his hotel reservations have been canceled. In need of housing, Vern and Margie take temporary domestic jobs as butler and cook in the nearby Chandler household. Unfortunately, the Chandlers' visiting cousin proves to be none other than Johnson. The Albrights are forced to keep up their servant charade, while Honeywell is pressured to replace the "absent" Vern with an ambitious member of the Chandler family.

Notes: This is a rare episode not directed by Hal Yates; here, series assistant director Nate Watt (1889–1968) takes the reins, with Edward J. Babille filling the assistant slot. Character actress Queenie Smith has some amusing moments as daffy Cousin Emily, who's prone to falling in love with butlers, and takes an immediate shine to Vern.

Quote: JOHNSON (upon discovering Vern's true identity): You mean to tell me that *you're* Vern Albright?
VERN: I didn't *mean* to tell you…

"The Newlyweds" (April 23, 1953)

Writers: G. Carleton Brown, Frank Fox, Audrey Lives. *Director*: Hal Yates.
Cast: Hillary Brooke (*Roberta Townsend*), George Nader (*Lt. Ralph Brooks*), Gloria Henry (*Norma Calkins*), Robert Neil (*Richard Calkins*)

Summary: Always-helpful Margie makes the mistake of putting the idea of jealousy into the heads of young newlyweds Dick and Norma Calkins. The resulting arguments—and smashed objects—have the tenth floor in an uproar, just as Margie is expecting a visit from her Marine beau. Misunderstanding builds upon misunderstanding until an annoyed Dick decides to give Margie, Vern and Roberta a taste of their own medicine.

Note: This episode introduces the recurring characters of the Calkins, who will be seen again a few weeks later in "Mrs. Margie Calkins." George Nader reprises his role as Margie's Marine beau. Gloria Henry (born 1923) played a featured role in Gale's film *Al Jennings of Oklahoma*.

"To Health with Yoga" (April 30, 1953)

Writers: Alan Woods, John Kohn. *Director*: Hal Yates.
Cast: Tom Browne Henry (*Professor Ambrose*), Hillary Brooke (*Roberta Townsend*), Don Hayden (*Freddie Wilson*), Betty Finley (*Cashier*)

Summary: Vern wants Professor Ambrose, who's written a bestselling book on yoga, as a client; Margie wants him to speak at her book club. Because the professor admits he's lonely in New York and plans to leave, Margie and Roberta pose as denizens of his home town, Elm Grove, Missouri. When both Vern and Margie show up at the vegetarian cafeteria where the professor lunches, she tries to keep her father from getting wise to her latest escapade.

Notes: Not one of the series' stronger episodes, this one ekes out a few laughs by having Margie, Roberta and Freddie assume awkward yoga poses, and by poking fun at a vegetarian diet, which is treated as quite exotic: The "Garden of Eden Special" at the professor's favorite restaurant consists of "homogenized prunes on a steamed spinach leaf, smothered with fig whip."

"Young Vern" (May 7, 1953)

Writers: G. Carleton Brown, Frank Fox, Audrey Lives. *Director*: Hal Yates.
Cast: Clarence Kolb (*George Honeywell*), Jacqueline Du Val (*Suzanne Gilbert*), Alphonse Martell (*Joe*), Pepi Lenzi (*Francois*), Willie Best (*Charlie*)

Summary: Hearing that a vacationing Roberta went dancing with a man "39 years old, with wavy red hair" makes Vern feel old. Margie tries to show him otherwise by having his hair dyed black, and asking her visiting young friend Suzanne to pretend she has fallen in love with him. When Vern turns the tables by announcing his plans to marry Suzanne, Margie counterattacks by "confessing" her long-standing crush on Mr. Honeywell.

Note: According to this script, Mr. Honeywell is 76 years old. Actor Clarence Kolb was a year away from his 80th birthday.

"A Horse on Vern" (May 14, 1953)

Writers: G. Carleton Brown, Frank Fox, Audrey Lives. *Director*: Hal Yates.
Cast: George O'Hanlon (*Bob Porter*), Harry Lauter (*Don Hadley*), Clarence Kolb (*George Honeywell*), Don Hayden (*Freddie Wilson*), Jack Rutherford (*Mr. MacAllister*), Willie Best (*Charlie*), "King" (*Horse*)

Summary: To impress Don, the newspaper reporter she's dating, Margie calls him with a real scoop: There's a horse roaming the tenth floor of the Carlton Arms. Unfortunately for her, the horse, which vanishes as soon as Don and his photographer Bob show up, was planted by Vern and Freddie, hoping to derail Margie's new relationship. To get even, Margie pretends that the incident has left her mentally unhinged and in need of a psychiatrist (impersonated by Bob) who assures Vern that his daughter can be cured—if her father does everything the doctor says.

Notes: Willie Best, as Charlie, has some funny reactions to the visiting horse, while Charles Farrell demonstrates that Vern can adopt Margie's gurgle in moments of crisis.

"Girl Against the World" (May 21, 1953)

>*Writers*: G. Carleton Brown, Frank Fox, Audrey Lives. *Director*: Hal Yates.
>*Cast*: Don Hayden (*Freddie Wilson*), Gertrude Hoffmann (*Mrs. Odetts*), Robert Lowery (*George Schuck*)

Summary: Freddie has written a play, *Girl Against the World,* but encounters nothing but rejection. When Vern refuses to show the script to his new client, theatrical producer George Schuck, Margie and her friends stage a real-life version that begins outside the producer's office door. Taking pity on "Gwendolyn," the impoverished heroine Margie is playing, Schuck sets her up in business with a hot dog stand, so that she can support her shoplifting grandmother (Mrs. Odetts) and delinquent cousin (Freddie). When Vern exposes Margie's game, he and Schuck decide to stage a little impromptu drama of their own.

Note: Guest player Robert Lowery (1913–1971) previously appeared with Gale in three films of the 1940s.

>*Quote:* VERN (assessing Freddie's play): It's great—right up to where it says "The curtain rises."

"Mrs. Margie Calkins" (May 28, 1953)

>*Writers*: G. Carleton Brown, Frank Fox, Audrey Lives. *Director*: Hal Yates.
>*Cast*: Hillary Brooke (*Roberta Townsend*), Robert Neil (*Richard Calkins*), Gloria Henry (*Norma Calkins*), Tracey Roberts (*Hazel Miller*), Don Hayden (*Freddie Wilson*), Willie Best (*Charlie*)

Summary: The Albrights' neighbor, young newlywed Richard Calkins, panics when his ex-girlfriend Hazel threatens to pay a visit and tell his wife Norma all about their past together. Adapting the plot of a movie Vern saw, Margie agrees to pose as Mrs. Calkins, while her father is charged with keeping Norma busy. "Mrs. Calkins," as played by Margie, succeeds in keeping the peace—until Hazel decides to take a vacant apartment in the building.

Note: We learn that Freddie gets ideas for his flowery love letters to Margie from the same book that Richard Calkins uses.

>*Quote*: MARGIE (to Richard): What does Hazel know that Norma doesn't know that Hazel's going to make sure that Norma does?

"Vern's New Girlfriend" (June 4, 1953)

>*Writers*: Robert Raff, Jim Bullock. *Director*: Hal Yates.
>*Cast*: Joan Shawlee (*Sandra Fleming*), Hillary Brooke (*Roberta Townsend*), Clarence Kolb (*George Honeywell*), Don Hayden (*Freddie Wilson*), Keith McConnell (*Carlton*)

Summary: Margie's dismayed to learn that Vern has fallen head over heels for glamorous three-time divorcee Sandra Fleming. With the help of Roberta, Mr. Honeywell and Freddie, Margie sets out to show her father that his new flame is a gold digger who would lose interest if she believed he no longer had any money.

Notes: This episode was scripted by two *Margie* crew members, music editor Robert Raff and sound editor Jim Bullock. Although early episodes had Margie opposed to her father's relationship with Roberta, here she's completely supportive when she believes (wrongly) that they might be getting married.

"Father's Little Helper" (June 11, 1953)

Writers: Frank Fox, G. Carleton Brown, Audrey Lives. *Director*: Hal Yates.

Cast: Gertrude Hoffmann (*Mrs. Odetts*), Clarence Kolb (*George Honeywell*), Andrew Tombes (*Mr. Hawkes*), Gertrude Graner (*Mrs. Hawkes*), Dian Fauntelle (*Miss Hansen*)

Summary: Greedy Mr. Honeywell tries to cut Vern out of a lucrative deal with Mr. and Mrs. Hawkes from Texas. When Margie learns that the Hawkeses are swindlers, selling rights to land that belongs to the Indians, she and Mrs. Odetts plan an uprising to take place in Mr. Honeywell's office.

Note: According to this script, Mrs. Odetts is part-Indian, the daughter of a Cherokee woman and a Union Pacific Railroad engineer.

Quote: MARGIE (explaining her plan to Vern): Don't you see, Dad, it's simple psychology.
VERN: Well, get yourself another psycho!

"Delinquent Margie" (June 18, 1953)

Writers: Alan Woods, John Kohn. *Director*: Hal Yates.

Cast: John Hubbard (*Bill Bronson*), Gertrude Hoffmann (*Mrs. Odetts*), Clarence Kolb (*George Honeywell*), Dick Cogan (*Car Salesman*)

Summary: Wanting $6000 from her trust fund to buy a new convertible, Mrs. Odetts convinces her conservative banker Mr. Bronson that she needs the money to help a young friend settle her gambling debt. Margie plays the role so convincingly that Mr. Bronson thinks Vern is the gangster who's threatening her, and punches him—twice. Both men are in for a surprise when Mr. Bronson turns up at Honeywell and Todd to discuss a business deal.

Note: This episode is a fun showcase for Gertrude Hoffmann's Mrs. Odetts, who doesn't think her convertible's top speed of 130 MPH is sufficient, and after buying it decides what she really needs is her own plane.

"A Mother for Vern" (June 25, 1953)

Writers: Alan Woods, John Kohn. *Director*: Hal Yates.

Cast: Florence Bates (*Lady Franklin*), Robert Edgecomb (*Charles Franklin*), Gertrude Hoffmann (*Mrs. Odetts*), Clarence Kolb (*George Honeywell*), Barbara Hill (*Secretary*)

Summary: Margie wants Vern's socially prominent client, Lady Franklin, to give her tickets to a ritzy cotillion ball. Lady Franklin decides to take her investment business to a rival firm, because of her friendship with the account executive's mother. Margie promptly converts herself into Vern's mother, who shows Lady Franklin a thing or two about having fun at any age.

Note: This was Florence Bates' second appearance in the series as a stuffy matron.

"Freddie's Formula" (July 2, 1953)

Writers: G. Carleton Brown, Frank Fox, Audrey Lives. *Director*: Hal Yates.

Cast: Norma Varden (*Emily Laneheim*), Don Hayden (*Freddie Wilson*), Clarence Kolb (*George Honeywell*), Charles Hall (*Delivery Man*), Willie Best (*Charlie*), William Frambes (*Bob Spaulding*), Ted Stanhope (*Clerk*), Jackie Park (*Girl*)

Summary: Freddie's ready to go into business with his "miracle hair dye." Margie and her boyfriend try out the formula on what they believe is a stray cat. It's actually Sir Hugo, a show animal that belongs to wealthy Miss Laneheim. Initially angry, Miss Laneheim sees that the dye works well, leading Honeywell to propose a business deal that will be lucrative for Freddie. First, however, he and Margie mix up a second batch, wanting to make sure the dye works on human hair. The mixture proves to have a serious side effect.

Notes: Fired yet again, Vern visits the local unemployment office, where he's shown the ropes by Freddie, who's practically a fixture there.

"The Truck Driver" (July 9, 1953)

Writers: G. Carleton Brown, Frank Fox, Audrey Lives. *Director*: Hal Yates.

Cast: Robert Keys (*Buck Foster*), Clarence Kolb (*George Honeywell*), Gertrude Hoffmann (*Mrs. Odetts*), Paul Maxey (*Bennsen*), Willie Best (*Charlie*)

Summary: A young truck driver stages a minor fender-bender in order to get Margie's name and number. Warned by Mr. Honeywell that he could be a fortune hunter, Margie decides to convince him that she and her father are quite poor. Unbeknownst to them, Buck Foster is actually the president of a trucking company, as well as the man with whom Mr. Honeywell hopes to close a lucrative deal.

Note: This is a slapstick-rich episode, highlighted by Vern and Buck's messy encounter with a broken water pipe in Mrs. Odetts' apartment and the impromptu use of a paint sprayer.

"Margie's Helping Hand" (July 16, 1953)

Writers: G. Carleton Brown, Frank Fox, Audrey Lives. *Director*: Hal Yates.

Cast: Clarence Kolb (*George Honeywell*), Don Hayden (*Freddie Wilson*)

Summary: Would-be do-gooder Margie takes an ad in the local newspaper, offering help to people in dire circumstances. What she gets for her trouble is a bootlegger posing as an inventor who makes fine perfume from rye and barley. Claiming a 600 percent profit margin, Oliver Westcott's deal even attracts the attention of Mr. Honeywell and a wealthy client—not to mention the police, who find his makeshift still set up at the Albrights' apartment.

Note: The accessible print of this episode has the wrong closing credits sequence attached, one taken from the later episode "Tugboat Margie." It credits actors, including Roy Roberts, who are not seen in this segment.

Quote: VERN: Margie, it's about time that you learn to appreciate money.

MARGIE: Oh, I do appreciate it. Give me some, and watch my eyes light up!

"Double Trouble" (July 23, 1953)

    Writers: Alan Woods, John Kohn. *Director*: Hal Yates.

    Cast: Gustaf Unger (*Tom Carter*), Bertel Unger (*Jerry Carter*), Clarence Kolb (*George Honeywell*), Gertrude Hoffmann (*Mrs. Odetts*)

Summary: Refusing to take Margie on his business trip to South America, Vern hires an actor, Tom Carter, to romance his daughter so that she won't mind staying behind. Margie, wanting to make her father afraid to leave her in New York, has the same idea, and unwittingly hires Tom's twin brother. Once she realizes that there are two Mr. Carters, Margie puts them both to work, trying to convince Vern he's having a breakdown and needs her to nurse him on the South American trip.

Notes: This season finale uses a clever twist on the "lookalike twin" gimmick, climaxing in a funny scene where the two brothers impersonate every single employee of the restaurant where Vern and Margie are having dinner. Given the logistics of the fast-paced episode, the producers opted to use twin actors, rather than rely on split-screen special effects. The audience's enthusiastic response, as recorded on the episode's laugh track, occasionally drowns out bits of dialogue.

Season Three

Beginning with this season, the closing credits list the names of featured actors, but not the characters they played. Where a definite identification could not be made, the names are presented at the end of the cast list, following a semi-colon.

"A Present for Dad" (September 2, 1953)

    Writers: Frank Fox, G. Carleton Brown, Audrey Lives. *Director*: Hal Yates.

    Cast: Don Hayden (*Freddie Wilson*), Gertrude Hoffmann (*Mrs. Odetts*), Clarence Kolb (*George Honeywell*), Willie Best (*Charlie*); Eugene Borden, John Mylong

Summary: Wanting a unique birthday gift for Vern, Margie decides to have her portrait painted. When Vern learns that Mrs. Odetts borrowed $1500 (the artist's fee) on Margie's behalf, he concludes that his daughter is in trouble. Jumping to the conclusion that the artist, Pierre Duval, is his daughter's new boyfriend, Vern decides she'd be safer married to Freddie.

Notes: This script revives a routine seen in previous episodes, where Vern pretends to be Margie's mom so that she can confide a problem she doesn't dare tell Dad. Comic highlights include Mrs. Odetts' impromptu gun safety lesson, which results in a hole in the wall of Vern's bedroom, plus Freddie once again making the plaintive complaint to camera, "This place confuses me!"

With this installment, the show began its Wednesday night run on NBC, sponsored by the Scott Paper Company. Of this season opener, *Variety* (September 11, 1953) said, "Miss Storm is spritely and charming ... [I]nitialer ... offers promise for regular entertainment later."

"Campus Homecoming" (September 9, 1953)

    Writer: Frank Gill, Jr. *Director*: Hal Yates.

    Cast: Cliff Ferre (*Roger Crane*), Douglas Wood (*Dean Owens*), Emory Parnell (*Curly*

Crane), Charles Meredith (*Cabot*), Jill [Jil] Jarmyn (*Sue Anders*), John Smith (*Fraternity Brother*), Bob Carraher (*Policeman*)

Summary: Margie wants to accompany Vern on his college homecoming visit, but he tells her it is purely a business trip. Snagging herself a date with the current president of Kappa Chi, Vern's old fraternity, she sees her dad and his friends (class of '22) whooping it up. Margie and her friends decide to reenact Vern's famous prank of years earlier, putting a bull in the dean's bedroom, unaware that her father's pals have had the same idea.

Notes: According to this script, Vern's college nickname was "Scooter." Improbably, the college dean from some 30 years earlier still holds the same position. This is an early credit for actor John Smith (1931–1995), who went go on to star on TV's *Laramie*. He made a second appearance on *Margie* during its final season.

Quote: VERN (describing Freddie): "Of all the irresponsible morons running around loose, that crewcut is the large economy size!"

"A Day at the Beach" (September 16, 1953)

Writers: Alan Woods, John Kohn. *Director*: Hal Yates.
Cast: Gertrude Hoffmann (*Mrs. Odetts*), Clarence Kolb (*George Honeywell*), Kristine Miller (*Norma Fairbanks*), George Wallace (*Bruce, the Lifeguard*), Henry Kulky (*Tough Guy*), Crystal Reeves (*Receptionist*), Stephen Wooten [Wootton] (*Boy at Beach*)

Summary: After Margie persuades Vern to call in sick so that they can spend Wednesday at the beach, Mr. Honeywell receives a visit from pretty Norma Fairbanks, a potential client who doesn't approve of playboy executives. Thanks to Mrs. Odetts' loose lips, both his boss and his prospective client track Vern down at the beach, where Margie tries to help him save his job.

Notes: In this episode, we get reminiscences from Mrs. Odetts about her first, second and fourth husbands.

Quote: MRS. ODETTS (accused of being nosy): Mr. Honeywell, do you think all I do is peek through keyholes?
HONEYWELL: That, and an occasional transom or two.

"My Little Bookie" (September 23, 1953)

Writer: Frank Gill, Jr. *Director*: Hal Yates.
Cast: Don Hayden (*Freddie Wilson*), Gertrude Hoffmann (*Mrs. Odetts*), Clarence Kolb (*George Honeywell*), Katherine [Kathryn] Card (*Mrs. Seaton*), Murray Leonard (*Louie*), Willie Best (*Charlie*)

Summary: Trying to keep the bonus he received at work a secret, Vern tells Margie times are hard and his job is in jeopardy. After Mrs. Odetts talks about men who marry rich widows for their money, Margie fears her father is romancing client Mrs. Seaton. When "Fast-Buck Margie" and her friends pose as the members of a gambling ring headed by Vern, they succeed in convincing not only the staid Mrs. Seaton, but also unscrupulous gangster Louie the Torpedo.

Notes: Once again Margie is angling to get a new car. Hillary Brooke's character, Roberta, has been AWOL thus far this season, and her photo is no longer in display in Vern's office.

"Go North, Young Girl" (September 30, 1953)

Writer: Nathaniel Curtis. *Director*: Hal Yates.

Cast: Clarence Kolb (*George Honeywell*), Gertrude Hoffmann (*Mrs. Odetts*), Bob [Robert] Lowery (*Steve*), Dick Simmons (*Tom*), Brad Johnson (*Dick*), John Halloran (*Henderson*), Belle Mitchell (*Woman at Trading Post*)

Summary: Vern is looking forward to a two-week fishing trip in the Canadian woods with Mr. Honeywell, but Margie wants a vacation in Hawaii. Sure she won't like roughing it, Honeywell offers to pay for the Hawaiian trip if Margie lasts a week at the campsite. Prompted by Mrs. Odetts to look for handsome trappers, traders or Mounties, Margie manages to find one of each, and with their surreptitious help she lives it up in style in the wilderness.

Notes: Robert Lowery makes his second *Margie* appearance. This episode, coming only two weeks after one in which Vern claimed he seldom took time off, finds Mr. Honeywell uncharacteristically urging his employee to embark on a vacation.

"Margie, the Writer" (October 7, 1953)

Writers: Frank Fox, G. Carleton Brown. *Director*: Hal Yates.

Cast: Don Hayden (*Freddie Wilson*), Clarence Kolb (*George Honeywell*), Gertrude Hoffmann (*Mrs. Odetts*), Charles Evans (*Police Commissioner*), Crystal Reeves (*Betty*); Lou Nova, Frank Richards, Paul Newlan

Summary: Vern's latest scheme to keep Margie out of trouble involves persuading her to become a writer. Working on a mystery story, Margie plans a visit to a waterfront dive, the Buccaneer Saloon, for the purpose of "mingling with cutthroats and riffraff." Tipped off by Freddie, Vern rents out the place for the evening, giving it the atmosphere of a genteel tea room and discouraging Margie—until she learns she was played.

"My Little Clementine" (October 14, 1953)

Writers: Frank Fox, G. Carleton Brown. *Director*: Hal Yates.

Cast: Clarence Kolb (*George Honeywell*), Gertrude Hoffmann (*Mrs. Odetts*), James Brown (*Bill*)

Summary: Shortly after Vern refuses to help Margie get a job as a secretary at Honeywell and Todd, she is surprised by a visit from her distant cousin Clementine. Vern assumes the newcomer is just Margie in a wig and glasses, until Clementine proves herself surprisingly efficient as Honeywell's new secretary. Realizing that, for once, she's being blamed for something she didn't do, Margie conspires with Clementine to leave Vern and his boss in a state of hopeless confusion.

Notes: This clever script plays on not only Vern's, but the *audience's* awareness of Margie's usual shenanigans, turning the expectation upside down. With the help of some split-screen photography, Gale plays both roles. Clarence Kolb, as Honeywell, has a funny line that closes out this episode. Actor James Brown (1920–1992), seen here as Clementine's fiancé, was about a year away from being cast in the lead (two-legged) role in *The Adventures of Rin Tin Tin*. He had previously played a small role in Gale's film *Between Midnight and Dawn*.

"That's the Spirit" (October 21, 1953)

    Writers: Alan Woods, John Kohn. *Director*: Hal Yates.

    Cast: Clarence Kolb (*George Honeywell*), Gertrude Hoffmann (*Mrs. Odetts*), Theresa Tudor (*Princess Nadja*), Lucien Littlefield (*Ghost Albright*), Charles Cane (*Policeman*)

Summary: Mr. Honeywell is planning to bring another executive vice-president into the firm, and Margie is distressed to see that her father lacks the gumption to stand up to his boss. With help from a clairvoyant, Margie makes Vern believe that the spirits of his ancestors are urging him to be more aggressive. Catching on to his daughter's latest scheme, Vern employs a ghost of his own to turn the tables on Margie.

"Margie's Phantom Lover" (October 28, 1953)

    Writers: Frank Fox, Jr., George Carleton Brown. *Director*: Hal Yates.

    Cast: Clarence Kolb (*George Honeywell*), Rip Callahan (*Bill Davenport*), Russell Hicks (*DeWitt Davenport*), Crystal Reeves (*Betty*), Willie Best (*Charlie*)

Summary: When Vern is unable to dissuade Margie from attending an auto race out of town, Mr. Honeywell suggests distracting her with a secret admirer. Margie's mystery man claims to have met her at a Honeywell and Todd party, so she combs through the client list looking for him. When she connects by telephone with young playboy client Bill Davenport, he's only too happy to be "Bright Eyes," and Vern tries to avert an in-person meeting.

    Note: According to this episode, Honeywell and Todd's telephone number is Dunbar 3-6862.

"Margie's Baby" (November 4, 1953)

    Writers: Charles Hoffman, G. Carleton Brown. *Director*: Hal Yates.

    Cast: Don Hayden (*Freddie Wilson*), Clarence Kolb (*George Honeywell*), Gertrude Hoffmann (*Mrs. Odetts*), Paul Maxey (*Mr. Hailey*), Jill Jarmon [Jil Jarmyn] (*Lynn Hailey Clarke*), Olan Soule (*Accountant*), Willie Best (*Charlie*), Deborah Ann Farrell (*Baby Clarke*)

Summary: Margie's pal Lynn has been in hiding for several months, not wanting her disapproving father to know she's married and has a baby. When Mr. Hailey, a Honeywell and Todd client, turns up unexpectedly, Margie pretends the baby is hers, and enlists Mrs. Odetts' help in hiding her for a few days. When Hailey visits the Albrights' apartment, Margie asks him not to tell Vern about "her" baby. The client decides to help her out by getting her "husband" Freddie a job—at Honeywell and Todd.

    Note: Gale Storm wrote a friendly letter to the editor of *Time* (November 23, 1953) after the magazine published a photo of her with Deborah Ann Farrell, the baby seen in this episode; according to *Time*'s caption, the baby was Gale's. Gale wrote, "The baby who appeared in the photo with me wasn't mine but six-month-old Deborah Ann Farrell (no relation to Charley), who was featured on one of our programs. I certainly didn't mind, and am sure Deborah Ann didn't, but my boys seemed to resent an intruder."

"A Slight Misunderstanding" (November 11, 1953)

    Writers: Frank Fox, G. Carleton Brown. *Director*: Hal Yates.

    Cast: Don Hayden (*Freddie Wilson*), Scott Elliott (*Richard Calkins*), Gloria Henry (*Norma Calkins*), Byron Foulger (*Mr. Carson*), Willie Best (*Charlie*)

Summary: Dick Calkins thinks his wife Norma is taking him for granted, so Margie suggests that they make her jealous. The staged embrace between Dick and Margie is witnessed not by Norma, but by Vern, who decides he'll move his daughter to Connecticut to break up her new romance. Norma misunderstands Vern's attempt to tip her off, and assumes he's expressing his own passion for her.

Notes: Jealousy is once again the theme in the Calkins' third and final *Margie* appearance. Actor Robert Neil, reprising the role of Dick, has changed his professional name, and is now known as Scott Elliott.

"Vern's Secret Fishing Place" (November 18, 1953)

Writer: Earl Baldwin. *Director*: Hal Yates.

Cast: Don Hayden (*Freddie Wilson*), Clarence Kolb (*George Honeywell*), Thurston Hall (*Carl Garris*), Barbara Morrison (*Garris' Secretary*), Dian Fauntelle (*Betty*)

Summary: Mr. Honeywell promises Margie a mink stole, and a week's vacation for her father, if she can keep Vern in town for the weekend, and away from a fishing tournament in Vermont (Honeywell hopes to win it). Margie's initial plan, to persuade Vern he has a Saturday appointment with an important client, backfires when it develops that Mr. Garris, a fellow fisherman, wants to attend the tournament. Trying to keep Garris and her father closer to home, Margie arranges for the client to overhear a young couple (herself and Freddie) rave about Vern's secret "fisherman's paradise" just an hour outside New York City.

"Comedy of Terrors" (November 25, 1953)

Writers: Edward E. Seabrook, Homer McCoy. *Director*: Hal Yates.

Cast: Don Hayden (*Freddie Wilson*), Clarence Kolb (*George Honeywell*), Lorin Raker (*Sidney Maple*), Lyle Talbot (*John Branton*), Dick Wessell [Wessel] (*Mr. Haskell*), Lee Turnbull (*Gerald*), Alan Aric (*Humphrey*)

Summary: Margie is worried for Vern's safety after he serves as jury foreman at the trial of a gangster, who vows revenge. Dismissing her fears, Vern sneaks out of the house to meet with a wealthy new client, Mr. Maple. Freddie recruits his pals Gerald and Humphrey to stand guard over the Albright apartment, where they punch out the bodyguard Vern hired, an assistant district attorney sent by Mr. Honeywell, and the timid Mr. Maple.

Notes: In the epilogue, Vern shows off the December 1953 issue of *Cosmopolitan* magazine, which features a cover story on Gale Storm. This is the first *Margie* script for writers Seabrook and McCoy, whose contributions to the series are infrequent, but usually make for above average episodes.

"What's Cooking?" (December 2, 1953)

Writer: Earl Baldwin. *Director*: Hal Yates.

Cast: Don Hayden (*Freddie Wilson*), Clarence Kolb (*George Honeywell*), Thurston Hall (*Mr. Crater*), Barbara Morrison (*Gertrude*), Dian Fauntelle (*Betty*)

Summary: Freddie's new job selling cookware door to door gets off to a bad start when he makes a mess of a demonstration meal at the Albrights' house. When Mr. Honeywell needs a caterer for a business dinner at his apartment, Margie unwisely decides that Freddie and his bad-tempered colleague Gertrude should get the job—unaware that the client owns a rival company.

Note: Veteran character actor Thurston Hall (1882–1958), whose film career dated back to the silent era, made this guest appearance while playing a recurring role as a banker on TV's *Topper* (1953–55).

"Vern's Two Daughters" (December 9, 1953)

Writers: Frank Fox, G. Carleton Brown. *Director*: Hal Yates.

Cast: Clarence Kolb (*George Honeywell*), Hillary Brooke (*Roberta Townsend*), Gertrude Hoffmann (*Mrs. Odetts*), Craig Hill (*Charles Morgan, Jr.*), Claude Allister (*Winston*), Willie Best (*Charlie*)

Summary: Vern is opposed to Margie's visit to a house party at Princeton, until a handsome young client arrives in town eager to meet her. After reversing himself and urging Margie to take the trip, Vern persuades Roberta to pose as his daughter for the evening. Realizing a scheme is afoot, Margie comes back home and walks into Vern's carefully planned dinner party, introducing herself as his younger daughter, Helen.

Notes: This cleverly plotted episode by the series creators uses many of the elements of the classic French bedroom farce, with slamming doors as well as quickly timed exits and entrances, but adds a few novel elements, including five duck dinners to somehow be served at seven places in two different apartments. Actor Craig Hill (1926–2014) went on to star in the syndicated adventure series *Whirlybirds*.

"Chubby Little Margie" (December 16, 1953)

Writers: Frank Fox, G. Carleton Brown. *Director*: Hal Yates.

Cast: Mabel Paige (*Amy McKenna*), John Stephenson (*Bill Carlin, Jr.*), Willie Best (*Charlie*)

Summary: Margie is reluctant to break her date with Lt. Ralph Brooks so as to entertain Bill, the visiting son of a client, expecting him to look like his homely father. With the help of Mrs. Odetts' visiting sister, Margie makes herself obese so that the young man will reject her, but lives to regret it when Bill proves to be quite handsome. Letting Bill in on the joke, Vern fills Margie's fat suit with helium before the big dance, making her so "light on her feet" she's in danger of floating away.

Notes: Character actress Mabel Paige (1880–1954) appears as Mrs. Odetts' sister, who's just as eager to join in Margie's latest scheme. Longtime series writers Fox and Brown give this episode some continuity with previous segments. Although he doesn't appear here, Margie is anticipating her date with the character played by George Nader in "The Two Lieutenants." This script, which begins with a similar premise to that of "Margie's Sister Sally" and "Homely Margie," takes a different turn when Vern dissuades his daughter from trying the same trick she did in those instances.

"Margie's Millionth Member" (December 23, 1953)

Writers: Frank Gill, Jr., Kenneth Noyes, G. Carleton Brown. *Director*: Hal Yates.

Cast: Don Hayden (*Freddie Wilson*), Clarence Kolb (*George Honeywell*), Ralph Dumke (*Calvin Burns*), Roger Pace (*Captain Stratosphere*), Paul Maxey (*Bertram Bolton*), David Saber (*Andy Harris*), Bill Sheldon (*Reporter*)

Summary: Margie's young neighbor Andy Harris is a devoted fan of the *Captain Stratosphere* TV show. To help him win a promotion to "space sergeant," Margie signs Vern up as a new member, not taking into account that the sponsor's chief rival is a Honeywell and Todd client. When Vern wins a prize as the show's millionth member, the sponsor and star show up to deliver it personally, forcing Margie to press Freddie into service as the substitute small fry.

Notes: *Captain Video*, a popular children's science fiction show of the era, often featured premiums provided by sponsors such as Post Cereals. Roland Reed Productions also produced *Rocky Jones, Space Ranger,* whose leading man, Richard Crane, later turned up on *Margie*. Actor Ralph Dumke (1899–1964) was a seasoned character actor well-suited to playing irascible businessmen, as he does here and subsequently in "Margie's Manproof Lipstick." Roger Pace (born 1930) makes the first of three appearances on *Margie*.

"Meet Mr. Murphy" (December 30, 1953)

Writers: Alan Woods, John Kohn. *Director*: Hal Yates.

Cast: Don Hayden (*Freddie Wilson*), Clarence Kolb (*George Honeywell*), Richard Garland (*Tom Shane*), William Forrest (*Mr. Branch*), Dian Fauntelle (*Betty*), Willie Best (*Charlie*), Cindy the Chimp (*Mr. Murphy*)

Summary: When Vern refuses to lend Margie $50 for one of Freddie's business ventures, she vows to raise the money herself. Visiting the Honeywell and Todd office, she's hired to babysit Mr. Murphy, a chimpanzee who's to star in a jungle movie. Vern despises having the chimp around the apartment and hides him away from Margie, not knowing that Mr. Honeywell's client is producing the movie in which Mr. Murphy will star.

Note: This episode provides a rare glimpse at a portion of Freddie's apartment.

"Vern Gets the Bird" (January 6, 1954)

Writers: G. Carleton Brown, Frank Fox. *Director*: Hal Yates.

Cast: Don Hayden (*Freddie Wilson*), Gertrude Hoffmann (*Mrs. Odetts*), Clarence Kolb (*George Honeywell*), Alvy Moore (*Harvey Woodruff*), Bob Carraher (*Policeman*), Willie Best (*Charlie*)

Summary: Honeywell and Todd client Harvey Woodruff, an amateur ornithologist, may not renew his contract, so that he'll be free to travel the world photographing birds. Margie, calling herself Agatha, persuades Woodruff to stay in New York and bird-watch with her, but the plan goes awry when they go on a late-night date in search of owls. Vern and Freddie, unaware of his identity, follow the couple to the park and give Harvey a black eye that may land them in jail.

Notes: Actor Alvy Moore, previously seen in "The Efficiency Expert," gives another effective performance as a "droop." The name of the eatery seen in this episode, the L'Estrange Restaurant, must be an in-joke reference to series production manager Dick L'Estrange.

Quote: FREDDIE (when Vern is being uncharacteristically nice to him): Why can't you treat me like this all the time?
VERN: That's impossible. You know I can't stand you.

"Vern Retires" (January 13, 1954)

Writers: G. Carleton Brown, Frank Fox. *Director*: Hal Yates.
Cast: Don Hayden (*Freddie Wilson*), Gertrude Hoffmann (*Mrs. Odetts*), Clarence

Kolb (*George Honeywell*), Harry Hayden (*Mr. Morton*), Dian Fauntelle (*Betty*); David Webster, Edward Clark

Summary: After an argument with Mr. Honeywell, Vern impulsively decides to retire. Looking forward to a life of leisure, he soon finds himself bored stiff. Margie plots to bring her father and his crotchety boss back together.

Note: This episode gives Honeywell and Todd receptionist Betty (Dian Fauntelle) more to do than she has ever had before.

"Health Farm" (January 20, 1954)

Writer: Frank Gill, Jr. *Director*: Hal Yates.
Cast: Clarence Kolb (*George Honeywell*), Don Hayden (*Freddie Wilson*), Dian Fauntelle (*Betty*), Anne Kimbell (*Doris Barron*)

Summary: Doris Barron, a beautiful young Honeywell and Todd client who's about to come into a sizable trust fund, invites Margie to accompany her to a health farm. To make sure Doris' new beau, Jeff, isn't a fortune hunter, the two young ladies trade identities, leading to trouble when Doris is arrested during a gambling raid. Vern, Mr. Honeywell and Freddie set out to infiltrate the health farm, wrongly believing that it's Margie, rather than her pal, who's preparing to elope with the young man who works there.

Quote: VERN: Now see here, Margie doesn't get into trouble with our clients every time.
HONEYWELL: Name one, for the giant jackpot and a trip to Honolulu!

"Day and Night" (January 27, 1954)

Writers: Jerry Adelman, George Carleton Brown. *Director*: Hal Yates.
Cast: Don Hayden (*Freddie Wilson*), Clarence Kolb (*George Honeywell*), Lester Mathews [Matthews] (*Albert Patterson*), Myra McKinney (*Mrs. Wallington*), Willie Best (*Charlie*), John Hedloe, Bill Sheldon (*Telephone Repairmen*)

Summary: After a dose of the usual pandemonium from the Albright apartment, new tenant Mrs. Wallington cancels her lease and threatens building manager Mr. Patterson with a lawsuit. Vern tells Margie her upcoming vacation to Sun Valley will be canceled if there are any more mishaps before she leaves. After unintentionally taking stuffy Mrs. Wallington for a hair-rising ride on the Carlton Arms' malfunctioning elevator, Margie dreams up a wild scheme to prevent Mr. Patterson from confronting her father.

Note: This episode introduces the character of Albert Patterson, manager of the Carlton Arms. He will return shortly in another episode, played by another actor.

"Mexican Standoff" (February 3, 1954)

Writers: Frank Gill, Jr., George Carleton Brown. *Director*: Hal Yates.
Cast: Gertrude Hoffmann (*Mrs. Odetts*), Eugene Iglesias (*Young Gregorio/Alfredo*), Vincent Padula (*Don Gregorio*)

Summary: Vern and Margie's host on a business trip to Mexico, Don Gregorio, tries to give the visitors to his hacienda the flavor of the old country. Their host's college-educated son catches a glimpse of Margie and ups the ante by posing as his "gay caballero" of a cousin, Alfredo. After Margie catches on to the gag, she conspires with her new admirer to attend a ball in Mexico City, with a plan that involves convincing Vern that the hacienda is being invaded by bandits.

Note: Once again, Vern, who should certainly know better by now, decides that Mrs. Odetts will make a proper chaperone to keep his daughter out of trouble.

"Margie's Manproof Lipstick" (February 10, 1954)

Writers: Frank Gill, Jr., George Carleton Brown. *Director*: Hal Yates.

Cast: Don Hayden (*Freddie Wilson*), Ralph Dumke (*T.J. Bradshaw*), Gladys Holland (*Mme. Gisselle*), Stephen Bekassy (*Gisselle's Husband*), Leon Tyler (*Harvey*)

Summary: Margie and Freddie are trying to sell "Permanently Yours," a lipstick that doesn't wear off for three months, invented by Freddie's chemist pal. Vern is furious when their interference jeopardizes a business deal, the merger of his client Mme. Gisselle's company with Hemisphere Cosmetics. When it develops that Mme. Gisselle is interested in the new lipstick, Vern makes amends with Freddie, whose friend neglected to tell him one important thing about his invention.

Note: Stephen Bekassy (1907–1995), Hungarian by birth, was often cast as a Frenchman, as he was here and in a second episode a few weeks later. He also employed a Gallic accent for his featured role in Gale's final film, *Woman of the North Country*.

Quote: MARGIE (caught by her father kissing Freddie): Please, Dad! I can explain if you'll just give me time to think of something!

"Margie Babysits" (February 17, 1954)

Writers: Jim Bullock, Robert Raff, George Carleton Brown. *Director*: Hal Yates.

Cast: Clarence Kolb (*George Honeywell*), James Burke (*Mr. Patterson*), Stuffy Singer (*Sidney Mortensen*), Marjorie Bennett (*Miss Flanagan*), Frank Jaquet (*Policeman*), Katherine Sheldon (*Mrs. Mortensen*)

Summary: Camera bug Margie unwittingly snaps a photo of an "old lady robber" who's posing as a cleaning lady to case the Carlton Arms. Wanting to retrieve the negative, the robber breaks into the Albrights' apartment the night that Margie and Vern are playing reluctant babysitters to the young grandson of an important client.

Note: Beloved character actress Marjorie Bennett (1896–1982), perhaps best-remembered as Mrs. Flagg in *What Ever Happened to Baby Jane?* (1962), is nicely spotlighted here as the seemingly sweet old lady who proves to have a criminal bent.

"Case of the Helping Hand" (February 24, 1954)

Writers: Frank Gill, Jr., G. Carleton Brown. *Director*: Hal Yates.

Cast: Hillary Brooke (*Roberta Townsend*), Clarence Kolb (*George Honeywell*), Robert Nichols (*Perkins*), Dian Fauntelle (*Betty*)

Summary: Vern worries that he is being shown up at the office by a new young employee, Perkins. Learning that Perkins is a fan of mystery novels, Margie and Roberta rope him into a "real-life mystery" that causes the young man to make a fool of himself with his boss. With Perkins put in his place, all seems right in the Albrights' world. Then Vern, who knows nothing of the trick his daughter and girlfriend pulled, invites his now-humbled colleague over for dinner.

Note: This episode has parallels with the previous installments "Young Vern," which found Margie's dad feeling old and past his prime, and "The Golf Game," in which Mr. Honeywell longs for "young blood" in the firm.

"Sleepwalking" (March 3, 1954)

Writers: Jerry Adelman, G. Carleton Brown. *Director*: Hal Yates.
Cast: Don Hayden (*Freddie Wilson*), Charles Cane (*Policeman*), Emil Sitka (*Max/Dr. Easton*)

Summary: Margie wants to move to a ground-floor apartment that's more luxurious than their current abode (and costs $50 per month more), but Vern refuses. With Margie pulling out all the stops to persuade her father he's a sleepwalker, and thus shouldn't live on an upper floor, Vern soon finds himself waking on a bench in Central Park. Catching on to his daughter's scheme, Vern turns the tables by telling Margie they're moving to a rundown farm on Long Island for his safety.

Notes: This script is a textbook example of the show's primary plot construction, what Margie refers to as "that old Albright game of teaching little Margie a lesson," inevitably followed by her retaliatory strike. One minor inconsistency finds Vern willingly taking sleeping pills, after saying in last week's episode that he didn't believe in using them.

"A Proposal for Papa" (March 10, 1954)

Writers: Frank Gill, Jr., G. Carleton Brown. *Director*: Hal Yates.
Cast: Clarence Kolb (*George Honeywell*), Don Hayden (*Freddie Wilson*), Lucien Littlefield (*J.P. Joiner*), Shirley O. Mills (*Muriel Joiner*)

Summary: Vern's new young secretary, the daughter of a client, is infatuated with him. Ordered by Mr. Honeywell to humor her until her father renews his contract, Vern panics when the young lady proposes marriage. When Margie's plan to make Vern unappealing falls short, she decides to counterattack by pretending to be in love with Muriel's hypochondriac father.

"Vern's Son" (March 17, 1954)

Writers: Jerry Adelman, George Carleton Brown. *Director*: Hal Yates.
Cast: Clarence Kolb (*George Honeywell*), Gertrude Hoffmann (*Mrs. Odetts*), Stuart Wade (*Jerry Walsh*), Wayne Taylor (*Slug*)

Summary: Honeywell and Todd's new client, Jerry Walsh, is a handsome former All-American football player, prompting Vern to claim he has a teenage son rather than a beautiful 21-year-old daughter. When Vern is unable to avert an in-person meeting, Margie assumes the role of "Mike," until Jerry offers to coach the boy in football. Margie runs in a ringer to bluff her way through football practice, but can't resist meeting Jerry as herself once she gets a look at him.

Note: Though she's usually inclined to defend Freddie, here Margie admits he's probably not bright enough to carry out the charade of being "Mike." Mrs. Odetts agrees, saying, "He's no Einstein." Margie retorts, "He's not even a beer stein. At least that has a head!"

"Daughter-at-Law" (March 24, 1954)

Writers: Edward E. Seabrook, Homer McCoy. *Director*: Hal Yates.
Cast: Don Hayden (*Freddie Wilson*), Herbert Heyes (*John J. Bascomb*), Tom Selden (*Gregory Brent*), Gil Lamb (*Counterman*); Al Nalbandian, Eddie Baker

Summary: When Vern chastises Margie for staying out too late, her new beau, young lawyer Gregory, offers to protect her legal rights as an adult. Vern, too, lawyers up, and soon Margie and her dad are waging a war armed with legal principles. After Margie's allowance is cut off, she sends her father a bill for her domestic services, causing him to retaliate with a spanking. Margie escalates the game by pretending to elope with Gregory so that she can be legally emancipated.

Notes: Writers Seabrook and McCoy manage to find a fresh and funny take on the endless power struggle between Margie and her dad. The spanking wouldn't sit well with modern audiences.

"The New Freddie" (March 31, 1954)

Writers: Jerry Adelman, George Carleton Brown. *Director*: Hal Yates.

Cast: Don Hayden (*Freddie Wilson*), Clarence Kolb (*George Honeywell*), Hillary Brooke (*Roberta Townsend*), Patricia Hitchcock (*Wife #1*), Jan Wayne (*Wife #2*)

Summary: At Mr. Honeywell's suggestion, Vern persuades Freddie to go from being "a human doormat" to "a caveman," sure that Margie will not like being dominated. Catching on to the gag, Margie pretends to have accepted Freddie's marriage proposal, and Vern in turn professes to be delighted. At the eleventh hour, Margie feels guilty about playing with Freddie's feelings and seeks Vern's help in letting him down easy.

Notes: Alfred Hitchcock's actress daughter Patricia (born 1928) appears in the climactic scene. Once again, it falls to Roberta to see through Margie's scheming more clearly than her father can.

Quote: FREDDIE (ready for the wedding): Remember, Vern, from now on she's *my* little Margie!

"Tugboat Margie" (April 7, 1954)

Writers: Frank Gill, Jr., George Carleton Brown. *Director*: Hal Yates.

Cast: Don Hayden (*Freddie Wilson*), Roy Roberts (*Captain Murdock*), Edmund Penney, Don McArt, Edgar Dearing (*Sailors*)

Summary: Both Vern and Freddie are called up for naval reserve duty. Much to his disgust, Vern finds that he has been assigned to a tugboat under the temporary command of Lt. Freddie Wilson. Bringing Margie aboard to show off, Freddie fails to notice when the ship sails, leaving him and her father to conceal the stowaway.

Notes: Roy Roberts' role as a ship's captain here is apropos, considering he will play one in Gale Storm's next series. His character, Captain Murdock, unexpectedly sympathizes with Vern, claiming he too has a daughter who has caused him "some frightening moments."

"En Garde" (April 14, 1954)

Writers: Frank Gill, Jr., Jerry Adelman, George Carleton Brown. *Director*: Hal Yates.

Cast: Hillary Brooke (*Roberta Townsend*), Clarence Kolb (*George Honeywell*), Stephen Bekassy (*Pepe*), Albert Cavens (*Second Actor*), Bob Carraher (*Policeman*)

Summary: Upset because Vern takes her for granted, Roberta accepts Mr. Honeywell's offer to hire an actor to give her beau some competition. Trying to show up suave Frenchman Pepe, Vern is trapped when his rival challenges him to a duel. Roberta and Margie learn what's afoot and hire an actor of their own to add a new wrinkle to the scenario.

Note: According to this script, Mr. Honeywell thinks Vern should marry Roberta, in part so that she can be a stepmother to Margie.

"Honeyboy Honeywell" (April 21, 1954)

Writers: Frank Gill, Jr., Jerry Adelman, George Carleton Brown. *Director*: Hal Yates.
Cast: Clarence Kolb (*George Honeywell*), Gertrude Hoffmann (*Mrs. Odetts*), John Eldredge (*Roger Kent*), Joan Blair (*Annette Gilmore*)

Summary: Margie decides that Mr. Honeywell, who's been driving Vern crazy at the office, needs a wife. Mr. Kent of the "400 Whist and Social Club" recognizes Honeywell as a "nice fat pigeon" and sets him up with grifter Annette Gilmore. Within days, Vern's boss has decided to sell the firm and marry Mrs. Gilmore. Margie must halt the nuptials.

"Careless Margie" (April 28, 1954)

Writer: Lee B. Henry. *Director*: Hal Yates.
Cast: Clarence Kolb (*George Honeywell*), Hillary Brooke (*Roberta Townsend*), Don Hayden (*Freddie Wilson*), Gabor Curtiz (*Manager*), Charles Meredith (*Carson*), Joel Marston (*Bank Teller*), Willie Best (*Charlie*), Creighton Hale (*Writer*)

Summary: After Vern chides Margie for being careless, she tries to prove her reliability by running a bank errand for Roberta involving $2500 in cash. Margie leaves her purse lying around Vern's office, enabling him to find the money and tempting him to "teach her a lesson." Overhearing Vern and his boss gloating over the missing cash, Margie enlists Freddie's help in making their business dinner at a posh restaurant memorable.

Note: According to this episode, the available balance in Margie's checking account, after depositing a dollar, is 55 cents.

"Vern on the Lam" (May 5, 1954)

Writers: Frank Gill, Jr., G. Carleton Brown. *Director*: Hal Yates.
Cast: Clarence Kolb (*George Honeywell*), Fortunio Bonanova (*Col. Luis Olveda*)

Summary: Sent to a small Central American country to obtain a client's signature on a contract, Vern is stymied when he is unable to produce his entry papers at the border. While Margie tries to contact the client, Luis Olveda, Vern panics and breaks out of custody, going on the lam in disguise. Olveda tracks the Albrights down at the local hotel, but Vern mistakes him for the chief of police and enlists Margie's help in evading him.

"Margie and the Shah" (May 12, 1954)

Writers: Frank Gill, Jr., G. Carleton Brown, Alan Woods, John Kohn. *Director*: Hal Yates.
Cast: Don Hayden (*Freddie Wilson*), Clarence Kolb (*George Honeywell*), Edgar Barrier (*Shah*), Donna Martell (*Samia*), Henry Corden (*Ahmed*), Ralph Sanford (*Policeman*)

Summary: Vern's old fraternity brother, now the shah of Zena, is coming to New York to arrange financing for some oil leases. Vern is initially thwarted from seeing his friend by the shah's secretary Ahmed, but Margie infiltrates the royal hotel suite. Disguising herself as a harem girl, Margie is caught in the act by her father, who enlists the shah's help in pretending she has caught his eye as a potential 66th wife.

Quote: MARGIE (told, after deliberately making herself ugly, that she reminds the shah of his first wife): [She] must have been a real Halloween broom jockey!

"Margie and the Bagpipes" (May 19, 1954)

Writers: Frank Gill, Jr., George Carleton Brown. *Director:* Hal Yates.
Cast: Don Hayden (*Freddie Wilson*), Clarence Kolb (*George Honeywell*), Andy Clyde (*Mr. MacPherson*), Tom Dillon (*Mr. MacIntyre*)

Summary: Wanting to join the Bonnie Sons of Scotland lodge, Mr. Honeywell acquires a rare set of bagpipes just like those of Mr. MacPherson, the club president. When Margie accidentally ruins MacPherson's pipes, Freddie tries to make amends by giving him Mr. Honeywell's set. After an angry Honeywell fires Vern, Margie and Freddie infiltrate the lodge hall, where she's mistaken for the "professional bagpipe player" Mr. MacPherson's expecting.

"Dutch Treat" (May 26, 1954)

Writers: Frank Gill, Jr., Jerry Adelman, George Carleton Brown. *Director:* Hal Yates.
Cast: Clarence Kolb (*George Honeywell*), George Meader (*Mr. Todd*), Lizz Slifer (*Laura Todd*), Hugh Sanders (*Roger Bracken*), Sheila James (*Kathy*), Howard Negley (*Inspector Brady*), Dee Aaker (*Peter*), Phillip Bonnell (*Bob*)

Summary: Mr. Todd comes home from Europe unexpectedly after a fight with his wife, who thinks he was having an affair with a German girl. With Mrs. Todd filing for a separation, and threatening to pull her money out of Honeywell and Todd, Vern and his colleagues are desperate to show her that Ilse was only a 12-year-old refugee her husband was sponsoring. When the real Ilse can't be located, Margie suggests hiring a child actress to fool Mrs. Todd, and then steps into the part herself at the last minute.

Notes: In the second act, when Mrs. Todd brings in some children to play with "Ilse," the boy who plays Bob is Gale's son Phillip. The other boy is the brother of child actor Lee Aaker, star of *The Adventures of Rin Tin Tin*.

SEASON FOUR

"Kangaroo Story" (September 1, 1954)

Writers: Frank Gill, Jr., George Carleton Brown. *Director:* Hal Yates.
Cast: Don Hayden (*Freddie Wilson*), Hillary Brooke (*Roberta Townsend*), Irving Bacon (*Mr. Townsend*), Donald Kerr (*Zookeeper*), Willie Best (*Charlie*)

Summary: Freddie spends his unemployment check buying a boxing kangaroo he thinks will make him money in show business. Refusing to babysit a kangaroo, Margie instead hides him temporarily in the vacant apartment next door. Roberta's staid father, visiting from Minnesota, meets Vern as he babbles about being punched by a kangaroo, and concludes that his daughter's boyfriend is a crazy drunk.

Notes: This silly—but fun—season opener gives Willie Best a more sizable role than usual. According to syndicated columnist C.E. Cupples (August 22, 1954), director Hal Yates assured his stars the kangaroo was harmless—right before the animal "lashed out with a combination right and left foot" that sent Yates "to the floor for the full count."

Variety (September 10, 1954), none too impressed with the "nonsensical" script, complained, "Miss Storm and Farrell, who deserve better material, and direction, try valiantly..."

"The All-American" (September 8, 1954)

Writers: Frank Gill, Jr., George Carleton Brown. *Director*: Hal Yates.

Cast: Gertrude Hoffmann (*Mrs. Odetts*), Fess Parker (*Lenny Crunchmeyer*), Ed Penney (*Jerry*); Ben Chapman, Ed Sweeny, Paul Savage, Pat Flaherty

Summary: The star football player Vern's been asked to recruit for his alma mater turns out to be Mrs. Odetts' nephew Lenny. Better equipped on the athletic field than in the classroom, Lenny nonetheless agrees to enroll, provided Margie comes along to tutor him. With a gleeful Mrs. Odetts as her chaperone, Margie goes back to school, where her charms throw the members of the football team into a jealous uproar.

Notes: This is one of the relatively few episodes in which Mrs. Odetts' first name is heard, as Lenny calls her Aunt Flo. Actor Fess Parker (1924–2010) makes an early television appearance as Lenny, about a year before Walt Disney cast him as Davy Crockett. Ben Chapman (1928–2008), seen as one of the ballplayers, had worked a few months earlier on *Creature from the Black Lagoon* (1954), donning the monster costume for scenes set on dry land.

"Vern's Guilty Feeling" (September 15, 1954)

Writers: Frank Gill, Jr., George Carleton Brown. *Director*: Hal Yates.

Cast: Paul Picerni (*Joe Brady*), Byron Foulger (*Dr. Crane*), Phil Van Zandt (*Frankie*), Hugh Sanders (*Deputy D.A.*), Lyle Latell

Summary: Vern wants Margie to bring her problems to him, so she concocts a story about gambling at a nightclub. Sure she's in love with the handsome croupier, Joe Brady, Vern tries to reform him by giving the young man a job at Honeywell and Todd, unaware that he's actually an undercover agent for the D.A.'s office. Vern frets when his new assistant tries to get the crooked nightclub owner as a client, while Margie keeps an eye on things by taking a job as a cigarette girl at the club.

Note: Actor Paul Picerni (1922–2011) would be best-known for his later television role as Agent Lee Hobson on *The Untouchables*.

"Star of Khyber" (September 22, 1954)

Writers: Frank Gill, Jr., George Carleton Brown. *Director*: Hal Yates.

Cast: Gertrude Hoffmann (*Mrs. Odetts*), Clarence Kolb (*George Honeywell*), Tom Avera (*Dick Taylor*), Tris Coffin (*Mr. Pandit*), Lucille Knox (*Gloria*), Henry Corden, Russ Conklin (*Henchmen*)

Summary: Margie wants to meet handsome private eye Dick Taylor, but he's preoccupied with his latest case, recovering a valuable emerald stolen from a maharajah. Trying to attract Dick's attention, Margie goes to a nightclub with Mrs. Odetts tricked out in Indian dress. Her plan is too successful for her own good when she catches the eye of the jewel thieves themselves.

Quote: HONEYWELL: Albright, are you crazy? Don't answer that, it's a waste of time.

"Parrot Gold" (September 29, 1954)

>*Writers*: Frank Gill, Jr., George Carleton Brown. *Director*: Hal Yates.
>*Cast*: Clarence Kolb (*George Honeywell*), Roger Pace (*Bob*), James Hayward (*John*), Maudie Prickett (*Martha*)

Summary: Rich, reclusive Jason Grimm died and left a trust fund for his beloved parrot Skipper, but the money can't be located. Learning that the parrot frequently says, "Time is money. Look in the clock," Margie concludes that this is a clue. At the late Mr. Grimm's spooky mansion, Margie, her gentleman friend Bob, Vern and Mr. Honeywell all try to solve the mystery, with the late owner's two resentful servants opposing them at every turn.

"Real George" (October 6, 1954)

>*Writers*: Frank Gill, Jr., George Carleton Brown. *Director*: Hal Yates.
>*Cast*: Gertrude Hoffmann (*Mrs. Odetts*), Clarence Kolb (*George Honeywell*), Cliff Ferre (*George Adams*), Harry Cheshire (*Jonathan Jones*), Roy Gordon (*George #4*)

Summary: Margie's new admirer, George, mistakenly sends flowers to Mrs. Odetts instead of his intended. Trying to keep her friend's feelings from being hurt, Margie persuades a visiting Texas oil man to pitch woo to Mrs. Odetts. Meanwhile, Mr. Honeywell, trying to keep Mrs. Odetts' money safe with Honeywell and Todd, reluctantly decides to present himself as the romantic "George" who has fallen for her.

Notes: This was actor Cliff Ferre's second stint as a love interest for Margie; he previously appeared as a fraternity boy in "Campus Homecoming." He returned a few weeks later in "Miss Whoozis." Harry Cheshire (1891–1968), cast here as the wealthy oil man, played a similar role in the *I Love Lucy* segment "Oil Wells." He made two more *My Little Margie* appearances before the season was out.

"Margie the Do-Gooder" (October 13, 1954)

>*Writers*: Frank Gill, Jr., George Carleton Brown. *Director*: Hal Yates.
>*Cast*: Don Hayden (*Freddie Wilson*), Shirley O. Mills (*Helen Seeley*), John Hubbard (*Major Tom Grady*), Jack Kelly (*Captain Cliff Seeley*); William Sheldon

Summary: Challenged by Vern to do a good deed for someone, Margie befriends a young newlywed crying in Central Park over her absentee husband. Thanks to Margie, Helen Seeley soon believes her husband Cliff has taken up with a stripteaser, when in fact he's on a secret Air Force mission. Things go from bad to worse when Vern and Freddie involve themselves, culminating in a late night rendezvous at an airfield where Margie's father and boyfriend are mistaken for enemy agents.

Note: Actor Jack Kelly (1927–1992) is best-known for his role as Bart on TV's *Maverick*.

"Convention Story" (October 20, 1954)

>*Writers*: Frank Gill, Jr., George Carleton Brown. *Director*: Hal Yates.
>*Cast*: Hillary Brooke (*Roberta Townsend*), Clarence Kolb (*George Honeywell*), Emory Parnell (*Mr. Parnell*), Lucille Barkley (*Gloria Knight*), William Lechner (*Ted Andrews*), Victor Sutherland (*Briggs*), Cecil Elliott (*Mrs. Parnell*)

Summary: Margie and Roberta tag along on Vern's business trip to Miami, to protect him from a husband-hunting widow. While Vern tries to cope with Parnell, a practical-joking colleague he can't afford to antagonize, the ladies inadvertently devote their best efforts to bothering the wrong widow. Concerned that she has cost her father the deal, Margie plots to get the upper hand with Mr. Parnell, which involves roping in Mrs. Parnell.

Note: This episode's running gag involves Parnell's hotel room, which much to the prankster's delight features a missing balcony and a doorway that drops visitors directly into the hotel pool.

"Shipboard Story" (October 27, 1954)

Writers: Frank Gill, Jr., G. Carleton Brown. *Director*: Hal Yates.
Cast: John Lupton (*Tony Stanley*), Roy Roberts (*Vaughn*), Dian Fauntelle (*Betty*), Barry Bernard (*Steward*)

Summary: Vern flatly refuses to take Margie on his business trip to London, even after she invents a story about being left alone in New York with a fortune-hunting fiancé. Margie decides to bolster her story by persuading Tony, a handsome young stranger, to play her fiancé, unaware that he's the Earl of Westbrook, with whom Vern is to meet in London. On the trip over, with Tony aboard, Margie and her father play tricks and counter-tricks on each other, aided and abetted by a steward whose loyalty changes every time money crosses his palm.

Note: This episode serves as a precursor to *Oh! Susanna*, with Gale aboard a cruise ship, a British-accented steward and an almost unrecognizable Roy Roberts (her *Susanna* co-star) playing a bearded passenger and exercise freak who butts heads with Vern.

"A Job for Freddie" (November 3, 1954)

Writers: Frank Gill, Jr., G. Carleton Brown. *Director*: Hal Yates.
Cast: Don Hayden (*Freddie Wilson*), Billy Gilbert (*Luigi*), Genevieve Aumont (*Lili Pontine*), Maurice Marsac (*Jacques*), Herb Vigran (*Reporter*)

Summary: Vern promises to double Margie's allowance if Freddie can hold a job for one week. Margie convinces the owner of Luigi's Café, where business is slow, that Freddie is a European maître d' named Dimitri who will attract a celebrity clientele. After reading a newspaper account of famed opera singer Lili Pontine, who has run away from her jealous husband, Margie decides to assume the role, not foreseeing that the real Lili will turn up.

Note: Comic actor Billy Gilbert (1894–1971), seen here as the excitable Luigi, had a long association with the Roach studios, playing supporting roles in the films of Laurel and Hardy and the *Our Gang* kids.

"The Switzerland Story" (November 10, 1954)

Writers: Frank Gill, Jr., George Carleton Brown. *Director*: Hal Yates.
Cast: Danny Richards, Jr. (*Jonathan Weatherby*), Archer MacDonald (*Jasper Weatherby*); Jack Rice, Douglas Wood

Summary: The Albrights arrive in Switzerland to obtain a client's signature on a contract. Trouble develops when Margie learns that the Weatherby who's there for a Swiss chess tournament is actually Jonathan, the younger brother of mountain climber Jasper, whose signature Vern needs. Margie colludes with Jonathan to lure his older brother to Switzerland, by making it appear that Vern set a new world record for climbing Mount Bagenbruck.

Note: This episode finds Margie meeting a ten-year-old whose ability to scheme and contrive mischief rivals even hers, causing her to say admiringly that he'll make the perfect husband for her when he grows up. Once again, Margie is campaigning for a new car.

"Big Chief Vern" (November 17, 1954)

Writers: Frank Gill, Jr., George Carleton Brown. *Director*: Hal Yates.
Cast: Clarence Kolb (*George Honeywell*), Gertrude Hoffmann (*Mrs. Odetts*), Eugene Iglesias (*Chief Bill Lightfoot*), Monte Blue (*John Lightfoot*)

Summary: Facing the prospect of Margie taking flying lessons in New York, Vern decides he'd rather bring her along on his trip to Oklahoma. To keep Margie occupied while he negotiates a deal for oil rights with the local Indians, he and Mr. Honeywell arrange for her and Mrs. Odetts to find a phony map showing buried treasure. Young Bill Lightfoot, Margie's guide, finally admits that he is in cahoots with Vern, but helps her get even by arranging a rigorous tribal ceremony to induct her duplicitous dad as a member of the Indian tribe.

Note: Previously seen as a native of Mexico in "Mexican Standoff," actor Eugene Iglesias returns, this time playing an American Indian. The actor was actually Puerto Rican.

"Vern's Winter Vacation" (November 24, 1954)

Writers: Frank Gill, Jr., George Carleton Brown. *Director*: Hal Yates.
Cast: Don Hayden (*Freddie Wilson*), Peter Leeds (*Emcee*), Edward Earle (*Dr. Farrell*); Helen Fosmore, Ralph Hodges

Summary: Freddie's new career as a "professional contestant" pays off when he wins the jackpot on *Love Conquers All* with a phony sob story about his secret wife and her disapproving father. Winning a trip to Palm Beach, Florida, Freddie needs Margie to come along as his "bride," but she's preparing to take a vacation in Bermuda with Vern. To persuade Vern to stop off in Palm Beach, where Margie can play Mrs. Wilson on a live broadcast of *Love Conquers All,* Margie pretends she has contracted amnesia and can remember no one except her beloved Freddie.

Notes: This episode parodies popular giveaway shows of the era such as *Queen for a Day.*

"San Francisco Story" (December 1, 1954)

Writers: Frank Gill, Jr., George Carleton Brown. *Director*: Hal Yates.
Cast: Emory Parnell (*Mr. Parnell*), Keye Luke (*Chang*), Rico Sato (*Mei Ling*), Richard Loo (*Mr. Tang*), Frank Kumagai (*Workman*)

Summary: Margie and Vern are on their way to San Francisco so that he can try to win the business of wealthy banker Mr. Tang, but Vern's rival Mr. Parnell has a trick up his sleeve. Parnell's assistant, Chang, befriends Margie on the train and dupes her into trying to help Tang's sheltered daughter elope with her boyfriend, which infuriates the client.

When the scheme proves successful, Parnell tries to manipulate Vern and Margie into leaving town quickly, before they can make amends with Tang.

Note: This episode reunites Gale with actor Keye Luke, one of her co-stars in the film *Let's Go Collegiate* (1941). Emory Parnell reprises his role from "Convention Story" as Vern's prankish colleague Mr. Parnell.

"Operation Rescue" (December 8, 1954)

Writers: Edward E. Seabrook, Homer McCoy. *Director*: Hal Yates.

Cast: Don Hayden (*Freddie Wilson*), Gertrude Hoffmann (*Mrs. Odetts*), Clarence Kolb (*George Honeywell*), Willie Best (*Charlie*), Dorothy Green (*Vera Wagner*), Lester Matthews (*Ralph Burton*), Dian Fauntelle (*Betty*), Jeanne Gray (*Claire Winthrop*), Joanne Jordan (*Miss Hennessey*)

Summary: Vern returns from a cruise with an unwanted fiancée, the result of a shipboard romance. Margie plots to shake the woman by persuading her that the Albright family is completely deranged. Unfortunately, she mistakes a female client for the fiancée, and puts on her performance for the wrong woman.

"Subconscious Approach" (December 15, 1954)

Writers: Jack Krutcher, G. Carleton Brown. *Director*: Hal Yates.

Cast: Don Hayden (*Freddie Wilson*), Clarence Kolb (*George Honeywell*), Nanette Bordeaux (*Countess de Lichtenfeld*), Lyle Latell (*Hotel Detective*)

Summary: When Mr. Honeywell forces Vern to cancel his business trip to Havana, Margie vows to make her father stand up to his boss. Inspired by the "Learn Spanish While You Sleep" records she's been using, Margie makes recordings she hopes will subconsciously stiffen her father's spine. Vern and his boss scheme to make Margie think her plan cost her father his job, but their efforts backfire when they give a seltzer spritzing to a client they assume is Margie in disguise.

Note: This script finds Honeywell making plans to attend a dog show, a follow-up mention of a hobby first described in the series pilot.

"The New Neighbor" (December 22, 1954)

Writers: Frank Gill, Jr., George Carleton Brown. *Director*: Hal Yates.

Cast: Charles Smith (*Clyde Lane*), Harry Cheshire (*Uncle Jim*), William Sheldon (*Moving Man*)

Summary: Vern hits the roof when Margie shows off her new $4200 fur coat, and tells her she must pay for it herself. When she meets a new neighbor, young Clyde Lane, he offers her a share in the proceeds of his new invention, the Lane Lullaby Lounge. In exchange, Margie must pose as Clyde's wife for three days, to appease his visiting uncle, who thinks his nephew is happily married and attending business school.

Notes: Guest player Charles Smith may be best-remembered for his role as Henry Aldrich's pal Dizzy in the 1940s Paramount film series. This is another segment filled with slapstick, as the recliner Clyde invented sends everyone who sits on it on a wild ride, and Vern gets doused with a bucket of water. Here we get a rare look at the back hallway that supposedly runs behind the Albrights' apartment, which looks different than the service porch we saw in previous episodes.

> *Quote:* VERN (in an unusually good mood after breakfast): Even the toast tasted different. What did you do to it?
> MARGIE: I gave it to you with only second-degree burns.

"Margie's Client" (December 29, 1954)

Writers: Frank Gill, Jr., George Carleton Brown. *Director:* Hal Yates.

Cast: Don Hayden (*Freddie Wilson*), Clarence Kolb (*George Honeywell*), Dian Fauntelle (*Betty*), Lucien Littlefield (*Jason Whaley*); Paul Maxey, Bill Baldwin, Donald Kerr, The Evans Brothers

Summary: Wanting to ditch their client Jason Whaley so they can sign his competitor, Vern and Honeywell sic Margie on him to wreak her usual havoc. As they hoped, Margie thoroughly angers Mr. Whaley, but she redeems herself when she saves him from a "burglar" (Freddie). Doing her best to insure that both Whaley and his rival, Mr. Grant, will do business with Honeywell and Todd, Margie invades a business convention dressed as half of a horse.

Note: After more than 100 episodes of doing it metaphorically, Margie finally succeeds here in literally making her father a horse's ass, as they don a costume built for two.

"Miss Whoozis" (January 5, 1955)

Writer: Nathaniel Curtis. *Director:* Hal Yates.

Cast: Clarence Kolb (*George Honeywell*), Cliff Ferre (*Cleve Harrison*), Elaine Riley (*Lois*), Fritz Feld (*Duval*), Ed Fury (*Hercules*)

Summary: Vern doesn't know about Margie's new gig as a fashion model, and Margie does not know that the dress designer is being financed by Honeywell and Todd. Annoyed that Cleve, the handsome photographer with whom she's working, can't seem to remember her name, Margie decides to get his attention by making him mad. Accepting another job, working alongside a bodybuilder, does the trick, but it also tips off the designer that Margie has violated her contract, and reveals to Vern just who the campaign's lead model is.

"Murder in Bermuda" (January 12, 1955)

Writers: Frank Gill, Jr., G. Carleton Brown. *Director:* Hal Yates.

Cast: Roy Roberts (*Sir Clyde*), Dorothy Patrick (*Pamela*), Liam Sullivan (*Alan Cotton*), Barry Bernard (*Inspector Plum*)

Summary: Vern's restful vacation in Bermuda is disrupted when Margie claims she saw a murder being committed in the hotel room across the way. What she actually witnessed was aspiring playwright Alan Cotton rehearsing a scene with his girlfriend Pamela, niece of the stuffy Sir Clyde. Since Pamela and Alan don't want her uncle to know about their plans, their cover-up results in the local police inspector thinking both Margie and her dad have gone around the bend.

Note: Roy Roberts gives another strong character performance here, as the blustery, nearsighted Britisher Sir Clyde.

"The Unexpected Guest" (January 19, 1955)

Writers: Frank Gill, Jr., George Carleton Brown. *Director:* Hal Yates.

Cast: Don Hayden (*Freddie Wilson*), Clarence Kolb (*George Honeywell*), Donald MacBride (*Withers*), Willie Best (*Charlie*)

Summary: With a week still to go on his vacation, Vern and Margie sneak into their own apartment, not wanting Mr. Honeywell to know they're in town. Unbeknownst to them, Mr. Honeywell has invited a client, Mr. Withers, to stay there in their absence, along with his rambunctious dog. Caught on the premises, Margie and Vern pose as the Albrights' maid and butler. When Mr. Honeywell finds out, he insists they keep up the ruse.

"Mardi Gras" (January 26, 1955)

Writers: Frank Gill, Jr., George Carleton Brown. *Director*: Hal Yates.
Cast: Clarence Kolb (*George Honeywell*), Hal Baylor (*Randolph*), Paul Harvey (*Mr. LeDuc*), Lyn Thomas (*Nurse*); Jim Hayward, Grady Sutton

Summary: Visiting New Orleans during Mardi Gras, Vern and Margie can't find lodgings, until she feigns a sprained ankle in client Mr. LeDuc's house. LeDuc's annoying brother-in-law Randolph, fond of practical jokes, arranges for Margie to get medical attention— in a maternity ward. Margie and Vern make amends with the client when they promise to scare Randolph into leaving town.

Note: The Gale Storm Show also had a Mardi Gras–themed episode.

"Vern's Mother-in-Law" (February 2, 1955)

Writers: Frank Gill, Jr., George Carleton Brown. *Director*: Hal Yates.
Cast: Clarence Kolb (*George Honeywell*), Leslie Turner (*Miss Joiner*)

Summary: Vern and Mr. Honeywell tell Margie that her impulsive nature was inherited from her maternal grandmother. A flashback takes us to 1930, where Vern is a recent college graduate courting Margie's mother-to-be, Cathy. Cathy's disapproving mother, also named Margie, asks her friend and investment counselor George Honeywell to consider giving the young man a job—if he can demonstrate that he has what it takes.

Notes: This change-of-pace episode gives a real workout to Charles Farrell and Clarence Kolb, both with their hair darkened to represent their younger days. Likewise, Gale, once again aided and abetted by split-screen photography and the use of an over-the-shoulder double, plays Margie and Margie's mother and grandmother. The three main actors are kept so busy that only one guest player is needed, the actress who plays Honeywell's 1930s receptionist. The script here places Vern's college graduation several years later than what was seen in the second-season episode "Campus Homecoming."

"Too Many Ghosts" (February 9, 1955)

Writers: Jack Crutcher, G. Carleton Brown. *Director*: Hal Yates.
Cast: Clarence Kolb (*George Honeywell*), Jon Shepodd (*Lord Tony Stanley*), Hallene Hill (*Mrs. Edith Bishop*), Gerald Oliver-Smith (*Blivens*), William Baldwin (*Phillips*)

Summary: Honeywell and Todd's client, a young British nobleman, is facing financial ruin unless he can unload some of his property. Challenged to find someone who wants to own a 15th century English castle, Margie succeeds in interesting a dotty older woman who wants it—if it's haunted. Margie and Lord Stanley's butler try to give Mrs. Bishop the spirits she craves; the chaotic results put the transaction in jeopardy.

Notes: Actor Jon Shepodd (1925–2017) was subsequently cast as Paul Martin on TV's *Lassie* for the 1957–58 season. Convincing as a British subject here, Shepodd was actually a native of Alabama. The August 24, 1955, rerun of this episode was *Margie*'s final prime time telecast.

"Make Up Your Mind" (February 16, 1955)

    Writers: Frank Gill, Jr., George Carleton Brown. *Director*: Hal Yates.
    Cast: Hillary Brooke (*Roberta Townsend*), Gertrude Hoffmann (*Mrs. Odetts*), Robert Nichols (*Wilbur Weems*), Tristram Coffin (*Dr. Wilton*), Peter Leeds (*Hospital Attendant*)

Summary: The Albrights' trip to Hawaii is jeopardized when Vern's indecisive client Weems reconsiders his decision to buy a pineapple plantation there. Margie, assuming the identity of beautiful native girl Aloha, rekindles Weems' interest in Hawaii, but first he wants to be treated by the same therapist who cured her indecision. Pressed into service as the dubious doc, Roberta almost seals the deal, until a jealous Vern mistakenly thinks her meeting with Weems is an incipient romance.

    Quote: VERN (busting Roberta's scheme): Okay, Roberta, I'll give you just two minutes to explain, and you'd better start at the beginning—which is bound to be Margie!

"Hawaii Story" (February 23, 1955)

    Writers: Frank Gill, Jr., George Carleton Brown. *Director*: Hal Yates.
    Cast: Hillary Brooke (*Roberta Townsend*), Kent Taylor (*Phillip Hubbard*), Margaret Irving (*Nan Carter*), Dian Fauntelle (*Betty*), Roger Pace (*Tom Carter*), Marya Marco (*Kalua*)

Summary: Annoyed when Mr. Honeywell forbids him to take Margie along on a business trip to Hawaii, Vern tells his daughter to cash in the tickets and use the money herself, claiming he's going to Alaska instead. Margie buys herself and Roberta tickets to the islands, where she inadvertently stumbles upon Vern's efforts to win aging movie star Nan Carter as his client. With Vern claiming to be younger in order to compete with his rival Phillip Hubbard for Nan's account, Margie decks herself out in pigtails and poses as his 12-year-old daughter.

    Notes: In its fourth season, the show was running low on handsome young actors to play suitors for Margie, or at least on ones who were affordable and reliable. This is Roger Pace's third go-round on the series. In a nice touch of continuity, Phillip Hubbard is employed by Conway and Staub, the firm mentioned in previous episodes as Honeywell and Todd's chief rival.

    Quote: HONEYWELL (in a memo Betty reads aloud): First, find out whether Knucklehead Albright has blabbed the client's name to Margie.

"Las Vegas Story" (March 2, 1955)

    Writers: Frank Gill, Jr., George Carleton Brown. *Director*: Hal Yates.
    Cast: Richard Crane (*Lee Barker*), Jan Shepard (*Nancy Porter*), Paul Harvey (*Jim Sledge*), Mira McKinney (*Woman Gambler*); Peter Leeds

Summary: In Las Vegas, Margie has been forbidden to gamble, since Vern's client Jim Sledge is vehemently opposed to it. Meeting a young lady at the hotel who entices her into playing the roulette table, Margie doesn't realize she's befriended the client's niece

Nancy. Identified by Sledge as the "professional shill" whom he spotted gambling with his niece, Margie tries to skip town—only to take refuge in the hotel's beauty contest.

Note: Actor Peter Leeds, a familiar character player on *Margie*, is billed in the closing credits, but not visible in surviving prints.

"Vern's Flying Saucer" (March 9, 1955)

    Writers: Frank Gill, Jr., George Carleton Brown. *Director*: Hal Yates.
    Cast: Clarence Kolb (*George Honeywell*), Archer MacDonald (*Chester*), John Hubbard (*Director*), Ralph Dumke (*Mr. Philpotts*), Peter Leeds (*TV Host*), Joanne Jordan (*Actress Playing Queen Venusia*); Richard Beals

Summary: Aspiring to an acting career, Margie gets a break when she meets her nerdy neighbor Chester, an astrophysicist who serves as technical adviser to a TV science fiction show, *Space Men*. With Chester's help, Margie lands her first acting gig on a live dramatic show. The slapstick mess that results infuriates the sponsor, who is Vern's new client. Temporarily grounded, Margie sneaks out when Chester gets her a role on *Space Men*, but the real drama begins when Vern and Mr. Honeywell follow her to the shoot, and a scene involving a Venusian spaceship.

Note: According to *Daily Variety* (February 15, 1955), casting director Frank Edmunds needed midgets for the spaceship scenes, but found that most of them were busy working on the Danny Kaye comedy *The Court Jester* at Paramount. "So the 'space men' in the Gale Storm–Charles Farrell yarn about flying saucers will be moppets instead."

"Margie's New Boyfriend" (March 16, 1955)

    Writers: Frank Gill, Jr., George Carleton Brown. *Director*: Hal Yates.
    Cast: Don Hayden (*Freddie Wilson*), Hillary Brooke (*Roberta Townsend*), Don Megowan (*Sgt. Jim McCarthy*), Dorothy Ford (*Sgt. Jane Smith*), Jack Rutherford (*Gen. Jeffers*), Dian Fauntelle (*Marine*); Harry Lauter

Summary: After another run-in with Freddie, Vern wants Margie to find "a real live he-man" to date. Visiting a Marine base, Margie recruits Sgt. Jim McCarthy, who proves to be so rough and tough that her father has second thoughts. Tricked into thinking Margie is going to elope with her Marine, Vern and Freddie infiltrate the base to stop her.

Notes: Actor Don Megowan (1922–1981), seen as Margie's he-man, may be best-known for playing the Creature from the Black Lagoon (in his scenes on dry land) in *The Creature Walks Among Us* (1956). Dian Fauntelle, usually seen as Honeywell and Todd receptionist Betty, turns up here in a small role as a lady Marine.

"Corpus Delicti" (March 23, 1955)

    Writers: Frank Gill, Jr., George Carleton Brown. *Director*: Hal Yates.
    Cast: Don Hayden (*Freddie Wilson*), Michael Fox (*Roland Roberts*), El Brendel (*George*), Willie Best (*Charlie*), Ruby Goodwin (*Housekeeper*)

Summary: Inside the old trunk she bought at a rummage sale, Margie finds a diary that seems to contain the confession of a murderer. Unbeknownst to her, the diary belonged to Vern's client Roland Roberts, an author who needs it to defend himself against a plagiarism suit. When he's unable to retrieve the diary, Roberts and Vern head to the movie studio where he once worked, and where Margie and Freddie are hot on the trail of the killer.

Note: This episode finds Charlie making a rare reference to "my wife."

"Mr. Uranium" (March 30, 1955)

 Writers: Frank Gill, Jr., George Carleton Brown. *Director*: Hal Yates.

 Cast: Clarence Kolb (*George Honeywell*), Irving Bacon (*Hank Brattle/"Smith"*), Frank Ferguson (*Jones*), John Smith (*Jim Brattle*), Harry Hines (*Proprietor*)

Summary: Mr. Honeywell is hot on the trail of a wealthy and eccentric client, a former uranium prospector who's holed up incognito in a trailer camp to get away from "city folk." Equipped with a dilapidated trailer supplied by his boss, Vern and Margie make camp in the same location. Vern cozies up to Mr. Jones, believing him to be the client, while getting off entirely on the wrong foot with Mr. Smith, who's actually the man he needs to impress.

 Notes: This fun episode is generously larded with slapstick, as Vern and "Mr. Smith" play a series of pranks on each other, and the Albrights rough it in their rickety trailer. Character actor Irving Bacon previously worked with Gale in *Freckles Comes Home*.

"The Big Telecast" (April 6, 1955)

 Writers: Frank Gill, Jr., George Carleton Brown. *Director*: Hal Yates.

 Cast: Don Hayden (*Freddie Wilson*), Clarence Kolb (*George Honeywell*), Dian Fauntelle (*Betty*), Muriel Landers (*Bertha Mardini*), Duke Johnson, Harry Johnson (*The Mandini Brothers*), Bill Sheldon, Joel Marston (*TV Crew*)

Summary: Margie's $400 investment in Global Amusement Enterprises makes her co-owner of a circus act, the Marvelous Mandinis, which features juggling twins, a bearded lady and two performing seals. Obliged to furnish housing for the performers, Margie boards them in the Albright apartment while Vern is away, unaware he's heading back into town to appear on a live TV interview show, *Important People*.

 Notes: This episode features a tie-in with *TV Guide* (Gale appeared on the April 23, 1955, cover). The fictional TV show depicted in this episode, *Important People*, is loosely modeled on Edward R. Murrow's popular interview program *Person to Person*.

"Margie's Recipe" (April 13, 1955)

 Writers: Frank Gill, Jr., George Carleton Brown. *Director*: Hal Yates.

 Cast: Clarence Kolb (*George Honeywell*), Willie Best (*Charlie*), Paul Maxey (*Russell Kaye*), Fred Sherman (*Member*)

Summary: Vern forbids Margie to audition her operatic voice for their dinner guest Mr. Kaye, head of the Civic Opera Foundation. Staying true to the letter of the law, Margie disguises herself as the Albrights' German cook Ilse Krautmeyer, singing lustily while serving a meal cooked by Charlie. Mr. Kaye, who loves the meal, asks "Ilse" to prepare it for the Manhattan Gourmet Society.

 Notes: This episode spotlights Willie Best as Charlie in a way that few, if any, others do. To the producers' credit, he is given billing that recognizes his contribution to the segment, rather than dropping his name to the bottom of the list of featured players as is usually done. According to the script, Charlie's "Chicken Bayou" (which Ilse redubs "Chicken Bavarian") is based on a recipe given him by his late grandmother, although he can't write it out for Margie because it relies heavily on "dabs, pinches and smidgens."

"Papa and Mambo" (April 20, 1955)

 Writers: Frank Gill, Jr., George Carleton Brown. *Director*: Hal Yates.

 Cast: Hillary Brooke (*Roberta Townsend*), Clarence Kolb (*George Honeywell*), Charlita

(*Pepita*), Teresa Tudor (*Mrs. Mendoza*), Dian Fauntelle (*Betty*), Tom Hernandez (*Hernando*)

Summary: With Vern's Honeywell and Todd contract up for renewal, he presses his boss to keep an old promise and step down, giving the presidency to Vern. Honeywell issues a challenge: whichever of them can win the account of wealthy widow Mrs. Mendoza will be president of the firm. Thinking the client is a fortune hunter chasing Vern, Margie and Roberta plot to cool off his new fling. They get active encouragement from the conniving Mr. Honeywell.

Note: Lots of costumes and assumed identities come into play here: Margie casting herself as a sergeant from the New York bunco squad, while Roberta assumes the persona of a San Francisco stripper named Bubbles.

"Matinee Idol" (April 27, 1955)

Writers: Frank Gill, Jr., George Carleton Brown. *Director*: Hal Yates.
Cast: Don Hayden (*Freddie Wilson*), Gale Robbins (*Lynn Loring*), John Hubbard (*Harold Clairmore*), Herb Vigram [Vigran] (*Danny*), Ferris Taylor (*Justice of the Peace*)

Summary: After reading a magazine article about Broadway actor Harold Clairmore, Margie is convinced she's his "Dream Girl." Going backstage to meet him, Margie gets a warm welcome, unaware that Clairmore is using the publicity to coax his leading lady, Lynn Loring, into marrying him. When a jealous Miss Loring learns the truth, she conspires with Margie to give their men a taste of their own medicine.

"Countess Margie" (May 4, 1955)

Writers: Frank Gill, Jr., George Carleton Brown. *Director*: Hal Yates.
Cast: Clarence Kolb (*George Honeywell*), Noreen Nash (*Countess Louise DuBois*), Joseph Kearns (*Mr. Roberts*), Roy Roberts (*Dr. Carr*), Michael Emmet (*Jeff Dale*)

Summary: Margie accompanies her pal, the Countess DuBois, to a rest home, where they trade identities to find out if the manager, Jeff Dale, is in love with the countess or with her money. When the countess, driving Margie's car, has an encounter with the police, Vern shows up to see what happened. With the help of a fellow resident who loves practical jokes, Margie and the countess conspire to keep Vern occupied until the situation with Jeff is resolved.

Notes: This episode is a partial remake of the previous segment "Health Farm." Busy character actor Joseph Kearns gives a lively portrayal of the eccentric patient Mr. Roberts, who enjoys posing as a doctor and "treating" unsuspecting visitors.

"Margie's Baseball Player" (May 11, 1955)

Writers: Frank Gill, Jr., George Carleton Brown. *Director*: Hal Yates.
Cast: Don Hayden (*Freddie Wilson*), Clarence Kolb (*George Honeywell*), Robert Easton (*Ozark Hoskins*), Harry Cheshire (*Mr. Brooks*), John Dierkes (*Minister*)

Summary: Honeywell and Todd client Mr. Brooks has invested $100,000 in a baseball player from Arkansas, Ozark Hoskins, who has fallen into a slump because he's homesick in New York. Margie arranges for the naïve young man to meet Southerners Margie Belle, her pappy and her dimwitted cousin (Margie, Vern and Freddie, respectively). Ozark's playing improves dramatically, thanks to the new friends he likes so much that he wants to move into their apartment and marry Margie Belle.

Note: This script has some very funny lines, although the derisive portrayal of "hillbillies" and the accompanying accouterments (blacked-out teeth, clotheslines and livestock in the living room) may not have gone over well with some viewers outside New York.

Quote: MARGIE BELLE (welcoming Ozark to the apartment): Let me have your hat, Ozark. This place has got little bitty rooms where they don't keep nothing but clothes.

"Vern's Butterflies" (May 18, 1955)

Writers: Frank Gill, Jr., George Carleton Brown. *Director:* Hal Yates.
Cast: Richard Crane (*Ted Stark*), Gil Lamb (*Toby*), Joe Besser (*Ernest Briggs*), Dian Fauntelle (*Betty*), Jack Rice (*Desk Clerk*)

Summary: Vern and Margie have been invited to spend a week at the lakeside inn managed by his old Navy buddy. At first reluctant to leave New York, because he's pursuing a new client who's a butterfly collector, Vern agrees to the trip when he's told that "Mr. Briggs" just checked in at the inn. While Vern exhausts himself chasing butterflies with the phony "Mr. Briggs," who's actually the inn's janitor, a new wrinkle develops when the real client turns up and hears that someone is impersonating him.

Note: Comic actor Joe Besser (1907–1988), known for his role as Stinky Davis on *The Abbott and Costello Show* as well as his stint with the Three Stooges, considerably enlivens this episode. He and Charles Farrell pair off well, with comic mayhem ensuing.

"Margie's Elopement" (May 25, 1955)

Writers: Herbert F. Margolis, William F. Raynor. *Director:* Hal Yates.
Cast: Don Hayden (*Freddie Wilson*), Clarence Kolb (*George Honeywell*), Nancy Hale (*Cindy Lou Rivers*), John Hiestand (*Mr. Rivers*), Joe Devlin (*Lieutenant*), Jimmy Hayes (*Tony Brown*), Ferris Taylor (*Justice of the Peace*)

Summary: Prospective client Mr. Rivers wants to whisk his daughter off to Europe, because he disapproves of her boyfriend. At Vern's suggestion, Rivers installs his daughter Cindy in the apartment next to the Albrights, under the watch of a private detective. Margie plots to help Cindy and her boyfriend Tony elope, resulting in chaos when Vern thinks it's his own daughter who's getting married.

The NBC Comedy Hour

In early 1956, Gale accepted a short-term job as the emcee of a struggling variety show, *The NBC Comedy Hour,* seen on Sunday nights opposite CBS' popular Ed Sullivan. She replaced Leo Durocher, who had hosted the January segments, the first of which *Variety* (January 11, 1956) termed "a potpourri of mediocrity." Early episodes showed ratings only half of what Ed Sullivan drew on the rival network. Of Gale's initial outing, reviewer Bob Foster wrote,

> NBC tried to add new life to ... *Comedy Hour* by hiring Hollywood's miracle girl, Gale Storm, to be the master of ceremonies. Miss Storm's appearance was excellent, but as usual they failed to back her up with much in the way of good comedy. Only the appearance of Jonathan Winters and Peter Donald, one of America's best story tellers, saved the show for Miss Storm. The rest was pretty pathetic.[20]

Gale's contract with Hal Roach for a new filmed sitcom prevented her from making a long-term commitment to *The NBC Comedy Hour*. "We've just completed the pilot," she told an interviewer that spring, "and once we're underway I'll have to give up my mistress of ceremony job on the *Comedy Hour*. But I'll never forget the things I've learned working with all those great comedians. They work harder than anyone else in show business."[21] In May, Steve Allen took over hosting the show, with its name changed to reflect his participation.

Episodes

February 5, 1956. Guests, "television personality Eddie Bracken; storyteller Peter Donald; Shecky Greene, young comedian making his television debut; monologist Georgie Kaye, and the *Comedy Hour*'s popular 'repeat' guest, Jonathan Winters."—*Bluefield (WV) Daily Telegraph*. *Variety* (February 6, 1956) said that Gale "carried off her double-duty chores as femcee and singer-dancer with taste and judgment." She sings "Teenage Prayer" and "Memories Are Made of This."

February 12, 1956. Guests, Jonathan Winters, Stan Freberg, Bert Wheeler, Tom D'Andrea.

February 19, 1956. Guests, Stan Freberg, Bill Thompson, Ben Blue, Hans Conried. "Miss Storm, pert and pretty as hostess, pleasantly intoned two tunes given inventive mounting with the gay cavorting of the dancers."—*Daily Variety*, February 20, 1956

March 4, 1956. Guests, Stan Freberg, Bert Lahr, Jonathan Winters, impressionist Dave Barry. "The laughs were few and far between ... the writing was woefully lacking in freshness or spark.... Gale Storm was her usual pert, cute self as mistress of ceremonies and her songs delightfully gay."—*Daily Variety*, March 5, 1956

March 11, 1956. Guests, Bert Lahr, David Burns, the Slate Brothers.

March 18, 1956. Guests, Stan Freberg, Jonathan Winters, dancer Harry Mimmo. "Show fell apart at the finish, with Storm and the comics practically ad libbing a full five minutes. The laugh spread wasn't there, which threw off the timing."—*Daily Variety*, March 19, 1956.

April 1, 1956. Guests, Cesar Romero, Stan Freberg, Jonathan Winters, Emmett Kelly.

April 8, 1956. Guests, Kaye Ballard, Cliff Arquette, Mort Sahl, Jonathan Winters.

The show was pre-empted on February 26 and March 25, 1956, for Max Liebman's monthly "Sunday Spectacular" specials.

The Gale Storm Show: Oh! Susanna

Cast: Gale Storm (*Susanna Pomeroy*), ZaSu Pitts (*Elvira "Nugey" Nugent*), Roy Roberts (*Captain Simon P. Huxley*), James Fairfax (*Cedric*)

Executive Producer: Hal Roach, Jr. *Producer*: Alex Gottlieb. *Based on Characters Created by* Lee Karson. *Production Supervisor*: Sidney Van Keuren. *Photography*: Eddie Fitzgerald, Lothrop Worth. *Production Coordinator*: William Sterling. *Production Managers*: William Beaudine, Jr., James W. Lane. *Assistant Directors*: Bernard L. Kowalski, Marty Moss, Maurice Vaccarino. *Editors*: Bert Jordan, Fred Maguire. *Art Director*: William Ferrari. *Set Decorators*: Hal Gausman, Kenneth W. Swartz, Charles Thompson. *Photographic Effects*: Jack R. Glass. *Music*: Leon Klatzkin. *Sound*: Charles Althouse, Frank McWhorter, Joel Moss. *Makeup*: Tom Case, Don Roberson, John Sylvester. *Hair Stylists*:

Carmen Dirigo, Shirley Madden, Betty Pedretti, Josephine Sweeney. *Wardrobe Supervisor*: Wally Harton. *Costumers*: Ann Helfgott, Fay Moore. *Casting*: Ruth Burch. *Script Supervisor*: Maggie Lawrence. *Technical Assistance and Cooperation*: American President Lines. *Miss Storm's Wardrobe*: Junior House of Milwaukee.

After the success of *My Little Margie,* Hal Roach, Jr., offered both of its stars an opportunity to appear in other shows for the company. Roach sold CBS the new sitcom *The Charles Farrell Show.* Like *My Little Margie,* it was introduced to the world as the summer replacement for *I Love Lucy.* The new series was based on Farrell's real-life background as proprietor of the Racquet Club in Palm Springs, California. Signed for featured roles in the series were Kathryn Card (who'd made a few *Margie* appearances) as Charles' housekeeper and character actor Richard Deacon as the club manager. Charles Winninger appeared as Farrell's dad. The series returned for a second summer run in 1957, but didn't attract a large enough audience to get onto the regular fall schedule.

Gale, under contract to Roach through February 1956, was warming to a concept developed by *Margie* writer Lee Karson. After reviewing several scripts submitted to her by Hal Roach, Jr., she sparked to the idea of *Oh! Susanna.* The concept, she told a *TV*

Aside from Gale, regulars on *The Gale Storm Show: Oh! Susanna* included James Fairfax (left) as Cedric, and ZaSu Pitts (right) as Nugey.

Guide interviewer, had scope. "We can go almost anywhere, land or sea. And it gives me a chance to sing. We don't drag the music in by the jowls, but about every fourth show it naturally fits into the plot without looking like a 'number' just for the number's sake."[22]

Serving as producer for the first three seasons was Alex Gottlieb (1906–1988), a movie producer and screenwriter who'd been closely associated for most of the 1940s with Abbott and Costello. *The Gale Storm Show* was Gottlieb's most successful sitcom venture; he also produced the series *Dear Phoebe* (NBC, 1954–55), *Love That Jill* (ABC, 1958) and *The Tammy Grimes Show* (ABC, 1966). The most prolific of the show's scriptwriters was Larry Rhine, teamed with either Bill Freedman or Milton Pascal. Rhine, who died in 2000 at the age of 90, enjoyed a long career ranging from radio (*Duffy's Tavern*) to his Emmy-nominated work for television's *All in the Family*. Other frequent contributors included John L. Greene and John Fenton Murray.

Comic actress ZaSu Pitts (1894–1963), who'd first worked with Gale 15 years earlier in the film *Uncle Joe,* was signed for the role of Susanna's best friend, the ship's manicurist and beauty operator, Elvira Nugent. She'd had a long association with Hal Roach Studios, having co-starred with Thelma Todd in more than two dozen shorts for them. Said Pitts, "When I first started working with Gale, I thought she was a sweet young thing and I thought maybe I ought to mother her. But I want to tell you I learned a lot from her.... Gale's zest for life and her ability to make us see the goofy side of life has rubbed off on all of us."[23] In 1959, Pitts received an Emmy nomination as Best Supporting Actress for her work as Nugey.

Gale suggested character actor Roy Roberts (1906–1975) for the part of her onscreen boss, Captain Simon P. Huxley. Roberts, with a long list of credits on Broadway and in films, had appeared as a guest player on *My Little Margie*, where he'd impressed Gale with his ability to play a variety of characters. He had just the right touch to play Gale's sometimes grumpy, stuffy boss, but in a way that allowed viewers to smile at her predicaments. In the 1960s, Roberts juggled recurring roles on three sitcoms: *Bewitched* (as Samantha's father-in-law, Frank Stephens), *The Beverly Hillbillies* (as rival banker Mr. Cushing) and *The Lucy Show* (as Mr. Mooney's boss, Mr. Cheever).

Character actor James Fairfax (1897–1961), previously seen in a featured role on the adventure series *Ramar of the Jungle,* was cast as steward Cedric. His film credits included small roles in *My Cousin Rachel* and *Mrs. Mike*. Fairfax, who was written out of the series in its fourth year, died about a year later of a heart attack in Tahiti, while appearing in MGM's *Mutiny on the Bounty.*

Filming of the series pilot was set for March 1956; before the show was even in the can, Nestlé (most recently Jackie Gleason's sponsor) had signed on to sponsor. The company promoted the show with ads promising "melody, hilarity and suspense in a program that promises to be one of the brightest new shows of the season."

Production of the first season episodes was complicated by Gale's unexpected pregnancy, ten years after giving birth to her third child. She was only a few weeks away from delivery that fall when she took part in preview showings for the press. Urged several times by executive producer Hal Roach, Jr., to stand and take a bow, Gale cracked, "He's just doing that because he knows how difficult it is for me to get up and down right now."[24] Gale took about a month's maternity leave that fall, before going back to work.

Gale's new series was assigned a time slot on CBS' Saturday night schedule. Her competition was Lawrence Welk (on ABC) and Sid Caesar (on NBC). *The Gale Storm Show* made its network bow on September 29, 1956, paired with another new comedy series, *Hey, Jeannie!*, starring Jeannie Carson. Said syndicated columnist Dick Kleiner (July 29, 1956), "The smart money is on Caesar."

Opening night reviews were mixed. *Daily Variety* (October 1, 1956) was dubious about the series premiere, saying, "It's going to take sturdier stuff than this to stay in the rat(e) race," finding Lee Karson and Phil Shuken's pilot script weak. The reviewer noted that Gale was "by far the prettiest of the comediennes, can sing a good song, spin around her classy chassis with charm and grace, read a line well and do just about anything the script calls for." A more favorable reaction came from syndicated columnist Bob Foster, who attended a preview showing of the premiere episode in September and reported, "It's going to be top TViewing [sic] and is bound to give Lawrence Welk and Sid Caesar a run for their money."[25]

In Chicago, critic Gabe Gabriel noted some criticisms of the show, but concluded that it "is still a fresh and sprightly entry for the new TV season and may very well prove to be one of the big items of the winter months. It has the qualities that can build a large and loyal following."[26] Columnist Jack O'Brian wasn't wowed either, but quoted an "amateur psychologist" of his acquaintance who said, "Keep an eye on that one. It has no serious problems, has its characters in stylish clothes and enviable, if not precisely believable, situations. I think the time is ripe for a good little feather-headed show with nothing important on its mind or script."[27] Charles Barton, who alternated with William A. Seiter as the show's regular director, told *TV Guide* that there would be a noticeable difference between Gale's first sitcom and the new one. "*Margie* was pretty broad stuff," he said. "We're going to put this one on a little higher level.... We're giving her more believable situations. As social directress aboard a luxury liner, she's got to be a girl of intelligence. She can't be completely scatterbrained, you know."[28] Gale concurred: "The characterization is different, even though she [Susanna] is prone to get everything in a mess from time to time. But this is credible, not silly, comedy. Also, the tempo isn't frantic."[29]

At the outset, though, not everyone could see the distinction clearly. "Gale's still little Margie in the new series," said syndicated columnist Erskine Johnson (October 1, 1956), "except for a chance to display her slick singing and dancing. The first stanza [episode] was Formula Margie—Miss Fix-It gets into hot water, Miss Fix-It gets out of hot water. Fans who zoomed *Margie* to sky-high ratings though should do the same for *Susanna*."

In May 1957, the *Los Angeles Times'* Walter Ames reported that Gale's show had been renewed for a second season, saying, "It appears as if Gale Storm again has fooled her critics. This won't be the first time because the boys in the know have been giving Gale the axe ever since she first ventured into television."[30] Added Erskine Johnson (August 24, 1957), "On an average of seven out of ten times, Gale beat the [Lawrence] Welk show in the rating battle and she helped carve R.I.P. on the tottering [Sid] Caesar's chest by drawing almost double his audience."

Producer Gottlieb told *Daily Variety* columnist Dave Kaufman (September 27, 1957) that second-season scripts would place a bigger emphasis on stories that contained heart-warming, human interest elements. "If we keep it in the straight situation comedy vein," Gottlieb said, "we will not only be imitating ourselves, but 5000 other series." The producer told another journalist, "What we're trying to do is keep the youngsters and add to the grownup audience."[31] Gottlieb was also seeking more big-name guest stars, hoping to make deals where Gale appeared on their shows in exchange for them doing likewise on *Oh! Susanna*.

In May 1958, *Variety* reported that Nestlé would continue its sponsorship of the series for a third season, with Lorillard taking the place of Helene Curtis as the alternate sponsor. Lever Brothers came aboard as an alternate sponsor in early 1959.

While all was well onscreen, behind the scenes things were rocky financially for Hal Roach, Jr., and his studio. In October 1958, Roach, in financial straits, sold *The Gale Storm Show* lock, stock and barrel to International Television Corporation for a price estimated at $2 million. The buyer obtained the ownership rights to 111 episodes already filmed, plus 38 forthcoming ones to be made under Roach's supervision. The lucrative sale didn't solve all his problems. *Variety* (January 8, 1959) reported that the William Morris agency had filed a lawsuit against Roach, alleging more than $300,000 outstanding in commissions owed. "Agency also obtained a writ of attachment which was levied on Roach's bank accounts, and filed in the County Recorder's Office against the Roach studio real property." Forewarned about the impending bankruptcy, Gale said, "We knew when they were going to lock the gates. We had to get all our sets off the lot and get them set up at Desilu."[32]

ITC succeeded in selling ABC the rerun rights for three years to *Oh! Susanna,* which would be added to the network's daytime schedule, as well as 26 fresh episodes to air in prime time. ABC paid $5 million for the package. ITC took out trade paper ads boasting of the $2 million profit the company had cleared through the deal. In April 1959, daily repeats of the show began on ABC. The network slotted the nighttime episodes to air at 7:30 p.m. on Thursdays, preceding *The Donna Reed Show.* A new sponsor was the Warner-Lambert Pharmaceutical Company, promoting its Listerine product; Gale filmed singing commercials built around the phrase, "Finish the job!" (urging viewers to supplement their use of toothpaste with mouthwash).

Though the transition was worrisome for the show's cast and crew, it unexpectedly presented the opportunity to make some changes Gale had wanted. Gale told a *TV Guide* reporter that she was dissatisfied with some aspects of her second series as it went along, despite its popularity. "I felt a sense of frustration about the show," she said. "I would read a script and want to *change* so many things! I felt that I was just 'busy Margie' again. Everything too broad, too strong."[33] She asked to have a screening of the original series pilot, so that she and her colleagues could assess how the show might have lost its way. The fee for scripts was raised from $2000 to $4000 per week, and the cast and crew were given a day in the production schedule to talk through any script or production problems before formal rehearsal got underway.

The Gale Storm Show launched its fourth season on ABC playing out episodes already filmed under producer Alex Gottlieb. But in August, ITC had veteran comedy writer Lou Derman (1914–1976), who'd just finished a successful run on CBS's *December Bride,* take the show's reins. *Daily Variety* (August 17, 1959) reported, "Derman's deal calls for him to produce six of the 26 Storm stanzas slated for ABC this fall, with options for the balance." Production of the series had been moved to the Desilu lot. Derman concurred with Gale's assessment of the show's shortcomings and, according to *Daily Variety*'s Jack Hellman (November 12, 1959), "All the wild improbabilities of the past three years will be tempered to more believable situations and Miss Storm will be given broader opportunities to act with feeling rather than clown through bizarre situations." Derman's work apparently pleased all involved, and ultimately he was credited as producer and story consultant for most of the Season 4 episodes. After the change at the top, actor James Fairfax was dropped from the cast and his character Cedric no longer mentioned. Instead, John Qualen made two guest appearances as steward Olaf Hansen, while Sid

Melton appeared in a few episodes as crew member Hal Miller. Two Season 4 episodes introduced viewers to Susanna's previously unseen parents, Henry and Bess Pomeroy.

As described in network publicity, "[Gale's] refreshing good looks enhance the captain's table, her vocal talents brighten every ship's party and her flair for making folks happy turns every moment into a wonderfully comic adventure." Captain Huxley is "in reality, a sentimental pushover for Susanna's wild and wacky schemes."[34]

Susanna spends most of her time either causing trouble, being in trouble, or trying to get out of trouble. Called to her boss' office in "Jailmates" (February 28, 1959), she is on the defensive as soon as Huxley announces that he wants to discuss "a matter of tremendous importance":

> SUSANNA: Well, I didn't do it, sir.
> HUXLEY: No, Miss Pomeroy...
> SUSANNA: Or, if I did it, I can explain it.
> HUXLEY: Miss Pomeroy, it is not...
> SUSANNA: Or if I can't explain it, well, I promise you I'll never do it again!

Always prone to take an interest in the problems of others, Susanna seems unable to remember, as Huxley puts it in one episode, "You are not Miss Lonelyhearts, you are not a nurse, and you are not a seagoing psychiatrist." Susanna, on the other hand, says, "After all, I am the social director on this ship, and if I let my passengers walk around unhappy, I'm not being very social, am I?"

According to an ABC press release, *The Gale Storm Show* gave its star an itch to travel for real. She said, "I'd like to hear Swiss yodeling in the Alps and see if Trinidad calypso singers really make up the verses as they go along. I'd like to visit the vineyards of France and see if they really stomp on the grapes with their bare feet to press wine. I'd like to try shish-kebab that tastes as foreign as it sounds. I've always wondered—what does a sacred cow look like?"[35] Still, when Gale had her first opportunity to actually travel on a luxury liner, courtesy of the American President Lines, she found it to be not quite what she was expecting. Standing on deck while a breeze blew, according to syndicated columnist Vernon Scott, "Gale jumped a foot in the air when the ship's horn loosed an ear-splitting blast." The startled actress cracked, "Stop the boat! I've got to go back for my eyelashes!"[36]

ABC publicity during the show's final prime time season was careful to label it as "a brand-new evening series," wanting to distinguish new segments from the daytime reruns. At the end of its fourth season, *The Gale Storm Show* ceased production, and left the prime time schedule. Daytime reruns continued into the early 1960s.

Gale Storm appeared in every episode as Susanna Pomeroy. ZaSu Pitts and Roy Roberts appeared in almost every episode as Nugey and Captain Huxley, and were billed in the closing credits each week. James Fairfax, as Cedric, was billed among the featured players in the episodes in which he appeared, and is listed below for every appearance that could be confirmed.

SEASON ONE

"Italian Movie Star" (September 29, 1956)
    Writers: Phil Shuken, Lee Karson. *Director*: William A. Seiter.
    Cast: James Fairfax (*Cedric*); James Lydon

Summary: "Miss Storm comes to the rescue of a young officer who has a personality considered too flat for a cruise ship by the ship's captain.... That's when Gale dons a blond wig to impersonate an Italian movie star and pretends to be entranced with the young officer."—*Racine* (WI) *Journal-Times*

Note: This episode reunited Gale with actor James Lydon, star of her first feature film *Tom Brown's School Days*. Lydon appeared in multiple episodes as an *Ocean Queen* crew member, a character later called Evans. Gale sings "Ain't Got a Worry in the World." The *Gale Storm Show* DVDs in circulation among collectors often contain an episode listed as "Italian Movie Star." But hit PLAY and you'll find, not this series opener, but "Stop, Thief," in which a jewel thief poses as an Italian film actor.

"The Chimpanzee" (October 6, 1956)

Writers: Al Gordon, Hal Goldman. *Director*: John Rich.

Cast: J. Pat O'Malley (*Rearden*), Lucie Lancaster (*Mrs. Rearden*), Dan Barton (*Gordon*), Eleanor Audley (*Passenger*), Eddie Parks (*Man*), James Fairfax (*Cedric*)

Summary: With the president of the cruise line, Mr. Rearden, and his wife aboard, Huxley is especially anxious for the trip to go smoothly. His best intentions are upset when Susanna agrees to hide in her cabin Bimbo, the chimpanzee Cedric bought for his nephew. Forced to find a new hiding place after Bimbo gets loose and creates havoc, Susanna unwittingly chooses the cabin to which the Reardens were just assigned.

"Passenger Incognito" (October 13, 1956)

Writers: Frank Gill, Jr., G. Carleton Brown. *Director*: John Rich.

Cast: Nancy Kulp (*Helga Peterson*), Paul Maxey (*Sylvester Rockwell*), Casey Adams (*Orchestra Leader*), Maurice Marsac (*Inspector*), Paul Bryar (*Detective Renaud*), James Fairfax (*Cedric*)

Summary: Feeling sorry for a drab, shy passenger, Susanna arranges for Nugey to give her a glamorous makeover and spread a rumor that she's a countess traveling incognito. The "new" Helga soon becomes the belle of the ball, but attracts the attention of two French policemen searching for a jewel thief.

Notes: It's old home week, with a script by Gale's longtime *Margie* writers and a guest appearance by actor Paul Maxey, seen often in her first series. Captain Huxley sounds a bit like a defeated Vern Albright when he says at the episode's conclusion, "Doesn't anything you do wrong ever turn out wrong for you?" Gale does a medley combining "Rock-a-Bye-Baby" with the upbeat "Rock the Cradle."

"Bonnie Lassie" (October 20, 1956)

Writers: Erna Lazarus, Nathaniel Curtis. *Director*: Charles Barton.

Cast: Lumsden Hare (*Kenneth MacNab*), Frank Wilcox (*Duncan Glowrie*), Irene Corlett (*Mrs. Hatfield*), Francis DeSales (*Hartley E. Benson*), Eric Wilton (*Horace*), James Fairfax (*Cedric*)

Summary: Innocently introducing two passengers, Susanna doesn't know that MacNab and Glowrie are members of Scottish families that have been feuding for generations. Glowrie wants to buy a historic gold cup that's in his rival's possession, but MacNab refuses to sell. Invited to be a guest at MacNab's castle, Susanna tries to settle the dispute.

Note: Gale's musical number features Harry Lauder's 1911 song "Roamin' in the Gloamin,'" with some specially adapted lyrics. Choreography is credited to Nick Castle.

"Too Many Maharanis" (October 27, 1956)

Cast: Narda Onyx

Summary: "Susanna Pomeroy ... poses as a maharani when the real one declines to attend a round of ship's parties.... Her troubles begin when Susanna learns two assassins are on board who plan to do away with the real maharani."—*Dallas Morning News*, June 16, 1959

Note: According to *Daily Variety* (June 29, 1956), other actors signed for this episode included Isabel Randolph, Lela Bliss, Doris Packer and William Pullen.

"Nicked in Naples" (November 10, 1956)

Writers: Lee Karson, Ben Gershman. *Director*: Charles Barton.

Cast: Jay Novello (*Alfredo Colucci*), Penny Santon (*Signora Scarlatti*), Philip Tonge (*Sir Twickenham*), Frank Nechero (*Bartender*), Paul Cesari (*Italian Chef*), The Carl Carelli Trio (*Nightclub Musicians*)

Summary: After coming into some money thanks to a raffle held aboard the *Ocean Queen*, Nugey decides to buy a business in Naples. Fast-talking Alfredo Colucci, proprietor of a local hotel, bilks her of $1350 for a nightclub that looks like a bustling enterprise, thanks to being populated with his friends and relatives. Susanna poses as a wealthy heiress who wants to buy the club herself—if Colucci can get it back from Miss Nugent.

Note: Gale's musical segment features her renditions of "Vieni Sue" and "Funiculi, Funiculà," choreographed by Nick Castle.

"The Immigrants" (November 17, 1956)

Writers: Bernard Ederer, Bob White. *Director*: William A. Seiter.

Cast: Harold Dyrenforth (*Peter Jezek*), Kaaren Verne (*Marya Jezek*), Peter Votrian (*Michael*), Jeri Lou James (*Anya*), James Lydon (*Hendricks*)

Summary: A family emigrating to America stows away on the *Ocean Queen*, so as to use their visas before they expire. Aware that Captain Huxley will not sympathize, Susanna hides them away in her cabin. When a head count reveals that there are four people too many on board, Susanna realizes the jig will soon be up.

Notes: Kaaren Verne (1918–1967), billed here as Karen Verne, was the ex-wife of actor Peter Lorre.

"Susanna Strikes Back" (November 24, 1956)

Writers: Larry Rhine, Bill Freedman. *Director*: William A. Seiter.

Cast: James Lydon (*Saunders*), Dick Elliott (*Mr. Bartlett*), Richard Collier (*Mr. Trumbridge*), Robert Cornthwaite (*Mr. Higgins*), Jean Bartel (*Miss Danbury*), Paula Winslowe (*Customer*)

Summary: Fed up with Susanna's shenanigans, Captain Huxley succeeds in having her transferred off the *Ocean Queen*. On dry land, she's none too successful training new social directors, but she gets an unexpected break in the sales office when she sells Mr. Bartlett 187 tickets on behalf of the Smilers Club of America. Winning the company's national sales contest, Susanna's prize is a cruise—on the *Ocean Queen*.

Notes: According to this script, Susanna and her friends are employees of Blue Anchor Lines (which will change in future episodes), and her middle name is Cordelia. James Lydon again plays a crew member, with a different character name than in the previous episode.

"Hold That Tiger" (December 1, 1956)

Cast: Raymond Bailey (*Mr. Carney*), Robert Clarke (*Jamil*), Rex Evans (*Rajah*)

Summary: "Suspecting that Captain Huxley ... is getting too old for his job ... the steamship company sends a new vice-president as a passenger to spy on the captain.... The captain appeals to [Susanna] for help but after he gets through the routine she sets for him—from doing the Charleston to big game hunting in Africa—the skipper is ready for retirement."—*Coshocton* (OH) *Tribune*, November 24, 1956

"The Witch Doctor" (December 8, 1956)

Writer: John L. Greene. *Director*: William A. Seiter.
Cast: Chuck Connors (*Ooma*), Tod Andrews (*Jim Madison*), Susan Morrow (*Lydia Vernon*), Barbara Slate (*Jane*), William Swan (*Bob*), James Fairfax (*Cedric*)

Summary: Handsome Jim Madison, too shy to approach women, is not enjoying his *Ocean Queen* voyage. While docked in Bali, Susanna persuades him to visit the local witch doctor (actually an ex–G.I. named Irving) and buy a love charm. The talisman gives Jim the confidence he needs to enlarge his social circle, to the dismay of Susanna, who wanted him for herself.

Note: Baseball player turned actor Chuck Connors (1921–1992) was still a couple of years away from his starring role in TV's *The Rifleman*.

"A Night in Monte Carlo" (December 15, 1956)

Writers: Larry Rhine, Bill Freedman. *Director*: William A. Seiter.
Cast: John Archer (*Lucky Malloy*), Peggy Knudsen (*Flo*), Stephen Bekassy (*Lazlo*), Eric Feldary (*Nikki*), Franco Corsaro (*Flaubert*), Arthur Brunner (*Croupier*)

Summary: Susanna and Nugey have no intention of gambling while they stay in Monte Carlo. But Nugey, trying to get change for the pay phone, manages to win big at the roulette table. Watching the ladies rake in the money, several denizens of the casino assume they have devised a winning system and go to extraordinary lengths to learn it.

Note: Actor John Archer (1915–1999) was a veteran of Gale's early film *City of Missing Girls*.

"Capri" (December 22, 1956)

Writers: Al Gordon, Hal Goldman. *Director*: Charles Barton.
Cast: Paul Picerni (*Sebastian*), Albert Villasainte (*Vittorio*), Tony Romano (*Antonio*), Damian O'Flynn (*Ship's Doctor*), Vincent Padula (*Waiter*), James Fairfax (*Cedric*)

Summary: When Nugey develops a psychosomatic backache just as the ship docks for a two-day stay at Capri, the ship's physician prescribes "equal parts of love and romance, affection and attention." Advised that the local hotel is crawling with handsome fortune hunters, Susanna manages to give two of them the impression that her friend Miss Nugent is extremely wealthy. Susanna's plan backfires when Nugey takes their attentions a bit too seriously, saying both gentlemen have proposed marriage to her.

Note: Gale duets with singer-guitarist Tony Romano (1915–2005) on "The Isle of Capri." Actor Paul Picerni is a veteran of *My Little Margie,* where he played one of Gale's many love interests.

"The Magician" (December 29, 1956)

Writers: Lee Karson, Elon Packard. *Director*: Charles Barton.
Cast: Alan Reed (*Zachary*), Lillian Culver (*Mrs. Guthrie*), Lowell Gilmore (*Hugo Higgins*), James Gavin (*Martin*), Frank Kreig (*Simmons*)

Summary: Doing a favor for a friend, Susanna arranges for the Great Zachary, a magician, to be booked as an entertainer on the *Ocean Queen*. Zachary is a hardcore kleptomaniac who spends his time relieving passengers of wallets and jewelry. Promising to reform, Zachary makes good use of his pickpocket skills one last time, to help a woman passenger being blackmailed.

Quote: HUXLEY: I can't remember anything you did wrong on this trip that upset me.
SUSANNA: Well, I'm glad your memory is slipping.

"Girls! Girls! Girls!" (January 5, 1957)

Writers: Erna Lazarus, Nathaniel Curtis. *Director*: Charles Barton.
Cast: Joi Lansing (*Kristine/Miss Lapland*), Pat McVey (*Harvey Reid*), Lisa Davis (*Miss England*), Joan Lora (*Miss Italy*), Shirley Russell (*Miss Spain*)

Summary: Contestants from the upcoming Miss Worldwide pageant are traveling to New York on the *Ocean Queen*. Pageant official Mr. Reid loses faith in Kristine, representing Lapland, when she runs in terror from a photographer. Susanna's efforts to help Kristine arouse the jealousy of the other contestants.

Notes: Blond bombshell Joi Lansing (1929–1972) died young of breast cancer, after a career encompassing numerous film and TV roles. This episode introduces a serious touch rare for *Oh! Susanna* when Kristine confesses that her fear of flashbulbs comes from childhood memories of World War II and her country being bombed.

"Desirable Alien" (January 12, 1957)

Cast: Glenn Langan (*Eric Brown*), Douglass Dumbrille (*Col. Bargo*)

Summary: Susanna "helps a prisoner escape and hides him aboard the *S.S. Ocean Queen*…"—*Corpus Christi* (TX) *Caller-Times,* January 6, 1957

Note: Not long after this guest appearance, actor Glenn Langan (1917–1991) was cast in his best-known role, as the plus-sized title character of the sci-fi film *The Amazing Colossal Man.*

"Foreign Intrigue" (January 19, 1957)

Summary: "Susanna … befriends a sweet, little, old lady passenger … not realizing she is a spy."—*Galveston* (TX) *Daily News,* November 8, 1959

"Goodbye Kiss" (January 26, 1957)

Summary: "Trouble begins when Susanna smuggles a young man aboard to say goodbye to his sweetheart; for good measure, Susanna is involved with a diamond smuggler."— Kokomo (IN) *Tribune*

"Super Snoop" (February 2, 1957)

 Writers: Larry Rhine, Bill Freedman. *Director*: William A. Seiter.
 Cast: Mira McKinney (*Mabel Thomas*), Reginald Sheffield (*Waldo*), William Pullen (*Anderson*), Ted Bliss (*Walter*), Charles Schrouder (*Singer*), James Fairfax (*Cedric*)

Summary: An unidentified crew member has been acting as a stool pigeon, reporting co-workers' minor rule infractions to the home office. Susanna, picking up a piece of Nugey's mail, jumps to the erroneous conclusion that she's the guilty party. Accompanied by Cedric, Susanna trails her roommate to a mysterious rendezvous in London, where she's actually having a blind date with a man referred to her by the International Lonely Hearts Club.

 Notes: In the scene at the Boar's Head Tavern in London, Gale performs an impromptu version of "There Is a Tavern in the Town." According to this script, there are 175 crew members aboard the *Ocean Queen,* which is now said to be operated by the American Eagle Lines.

"Checkmate" (February 9, 1957)

 Cast: Morey Amsterdam (*Mr. Agnew*), David Stollery (*Jonathan*)

Summary: "Susanna is disturbed to learn that a 14-year-old boy has developed a crush on her. She is persuaded not to discourage him when she learns he is en route to the international chess matches. It seems U.S. prestige in the chess world depends on his peace of mind!"—*TV Guide*

"Swiss Miss" (February 16, 1957)

 Writers: Larry Rhine, Bill Freedman. *Director*: Charles Barton.
 Cast: John Banner (*Hans Schlosser*), Ernest Sarracino (*Boticelli*), Marjorie Bennett (*Mrs. Caldwell*), Sven Hugo Borg (*Appelmann*), Jimmy Karath (*Otto Schlosser*)

Summary: Thanks to Susanna's carelessness, the cuckoo clock presented to Captain Huxley by grateful passengers gets a dunking in the ship's pool. Sneaking the clock off the ship to get it repaired, Susanna learns that it is an original that can only be fixed by its maker, who lives in a remote Swiss village. Arriving during the town's annual William Tell Day, Susanna tries to persuade Herr Schlosser to fix the clock immediately, which lands her in the midst of the pageant with an apple on her head.

"The Blarney Stone" (February 23, 1957)

 Writers: Bill Freedman, Larry Rhine. *Director*: Charles Barton.
 Cast: Woodrow Chambliss (*Martin Morley*), Sarah Selby (*Catherine Ericson*), James Flavin (*Attendant*), Hazel Shermet (*Miss Magruder*), James Burke (*Sergeant*)

Summary: Tongue-tied Irishman Martin Morley has never been able to profess his love for his friend Catherine, who has now accepted a marriage proposal from another man. His plans to kiss the Blarney Stone while in Ireland, in hopes of gaining the gift of elo-

Morey Amsterdam is the guest star in "Checkmate," a first-season episode of *The Gale Storm Show: Oh! Susanna*.

quence, are disrupted when he is injured while dancing a jig with Susanna. Since Martin is unable to visit the stone, Susanna schemes to bring a piece of it back to the ship.

Notes: Actress Hazel Shermet (1921–2016), seen as a passenger with a dubious singing voice, was the wife of writer Larry Rhine. Gale sings Arthur Colahan's "Galway Way," to Nick Castle's choreography.

"Volcano" (March 2, 1957)

Writer: John Fenton Murray. *Director*: William. Seiter.
Cast: Robert Warwick (*King Maururu*), James Lydon (*Evans*), Kem Dibbs (*Makala*), Lani McIntire, Faipaua Misilagi (*Knife Dancers*)

Summary: On a tropical island, Susanna unwittingly offends the locals by tossing a pebble into a long-dormant volcano. When the volcano threatens to erupt, the king and his son welcome Susanna to the royal family—so they can appease the gods with a human sacrifice.

Note: According to this script, there are 912 passengers aboard the *Ocean Queen*.

"Indian Giver" (March 9, 1957)

Writer: Hal Fimberg. *Director*: William A. Seiter.

Cast: John Hoyt (*Tom Lightfoot, Sr.*), Douglass Dumbrille (*Chief Chattahoochee*), Richard Garland (*Tom Lightfoot, Jr.*), Helen Mayon (*Mrs. Pool*), Jonathan Hole (*Mr. Pool*), Lester Miller (*Medicine Man*)

Summary: As Susanna prepares to take passengers on a tour of the Everglades, Nugey sees a newspaper headline declaring that the Seminole Indians are at war with the U.S. The story is a publicity stunt designed by young Seminole (and Princeton graduate) Tom Lightfoot, Jr., trying to drum up business for his father's trading post. Tom and his friends give the tourists a thrill by having them "captured" during their tour. Complications arise with the arrival of Chief Chattahoochee, a traditionalist who completely eschews modern ways.

Notes: Roy Roberts does not appear in this episode. Tom Lightfoot, Sr., is seen reading the October 6, 1956, issue of *TV Guide*, with Gale on the cover.

"Susanna, the Chaperone" (March 16, 1957)

Cast: Joan Swift (*Grace*)

Summary: "Susanna is appointed chaperone to four lovely young ladies and is warned to keep them away from a group of Navy frogmen…. Susanna does her best until she discovers that an old boyfriend is leader of the group."—*Galveston* (TX) *Daily News*, November 8, 1959

Note: Gale sings "On Moonlight Bay."

"Gypping the Gypsies" (March 23, 1957)

Writers: Bill Freedman, Larry Rhine. *Director*: William A. Seiter.

Cast: Anthony Dexter (*Ramon*), Peter Coe (*Bardo*), Lou Krugman (*Ali*), Joan Lora (*Carla*), Irene James (*Lolita*), James Fairfax (*Cedric*)

Summary: Susanna and Nugey are kidnapped by a band of gypsies who believe they are wealthy. Captain Huxley assumes the ransom note they send for his employees' safe return is a gag, and ignores it. Just when Nugey fears they will never escape, Susanna begins to make herself unpopular at the gypsy camp by showing the women how downtrodden they are.

"Maid in Sweden" (March 30, 1957)

Writers: Bill Freedman, Larry Rhine. *Director*: William A. Seiter.

Cast: Isabelle Dwan (*Ingrid Johansen*), Whit Bissell (*Ralph Burkle*), John Yates, Jr., Chuck James, Guy Way (*Muscle Men*), James Fairfax (*Cedric*)

Summary: In Stockholm, Cedric tries to escape the attentions of a marriage-minded woman who has her eye on him. Interceding on his steward's behalf, Captain Huxley succeeds only in diverting Ingrid's attention to himself. Desperate to cool down the captain's unwanted romance, Susanna stages a "Mr. Ocean Queen" contest to help their ardent passenger meet an eligible bachelor.

Note: Character actor Whit Bissell (1909–1996), taking a break from playing mad scientists in films like *I Was a Teenage Werewolf* (1957), appears as hypochondriac passenger Mr. Burkle, whose favorite reading material is a book entitled *Be Sick and Enjoy It*.

"Trouble in Trinidad" (April 6, 1957)

Writers: John Fenton Murray, Benedict Freedman. *Director*: Charles Barton.

Cast: Don Beddoe (*Mr. Doff*), James Lydon (*Evans*), Ted de Corsia (*Ross*), Peter Mamakos (*Portera*), Claude Allister (*Sir Henry Ogelthorpe*), Chet Stratton (*Inspector Griffin*), "Calypso Mac" and His Boys

Summary: Susanna tries to help a passenger who needs to record some authentic Calypso music, but can't get around because of a sprained ankle. Sneaking into Trinidad after midnight, Susanna makes a late night stop at the Club Luis. While there, she meets a former crewman who's seeking revenge on Captain Huxley, and talks her into carrying onboard some cigars that could send Susanna's employer sky-high.

Notes: Noted songwriters Ray Evans and Jay Livingston are credited with the Calypso number "Bing, Bang, Bong," heard in this episode. According to one columnist, "Gale Storm's producers ... want to get in on the current calypso craze," and commissioned the number, with a Dot Records release planned to coincide with the telecast.

"Model Apartment" (April 13, 1957)

Writer: John Fenton Murray. *Director*: William A. Seiter.

Cast: Charles Arnt (*Mr. Smead*), Carol Kelly (*Carol*), Johnny Silver (*Superintendent*), Peter Adams (*Party Guest*), Peter Damon (*Maharajah*), James Fairfax (*Cedric*)

Summary: After three and a half months at sea, Susanna is eager to get home to her cozy New York apartment. But on arrival, she and Nugey discover that the fashion model who sublet it during Susanna's absence not only redecorated, but left behind a plethora of furs and other gifts from her busy romantic life. Invited by Captain Huxley to pay an impromptu visit, Mr. Smead, the cruise ship's new personnel director, concludes that the staff of the *Ocean Queen* is masterminding a smuggling ring.

Note: A nice change-of-pace episode that takes place almost entirely off the ship, and provides a few details of the crew members' lives away from work.

"Singapore Fling" (April 20, 1957)

Writers: Larry Rhine, Bill Freedman. *Director*: Charles Barton.

Cast: Paul Dubov (*Harry Gregory*), Keye Luke (*Chong*), Sandra Stone (*Agnes Gregory*), Christian Drake (*Jim Gregory*), Charles Irwin (*Barker*), Warren Lee (*Charlie*)

Summary: Susanna is assigned the task of assigning Captain Huxley's new mynah bird to talk. Despite her best efforts, her feathered friend learns only one phrase: "Susanna says Captain Huxley's off his rocker!" Determined to trade in the bird for a more trainable lookalike, Susanna makes the rounds of a gift shop, a carnival and a vaudeville show in search of a ringer.

Notes: Once again, Gale works with Keye Luke, with whom she first crossed paths in *Let's Go Collegiate*. He will make another *Susanna* appearance during the show's second season. Actor Christian Drake (1923–2006) was the leading man in the syndicated series *Sheena, Queen of the Jungle* (1955–56).

"The Parisian Touch" (April 27, 1957)

Writers: Larry Rhine, Bill Freedman, Erna Lazarus, Nathaniel Curtis. *Director*: Charles Barton.

Cast: Dick Elliott (*Mr. Smith*), Elvia Allman (*Mrs. Smith*), Gil Frye (*M. Jolie*), Ramsay Hill (*M. Martine*), Georgette Duval (*Yvette*), Vincent Padula (*M. Duprez*)

Summary: In Paris, a crook sells Susanna a cheap painting he convinces her is valuable, hoping she will carry it aboard the *Ocean Queen*. Not knowing her work of art is covering a stolen Rembrandt, Susanna impulsively sells it to an American man seeking a gift for his wife. After the painting changes hands a few more times, Susanna races from the Blue Devil Café to an auction house, with a growing cast of characters trying to get hold of the supposedly worthless picture.

Note: Gale sings Cole Porter's "I Love Paris" and takes part in an Apache dance routine.

"Action in Acapulco" (May 4, 1957)

Writers: Larry Rhine, Bill Freedman, Frank Fox, Warren Spector. *Director*: William A. Seiter.

Cast: Henry Kulky (*Mike*), Harry Antrim (*J.C. Osborne*), Lennie Bremen (*Moose*), William Pullen (*Anderson*), Don Diamond (*Ramos*)

Summary: Expecting a visit from company vice-president J.C. Osborne, Captain Huxley decides not to risk having Susanna underfoot. He sends her into Acapulco on a wild goose chase, to deliver "a secret message of the utmost importance" to someone he made up. On arrival, Susanna learns that, with a 20-peso reward at stake, countless men profess to be "Pepe Jose Manuel Lopez," but when she meets Mr. Osborne, she decides he fits the description perfectly.

"Wedding in Majorca" (May 18, 1957)

Writers: Larry Rhine, Bill Freedman. *Director*: Charles Barton.

Cast: Nancy Hadley (*Vicki Chapman*), Jean Carson (*Miss Kavenaugh*), Oliver Cliff (*Washburne*), Anthony DeMarco (*The Duke*), Manuel Paris (*Sebastian*), James Fairfax (*Cedric*)

Summary: Passenger Vicki Chapman is traveling to Spain, where she will wed a duke in a lavish wedding attended by the socially prominent. Nugey longs to attend, but Susanna fails to get an invitation extended. Unsuccessful as wedding crashers dressed to the nines, Susanna and Nugey's backup plan finds them sneaking in the servants' entrance, where they are promptly put to work.

Note: Actress Nancy Hadley (born 1931), with multiple TV guest roles on her résumé, was cast as a love interest for Joey Bishop on the first season of his 1961–65 sitcom, *The Joey Bishop Show*.

>   *Quote*: VICKI (declining Susanna's offers to play deck games): I'm not a regular cruise passenger. I'm on my way to be married.
>   SUSANNA: Well, how about boxing lessons?

"Sing, Susanna, Sing" (May 25, 1957)

>   *Writers*: Bernard Ederer, Bob White, Alex Gottlieb. *Director*: William A. Seiter.
>   *Cast*: Craig Stevens (*Tom Burnett*), Lillian Bronson (*Miss Carver*), James Flavin (*Mr. Ellis*), Peter Coe (*Francisco*), Don Diamond (*Chief of Police*), Norman Levitt (*Reyes*), Gordon Clark (*Pimo*)

Summary: A handsome tour guide is about to lose his job, having claimed language skills he doesn't possess. A sympathetic Susanna joins his tour of a Caribbean island, bluffing her way through with the use of a guidebook. The communications barrier hits a serious snag when the group mistakenly invades the hideaway of a band of heavily armed revolutionaries.

>   *Note*: Gale sings "Dark Moon."

"Stop, Thief" (June 1, 1957)

>   *Writers*: Hal Fimberg, Alex Gottlieb. *Director*: William A. Seiter.
>   *Cast*: Brad Dexter (*Dude*), Sammy White (*Blackie*), Mario Siletti (*Mario Bonetti*), Don Orlando (*Giuseppe*), James Fairfax (*Cedric*)

Summary: Hearing that a well-known Italian actor is among the passengers, going incognito, Susanna and Nugey are determined to ferret him out. Also on board is Dude, a suave jewel thief whom Susanna mistakes for the movie star. When she confides in Dude that she is on the trail of a criminal, he decides to confuse the issue by planting a valuable piece of jewelry on the unsuspecting actor.

>   *Quote*: HUXLEY: Miss Pomeroy, why is it that every time I lose my head and ask for your help, things get complicated?

"'Alp, 'Alp" (June 8, 1957)

>   *Writer*: John Fenton Murray. *Director*: William A. Seiter.
>   *Cast*: Richard Webb (*Rene*), Grant Withers (*Oliver Wade*), Irene Seidner (*Old Lady*), Edythe Case (*Jessica*), James Fairfax (*Cedric*)

Summary: Captain Huxley challenges his old college rival, Oliver Wade, to a mountain-climbing competition in Switzerland. On arrival, the captain's climbing guide is more interested in romancing Susanna than aiding his client. Wanting to gain an advantage, Huxley arranges for Wade to experience "my deadly Pomeroy bomb."

>   *Note*: Actor Richard Webb (1915–1993) was best-known as the hero of TV's *Captain Midnight*.

"A Hit in Tahiti" (June 15, 1957)

>   *Writers*: G. Carleton Brown, Frank Gill, Jr., Alex Gottlieb. *Director*: Charles Barton.
>   *Cast*: Steve Dunne (*Mr. Ames*), Lila Lee (*Mrs. Mason*), James Fairfax (*Cedric*)

Summary: Passenger Mrs. Mason, the wife of an important executive with the steamship line, wants to break into the movies. Susanna charms movie producer Mr. Ames, about to shoot his film *That Night in Tahiti,* into giving Mrs. Mason a small role. When the actress playing native girl Leilani is sidelined by measles, Susanna finds herself taking part in the film as well.

Notes: Actress Lila Lee (1901–1973) was a former silent screen star whose films included *Blood and Sand* opposite Rudolph Valentino. Gale sings "My Isle of Golden Dreams."

Season Two

"Pat on the Back" (September 14, 1957)

Writer: Alex Gottlieb. *Director*: William A. Seiter.

Cast: Pat Boone (*Himself*), Leonard Carey (*Mr. Evergreen*), Ray Montgomery (*Dr. Jones*), Paul Hahn (*Purser*)

Summary: Singer Pat Boone is traveling on the *Ocean Queen*, under doctor's orders to rest his singing voice. Wanting him to perform for the passengers, Susanna decides to have him lip-synch to his records. When he's diagnosed with the measles, and confined to sick bay, she has to develop a backup plan.

Notes: Pat Boone (born June 1, 1934), was under contract to Dot Records, as was Gale, and was promoting his new ABC series for Chevrolet. Here he's heard singing "There's a Gold Mine in the Sky" and "Remember You're Mine," as well as dueting with Gale on "Would You Like to Take a Walk?" Gale also sings "Love by the Jukebox Light."

"Susanna Plays Cupid" (September 21, 1957)

Writer: Alex Gottlieb. *Director*: Charles Barton.

Cast: Jim Backus (*Arthur Hutchins*), Eleanor Audley (*Edith Gardner*), Robert Carson (*George*), James Fairfax (*Cedric*)

Summary: Nugey thinks her recurring dream of getting married will come true when she meets passenger Arthur Hutchins. Susanna uses an advice-to-the-lovelorn column ("Dear Dora") in the ship's newspaper to help things along, but inadvertently brings Hutchins together with another woman. With Nugey now not speaking to her, Susanna enlists Hutchins' help in persuading her pal that he wasn't worth having anyway.

Notes: Jim Backus (1913–1989) played leading man to Joan Davis in *I Married Joan* (1952–55), a popular sitcom that was often teamed with Gale's *My Little Margie* on NBC's Wednesday schedule.

"Pirate Treasure" (September 28, 1957)

Writers: G. Carleton Brown, Frank Gill, Jr., Alex Gottlieb. *Director*: William A. Seiter.

Cast: Madge Blake (*Mrs. Otis*), Mark Dana (*Jerry Allen*)

Summary: "A letter written in blood and sealed with a skull and crossbones sends Susanna Pomeroy on a search for buried treasure."—*San Rafael* (CA) *Daily Independent-Journal*

"Susanna Strikes Oil" (October 5, 1957)

Writers: Mel Diamond, Ben Gershman. *Director*: William A. Seiter.

Cast: Michael St. Angel (*Bill Eldredge*), Dan Seymour (*Sheik Abdul Hamid*), Rudolph Anders (*Strasser*), Robin Morse (*Dubroff*), James Fairfax (*Cedric*)

Summary: The predictions of Nugey's fortuneteller seem to be coming true when a passenger, Mr. Eldredge, is hotly pursued by enemy agents, seeking his map of oil-rich Arabian lands. Susanna suggests burning the map after Cedric memorizes it, which works until a conk on the head affects the steward's memory. The foreign agents try to ingratiate themselves with the local sheik by bringing him a bride: Susanna.

Note: Gale's hillbilly-styled musical number features Burton Lane's song "Feudin' and Fightin'," with choreography by Nick Castle.

"It's Only Money" (October 12, 1957)

Writer: Alex Gottlieb. *Director*: William A. Seiter.
Cast: John Russell (*Gary Donovan*), James Fairfax (*Cedric*)

Summary: A radiogram from home misleads Susanna into thinking that she's inherited a fortune from her uncle. Thanks to Nugey's big mouth, the news finds its way to Captain Huxley, who develops a new fondness for his social director, and to passenger Gary Donovan, a fortune hunter posing as a Texas oil man. When Susanna's bubble is burst, she decides to smoke out her would-be suitor's intentions.

Notes: "Special Guest Star" John Russell (1921–1991) starred in the popular Western series *Lawman* (ABC, 1958–62). This episode features a rare glimpse of the *Ocean Queen*'s swimming pool, or at least a corner of it, allowing an opportunity to put Gale and Russell into bathing suits.

"Honolulu Honeymoon" (October 19, 1957)

Writers: Hal Fimberg, Alex Gottlieb. *Director*: William A. Seiter.
Cast: Linda Leighton (*Penny Carlton*), Dan Jenkins (*Himself*), Patrick Waltz (*Rock Rollins*), James Fairfax (*Cedric*)

Summary: *TV Guide* Hollywood editor Dan Jenkins and his female photographer Penny are en route to Hawaii, to cover the shooting of a new series starring Rock Rollins. After Penny tells Susanna she has a yen for Captain Huxley, the social director decides to play matchmaker. Susanna leads her boss to believe that Penny is a wealthy heiress, unaware that this is actually the case.

Notes: Dan Jenkins, a fixture at *TV Guide* through the mid–1960s, does a fine job as an actor here, lacking the stiffness and self-consciousness that often afflicted minor celebrities cast as themselves.

Quote: SUSANNA (told that the new series will be set aboard an ocean liner): Oh, like *The Gale Storm Show*.
HUXLEY: Well, who's she?
SUSANNA: Oh, you know. She's that girl people say I look like.
HUXLEY: Well, there couldn't be two of you!

"Susanna's Baby" (October 26, 1957)

Writer: Alex Gottlieb. *Director*: William A. Seiter.
Cast: Joyce Taylor (*Lizabeth Jones*), Coulter Irwin (*Purser*), Susanna Bonnell (*Susie*), James Fairfax (*Cedric*)

Summary: The *Ocean Queen*'s all-honeymooner cruise has two unusual passengers: Mrs. Jones, already married for three years, and her baby daughter Susanna. The Joneses couldn't afford passage for both husband and wife, so Mr. Jones stayed behind, getting Nugey to smuggle their daughter aboard. Susanna and Nugey hide the baby in their cabin until her mother can be located.

Notes: Gale's daughter Susanna, not quite one year old, makes her TV acting debut in an episode her mother described as a favorite. As Gale recounted in 1993, she was concerned about her baby's ability to act naturally in an unfamiliar and busy environment, but needn't have been. Called upon to sing her daughter a lullaby, Gale boasted, "She went to sleep on cue!" Gale sings "I Cried for You" and "Now I Lay Me Down to Sleep."

"A Lass in Alaska" (November 2, 1957)

Writers: Larry Rhine, Bill Freedman. *Director*: William A. Seiter.

Cast: William Bishop (*Dan Marshall*), Irving Bacon (*Crackers*), Queenie Leonard (*Mrs. Magruder*)

Summary: With the *Ocean Queen* docked in Alaska, Susanna, Nugey and the captain try their luck at trout fishing. Handsome Dan Marshall, a champion fisherman, is bored with talk of the sport, and doesn't rise to the bait when Susanna tries to impress him with her expertise. Later, she and Nugey unwittingly cook the fish Captain Huxley planned to enter in a competition.

Notes: Actor William Bishop (1918–1959) previously starred in the NBC sitcom *It's a Great Life*, filmed on the Roach lot.

Quote: HUXLEY: Boy, the way you women sharpen your claws, it's amazing that any man can escape marriage.
NUGEY: I can personally account for 16 who did.

"The Phantom Valise" (November 9, 1957)

Writer: John Fenton Murray. *Director*: William A. Seiter.

Cast: Robert Rockwell (*Dan*), Percy Helton (*Waldo*), James Lydon (*Evans*), Joe Cranston (*Anderson*), Peter Bonnell (*Bobby*), Paul Bonnell (*Barry*), James Fairfax (*Cedric*)

Summary: A plaid valise containing a wad of cash turns up in Susanna and Nugey's quarters, but it vanishes before they can show it to Captain Huxley. After it reappears and disappears several more times, the crew members learn that a private detective is on board, in search of a crook who swindled a wealthy widow of her money. The presence of another valise, containing two young passengers' pet frogs, complicates the search.

Notes: Only a few weeks after their young sister appeared on the show, Gale's sons Peter and Paul play the two boys trying to keep their frogs hidden. According to syndicated columnist Earl Wilson (November 9, 1957), Gale's propensity for getting her kids on camera prompted one wiseacre to say, "I understand they're changing the name of this show. They're calling it *One Woman's Family*." Actor Joe Cranston (1924–2014) made multiple appearances on *The Gale Storm Show*, usually seen as Captain Huxley's assistant Anderson.

"For Money or Love" (November 16, 1957)

Writer: John L. Greene. *Director*: William A. Seiter.

Cast: Diane Brewster (*Julia*), Floyd Simmons (*Robert Wentworth III*), Pierre Watkin (*Mr. Fleming*), Robert Regas (*Carlos*), James Fairfax (*Cedric*)

Summary: Passenger Robert Wentworth III is due to inherit $15 million from his grandfather, but the trustees of his estate must approve any woman he wants to marry. Captain Huxley, after receiving a wire from the president of the line, asks Susanna to break up Wentworth's shipboard romance, unaware that she's the woman in question. Learning that her new beau recently broke up with his fiancée, Susanna decides to find out whether he is over his relationship with Julia.

Notes: Gale sings "A Rainy Night in Rio" and an original song by William B. Templeton and Leon Klatzkin, "The Name of My True Love." In this episode, Nugey fancies herself a novelist and is penning a tome based on her best friend's life, with a heroine named "Susquehanna Pomerantz."

"Aladdin's Lamp" (November 23, 1957)

Writer: John Fenton Murray. *Director*: William A. Seiter.
Cast: Richard Avonde (*Rick*), John Harmon (*Max*), Nacho Galindo (*Rahim*), Rodolfo Hoyos, Jr. (*Hassan*), James Fairfax (*Cedric*)

Summary: While visiting Pakistan, Captain Huxley chides Nugey for wasting her money on an "authentic Persian magic lamp." Unbeknownst to them, two crooks are seeking the lamp, one of seven in which their confederate hid clues to the whereabouts of some stolen money. A visit to Rahim's shop, where the lamp was purchased, leads Huxley and the ladies into danger when Susanna senses there's a reason the shopkeeper is so eager to buy it back.

Note: This is one of writer John Fenton Murray's stronger scripts for the series, providing both laughs and a fast-moving (if far-fetched) plot.

"The Kid from Korea" (November 30, 1957)

Cast: Warren Hsieh (*Lee*)

Summary: "Susanna and Nugey use every conceivable trick to keep a young Korean waif hidden from the angry captain of the S.S. *Ocean Queen* after he learns of the young stowaway's presence on board."—Hagerstown (MD) *Morning Herald*

"Mardi Gras" (December 7, 1957)

Cast: Mike Connors (*Jerry Moss*), Neil Hamilton (*Herbert Pascal*), Lillian Culver (*Miss McIntyre*)

Summary: "The S.S. *Ocean Queen* docks in New Orleans and Susanna and Nugey face the prospect of missing the Mardi Gras."—San Rafael (CA) *Daily Independent-Journal*

"Dutch Treatment" (December 14, 1957)

Writers: Larry Rhine, Bill Freedman. *Director*: William A. Seiter.
Cast: Charles Lane (*Dr. Charles Pierce*), King Donovan (*Rupert*), Kurt Katch (*Vandermeer*), John Bleifer (*Schneider*), Marjorie Bennett (*Mrs. Billingsley*), James Fairfax (*Cedric*)

Summary: Captain Huxley invites his old schoolmate, a psychiatrist, to observe Susanna and see "what makes her tick." To the captain's disappointment, Dr. Pierce diagnoses her as "a normal, energetic, exuberant young woman with a well-developed sense of humor."

He may change his opinion after Susanna and Nugey show up at the conference where he's giving a lecture, convinced that the doctor is a lunatic planning to blow up the place.

Note: The similarity of the titles occasionally causes this episode to be confused with "Dutch Treat" (March 14, 1959), which takes place in Amsterdam.

"Susanna Goes Native" (December 21, 1957)

Writer: John L. Greene. *Director*: William A. Seiter.

Cast: Liam Sullivan (*Prof. Alexander*), Sig Ruman (*Prof. Rudolph*), Fortunio Bonanova (*Tomba*), Dick Miller (*Sparks*)

Summary: "When native headhunters mistake Susanna for a goddess from the sea who can perform miracles, she enjoys her reign until she discovers she has to designate her wondermaking talents to prevent a scalping party."—*Oneonta* (NY) *Star*

"Friday the Thirteenth" (December 28, 1957)

Writer: Rik Vollaerts. *Director*: William A. Seiter.

Cast: Cheerio Meredith (*Melinda Cummings*), Junius Matthews (*Justin MacRae*), James Fairfax (*Cedric*)

Summary: Susanna and Nugey are touched by the plight of a sweet elderly passenger, Miss Cummings, who tells them she spent her life savings on a one-way passage to Singapore, where she expects to die. Taking up a collection from passengers and crew, Susanna and her friend present Miss Cummings with more than $1000 in cash. But when they learn that she is actually a shrewd confidence woman who regularly plays this game on luxury liners, Susanna determines to exploit Miss Cummings' superstitions to trick her into giving the money back.

Note: Gale sings Allan Roberts and Doris Fisher's "Some Rain Must Fall."

"The Ouija Board" (January 4, 1958)

Writer: Henry Sharp. *Director*: William A. Seiter.

Cast: Mark Dana (*Vance Carter*), A.E. Gould Porter (*J. Luther Replogle*), Colin Campbell (*Eustace Dibble*), Hal Callie (*Geoffrey Pilkington*), Joe Cranston (*Anderson*), James Fairfax (*Cedric*)

Summary: Susanna and Nugey's Ouija board predicts that they will meet three bearded men, one of whom will be dangerous. Indeed, mad bomber Eustace Dibble is stowed away on the *Ocean Queen,* armed with explosives that he hides in the captain's bust of John Paul Jones. Susanna's interest in handsome Scotland Yard agent Vance Carter doesn't prevent her from playing detective, though Huxley scoffs at her warnings about the bomber.

"Angela, the Angel" (January 11, 1958)

Writers: John Fenton Murray, Margaret Jennings. *Director*: William A. Seiter.

Cast: Evelyn Rudie (*Angela Stuyvesant*), Queenie Leonard (*Lady Orkin*), Joe Cranston (*Anderson*), James Fairfax (*Cedric*)

Summary: The *Ocean Queen* is transporting a wealthy, snobbish little girl who's never been allowed to have fun. With fond memories of her own childhood, Susanna decides Angela deserves a chance to be "a normal little girl." Angela happily learns all about blue jeans, football and a variety of other pastimes. Captain Huxley is concerned that her aunt, who's meeting the ship at the end of the voyage, will disapprove.

Note: Child actress Evelyn Rudie (born 1949) was an Emmy nominee for her performance as Kay Thompson's Eloise in an episode of *Playhouse 90*.

"Lovey-Dovey" (January 18, 1958)

Writer: Hal Fimberg. *Director*: William A. Seiter.

Cast: Russell Arms (*Gary Stewart*), Vera Vague (*Mrs. Winslow*), Judy [Judi] Meredith (*Phyllis Winslow*), James Fairfax (*Cedric*)

Summary: Passenger Mrs. Winslow is taking her daughter Phyllis on a trip to get her away from her boyfriend Gary Stewart, a guitar player whom the mother considers unsuitable. Little does she know that Gary has just been hired by Susanna as a shipboard performer. Knowing Mrs. Winslow is highly superstitious, Susanna assumes the identity of fortune-teller Madame Oracle to pave the way for Phyllis and her beau to be together.

Notes: Singer-actor Russell Arms (1920–2005) was known to 1950s TV audiences for his performances on *Your Hit Parade*. He and Gale team for the song "Lovebirds," credited to Bob Russell and Ben Oakland (with choreography by Nick Castle), while she sings "Winter Warm," from her album.

"The Case of the Chinese Puzzle" (January 25, 1958)

Writers: John Fenton Murray, Robert Gottlieb. *Director*: William A. Seiter.

Cast: Keye Luke (*Henry Ling*), Douglas Fowley (*Doyle*), Ray Walker (*Snyder*), Lisa Lu (*Fan Toy*), Gai Lee (*Rickshaw Driver*), James Fairfax (*Cedric*)

Summary: Passenger Henry Ling entrusts a Chinese puzzle box to Susanna and Nugey for safekeeping, saying his life may be in danger. Recruited to deliver the box to a shop in Hong Kong, the ladies realize too late that they are unwittingly aiding a thief. Retrieving the priceless ruby that is secreted within the box turns into a potentially explosive situation in a shop stocked with fireworks.

Note: As in his *My Little Margie* appearance, Keye Luke's natural likability is used to draw suspicion away from a character who's up to no good.

"Royal Welcome" (February 1, 1958)

Writers: Bill Freedman, Larry Rhine. *Director*: William A. Seiter.

Cast: Beryl Machim (*Mrs. Montaigne*), Molly Roden (*Hilda*), Don Kennedy (*Hodgkins*), Joe Cranston (*Anderson*), James Fairfax (*Cedric*)

Summary: Feeling unappreciated on the *Ocean Queen*, Nugey hires a company to research her family tree. The response letter, steamed open by Susanna and Cedric, reveals that she comes from "just good, honest working people." Knowing her friend will be disappointed, Susanna mugs up a tonier background for the beloved beautician, but regrets it when Nugey turns into a snob overnight.

Note: This episode puts the spotlight on ZaSu Pitts, who delivers an endearing comic performance.

"Susanna Takes a Husband" (February 8, 1958)

Writers: Larry Rhine, Bill Freedman. *Director*: Norman Z. McLeod.

Cast: Margaret Hamilton (*Mrs. Gibney*), William Roerick (*Charles Martindale*), Maurice Marsac (*Gautier*), Kitty Larsen (*Darlene*), James Fairfax (*Cedric*)

Summary: While performing at a charity bazaar, Susanna meets the mother of an old classmate and rival, Emily. To impress Emily's mother, whose plane is to depart shortly, Susanna invents a wealthy husband for herself. When Mrs. Gibney's stay is extended, Susanna tries to maintain the fiction that she is the wife of rich passenger Mr. Martindale.

Note: Famed character actress Margaret Hamilton (1902–1985), best-known for her role in *The Wizard of Oz,* plays the snobbish mother of Susanna's classmate. Gale sings "Pennies from Heaven."

"Taking Ways" (February 15, 1958)

Writers: Larry Rhine, Bill Friedman. *Director*: Norman Z. McLeod.
Cast: June Vincent (*Charlene Hendrix*), Richard Shannon (*Bert Runyan*), Robert Riordan (*Gillespie*), Nestor Paiva (*Judge*), James Fairfax (*Cedric*)

Summary: Traveling on the *Ocean Queen* are a charming woman who happens to be a kleptomaniac, and Runyan, the private detective who's been retained by her family to keep her out of trouble. Though Runyan tries to remain inconspicuous, matchmaker Susanna insists on bringing the two together, and they hit it off. After a newspaper article causes Susanna and Nugey to mistake Runyon for a notorious Bluebeard, they take the law into their own hands, unwittingly leaving Miss Hendrix free to embark on a stealing spree in Barcelona.

Note: Although the closing credits list the character's name as Joe Runyan, he's called Bert within the episode itself.

Quote: HUXLEY: Cedric, I'm going ashore. There's some trouble; the usual reason.
CEDRIC: Oh, give my regards to Miss Pomeroy.

"Ride 'Em Cowgirl" (February 22, 1958)

Writers: Bill Freedman, Larry Rhine. *Director*: Norman Z. McLeod.
Cast: Ken Clark (*Steve Madison*), Lois Corbet (*Flora Madison*), Edward Colemans (*Senor Valdez*)

Summary: Wealthy widow Mrs. Madison has attracted the romantic attentions of Captain Huxley, while her handsome son Steve appeals to Susanna. Steve seems to have eyes only for the horse he bought overseas, until Susanna convinces him she's a skilled rider herself. During a stop at Valparaíso, Chile, the Madisons and their dates are the guests of a ranch owner who invites Susanna to demonstrate her riding prowess on his horse.

Note: Actress Lois Corbet (sometimes spelled Corbett) was the wife of longtime Jack Benny cohort Don Wilson.

"Bye Bye Banshee" (March 1, 1958)

Summary: "'Little ghosts' take Susanna and Nugey snooping through a farmhouse in Ireland in search of banshees and leprechauns."—*Pasadena Star-News*

Note: *Daily Variety* (January 31, 1958) reported that actors Harry Shannon, Hilda Plowright, Charles Irwin, Kendrick Huxham, Barry O'Hara and Coleman Francis had been cast in this episode.

"A Beautiful Friendship" (March 8, 1958)

Writer: John Fenton Murray. *Director*: Norman Z. McLeod.

Cast: Addison Richards (*J. Bromley Dorne*), Joe Cranston (*Anderson*), James Fairfax (*Cedric*)

Summary: Cynical Captain Huxley is unimpressed by passenger J. Bromley Dorne's book *The Power of Positive Friendship.* Wanting to prove a point, Huxley bets the author $100 that he can cause a rift in the seemingly rock-solid friendship of Susanna and Nugey. Aware that the ladies have insured their lives in each other's favor, Huxley succeeds in planting suspicions between the two, until Susanna catches on and turns the tables.

Note: This premise could easily have been a *My Little Margie* episode, with Gale's character devising a scheme to pay her father figure back for trying to put one over on her.

"Ghosts Aboard" (March 15, 1958)

Writers: Hal Fimberg, Rik Vollaerts. *Director*: Norman Z. McLeod.

Cast: Ralph Dumke (*Clem Thompson*), Ruth Lee (*Mrs. Thompson*); David Frankham

Summary: "Susanna and Nugey discover that the ghost of a British nobleman is an unlisted passenger…. When Captain Huxley learns that the ghost has taken up residence in Hold No. 8, he orders the two girls to spend the night in the hold and trap the ghost!"—*El Paso* (TX) *Herald-Post*

Notes: This is the first of two appearances by British actor David Frankham (born 1926). Asked nearly 60 years after the fact, he remembered his work on Gale's show as "uneventful, professional and pleasant," adding, "It's always easier to remember the *bad* experiences working on a show!" He recalled buying Gale's 45 rpm record "Memories Are Made of This" so as "to have a memento of … a very pleasant experience."

"How to Catch a Man" (March 22, 1958)

Writers: Henry Sharp, Robert Gottlieb. *Director*: Norman Z. McLeod.

Cast: Tom Helmore (*Ralph Emory*), Betty Lynn (*Sylvia Powell*), James Fairfax (*Cedric*)

Summary: Business executive Ralph Emory is too busy working to take part in the ship's social activities, or to notice that his secretary Sylvia is in love with him. Susanna succeeds in getting the buttoned-up Mr. Emory to unwind, and coaches him as to how to propose marriage, unaware she's now the object of his affections. Susanna decides to turn herself into "a rock'n'roll playgirl" so that her unwanted beau will change his tune.

Notes: Gale sings "Farewell to Arms" and "I've Got a Feeling," both from her album. A funny dream sequence finds Roy Roberts' Captain Huxley as the singing minister at Susanna's wedding to a nonplussed Emory. Betty Lynn (born 1926) is best-known for her recurring role as Thelma Lou on *The Andy Griffith Show*. Nick Castle is credited for choreography.

"Our Dear Captain" (March 29, 1958)

Writers: Bill Freedman, Larry Rhine. *Director*: Norman Z. McLeod.

Cast: Robert Burton (*Captain Jenkins*), Molly Roden (*Gladys*), Don Kennedy (*Hodgkins*), Ralph Smiley (*Barney*), Kay Hayden (*Mrs. Sheridan*), James Fairfax (*Cedric*)

Summary: The employees' organization SDDNCCS (the Sons and Daughters of Neptune Clam Chowder Society) is planning its Hi-Jinks show, featuring Susanna's skit lampooning

Captain Huxley. Trying to get permission to use the ship's main lounge for the show, Susanna inadvertently makes her boss think he's been invited to join the society. After Huxley is blackballed by the members, Susanna plots to hold the Hi-Jinks while he is ashore.

Note: The Hi-Jinks show features a spoof of Gilbert and Sullivan's H.M.S. *Pinafore,* with Cedric taking the role of the captain.

"Susanna and the Pirates" (April 5, 1958)

Cast: Don Durant (*Philip Casper*), Paul Maxey (*Commodore Whitehead*), Joe Cranston (*Anderson*), Frank Kreig (*Pirate Guard*)

Summary: "When the steamship line's commodore comes to hold an inspection on Capt. Huxley's ship he is kidnapped by 'pirates.'"—*Mansfield* (OH) *News-Journal*

"Happily Unmarried" (April 12, 1958)

Writers: Alex Gottlieb, Hal Fimberg, Rik Vollaerts. *Director*: Norman Z. McLeod.
Cast: Burt Mustin (*Samuel Jordan*), Mary Young (*Priscilla Jordan*), James Fairfax (*Cedric*)

Summary: Susanna is planning an elaborate party to celebrate the 50th wedding anniversary of passengers Samuel and Priscilla Jordan, until a radiogram drops the bombshell announcement that they were never legally wed. Newly single, Priscilla takes her own cabin and rebuffs Samuel's entreaties to make their union legal. Susanna resolves to make the bachelorette jealous with the introduction of the Countess Nugent.

Note: Gale sings Harold Adamson and Walter Donaldson's "You" as well as "It Had to Be You." Burt Mustin (1884–1977) still had ahead of him another two decades of playing elderly men on TV, wrapping up his career in the 1970s with a recurring role on *Phyllis*.

"Bamboozled in Bombay" (April 26, 1958)

Writers: Larry Rhine, Bill Freedman. *Director*: Norman Z. McLeod.
Cast: Paul Picerni (*Bengali*), Jack Kruschen (*Akbar*), Charity Grace (*Mrs. Hathaway*), Diana Crawford (*Girl*), James Fairfax (*Cedric*)

Summary: Captain Huxley laughs at Susanna and Nugey for being taken in by "the foremost mystic in all Bombay," who happens to be equipped with "a walkie-talkie turban." Susanna evens the score by feeding the phony fakir enough information to do a detailed reading on Huxley, but she's taken aback when the captain hires Bengali to entertain the passengers on the *Ocean Queen*. Reluctant to confess her own part in the con man's charade, Susanna watches in increasing annoyance as he rooks the passengers, until she finally resolves to put him out of business.

Note: Paul Picerni makes his second *Susanna* appearance, playing the fake fakir who's actually a native of Brooklyn.

"Not So Innocents Abroad" (May 3, 1958)

Writers: Roland MacLane, Dick Conway, Alex Gottlieb. *Director*: Charles Barton.
Cast: Yvonne Lime (*Ann Radford*), Edward [Edd] Byrnes (*Phil Ellsworth*), Ruth Perrott (*Mrs. Radford*), Kem Dibbs (*Mark Roberts*), John Indrisano (*Bolo*), James Fairfax (*Cedric*)

Summary: Snobbish Mrs. Radford takes her daughter Ann on a cruise to separate her from a boyfriend, an Army private she considers unsuitable. Private Ellsworth sneaks on board to see Ann off, but inadvertently becomes a stowaway. With Susanna's help, Phil borrows the identity of a no-show passenger named Mark Roberts and succeeds in winning over Ann's mother. The unexpected appearance of the real Mr. Roberts complicates matters.

Note: Gale sings a few snatches of Epes Sargent's "A Life on the Ocean Wave."

"A Date with a Wolf" (May 10, 1958)

Cast: Frank Puglia (*Captain Flores*), Rick Jason (*Vincente*)

Summary: "Nugey joins a lonely hearts club and is immediately proposed to…"—*Mansfield* (OH) *News Journal*, May 3, 1958

"Beat the Band" (May 31, 1958)

Writers: Bill Freedman, Larry Rhine. *Director*: William A. Seiter.
Cast: Steven Geray (*Kurt Dolfas*), Kay Kuter (*Yasha*), Sam Wolfe (*Sasha*), O.Z. Whitehead (*Tasha*), James Fairfax (*Cedric*)

Summary: As soon as Captain Huxley finishes chiding Susanna for hiring inferior musicians, Nugey tries to get her new gentleman friend Kurt's quartet a gig. Susanna decides that Kurt and his band can take the place of the jazz group Huxley hired, but it quickly becomes apparent that the substitute musicians are more attuned to Mozart than bebop. After enlisting Cedric to claim that the band's instruments were all swept overboard, Susanna thinks the musical program is kaput. But Huxley won't give up so easily.

Notes: Gale sings Stanley Styne and Buddy Bregman's "I Just Can't Get Enough of You," to Dolores Blacker's choreography.

SEASON THREE

"Diamonds Are a Girl's Best Friend" (September 6, 1958)

Writer: Alex Gottlieb. *Director*: William A. Seiter.
Cast: John Agar (*Lt. Arnold Van Dyke*)

Summary: "Susanna falls in love with an Air Force officer who thinks she is his fiancée who disappeared five years ago. Susanna finds her double and loses her lieutenant."— *Provo* (UT) *Daily Herald*, September 1, 1958

Note: Gale sings "Soon I'll Wed My Love" and "South of the Border." Guest star John Agar (1921–2002) previously worked with Gale in the film *Woman of the North Country*.

"Happy Birthday, Captain" (September 13, 1958)

Writer: John Fenton Murray. *Director*: William A. Seiter.
Cast: Robert Emmett Keane (*Mr. Benedict*), Joe Cranston (*Anderson*), Eugene Borden (*Henri*)

Summary: "Captain Huxley has a birthday and seems determined to block any surprise parties."—*Mansfield* (OH) *News-Journal*

Film actor John Agar was Gale's love interest in the Season Three opener, "Diamonds Are a Girl's Best Friend."

"The Truth Machine" (September 20, 1958)

Cast: Charles Herbert (*Montgomery Flack*), Elvia Allman (*Mrs. Carter*), Howard McNear (*Diogenes Jones*).

Summary: "Indignant over Susanna Pomeroy's white lies, a passenger on the S.S. *Ocean Queen* threatens to have her fired."—*Oneonta* (NY) *Star*

"Hayride Ahoy" (September 27, 1958)

Writers: Larry Rhine, Bill Freedman. *Director*: William A. Seiter.

Cast: Edgar Buchanan (*Jasper Stokes*), George Cisar (*Murray Fenton*), Ben Bancroft (*Mr. Westover*), Carlos Romero (*Perez*), James Fairfax (*Cedric*)

Summary: Susanna's idea of an essay contest to win a cruise on the *Ocean Queen* works beautifully—until the winner shows up. Iowa farmer Jasper Stokes is having a miserable time, and nothing the crew members try seems to cheer him up. Fearing unfavorable publicity, Susanna arranges to bring the accouterments of a working farm to the ship, so that Mr. Stokes will feel more at home.

Notes: Gale sings Earl Lebieg's "Sleep" and a version of "Old MacDonald's Farm" with special lyrics. Choreography of the square dance number is credited to Carmen Clifford. Edgar Buchanan (1903–1979), known to Baby Boomers as Uncle Joe Carson on *Petticoat Junction,* was also the star of a syndicated Western series, *Judge Roy Bean*. The plot of this episode is reminiscent of the 1937 Bing Crosby-Martha Raye comedy *Waikiki Wedding*.

"Painted in Paris" (October 4, 1958)

Cast: Howard Wendell (*Hamilton Reese*), Paul Maxey (*J. Walter Martin*)

Summary: "Susanna Pomeroy's scheme to coax Captain Huxley into taking up art backfires when the captain resigns his post aboard the *S.S. Ocean Queen*."—*Oneonta* (NY) *Star*

"The Sweepstakes Ticket" (October 11, 1958)

Writers: Phillip Shuken, John L. Greene. *Director*: William A. Seiter.

Cast: John Qualen (*Clancy*), Dick Miller (*Sparks*), Joseph Martarano (*Whitey*), James Fairfax (*Cedric*)

Summary: When kindly steward Clancy wins $140,000 in the sweepstakes, two dishonest radio operators plot to claim the ticket for themselves. Their phony radiogram persuades Cedric that he actually won, while Clancy willingly relinquishes the winning ticket, unaware of its value. Cedric proceeds to make a nuisance of himself, going from lowly steward to obnoxious passenger, until Susanna stumbles on the truth and uses her feminine wiles to set things right.

Note: Beloved character actor Dick Miller (born 1928), veteran of Roger Corman drive-in movies like *Not of This Earth* (1957), appears as the lecherous, larcenous Sparks.

"Secret Assignment" (October 18, 1958)

Writers: Larry Rhine, Bill Freedman. *Director*: William A. Seiter.

Cast: Raymond Greenleaf (*Mr. Ludlow*), John Holland (*Greco*), Richard S. Davies (*Weber*), Eleanor Luckey (*Carmen*), Morgan Jones (*Durant*)

Summary: Receiving a summons from the Navy 15 years after his wartime service, Captain Huxley assumes he's being offered a new post, and the *Ocean Queen* crew plans a going-away party for him. When it develops that the Navy only wanted him to settle a debt for a lost typewriter, Huxley is embarrassed to come clean, and tells Susanna he's involved in a secret mission, "Operation Typewriter." Overhearing Susanna talk to Nugey about this, some criminal types plot to wrest the military secrets from Huxley during a stop in Lisbon.

Notes: Gale sings Nelson Riddle's "Lisbon Antigua (In Old Lisbon)," with choreography credited to Carmen Clifford.

"Heaven Scent" (October 25, 1958)

Writer: John Fenton Murray. *Director*: William A. Seiter.
Cast: Jacques Bergerac (*Roland Giroux*), Patricia Michon (*Gertie*)

Summary: Susanna is eaten alive with curiosity when Nugey makes secret purchases in every port they visit. Turns out Susanna's roommate has been inspired by passenger Roland Giroux, a perfume manufacturer, to create her own scent. The resulting "Fleur de Elvira" proves to be something of a love potion, tempting Susanna to test it on the handsome and wealthy M. Giroux.

Note: This episode features a rare look at the bathroom in Susanna and Nugey's cabin, where they mix up perfume in the tub. According to a *TV Guide* photo feature (October 25, 1958), producer Alex Gottlieb played a gag on guest star Bergerac, arranging to have a bit player in one scene replaced by the actor's then-girlfriend, Oscar winner Dorothy Malone.

"Love and Kisses" (November 1, 1958)

Writers: Larry Rhine, Bill Freedman. *Director*: William A. Seiter.
Cast: Andra Martin (*Helen Phillips*), Martin Freed (*Mike Sloan*), Michael Ross (*Haggarty*), Herbert Lytton (*J.H. Dodson*), James Fairfax (*Cedric*)

Summary: Susanna tries to help passenger Helen Phillips find the handsome man she met at boarding, who seems to have vanished. The gentleman in question is Mike Sloan, who works in the ship's engine room, and isn't allowed to mingle with passengers. Thanks to a borrowed dinner jacket and Susanna's sneaky plan, Helen and Mike are reunited at the ship's dance. Complications develop when Captain Huxley thinks Mike is a well-known investment counselor.

"You Gotta Have Charm" (November 8, 1958)

Writers: Larry Rhine, Bill Freedman. *Director*: William A. Seiter.
Cast: Jack Mulhall (*Walter Stewart*), Carol Morris (*Marsha*), Warren Frost (*Jerry*), Sandra Wirth (*Carol*), Paula Winslowe (*Mrs. Kirby*)

Summary: Nugey is attracted to passenger Walter Stewart, but he doesn't seem to return her interest. After applying the advice from the book *How to Make Yourself Charming*, things perk up, but trouble develops when Stewart falls for Susanna instead. On a nightclub outing in Rio, Susanna resolves to turn his attention back in Nugey's direction.

Notes: This episode features excerpts from songs heard on the "Gale's Great Hits" album, including "Ivory Tower" and "Memories Are Made of This." The major production number, with choreography credited to Carmen Clifford, features Irving Berlin's "Heat Wave." The story is reminiscent of the previous season's "How to Catch a Man."

"The Case of the Music Box Thief" (November 15, 1958)

Summary: "Susanna Pomeroy employs some unusual sleuthing tactics to unmask a phantom burglar."—*Oneonta* (NY) *Star*

"Susanna the Matchmaker" (November 22, 1958)

Writer: Joel Kane. *Director*: William A. Seiter.

Cast: Maria Palmer (*Mme. Jaubert*), Rita Lynn (*Miss Chapman*), Claire Carleton (*Mrs. Jarvis*), James Fairfax (*Cedric*)

Summary: Reading in his hometown newspaper that his old flame is marrying another man, Captain Huxley feels depressed and over the hill. Trying to build his confidence, Susanna persuades three female passengers that the captain has eyes for them. Unfortunately, the newly energized and cocky captain drives his crew members crazy, causing Susanna to shift course.

"Adventure in Alaska" (December 6, 1958)

Cast: Thomas B. Henry (*Brooks*), Nancy Millard (*Nora*)

Summary: "A couple of con men visit ... and manage to unload an Alaskan ghost town on the girls. However, a little scheme works for [Susanna] and her 'rebuilt' town snares the crooks."—*Long Beach* (CA) *Press-Telegram*

"Robot from Inner Space" (December 13, 1958)

Writer: John Fenton Murray. *Director*: William A. Seiter.

Summary: "There's a robot traveling in the baggage room and [Susanna] turns it loose.... Unable to fully master the controls, she creates a certain amount of havoc aboard the luxury ship."—*Long Beach* (CA) *Press-Telegram*

Note: This episode's "guest star" is Robby the Robot, the 7'6" robot built for the film *Forbidden Planet* (1956).

"Don't Give Up the Ship" (December 20, 1958)

Writer: John Fenton Murray. *Director*: William A. Seiter.

Cast: Keith Andes (*Gilbert Leeds*), James Lydon (*First Officer Evans*), Tom Palmer (*Mr. Cameron*), Frances Mercer (*Mrs. Cameron*), James Fairfax (*Cedric*)

Summary: When the ship docks, Susanna is looking forward to being reunited with her fiancé Gilbert Leeds, whom she agreed to marry after only three dates in New York. When Gilbert admits he was engaged once before, to a woman who was a social director on a cruise ship, Susanna is afraid to admit she has the same occupation. Gilbert comes aboard the *Ocean Queen* as a passenger, forcing Susanna to pretend she, too, is on a cruise—with her "Aunt Nugey."

"Make Mine Music" (December 27, 1958)

Cast: Salvatore Baccaloni (*Arturo Romano*)

Summary: "Susanna Pomeroy invites leading basso of the Metropolitan Opera Salvatore Baccaloni to entertain passengers aboard the S.S. *Ocean Queen*."—*Oneonta* (NY) *Star*, November 27, 1958

Note: According to *Daily Variety* (October 29, 1958), the segment cast Baccaloni as a janitor.

"How to Make Enemies" (January 3, 1959)

Writers: Rik Vollaerts, Hal Fimberg. *Director*: Norman Z. McLeod.
Cast: Ralph Dumke (*Clem Thompson*), Ruth Lee (*Mrs. Thompson*), David Frankham (*David Wells*)

Summary: A foggy night aboard the *Ocean Queen* is marked by the appearance of a ghost—or is it? Passenger Clem Thompson and his wife are returning from England after buying the ancestral English home of the Belleview family and its furnishings. Realizing the ghost in question is David Wells, a Belleview descendant who hopes to frighten Thompson into selling back the family possessions, Susanna offers the spooky assistance of herself and Nugey.

Note: Guest player Ralph Dumke was a veteran of multiple appearances on *My Little Margie*.

"One Captain Too Many" (January 10, 1959)

Writers: Bill Freedman, Larry Rhine. *Director*: William A. Seiter.
Cast: Charles Lane (*Captain*)

Summary: "Susanna Pomeroy and Nugey regard Capt. Huxley's transfer from the S.S. *Ocean Queen* as a new lease on life until they discover that his replacement is a hard-boiled skipper who will not tolerate their shenanigans."—*Marion* (OH) *Star*

"On the Dot" (January 17, 1959)

Writer: Alex Gottlieb. *Director*: William A. Seiter.
Cast: Billy Vaughn (*Himself*)

Summary: "Special guest star Billy Vaughn books passage incognito ... but Susanna Pomeroy ferrets him out and persuades him to join her in a festival of songs."—*Somerset* (PA) *Daily American*

Note: The episode title is a punning reference to Dot Records, where Gale recorded with the assistance of guest star Vaughn.

"The Honeymoon Suite" (January 24, 1959)

Cast: Dan Jenkins (*Himself*); Diane Jergens, Doug McClure

Summary: "After arranging a luxury cruise ... for a prize-winning 'dream couple,' [Susanna] is surprised to find herself in the role of matchmaker... [She] learns they are not married, and that they entered the contest for a chance to travel, [so] she has them pose as honeymooners for the benefit of Capt. Huxley and a magazine reporter."—*Victoria* (TX) *Advocate*, January 18, 1959

"It's Murder, My Dear" (January 31, 1959)

Writer: Alex Gottlieb. *Director*: William A. Seiter.
Cast: Boris Karloff (*Himself*), Frank Cady (*Director*), Tom Kennedy (*Officer*), Geraldine Hall (*Nurse*), Ray Montgomery (*Dr. Jones*), Frank Krieg (*Henderson*)

Summary: Confined to sick bay by Captain Huxley, Nugey is despondent over missing a chance to visit a TV studio. Susanna helps her friend go AWOL and they pay a visit to the Hal Roach Studios, where actor Boris Karloff is filming scenes for his new TV series.

Seeing a Karloff lookalike fire a shot at him, Susanna and Nugey try to solve the mystery of who's trying to kill the beloved horror movie actor.

Notes: This fun episode includes footage shot on the Roach lot, including a look at "Lake Laurel and Hardy," the water tank where so many of the comedians' scenes were filmed. Karloff is promoting his anthology series *The Veil*, produced at the Hal Roach Studios, which ceased production after less than a dozen episodes. ZaSu Pitts makes a cameo appearance as herself, with Susanna noting her resemblance to Nugey. Discussing guest star Karloff, producer Alex Gottlieb told syndicated columnist Erskine Johnson (December 23, 1958), "He has an amazing inner sense of comedy."

Quote: TV DIRECTOR (after meeting Susanna and Nugey): What a pair of characters! They'd be great in a television series, but who'd believe them?

"Battle of the Bull Run" (February 7, 1959)

Writers: Larry Rhine, Bill Freedman. *Director*: William A. Seiter.

Cast: Elena Verdugo (*Jenifer Smith*), Scott Elliott (*Danny*), Gilbert Frye (*Jack*), Don Orlando (*Cabrillo*), James Fairfax (*Cedric*)

Summary: Passenger Jenifer Smith, a beautiful bullfighter, inspires Susanna to perform a musical number about bullfighting in her floor show. Seeing Susanna borrow all the accouterments a bullfighter needs, Nugey jumps to the conclusion that her pal means to try the real thing when they dock in Barcelona. In fact, Susanna has just been invited to watch Jenifer in action, but before the afternoon is over, all the denizens of the *Ocean Queen* find themselves in the ring with a live bull.

Notes: Gale performs Nicola Salerno and Renato Carosone's song "Torero" in a routine choreographed by Nick Castle. She also sings a lullaby she calls "Rock-a-bye Bully." Special Guest Star Elena Verdugo (1925–2017) starred in the early TV sitcom *Meet Millie* (CBS, 1952–56), but may be better known to Baby Boomers as Nurse Consuelo Lopez on ABC's *Marcus Welby, M.D.* (1969–76).

"Jailmates" (February 28, 1959)

Writer: Joel Kane. *Director*: William A. Seiter.

Cast: Lorne Greene (*Constable Barnaby*), Ashley Cowan (*Sergeant Quimby*), Vera Denham (*Nurse Pennington*), Nancy Millard (*Manicurist*), James Fairfax (*Cedric*)

Summary: Captain Huxley is planning a surprise party to commemorate Nugey's fifteenth anniversary on the *Ocean Queen*, but plans go awry when he upbraids her about an incident in the beauty salon, causing her to quit in a huff. With two days in port before the ship sails, Susanna is charged with bringing her friend back. To avoid Susanna, Nugey gets herself booked in the local jail for 48 hours, leaving her friend to try to infiltrate the lockup.

Note: Lorne Greene (1915–1987), seen as the frustrated law enforcement officer beleaguered by both Nugey and Susanna, was only a few months away from being cast in a starring role on TV's *Bonanza*.

"An Old Chinese Custom" (March 7, 1959)

Director: William A. Seiter.

Cast: James Hong (*Fred Kim*), Nico Minardos (*Ramon*)

Summary: "When Susanna Pomeroy saves a Chinese boy from a knife-wielding thief, the youth insists his life, according to Chinese custom, belongs to her."—*Hagerstown* (MD) *Morning Herald*

"Dutch Treat" (March 14, 1959)

Writers: Bill Freedman, Larry Rhine. *Director*: William A. Seiter.

Cast: James Fairfax (*Cedric*); Margriet Bekker, Heinrich Bekker, Trudi Ziskind, Roberta Kay, Peter Bourne, Fred Essler

Summary: "Susanna inherits a broken-down windmill in Amsterdam, quits the ship, and opens a restaurant. Captain Huxley schemes to get her back on board."—UCLA Film and Television Archive

"Alias Susanna Valentine" (March 21, 1959)

Writers: Bill Freedman, Larry Rhine. *Director*: William A. Seiter.

Cast: Harry Jackson (*Mr. Pinkley*), Lillian Culver (*Mrs. Weaver*), Paul Bryar (*Tompkins*), Dette LaRue (*Yvonne*)

Summary: Captain Huxley writes his annual report to the company on the ship's personnel, giving Susanna and Nugey high marks. Meanwhile, Susanna dictates a joking letter to Nugey, naming their boss "Nincompoop of the Year." When the offending letter finds its way into the same envelope as Huxley's report, Susanna tries every trick at her disposal to retrieve the damaging document from the purser's safe.

"Clip That Coupon" (March 28, 1959)

Writers: Larry Rhine, Bill Freedman. *Director*: William A. Seiter.

Cast: Nancy Millard (*Nora*), Robert Anderson (*Hodgkins*), Jonathan Hole (*Mr. Archer*), Stephen Roberts (*Mr. Wentworth*), Mike Keene (*Mr. Hartman*), James Fairfax (*Cedric*)

Summary: When Nugey's friends give her $35 for her birthday, Huxley suggests that she invest it. Taking his advice, Nugey acquires one share of stock in the steamship line, and as a stockholder promptly urges economy. Huxley's idea for saving money is to cancel the annual "Employee Hi-Jinks," but his wasteful expenditure on a huge supply of chopsticks may help Susanna change his mind.

"Who Stole That Melody?" (April 4, 1959)

Writers: G. Carleton Brown, Frank Gill, Jr. *Director*: William A. Seiter.

Cast: Buddy Bregman (*Danny Simmons*), Jerome Cowan (*Skitch Mason*), Joe Cranston (*Drummer*), James Fairfax (*Cedric*)

Summary: Successful record executive Skitch Mason is on board to get away from his work, but Susanna wants to sell him a tune written by crew member Danny Simmons. Forbidden by Captain Huxley to bother Mason, Susanna plots to somehow have him hear the music. A plot to pipe the music into the ship's gymnasium backfires when Huxley hears it, begins to hum it and interests Mason in "his" song.

Notes: Seen as the novice songwriter, Buddy Bregman (1930–2017) enjoyed a successful career as a composer, arranger and music director. Gale sings "Break It to Me Gently."

"Susanna, the Babysitter" (April 11, 1959)

    Writers: Phillip Shuken, John L. Greene, Margaret Jennings. *Director*: William A. Seiter.

    Cast: Steven Hammer (*Larry Hoffman*), Susan Reilly (*Carrie Hoffman*), Nancy deCarl (*Buzzy Hoffman*), Gregory Irvin (*Frank Hoffman*), Gina Gillespie (*Joan Hoffman*), Norma Varden (*Miss Gompers*), Jack O'Hara (*Officer*), James Fairfax (*Cedric*).

Summary: The *Ocean Queen* is playing host to the five bratty children of a company vice-president. Just before sailing, their frustrated governess quits. Captain Huxley decides that Susanna is the perfect candidate to take charge of the unruly fivesome.

Season Four

"One, Two, Ski!" (October 1, 1959)

    Writers: Larry Rhine, Bill Freedman. *Director*: William A. Seiter.

    Cast: Gene Nelson (*Chris*), Anna Lisa (*Helga*), Bob Hopkins (*Mr. Willis*), Cosmo Sardo (*Waiter*), James Fairfax (*Cedric*).

Summary: On vacation at a ski lodge, Susanna and Nugey learn that the men guests look down on "snow bunnies," i.e., women who come for romance but can't ski. Attracted to a handsome ski instructor, and jealous of blonde Helga, a champion skier, Susanna tries various ploys to suggest her expertise on the slopes without actually demonstrating it.

Notes: This season opener's "Special Guest Star" Gene Nelson is also credited with the choreography for Gale's musical number "Let It Snow," which features custom lyrics that turn the song into "Let 'Em Ski!" *Variety*'s review (October 7, 1959) was largely a pan: "[It's] designed to appeal to the 12-year-old sense of humor.... [Gale[endows her chore with just the sort of scatterbrained lovableness it requires."

"The Card Sharp" (October 8, 1959)

    Writers: Larry Rhine, Bill Freedman. *Director*: James V. Kern.

    Cast: William Frawley (*Jim Comstock*), Lillian Bronson (*Emily Albright*), Helen Kleeb (*Myrtle Buff*), Fred Kruger (*Henry Buff*), Ben Weldon [Welden] (*Muggsy*).

Summary: Unbeknownst to anyone but Captain Huxley, company detective Jim Comstock is aboard on an undercover mission to root out card sharps. Drawn into a poker game with passenger Mr. Buff, Comstock unwittingly shows off his expertise, arousing Susanna's suspicion. After boning up on card tricks, Susanna is ready to expose Comstock as a card sharp, which may derail his burgeoning romance with another passenger.

Note: Billed as Special Guest Star, *I Love Lucy*'s William Frawley (1887–1966) was then nearing the end of his run playing Fred Mertz in hour-long Lucy specials, but hadn't yet been signed to play Bub on *My Three Sons*.

"The Million Dollar Mutt" (October 15, 1959)

    Writers: Larry Rhine, Bill Freedman, Charles Hoffman. *Director*: Richard Kinon.

    Cast: Frank Albertson (*Stevens*), Don Diamond (*Captain Alicante*), James Fairfax (*Cedric*).

Summary: In Hollywood, Susanna and Nugey are followed by a dog who stows away atop their taxi. When the dog follows them aboard the *Ocean Queen*, Susanna must hide him from Captain Huxley. Unbeknownst to Susanna and her crewmates, the dog in question is a performer for the Walt Disney Studios, and his handlers think he has been kidnapped.

Notes: According to the closing credits, "The Shaggy Dog appears by arrangement with Walt Disney." This episode is a promotional tie-in for the Disney film *The Shaggy Dog* with Fred MacMurray, then in theaters. Director Richard Kinon (1924–2004) went on to direct multiple episodes of that 1970s counterpart to Gale's sitcom, *The Love Boat*.

"Come Back, Little Beatnik" (October 22, 1959)

Writers: Larry Rhine, Bill Freedman. *Director*: William A. Seiter.
Cast: Jerry Colonna (*Mischa Morningstar*), Richard Deacon (*Zonko*), Joseph Conley (*Cool*), James Fairfax (*Cedric*)

Summary: Passenger Mischa Morningstar is an author who, after finishing his book *The Universe Must Go*, says he has nothing else to write about. Susanna suggests he observe the passengers and crew for inspiration, resulting in an article in which he writes, "Everything is a symbol. Susanna Pomeroy is a symbol of the evil of regimentation." Afraid the article will cause her to lose her job, Susanna follows Morningstar to a meeting with his publisher at a beatnik joint called The Weeping Turnip.

Notes: Gale sings "Blues in the Night." Morningstar's article depicts Susanna as bossing passengers around, forcing them to engage in strenuous activities when they'd rather relax: "Two men want to play checkers but they are *pomeroyed* into inhaling and exhaling." Comic-musician Jerry Colonna (1904–1986), billed as "Special Guest Star," was a slightly odd choice at age 55 to play a representative of the youth-infused beatnik movement. An archival copy of this episode on videotape is held by the UCLA Film and Television Archive.

"Calling Scotland Yard" (October 29, 1959)

Writer: John Fenton Murray. *Director*: William A. Seiter.
Cast: Edward Ashley (*Michael*), Lily Kemble Cooper (*Lady Thornbury*), Milton Frome (*Neville*), Alan Caillou (*Eric Scott*), Hilda Plowright (*Maude*), Stanley Fraser (*Inspector Clayton*), John van Dreelen (*Thornbury*)

Summary: Susanna is being romanced by a charming British passenger, but Huxley's friend, a police inspector, warns him that the man is a potential lady-killer whose previous fiancées have all mysteriously disappeared. Invited to visit the Thornburys' ancestral home, Susanna and Nugey find a spooky house, creepy servants, mysterious moans and a dog named Satan. With Huxley and Inspector Clayton hot on the trail, Susanna and Nugey try to escape from the mansion before a wedding can take place.

"Happy Horoscope" (November 5, 1959)

Director: William A. Seiter.
Cast: Allyn Joslyn (*Mr. Bradshaw*), Lillian Culver (*Mrs. Page*); Ray Montgomery

Summary: "In a slightly mistaken case of predicting the future by the stars Nugey reads the wrong person's horoscope, and creates near disaster for Capt. Huxley..."—*Hope* (AR) *Star*, November 7, 1959

"Nugey, Come Home" (November 12, 1959)

Writers: Larry Rhine, Milton Pascal. *Director*: Richard Kinon.

Cast: Mabel Rea (*Candy Cortez*), Emil Sitka (*Pierre*); Ben Wright, Maida Severn, Helene Haigh, Arlen Stuart

Summary: Miss Larsen, the ship's librarian, is leaving to get married when they dock in New York. Nugey wants the job, Captain Huxley says no and Nugey, miffed, leaves the *Ocean Queen*. Huxley hires a sexy new beauty operator, Candy Cortez, who becomes Susanna's roommate. With a little help from Susanna, Huxley quickly tires of Candy, "that scatterbrained, hip-twisting man-trap." Susanna finds that Nugey has taken a new job—in a beauty parlor for dogs.

Note: Synopsis based on a reading of the script (dated 9/9/59), part of the Lou Derman collection at UCLA. This episode finds Nugey reassigned to work in the ship's souvenir shop, a job change that will be reflected in future scripts.

"The Swedish Steward" (November 19, 1959)

Writers: Joel Kane, Bill Freedman.

Cast: John Qualen (*Olaf Hansen*)

Summary: New steward Olaf Hansen is eager to please, but becomes a nervous mess any time Captain Huxley is in sight. Despite Susanna's best efforts, Olaf keeps bumbling, and Huxley fires him. But the captain is forced to track down his departed employee when he learns that an important company executive wants to meet him.

Note: Synopsis based on a reading of the script, part of the Lou Derman collection at UCLA. Guest player John Qualen had appeared as a different steward in "The Sweepstakes Ticket" about a year earlier.

Quote: SUSANNA (when Huxley scolds her for slacking off): If you'd been here a minute sooner, you would have caught us working!

HUXLEY: Really? What a pity. The first time in three years and I had to miss it!

"Goodbye, Doctor" (November 26, 1959)

Writers: Joe Quillan, Martin A. Ragaway. *Director*: James V. Kern.

Cast: Rolfe Sedan (*Dr. Eugene Reynolds*), Marjorie Bennett (*Mrs. Bender*)

Summary: Reynolds, the ship's doctor, is a bachelor who's kept to himself and avoided women since he was jilted many years before. When the ship develops engine trouble near an uncharted South Seas island, Susanna, Nugey and Reynolds go ashore. Learning that the island is populated by beautiful young ladies who lack male companionship, Reynolds refuses to return to the *Ocean Queen*, declaring he'll adopt the life of a beachcomber.

Notes: Veteran character actor Rolfe Sedan (1896–1982), best-known for his recurring role as the beleaguered mailman on *The George Burns and Gracie Allen Show*, has one of his more sizable roles here as the bachelor doctor. He's ably supported by Marjorie Bennett (1896–1982), playing a hypochondriac patient.

"Family Reunion" (December 3, 1959)

Writers: Milton Pascal, Larry Rhine. *Director*: James V. Kern.

Cast: Hope Summers (*Angie Kirkham*), Willis Bouchey (*Henry Pomeroy*), Eleanor Audley (*Bess Pomeroy*), James Fairfax (*Cedric*)

Summary: While visiting her parents during a stop at San Diego, Susanna is made to feel guilty by their nosy neighbor Miss Kirkham, who tells her the Pomeroys are "in their declining years" and need her. Susanna quits her job so that she can stay home and coddle her parents. The Pomeroys are confused by her suffocating attentions, until Miss Kirkham mentions the little talk she had with their daughter.

Notes: Synopsis based on a reading of the script (dated 10/12/59), part of the Lou Derman collection at UCLA. Eleanor Audley and Willis Bouchey reprised their roles as Susanna's parents in "Mother Steps Out." Gale sings "Far Away Places."

Quote: NUGEY (insisting she can keep a secret): You know me. I'm like a clam.
SUSANNA: Yes, but every time you start talking, I wind up in the soup.

"Wedding at Sea" (December 10, 1959)

Writers: Martin A. Ragaway, Joe Quillan. *Director*: Richard Kinon.
Cast: Ron Hagerthy (*Sgt. Rickie Hyland*)

Summary: On his way back from Italy, Sgt. Rickie Hyland pines for his Italian girlfriend Maria Poccoza, who was promised to another man in an arranged marriage. When Maria is discovered stowing away on the ship, Susanna suggests that the couple get married before arriving in America, so that she won't be deported. After some persuasion, Captain Huxley agrees to perform the ceremony. An impending hurricane may prevent the wedding.

Note: Synopsis based on a reading of the script (dated 10/18/59), part of the Lou Derman collection at UCLA.

Quote: SUSANNA (asked to keep Maria's secret): Don't worry. The only thing I ever say to the captain is: "I'm sorry, sir. I won't do it again."

"Spanish Souvenir" (December 17, 1959)

Writers: Larry Rhine, Milton Pascal. *Director*: Richard Kinon.
Cast: Howard McNear (*Mr. Parker*), Henry Corden (*Pintero*)

Summary: With Nugey discouraged by poor sales in the souvenir shop, Susanna takes it upon herself to teach her friend some principles of salesmanship. She succeeds too well, resulting in Nugey accidentally selling a departing passenger a rare, hand-painted plate that Susanna was holding for its owner. With only a few hours to spare, Susanna and Nugey travel by bus to a remote village where they've been told a duplicate of the plate can be found.

Notes: Synopsis based on a reading of the script (dated 10/12/59), part of the Lou Derman collection at UCLA.

"Captain Daddy" (December 24, 1959)

Writers: Lou Derman, Joel Kane. *Director*: Richard Kinon.
Cast: Ruth Perrott (*Henrietta Stewart*), Frank Killmond (*Melvin Stewart*), Chris Essay (*Maître d'*)

Summary: Running into an old girlfriend, Henrietta, whom he considers a "human leech," Captain Huxley improvises a wife and daughter to avoid reviving their relationship. Unbeknownst to him, Susanna and Nugey meet Henrietta in a restaurant and persuade her and her teenage son Melvin to book passage on the *Ocean Queen*. Huxley presses

Nugey and Susanna into service to pose as his wife and daughter, but a new complication arises when Melvin falls for "teenybopper" Susanna.

Notes: Synopsis based on a reading of the script (dated 10/12/59), part of the Lou Derman collection at UCLA. Gale sings "Darling, Je Vous Aime Beaucoup." According to this script, Nugey's recommended reading for nervous passengers is a tome titled *Famous Shipwrecks of History*.

"Susanna's True Confession" (December 31, 1959)

Director: William A. Seiter.
Cast: Robert Q. Lewis (*Tom Hobart*)

Summary: "Nugey ... writes a story for a confession magazine titled 'I Stole Men's Hearts So I Could Steal Their Money' and signs Susanna's ... name to it. The magazine editor goes aboard the *Ocean Queen* to observe Susanna's alleged operations, and Susanna finds herself suspect when a rash of burglaries take place."—Dallas (TX) *Morning News*

"African Drums" (January 7, 1960)

Writers: Milton Pascal, Larry Rhine. *Director*: Richard Kinon.
Cast: Oscar Beregi (*Sandar*), Robert Griffin (*Severaid*), James Fairfax (*Cedric*)

Summary: In Algiers, Huxley and the crew are on their best behavior during the visit of a company vice-president. When Susanna and Nugey decide to go ashore, Huxley warns them to be back on time. Accused of shoplifting in a souvenir shop, the ladies find themselves behind bars less than an hour before the *Ocean Queen* sails.

Notes: Synopsis based on a reading of the script (dated 11/10/59), part of the Lou Derman collection at UCLA.

Quote: SUSANNA (describing dour Mr. Severaid): He looks like he put on a new shirt this morning and forgot to remove the pins.

"No Tears for the Captain" (January 14, 1960)

Writers: Larry Rhine, Milton Pascal. *Director*: James V. Kern.
Cast: Liam Sullivan (*Henderson*), James Fairfax (*Cedric*)

Summary: Without a first mate, grouchy, overworked Captain Huxley is terrorizing the staff. But when the new man Henderson arrives, he's so popular with the crew that Huxley's feelings are hurt. Susanna steps into action to insure that their captain is made to feel important.

Notes: Synopsis based on a reading of the script (dated 11/9/59), part of the Lou Derman collection at UCLA. This script has a sizable role for Cedric, who's been mostly absent this season. The episode, which takes place in Panama, finds Susanna in charge of planning a "Crossing-the-Equator Party."

"Love, By Yiminy!" (January 21, 1960)

Writers: Bill Freedman, Joel Kane. *Director*: James V. Kern.
Cast: John Qualen (*Olaf Hansen*), Sid Melton (*Hal Miller*)

Summary: Olaf, the shy steward, has fallen in love with Jeanette Bartlett, who works in the ship's flower shop. Jeanette happily accepts his invitation to the employees' dance, but the romance is over before it begins when two of his practical-joking co-workers booby-trap the candy and flowers he gives her. Susanna schemes to set things right by making the guilty party clear Olaf's name with Jeanette.

Notes: Synopsis based on a reading of the script (dated 11/23/59), part of the Lou Derman collection at UCLA. John Qualen reprises his role from "The Swedish Steward."

"A Trip for Auntie" (January 28, 1960)
Writers: Bill Freedman, Joel Kane. *Director*: Richard Kinon.

Summary: Visiting her Aunt Martha and Uncle Will Benson, Susanna tries to persuade them to take a cruise as a second honeymoon, but her uncle balks at the cost. When Captain Huxley's travel slides of the Orient fail to entice him, Susanna tries taking the elderly couple to an atmospheric restaurant, the Jade Pagoda. Trying to apply the finishing touch, Susanna and Nugey sneak into the kitchen to insert a pertinent message into Uncle Will's fortune cookie.

Notes: Synopsis based on a reading of the script, part of the Lou Derman collection at UCLA. Gale sings "If You Were the Only Boy in the World."

Quote: SUSANNA: Sir, accidents will happen.
HUXLEY: But you seem to make appointments with them!

"Birthday for Gino" (February 4, 1960)
Writers: Larry Rhine, Milton Pascal. *Director*: Richard Kinon.
Cast: Bart Bradley [Braverman] (*Gino*), Tom Andre (*Mario*), Alan Roberts (*Giuseppe*); Don Orlando, Oreste Seragnoli, Bill Justice, Ernesto Milinari.

Summary: While in Naples, Susanna persuades Captain Huxley to entertain three young Italian boys aboard the *Ocean Queen*. Huxley enjoys their visit until he realizes that one of them, Gino, stole his gold watch. Knowing it is Gino's birthday, Susanna arranges for him to have a party, hoping she can persuade him to return the watch before Huxley goes to the police.

Notes: Synopsis based on a reading of the script (dated 11/27/59), part of the Lou Derman collection at UCLA. Young guest star Bart Bradley continued acting into adulthood under his real name, Bart Braverman. He played a regular role on TV's *Vega$*.

Quote: SUSANNA (coaxing Huxley into letting the boys meet him): Remember when you were a child, sir? And you wanted to meet Babe Ruth....
Douglas Fairbanks ...
NUGEY: Ulysses S. Grant?

"S.O.S. Dad" (February 11, 1960)
Writers: Bill Freedman, Joe Quillan. *Director*: James V. Kern.
Cast: Andre Phillips (*Larry Hackett*), Luis Van Rooten (*Pop Hackett*)

Summary: On a stopover in Miami, the ship's orchestra leader Larry Hackett is dismayed to find that his father, a retired *Ocean Queen* crew member, has put his life savings into an unsuccessful restaurant, the Blue Goose. Susanna devises a scheme to make the previous owner, Mr. Gorman, want to buy it back, borrowing the crew of the *Ocean Queen* to populate the place with staff and customers. Gorman arrives at the bustling restaurant for a meeting with his new "client," a sugar daddy (Huxley) who wants to buy the place for his chorus-girl sweetheart (Susanna).

Notes: Synopsis based on a reading of the script (dated 12/7/59), part of the Lou Derman collection at UCLA.

"Mother Steps Out" (February 18, 1960)
Writers: Larry Rhine, Milton Pascal. *Director*: James V. Kern.
Cast: Eleanor Audley (*Bess Pomeroy*), Willis Bouchey (*Henry Pomeroy*)

Summary: At home in San Diego, Susanna finds her father Henry frustrated because his wife Bess is too busy with her club activities to spend any time with him. Susanna suggests that Henry needs a hobby of his own and enlists her friend, photographer Dick Marshall, to turn him into a camera bug. When beautiful Honey La Verne shows up to be Henry's model, Bess reacts just as Susanna hoped she would.

Notes: Synopsis based on a reading of the script (dated 12/14/59), part of the Lou Derman collection at UCLA.

"Captain Courageous" (February 25, 1960)
Writers: Larry Rhine, Milton Pascal. *Director*: Earl Bellamy.
Cast: Nancy Kulp (*Gertrude Fenton*), Harry Antrim (*Horace Fenton*)

Summary: Horace Fenton, an executive with the steamer line, pressures Huxley into hiring his niece Gertrude as the ship's social director. With Susanna reassigned to the souvenir shop, and Nugey turned into a stewardess, nobody's happy. Susanna devises a plot to remind Captain Huxley about his wartime bravery (about which he loves to brag) and shame him into standing up to Mr. Fenton.

Notes: Synopsis based on a reading of the script (dated 12/28/59), part of the Lou Derman collection at UCLA. According to this script, Susanna has been social director on the *Ocean Queen* for "over five years."

"One Coin in the Fountain" (March 3, 1960)
Writers: Bill Freedman, Herb Finn. *Director*: William A. Seiter.
Cast: Sid Melton (*Hal Miller*), Arlen Stuart (*Amy*), Nestor Paiva (*Pablo*), Rodolfo Hoyos (*Officer Hernando*), Natividad Vacio (*Ramon*), Salvador Baguez (*Officer*)

Summary: In Acapulco, Captain Huxley entrusts Susanna with picking up a rare coin from a local shop. Pausing to pose for a picture at the town's historic wishing well, Susanna drops the coin into the water. After Nugey comes down with a cold, Susanna talks two other crew members into a late-night mission to retrieve the coin from the well.

"Made in Hong Kong" (March 10, 1960)
Writers: Si Rose, Seaman Jacobs. *Director*: Austen Jewell.
Cast: Sid Melton (*Hal*), Philip Ahn (*Lee Sing*), Noel Toy (*Mrs. Sing*), Warren Hsieh (*Lin Sing*), Maurice Dallimore (*Mr. Bruce*), Roy Wright (*Mr. Elliot*)

Summary: In Hong Kong, a stowaway jumps overboard wearing Captain Huxley's best suit. Needing a replacement for a dinner with the ambassador, Huxley visits Lee Sing's shop, where he's promised a new suit in a few hours. When the new suit is lost, Susanna smuggles Mr. Sing and his family on board so that another can be made. Just then, Huxley is visited by an immigration official.

"It's Magic" (March 17, 1960)
>*Writers*: Herb Finn, Bill Freedman. *Director*: Bob [Robert] Altman.
>*Cast*: Alan Mowbray (*Hadley N. Dexter*), Lillian Culver (*Mrs. Dexter*), Sid Melton (*Hal Miller*)

Summary: On a stopover in England, Susanna gets into a fender-bender with stuffy businessman Hadley Dexter. When Mr. Dexter visits the *Ocean Queen* to complain about her, Susanna coaxes crew member Hal into posing as the captain while Huxley is ashore. Seeing props from Huxley's magic act in the office, Dexter pressures the impostor captain to perform at his lodge meeting.

>*Notes*: Synopsis based on a reading of the script (dated 1/18/60), part of the Lou Derman collection at UCLA. This is the only episode directed by Robert Altman (1925–2006), later the Oscar-nominated director of films like *MASH* and *Nashville*.

"Show Biz" (March 24, 1960)
>*Writers*: Milton Pascal, Larry Rhine. *Director*: James V. Kern.
>*Cast*: Jack Albertson (*Freddy Morell*), Mel Prestidge (*Malekaya*)

Summary: In the Fiji Islands, Susanna finds an old family friend, ex-vaudevillian Freddy Morell, whose show business career ended after the death of his wife and partner Ruby. Susanna persuades Captain Huxley to give Freddy free passage back to the States, in exchange for his performing services. Freddy proves to be lost onstage without Ruby, so Susanna steps in to give him back his confidence.

>*Note*: This episode nicely showcases the comic and hoofing abilities of Jack Albertson (1907–1981). Unlike the character he plays here, Albertson went on to triumphs in his later career, winning an Oscar for *The Subject Was Roses* and starring on TV's *Chico and the Man*. He teams with Gale for "Nobody's Sweetheart" (Billy Meyers, Elmer Schoebel, Gus Kahn, Ernie Erdman), while she solos on "April Showers" (B.G. DeSylva, Louis Silvers). Choreography is credited to Miriam Nelson and Howard Krieger. This was the series' final original episode to air.

Series Pilots

Mr. and Mrs. Detective

Aired as an episode of ABC's *Hollywood Premiere Theatre* on September 27, 1950, *Mr. and Mrs. Detective* (also known as *Mystery and Mrs.*) was a pilot for a regular series, reuniting Gale with Don DeFore, her *It Happened on 5th Avenue* leading man. As a listing in that day's *Long Beach* (CA) *Independent* described it, "DeFore and Gale Storm are featured in a who-dun-it…. As a Mr. and Mrs. team they set out to solve a murder and follow the same story line as radio's innumerable detective teams." The show was produced by Al Aimer and featured Robert Shayne and Eve Whitney in supporting roles.

According to TV historian Vincent Terrace, Gale's character was Sally Fame, "young, beautiful, and somewhat trouble-prone, [who] enjoys the thrill of a case but often plunges into sometimes dangerous situations without thinking first. She does have a keen sense for crime-solving and often relies on her feminine intuition to help … uncover the clues they need to solve a crime." *Daily Variety* (September 28, 1950) said, "DeFore registered heavily as the super-sleuth and Miss Storm gathered all available luster as his wife and capable assistant.... Program derived full strength from a stout script by Cal Phillips..."

After that initial airing, nothing more was heard of the prospective series. In 1954, DeFore—then happily settled in as neighbor Thorny on ABC's *The Adventures of Ozzie and Harriet*—recalled of *Mr. and Mrs. Detective*, "We were told that we would have to do it live. Gale turned it down a few hours after I did.... I wonder where we'd both be if we had said we'd do that other show."[37]

The Gale Storm Show: A-OK, O'Shea

Absent from weekly prime time television since the cancellation of *The Gale Storm Show: Oh! Susanna* in 1960, Gale was ready to get back to work two years later. Syndicated columnist Erskine Johnson (July 5, 1962) reported that she was "on the comeback trail after a year's illness." In early 1963, with two successful sitcoms under her belt, and still showing great popularity in reruns, Gale signed with Desilu Productions to star in *A-OK, O'Shea*, a pilot for a new series. Lee Karson, who had developed *The Gale Storm Show: Oh! Susanna*, also created the new format and co-authored (with Ray Allen) the pilot script "Vocal Boy Makes Good." He was also tapped to serve as producer.

The proposed series would cast Gale as Captain Daphne O'Shea, a member of the Women's Army Corps serving as Assistant Special Service Officer at Fort Klondike, Alaska. Other regularly featured characters would be Daphne's boss, Major Bruce Wingfield, Staff Sergeant Irving Oomiak ("a young, wily Eskimo"), Sergeant Cabot Caldwell, who would be Daphne's assistant, and a "plain-looking clerk-typist," Corporal Edna Trimble. Life is pretty dreary for the men and women of Fort Klondike, with the best option for entertainment at the Officers' Club the umpteenth showing of the silent film *Tillie's Punctured Romance*.

In the initial script, Daphne tries to boost the company's morale by having pop singer Bobby Tyler, "the most famous G.I. in the army," assigned to Fort Klondike. Little does she know that the spoiled celebrity has been causing trouble everywhere he's assigned, so that Army brass are only too happy to dispatch him to Alaska. When the arrogant Tyler proves equally unpopular in his new post, it falls to Daphne to set him straight.

The role gave Gale ample opportunity for physical comedy, with one scene finding her character "upside down suspended from a rafter, her arms and legs twined around it, hanging on for dear life." She later takes the reins of a dogsled racing out of control through the wintry landscape. A running joke throughout the script concerns a suit of warming "electric underwear," which malfunctions during Daphne's sled ride. Coming to rest in a snow bank after a wild ride, Daphne surfaces long enough to say, "Don't just stand there. Come down here and turn off this crazy underwear!"

A-OK, O'Shea was to be a candidate for the 1963–64 television season, and filming of the pilot was scheduled for mid–February 1963. But *Variety* (February 20, 1963) reported that both Gale's pilot and another, *I Married a Martian*, to star Bob Cummings and Julie Newmar, were shelved; an unnamed studio source explained that "the elements weren't right."

Margie's Little Margie

On March 1, 1974, *Variety* reported that Gale and her husband Lee, in conjunction with writer Lee Karson, had formed a company called Showtime Productions to develop properties for television. Karson, in consultation with the Bonnells, developed a six-page prospectus for a new comedy series that would be a sequel to *My Little Margie*.

Margie's Little Margie, as Karson had named his concept, found Margie Albright, some 20 years later, now widowed and known as Margie Mayfield, a university English professor living and working in Southern California. (Apparently Margie married a man named Fred, though not Freddie Wilson.) In middle age, Margie had become "an attractive, extremely likable woman, warm-hearted, rather sophisticated ... but with strongly held, traditional views on morality, ethics and standards of conduct." Though Margie had mellowed with the years, history was repeating itself with her daughter Margaret, Jr., a rebellious teenager just as capable of wreaking havoc as her mother had been. Clashes between mother and daughter would be frequent, and at times would show that the supposedly older and wiser Margie "can still turn into the schemer we remember, still the perpetrator of outrageous plans."

Expected to make occasional appearances in the series was Charles Farrell's Grandpa Vern, now "a high-flying senior citizen playboy" living the life of Riley as the owner of the Palm Springs Racquet Club. (Karson noted that Farrell, in addition to reprising his role, would make the Racquet Club facilities available for filming as needed.) Stories for the show would follow not only Margie's relationship with her daughter, but also her life on campus, interaction with students and even some romantic possibilities of her own.

Karson's proposal emphasized that the program was designed both to capitalize on Gale's popularity as a television star since the 1950s, while introducing more contemporary elements that, in theory, would make it fit on a network schedule at a time when *All in the Family* and other shows of its ilk were popular.

Karson's agent submitted the proposal to Harry Ackerman, who was nearing the end of his 16-year stint as vice-president in charge of production at Screen Gems. Ackerman, who'd been a highly placed CBS executive during Margie's original run, might have been expected to warm to the project. But Ackerman would be shown the door before the year was out, and apparently nothing came of *Margie's Little Margie*.

Television Guest Appearances

Pantomime Quiz. CBS, August 20, 1951. Guest stars Gale Storm, Peggy Dow, Bruce Bennett and Jack Smith "match wits with show regulars Adele Jergens, Fritz Feld, Vincent Price and Jackie Coogan."—*Annapolis* (MD) *Evening Capital*, August 18, 1951

The Bigelow-Sanford Theatre. "Mechanic on Duty." DuMont, September 6, 1951. Gale Storm and Gene Raymond star in "the tale of a wayside garage run by a female mechanic. He learns a new policy in charging customers for repair work."—*Long Beach* (CA) *Independent*, August 29, 1952. Gale, said *Billboard* (September 15, 1951), played "an expert mechanic who owned her own garage, and properly despised anyone who wasn't mechanically inclined.... Storm made a fem mechanic extremely gratifying, even with grease on her nose." The filmed show was repeated in August 1952 on *Footlights Theater* and December 1953 on *Hollywood Half-Hour*.

The Colgate Comedy Hour. NBC, October 14, 1951. Hosts Bud Abbott and Lou Costello welcome guests Gale Storm and her movie leading man Phil Regan. In a sketch, Costello wants to marry Gale, but must first prove himself worthy. Gale sings "If I Were a Bell." Said *Variety* (October 17, 1951), "Regan, playing a competition for Costello for attentions of Miss Storm, did a pleasing bit of song-selling and Miss Storm did likewise."

The Bigelow-Sanford Theatre. "Hot Welcome." DuMont, November 12, 1951. Cast: Richard Denning, Gale Storm, Elizabeth Patterson. "This is the story of a strange encounter in a gas station in the desert near Las Vegas, involving a reformed gangster, his press agent, his fiancée and an eccentric old woman."—*San Antonio* (TX) *Light*, August 15, 1955. Said *Daily Variety* (November 13, 1951), "There's little to recommend 'Hot Welcome' beyond its modest pretentions.... Cast of four tries hard to give the plot some semblance of plausibility, but what worms out of the typewriter is more contrivance than factual probability." After its initial airing, the 30-minute filmed drama was repeated in later years as part of various TV anthology shows, including *Summer Night Theatre* (1953) and *Hollywood Half-Hour* (1955).

Pantomime Quiz. NBC, February 20, 1952. Guests, Gale Storm, Reginald Gardiner, John Barrymore, Jr., and Jean Wallace; regular panelists, Hans Conried, Jackie Coogan, Adele Jergens.

The Unexpected. "The Puppeteers." ABC, November 26, 1952. Cast: Gale Storm, Paul Frees, Robert Hutton. Tension arises between two puppeteers, who are brothers, when one has difficulty accepting the other's impending marriage. Gale plays the fiancée, who summons the police when her husband-to-be vanishes. *Variety* (November 26, 1952) thought this only "passable telefare," but noted, "Gale Storm rises above her material, again proving her top capability."

The Bob Hope Show. NBC, December 15, 1953. Gale and actor-dancer Gene Nelson are among Hope's guests in this musical comedy special. Gale does a skit with Bob (there's a cameo appearance by Charles Farrell) and performs musically on "Walking My Baby Back Home" (with Hope), "Silver Bells" (with Hope and Nelson) and "I'm in Love with a Wonderful Guy." The show was billed in advance publicity as Gale's television singing debut, which was misleading considering her occasional warbling on *My Little Margie* and the video showings of her early Monogram movies.

The Colgate Comedy Hour. NBC, November 28, 1954. Host Gordon MacRae welcomes guests Gale Storm, comedian Gene Sheldon and film actress Debra Paget. This broadcast proved important to Gale's career, as it was here that her soon-to-be record producer Randy Wood saw her perform and became interested in signing her to a contract.

This Is Your Life. NBC, April 29, 1955. Host Ralph Edwards surprises his guest, Gale, with an overview of her life. Guests, aside from husband Lee, include her mother Minnie Cottle, all four of her siblings, two of her high school teachers, and *Margie* co-star Charles Farrell. Near the end of the telecast, much of which Gale has spent awash in tears, her three sons are introduced.

Dateline: Disneyland. ABC, July 17, 1955. Art Linkletter, Bob Cummings and Ronald Reagan host this live telecast covering the dedication of Disneyland in Anaheim, California (and promoting Disney's new fall series on ABC). Gale and her sons are given a tour of Frontierland.

The Perry Como Show. NBC, October 8, 1955. Gale, Marion Lorne and Paul Winchell are Como's guests, along with the Ghezzis, comedic acrobats.

What's My Line? CBS, October 9, 1955. Gale is a panelist, along with Dorothy Kilgallen, Bennett Cerf and Robert Q. Lewis. Contestants include the first man commissioned to the Army Nurse Corps and a rodeo trick rider.

Robert Montgomery Presents. "Tomorrow Is Forever." NBC, October 17, 1955. Gale stars in this live one-hour broadcast, "a heartrending Enoch Arden story concerning a lovely young woman whose first husband is 'killed' in the First World War—but he returns 20 years later, altered beyond recognition."—*Hammond* (IN) *Times*. This is a television adaptation of the 1946 film starring Claudette Colbert, Orson Welles and George Brent. Gale's leading men in the video version are William Windom and Robert Ellenstein.

Celebrity Playhouse. "Mink Does Something for You." CBS, October 25, 1955. Gale Storm, Keith Andes, Eleanor Audley. "Girl wears employer's mink coat, boy borrows his boss' Jaguar car, they meet, are caught, wind up in court and in love."—*Long Beach* (CA) *Press-Telegram*

Ford Theater. "Johnny, Where Are You?" NBC, November 3, 1955. Gale plays a young wife who fears her husband (Keith Andes) is reigniting an old flame with an ex. *Variety* (November 7, 1955) thought the script weak, adding, "[Gale's] mannerisms and girlish charm aren't able to salvage many laughs, despite frantic mugging." Featured players include Alix Talton, Frances Robinson and Elliott Reid.

The Milton Berle Show. NBC, November 29, 1955. This trouble-plagued episode found Berle and his originally booked guest star Eddie Cantor too ill to perform, leaving comedian Jan Murray to step in as host. Gale sings "I Hear You Knockin'." Berle is seen via clips from previous episodes.

The Perry Como Show. NBC, January 28, 1956. Gale, Julius LaRosa, Buddy Hackett and Tuesday Weld are Como's guests.

Shower of Stars. "Cloak and Dagger." CBS, March 14, 1957. Producer-Director: Ralph Levy. Writers: Hugh Wedlock, Howard Snyder. Cast: Jack Benny, Gale Storm, Lawrence Welk, Hedy Lamarr, the Sid Krofft Marionettes, Jacques d'Amboise, William Lundigan (announcer). This variety show aired live and in color. Jack Benny introduces Gale, who sings "You Make Me Feel So Young." Benny tells her, "Miss Storm, you really sing up a Gale!" The show's second half features a sketch set in a Lisbon café said to be "the hotbed of international intrigue." Gale, playing the café's chanteuse, Sonya, sings "Just in Time."

This Is Your Life. June 12, 1957. Gale makes a return visit to Ralph Edwards' show to take part in a salute to Jesse L. Lasky, whose *Gateway to Hollywood* program brought her to Hollywood in 1940.

The Dinah Shore Chevy Show. October 27, 1957. Gale is a guest star on Shore's live variety hour, along with Boris Karloff and Bob Cummings.

What's My Line? CBS, November 10, 1957. Gale appears as the mystery guest. Using a high-pitched, squeaky voice, she succeeds in stumping panelists Arlene Francis, Dorothy Kilgallen, Bennett Cerf and Robert Monkhouse. Even after determining that she's a singer-actress currently starring in her own weekly series, they can't put the clues together. Asked in a *TV Guide* interview (April 5, 1958) about this appearance, Gale said, "The panel got extremely irritated with me because they couldn't guess who I was."

The Big Record. CBS, November 13, 1957. Hostess Patti Page introduces guests Gale, Bill Haley, Guy Mitchell and Harry James.

The Pat Boone Chevy Showroom. ABC, June 25, 1958. Gale and Pat sing duets of "Yatata, Yatata" and "Hollywood or Bust."

The Ed Sullivan Show. CBS, September 21, 1958. Gale Storm, Phil Silvers, Danny Thomas, Spring Byington, Arthur Godfrey and others preview their shows and the new fall season on CBS.

The Dinah Shore Chevy Show. NBC, December 21, 1958. Gale, along with John Raitt, Burl

Ives and the Mormon Choir of Southern California were guests on Dinah's holiday show. Gale sings "Winter Warm." According to *Daily Variety* (December 23, 1958), the "Christmas spirit was represented with style, grace and imagination."

Person to Person. CBS, May 1, 1959. Host Edward R. Murrow "visits" Gale at home in this installment of the long-running interview series.

Here's Hollywood. NBC, October 31, 1960. "The program is devoted to pianist Roger Williams' party for children of his neighbors. Attending ... will be Steve Allen, Gale Storm and Julie London, among others..."—*San Antonio* (TX) *Express*

Home for Christmas. NBC, December 18, 1960. Roy Rogers and Dale Evans headline this special. "Reunion around the Christmas tree of the big Rogers family, as daughters, granddaughters, Gale Storm, Doug Fairbanks, Jr., Trigger, Jr., and Sons of the Pioneers gather round."—*Joplin* (MO) *Globe*

The Garry Moore Show. CBS, February 7, 1961. Guests, Gale Storm, Mel Tormé, Bill Dana, Billy Gilbert. "Gale Storm joins Moore, Carol Burnett and Durward Kirby in a comedy sketch titled 'Lady Dither,' which satirizes a particular type of English drawing room comedy."—*Dubuque* (IA) *Telegraph-Herald,* February 3, 1961

The Tonight Show. NBC, August 6, 1962. Guest host Merv Griffin welcomes Gale Storm, Henny Youngman and golfer Sam Snead.

Burke's Law. "Who Killed His Royal Highness?" ABC, February 21, 1964. Guest stars: Gale Storm, Linda Darnell, Sheldon Leonard, Elizabeth Montgomery, Bert Parks, Mickey Rooney, Telly Savalas. Gale plays flirtatious Honey Leeps, proprietress of a nightclub frequented by the murder victim. She does a song-and-dance number, "Baby Face," teamed with Parks, who plays her jealous husband.

You Don't Say. NBC, September 14–18, 1964. Gale and Robert Horton were celebrity panelists on this daytime game show hosted by Tom Kennedy, in which contestants tried to guess the name of a famous person.

Burke's Law. "Who Killed Wimbledon Hastings?" ABC, February 3, 1965. Guest stars: Gale Storm, Nick Adams, Edgar Bergen, Debra Paget, Marie Wilson, Nancy Wilson. Burke investigates the murder of a tennis champion killed by an exploding ball.

I'll Bet. NBC, September 1965. Jack Narz hosted this short-lived daytime game show, in which celebrity couples competed against each other to win prizes for home viewers. Gale and Lee played opposite actor-comedian Harvey Lembeck and his wife.

Gypsy. Syndicated, May 1967. Gale and Robert Goulet were the guests on Gypsy Rose Lee's talk show.

The America's Junior Miss Pageant. NBC, May 6, 1969. Gale and June Allyson were judges on the five-member panel; Mike Douglas emceed.

The Steve Allen Show. Syndicated, March 1969. Guests, Gale Storm, Milton Berle.

The Steve Allen Show. Syndicated, January 1970. Guests, Gale Storm, London Lee, Josh White, Jr.

The Movie Game. April 23, 1970. Celebrities answer movie trivia questions to win prizes for home viewers in this daily syndicated game show, hosted by Sonny Fox. Gale was a guest panelist.

The Mike Douglas Show. Syndicated, September 1971. Gale is among Mike's guests, along with co-host Jim Backus, Paul Harvey and Natalie Schafer.

The Emmy Awards. CBS, May 14, 1972. Johnny Carson hosted the 24th annual ceremony; Gale was a presenter.

Celebrity Bowling. Syndicated, 1975. Producers: Joe Siegman, Don Gregory. Director: Don

Buccola. Jed Allan hosts this game show in which stars bowl to win prizes for contestants. In this episode, Gale and *Mary Tyler Moore Show* actor Ed Asner are on one team, competing against Jan Murray and Elena Verdugo.

Donny and Marie. ABC, September 24, 1976. The second-season opener of Donny and Marie Osmond's musical variety series features a "Salute to Television's Giants," with Gale one of the many celebrities seen briefly, along with Milton Berle, Arthur Godfrey and Desi Arnaz.

CBS: On the Air—A Celebration of 50 Years. CBS, March 26–April 1, 1978. Gale is one of more than 100 current and former network performers appearing in a lavish tribute to CBS's 50th anniversary of broadcasting.

The Love Boat. "Never Say Goodbye/A New Woman/Trial Romance." ABC, November 3, 1979. Director: Gordon Farr. Guest stars: Gale Storm, Louis Nye. A mature woman who's never been married, Rose Kennycott, is interested in romance, but feels she doesn't know the rules of the game. "I never what to say to men," she tells Julie. "When the sexual revolution took place, I must have been behind enemy lines." Julie tries to play matchmaker for Rose and fellow passenger Barney Briscoe, but her efforts go wrong. Rose takes Julie's advice on being more aggressive and applies it to the wrong man (ship's doctor Adam Bricker), while Julie's efforts to chat up Mr. Briscoe make him think she's flirting with him.

It's only fitting that Gale was invited to play a guest role on *The Love Boat,* basically a 1970s version of her *Gale Storm Show,* and that many of her scenes are played with Lauren Tewes, whose character is the Pacific Princess' equivalent of Susanna Pomeroy. The script offers her varied moments to play, including some teary ones, as well as a comic misfired seduction of Bernie Kopell's Dr. Bricker.

The John Davidson Show. Syndicated, August 1980. Gale is John's guest. Also appearing: co-host Gil Gerard, Dick Clark and soap opera actress Victoria Mallory.

Tomorrow with Tom Snyder. NBC, December 17, 1981. Gale is a guest on Snyder's late-night talk show, along with cable magnate Ted Turner and comedian Rip Taylor.

Over Easy. PBS, May 1982. Hugh Downs hosts this Public Broadcasting talk show aimed at older Americans. In this episode, Gale and actress Jan Clayton (*Lassie*) share their experiences with alcoholism.

All-Star Party for "Dutch" Reagan. CBS, December 8, 1985. President Ronald Reagan was feted by Golden Age Hollywood celebrities, including Gale, James Stewart, Charlton Heston, Frank Sinatra, Fred MacMurray and others in this fundraiser for Variety Clubs. The broadcast ranked among the Top Ten shows in that week's TV ratings.

Hour Magazine. Syndicated, November 5, 1986. Gale is interviewed by host Gary Collins on this episode of the long-running daytime talk show. Other guests are *60 Minutes'* Ed Bradley and actor Roy Scheider.

The Love Boat. "Who Killed Maxwell Thorn?" ABC, February 27, 1987. Director: Kim Friedman. Gale made a cameo appearance in this two-hour segment that takes the form of a *Ten Little Indians*–like murder mystery.

Win, Lose or Draw. NBC, February 1988. Gale was a celebrity guest on the daytime game show, along with fellow singers Bobby Rydell, Fabian and Mary Wells.

Murder, She Wrote. "Something Borrowed, Someone Blue." CBS, January 8, 1989. Writer: Philip Gerson. Director: John Llewellyn Moxey. Cast: Angela Lansbury, Patricia Barry, Ray Buktenica, Conchata Ferrell, Michael Horton, Rick Hurst, Bill Macy, Howard Morris, Betsy Palmer, Eugene Roche, Gale Storm, Debbie Zipp.

Back in the spotlight after publicly acknowledging her recovery from alcoholism, Gale appeared on talk shows, including *The John Davidson Show* in 1980.

Jessica Fletcher is attending the wedding of her nephew Grady, to be held at the mansion of his fiancée's parents, the Mayberrys. Before the ceremony can begin, the Mayberrys' obnoxious housekeeper is found dead, with a meat tenderizer in her back. With the grounds sealed off, it's obvious that the murderer is either a wedding guest or a member of the Mayberrys' staff. Jessica helps the none-too-sharp local police chief investigate.

In her final professional acting performance, Gale has a fairly sizable guest role as the bride-to-be's flighty, somewhat high-strung mother Maisie. Gale's character introduces some comedy reacting to various setbacks and challenges with outbursts like (to Eugene Roche as her husband), "It's the end of the world, that's all, the end of the world!" Later, she reacts to another situation by saying, "What are you trying to do, ruin the rest of my life?"

Hal Roach: Hollywood's King of Laughter. Disney Channel, 1994. Gale is interviewed in this documentary about Hal Roach, Sr., and is seen in *My Little Margie* excerpts.

ShirleyMania. Fox News Channel, 2002. This documentary traces the influence and ongoing popularity of child star Shirley Temple. In a brief appearance shot at the Hollywood Collectors' Show, Gale describes her as "absolutely a joy to behold."

IV

Radio

Gateway to Hollywood

Gale Storm's introduction to network radio—as well as her first nationwide exposure—came in the late 1930s with this CBS series, a precursor to *Star Search*. Longtime Hollywood producer Jesse L. Lasky devised the show, which made its debut under the sponsorship of the Wrigley Company on January 8, 1939. An ad in *Daily Variety* (January 6, 1939) described the show: "Youngsters brought here from all over America and supported by the great stars of Hollywood in a series of shows to find new faces for the screen." The contest was open to women between the ages of 18 and 26 and men between 20 and 30. *Variety* (January 11, 1939) was unimpressed by the premiere broadcast, featuring guest star Miriam Hopkins, calling it "flat-footed and feeble," not to mention "boresome."

Over the course of the show's 1939 run, three 13-week competitions were completed. The second concluded in the summertime, when finalists were awarded the names John Archer and Alice Eden. In preparation for the third and final round of competition, Lasky arrived in Texas in August 1939. He made personal appearances in Fort Worth, Houston, San Antonio and finally Dallas. Eighteen young people from Texas were sent on to Hollywood, including 17-year-old Josephine Cottle.

Josephine, winning the statewide competition in Houston, made her first appearance on the October 22, 1939, broadcast, along with five other Texas finalists. Film actors Leo Carrillo and Cliff Edwards appeared in skits with the contestants.

On the December 31, 1939, broadcast, the six finalists performed in a play titled "From the Mountain Top" with actor H.B. Warner. Lee and Josephine are the first of the three couples to perform, in a script that calls for romance, anger and tears. Among the judges, whom Lasky announces have been tasked with choosing winners based on "photographic qualities, personality and dramatic abilities," are RKO director Frank Woodruff and makeup artist Mel Berns.

In the program's final few moments, Cottle and Lee Bonnell are declared the winners, with only one judge (RKO talent executive Julius Evans) preferring another ingénue, Sally Cairns, in Jo's place. Both young people are awarded contracts as RKO featured players, with "Gale Storm's" first picture for the studio to be *Tom Brown's School Days*. Lee and Josephine (now Gale) accept congratulations, with Lee doing most of the speaking as Gale is fighting back tears.

Family Theater

Over a period of several years, Gale made multiple appearances on this dramatic anthology series produced and aired by the Mutual Broadcasting System. The series had an explicitly religious theme, and frequently reminded listeners about the importance of family prayer. Gale starred in several episodes, as well as hosting a few other broadcasts.

"Out of the Wilderness." Mutual, February 12, 1948. Director: David Young. Writer: Jack Price. Cast: Gale Storm (Nancy), Bill Williams (Tom); with Paul Frees, Joe Du Val, Dick Ryan, Peter Rankin, Marylee Robb, Marjorie Bennett. Hostess Maureen O'Hara introduces the story of Tom and Nancy, young Kentuckians in the early 1800s who, as the announcer says, "were the spirit of these early settlers whose outstanding deeds were the simple events of their everyday lives." The final scene finds the young couple welcoming their second child, a son who will grow up to carry out a great destiny. Gale plays the "small, pretty brunette" who inspires Tom to complete his journey to manhood and help settle the still-new community.

"The Unsung Hero." Mutual, May 27, 1948. Director: David Young. A drama depicting the story of how Memorial Day came to be. Lee Bonnell plays General John A. Logan, who in the aftermath of the Civil War realizes that those who lost their lives in military service should be recognized and honored. Gale plays his supportive wife Mary. Mona Freeman is the hostess.

"Brannigan's Bat." Mutual, September 23, 1948. Gale co-starred with Stephen Dunne in "a timely story of pennant race baseball ... of a rookie outfielder, horse-collared at the plate, who snaps a horrendous slump to blast his way to league batting leadership and becomes the team's star."—*Cedar Rapids* (IA) *Gazette*. Jeanne Crain is the hostess.

"The Valiant Lady." Mutual, April 26, 1950. Gale stars as Margaret of Hereford, an 11th-century English noblewoman who stands up defiantly against William the Conqueror. Supporting Gale are Dan O'Herlihy and William Conrad.

"The Stephen Foster Story." Mutual, October 4, 1950. A dramatization of the life of the famed composer, with Stephen McNally in the title role. Gale serves as hostess, introducing the drama and delivering a closing message about family prayer.

"The Kiddie Story Story." Mutual, September 19, 1951. Jane Wyatt stars as a cynical newspaper reporter determined to expose the harm of giving children fantasy stories instead of realistic literature. Jeff Chandler plays the author she confronts. Gale serves as hostess.

"Hackie." Mutual, January 13, 1954. "A fare to the fights at Madison Square Garden brings back Hank's memories of experiences in the fight game and he finds himself relating his tale of dreams of glory and disappointment to his passenger."—*Brownwood* (TX) *Bulletin*. Gale introduces the drama, which stars Michael O'Shea, her *Underworld Story* co-star.

"U.F.O." Mutual, October 13, 1954. A group of delegates from countries around the world travel to an uncharted Pacific island to make contact with visitors from outer space. Gale is the hostess.

My Little Margie

Producer-Director: Gordon T. Hughes. *Based on Characters Created by* Frank Fox. *Announcers*: Roy Rowan (program); Ken Roberts (commercials). *Sponsor*: Philip Morris.

Aired Sundays at 8:30 p.m. on CBS. First aired December 7, 1952. Last aired June 26, 1955.

Although many early television shows were adapted from popular radio programs, *My Little Margie* was one of the relatively few programs to make the switch in reverse. The sudden popularity of TV's *Margie* upon its 1952 debut inspired Philip Morris to develop a radio version. It came along at a time when network radio was beginning to struggle against the fast-growing popularity of television.

On November 13, 1952, syndicated columnist Erskine Johnson reported, "Charles Farrell and Gale Storm just cut an audition platter of TV's *My Little Margie* as a radio show for TV-less cities." Less than a month later, the show made its bow on CBS Radio, in a transcribed version. In charge of the radio version was producer-director Gordon T. Hughes (1909–1999), whose previous credits included *My Favorite Husband* and *Broadway Is My Beat*. According to a 1953 listing in *Sponsor* magazine, radio's *Margie* had a weekly production budget of $4000. The radio version premiered on CBS's Sunday night lineup on December 6, 1952, airing at 8:30 p.m. (EST), after *Our Miss Brooks*. CBS publicity described the lead characters as "a 21-year-old who's determined to make her father behave himself," and "the dashing, debonair father who refuses to recognize the fact that he's not quite as young as he used to be."

While Storm and Farrell reprised their starring roles from the TV version, an entirely different supporting cast was featured. Cast as Mrs. Odetts was Verna Felton (1890–1966). Although Felton may be best-remembered as Hilda Crocker on TV's *December Bride,* she was also a veteran radio actress whose credits included *The Jack Benny Program, The Joan Davis Show* and *The Great Gildersleeve.* A running gag on the radio show has Mrs. Odetts bursting into the Albrights' apartment unannounced, joining whatever conversation is underway in midstream (after listening at the keyhole).

Veteran actress Verna Felton (right) took the role of Mrs. Odetts when *My Little Margie* was adapted to radio.

Gil Stratton, Jr. (1922–2008), assumed the role of Freddie Wilson, here depicted as more of a wisecracking smart aleck than Don Hayden's TV version. Stratton's Freddie jovially refers to himself as "America's contribution to the finer things of life," and bursts into laughter at his own remarks. Stratton recalled to author Fredrick Tucker in 2005, "*My Little Margie* probably had the worst scripts in the world; they were not very funny. And I remember Verna and I did everything but drop our pants onstage to get laughs, and make it sound like it was funny even though there wasn't anything there to laugh at, really."[1]

Their characterizations on radio are even broader than in the video version. The sight gags, costumes and physical comedy that earned laughs on the TV screen had to be replaced largely by jokes. More so than on TV, the writers emphasize gags, with insults flying in every direction during a typical episode. When Vern tells Freddie, "You talk like an idiot," brassy Freddie promptly retorts, "I've got to, so you can understand me!" Heard less frequently was Vern's boss Mr. Honeywell, played here by Will Wright. Charlie the elevator operator was dropped altogether. A recurring character created for the radio show was Vern's Southern-accented girlfriend Connie Carter, usually voiced by Shirley Mitchell. The TV show's standard epilogue, which ends with Vern saying, "That's my little Margie!" was not a regular feature of the radio program, though the phrase is heard occasionally.

While featuring largely the same set of characters as the TV comedy, radio's *Margie* inevitably had a different feel. *Daily Variety* (December 8, 1952) wasn't wowed by the premiere episode, but acknowledged that it "may level off as a good Sunday night entry," acknowledging that the studio audience had greeted it with enthusiastic applause. The show would find its way into radio's Top Ten during its run, and introduced some new listeners to the Albrights. Charles Farrell told a journalist in 1954 that "many of the radio fans don't know it's on TV."[2]

On March 23, 1953, *Time* magazine reported that, in a record-setting feat, CBS had all of the Top Ten radio shows in both nighttime and daytime hours, completely shutting out its rivals. *My Little Margie* held seventh place on the list of highly rated prime time shows. A few months later, it had jumped to #3 in the ratings, as reported in *Variety* (October 29, 1953).

The show received some unwelcome attention that same year, when a lawsuit was filed in Superior Court by the producers of the soon-to-be-released film *Cat-Women of the Moon*, starring Sonny Tufts and Marie Windsor. Supposedly *Margie* writer Lee Karson had visited the set of the film during production and subsequently turned out a radio episode that, said the plaintiffs, "constituted an infringement, plagiarism, unauthorized use of story and unfair competition in that [they] claim that cannot now use the vehicle for radio."[3]

Beginning in the fall of 1953, the radio *Margie* was heard even more widely, when sponsor Philip Morris made a deal to supplement the Sunday airing on CBS with a secondary play on more than 400 Mutual Radio stations. The Mutual deal allowed the sponsor to reach potential customers in a number of smaller cities that didn't yet have a television station. MBS affiliates were required to observe a four-day delay following the CBS broadcast, resulting in a Thursday slot on those stations.

After serving as *Margie*'s sole sponsor for much of its radio run, Philip Morris agreed to share the load in December 1954, having found it more cost-effective to spread its advertising among multiple programs. Soon Gale was pitching Campana's Solitair "cake makeup."

In the summer of 1955, with television continuing to encroach upon radio's audience, CBS executives were said to be taking a hard look at numerous prime-time weekly shows.

"Among the old radio reliables who may not be back next season are Jack Benny and Bob Hope, busy with TV, and the radio version of *My Little Margie*."[4] *Margie* had its final radio broadcast in June 1955, a few weeks before the video version last aired in prime time on NBC-TV. *Margie's* Sunday CBS slot, as of July 3, was given over to a summer musical show spotlighting Gary Crosby.

Surviving Episodes

Although the radio *My Little Margie* lasted from 1952 through 1955, roughly concurrent with the TV series, only a relatively small number of episodes survive. Many of the surviving episodes are transcriptions made for the Armed Forces Radio and Television Service. These recordings have had commercials deleted, and the closing credits are typically missing as well. For this show, AFRTS staff filled out the time with a musical bridge featuring "Margie," the 1920 popular song by Conrad, Robinson and Davis.

The following episodes are readily available through online sites or from Old Time Radio vendors. In most cases, the episode titles have been supplied by sellers, or radio enthusiasts, and may not match those on the original scripts. Because the actual titles are often unknown, some compilations contain more than one version of the same episode, with only an alternate title to distinguish them.

"Princess Margie" (December 14, 1952)

Summary: Vern complains when Margie prefers Freddie's attentions to those of a young nobleman she recently met. Margie consults a genealogist who tells her she is descended from royalty of a defunct Balkan empire—on her mother's side—and promptly adopts the appropriate airs. Tiring of seeing his daughter pose as royalty, Vern plots to make her reconsider.

Notes: Written by Lee Karson and Maurice Richlin. Veteran character actors Hans Conried and Sheldon Leonard play Boris and Joe, respectively. The Philip Morris commercials promote cigarettes in the "holiday carton" as Christmas gifts. Margie's "gurgle," by now familiar to TV audiences, is heard.

Quote: VERN (complaining about Margie's preference for Freddie): I'd rather have a count than a no-account!

"Timmy's Christmas" (December 21, 1952)

Summary: Learning that their paperboy, Timmy, lives in a poor neighborhood where there are few Christmas gifts, Margie and her father decide to spend their holiday money treating the less fortunate. Accompanying the Albrights on their shopping spree is Honeywell's bratty, mischievous nephew, Ronald Wetherby III, who doesn't believe in Santa Claus. A timely dream convinces Ronald to rethink his views, leading to a happy holiday for all.

Quote: MARGIE: Freddie, did you get anything for my stocking?
FREDDIE: What for? I'm satisfied with what's in 'em now!

"Freddie the Prizefighter" (March 8, 1953)

Summary: After Freddie loses yet another job, he tries a career as a boxer. Margie persuades his first opponent, "Killer" Jenkins, to let her boyfriend win. Unaware that the fight was fixed, Vern jeopardizes his job by encouraging Mr. Honeywell to place a sizable bet on Freddie's next bout.

Notes: Written by Lee Karson and Jack Harvey. Cast members include Herb Butterfield and Charlie Cantor. Series announcer Roy Rowan doubles as the color announcer for Freddie's fight with Jenkins.

> *Quote*: MARGIE (bragging about Freddie's new job): And how much do you think he earns?
> VERN: About half what they pay him.

"Thanksgiving Show" (November 26, 1953)

Summary: Vern's old pal, a war correspondent, asks him to care temporarily for Elsa, an 11-year-old refugee he has sent to the U.S. Elsa arrives amidst preparations for the Albrights' Thanksgiving dinner, and her sweet nature helps Mr. Honeywell's bratty nephew, Ronald, understand the meaning of the holiday.

Note: This episode has some unusually serious moments (among the usual gags), as Elsa tells the Albrights her father died in a concentration camp.

Quote: Margie (describing Vern): When it comes to women, he's got a head like a doorknob ... anyone can turn it!

"My Son, My Son" (February 21, 1954)

Summary: Even after borrowing Vern's formal wear, Freddie can't make a good enough impression to land a solid job. Margie suggests that belonging to a well-respected family might give her boyfriend confidence, and persuades Vern to pretend to adopt Freddie. Freddie proceeds to make himself at home in the Albright apartment, to Margie's amusement, until he invokes his brotherly privileges to interfere in her love life.

Note: Also known as "Freddie Is Adopted," this episode also aired on Thursday, March 25, 1954, on Mutual Radio affiliates. This is a pretty wild plot even by *Margie*'s standards, and doesn't take into account that we met Freddie's perfectly respectable parents in an early TV episode.

"Margie Gets Freddie a Job" (July 18, 1954)

Summary: Vern challenges Freddie to get a job, which he does—until he's fired on the first day. Next Margie finds her boyfriend a position at Farley's Department Store. But when Mr. Honeywell learns that a wealthy client is Freddie's uncle, and wants the young man to learn the investment business, Vern and Margie try to persuade him to give up his cushy gig at the store.

Notes: This episode finds Freddie landing what must be his ideal job—lying in a store window wearing his pajamas, demonstrating mattresses. Frank Nelson is heard as a personnel manager.

"Stolen Pearls" (November 28, 1954)

Summary: The Albrights' lease is up for renewal, but they want the apartment redecorated before they sign. After Mrs. Odetts tells them that the former tenant was "Big Jim," a notorious jewel thief, Margie has her spread the rumor that there are unrecovered gems hidden in the walls. Margie's plot to make landlord Mr. Blandish tear out the walls (and

then be forced to redecorate) goes awry when former members of Big Jim's gang show up to retrieve the pearls.
>   Quote: MRS. ODETTS: I never got a pearl out of an oyster, but I once got a diamond out of an old crab.

"Thirty Days to Live" (December 12, 1954)

Summary: Misunderstanding an overhead conversation between her father and Mr. Honeywell, Margie jumps to the conclusion that Vern is seriously ill and has a month to live. Wanting her father to see her safely married before he dies, Margie decides to become Mrs. Freddie Wilson.
>   Note: Written by Lee Karson and Jack Harvey.
>   Quote: MARGIE: Freddie, make me happy! Marry me!
>   FREDDIE: Well, make up your mind! Which do you want me to do?

"Margie's Superstition" (February 20, 1955)

Summary: After dreaming three nights in a row that she inherited a fortune, superstitious Margie fully expects it to happen. Vern tries to persuade her otherwise by sending her a lawyer's letter promising her an inheritance from "Death Valley Pete," which proves to be nothing but an old trunk full of razor blades. Wanting to get even, Margie arranges for Vern to find a map that supposedly shows treasure buried in Central Park, unaware that it was actually drawn by two ex-convicts who show up to reclaim the stolen money they hid there.
>   Note: Written by Jack Harvey and Lee Karson. Lou Krugman and Herb Vigran play the crooks, Lefty Louie and Flathead Nelson; Ken Christy portrays the policeman.

"Miss Guided Missile Contest" (March 13, 1955)

Summary: While vacationing in Las Vegas, Margie fixes her father up with a woman named Sheila. Airman Lt. Bruce Howard romances Margie and persuades her to enter a pageant at his air base, to be named "Miss Guided Missile." When it develops that Sheila also wants to win the contest, Vern plots to make Margie drop out of the competition.
>   Notes: Written by Lee Karson and Jack Harvey. Guest players include George Neise as Lt. Bruce Howard, Hans Conried as a professor, Jeanne Tatum as Sheila Grant and Frank Nelson as the hotel clerk. Gale and Charles Farrell do a commercial, as "themselves," for the sponsor's Solitaire cake makeup.

"Crooked Campaign Manager" (June 6, 1955)

Summary: While vacationing at their farm in the country, Vern is persuaded to run for mayor. Sleazy Johnny Velvet, who operates a nearby roadhouse, warns Margie that her father will be hurt if he wins. Having encouraged her father to seek political office, Margie now has to do her best to ruin his chances of winning.

"Camping on the Roof" (June 12, 1955)

Summary: The Albrights' getaway to the mountains has to be postponed when Vern has an opportunity to see a longtime prospective investor, Mr. Green. Margie decides she doesn't want to go, since she will be separated from Freddie, and doesn't relish Vern's idea of roughing it in the wilderness. Vern tries to orient his daughter and Mrs. Odetts to the outdoor life by setting up a makeshift camp on the roof of their apartment building.

    Notes: Written by Lee Karson. Also known as "A Trip to Silver Lake."

"Station KREJ" (July 31, 1955)

Summary: Challenged to help Freddie get ahead in business, Vern buys a 1000-watt radio station for him to manage. When it becomes clear that the station has no paying sponsors, the new owners are forced to let most of the staff go. Margie, Vern, Freddie and Mrs. Odetts take on the challenge of providing all the station's daily programming, from a soap opera to a show offering relationship advice.

    Notes: The station's call letters, backward, spell a word that sums up Vern's opinion of Freddie.

    Quote: VERN (recalling his humble beginnings in the business world): I used to walk to work behind a streetcar, just to save a nickel.
    MARGIE: Why didn't you walk behind a taxi, and save 80 cents?

"Vern Reunites with Old Friends" (date unknown)

Summary: Vern and his daughter are pleased when their old friends, the Davises, return to New York. An argument about golf causes a rift between Vern and Hank Davis, while Hank's daughter Babs quarrels with Margie after they both run for the chairmanship of the Young Debs' dance committee. A confused Freddie tries to keep up as relationships between the Albrights and the Davises change almost hourly.

"Love's Trouble" (date unknown)

Summary: Vern has had a quarrel with his girlfriend Connie, while Margie is on the outs with Freddie. The men decide to make their ladies jealous by hiring two actresses, Tillie Smith and Millie Brown, to act as their dates. When Mrs. Odetts spills the beans, Margie and Connie arrange a surprise to interrupt the romantic dinner their boyfriends have staged.

    Quote: CONNIE: There's only one thing that makes me hesitate to call [Vern] a bare-faced liar.
    MARGIE: What's that?
    CONNIE: His mustache!

"Connie Returns from Europe" (date unknown)

Summary: Vern is anxiously awaiting the arrival in New York of Connie, who's been traveling in Europe. When Connie shows up with a titled Englishman, Lord Cyril Poindexter, in tow, Vern is jealous of this new rival. Margie thinks she can break up Connie's new relationship by making a play for Cyril, but when that fails she decides to get her father a title of his own.

    Quote: MARGIE: Here, let me put my head on your shoulder.
    CYRIL: You mean it comes off?!

"Quiz Show" (date unknown)

Summary: Freddie gives the Albrights and Mrs. Odetts tickets to attend a radio quiz show, where all four of them are chosen as contestants. Winning contestant Margie gets a free trip to Hawaii, but her fun is spoiled when an overprotective Vern lays down too many rules about her behavior and activities. Scheming Margie arranges for the group to be stranded on a small island, where the "natives" (actually members of the hotel band) pronounce her queen.

Notes: Actor Frank Nelson plays the bombastic quiz show host Dr. Quizem. This episode is also known as "Hawaii Trip."

Quote: DR. QUIZEM (leering at Margie): Well, Miss Albright, you're certainly looking lovely tonight!
MARGIE: Thanks, Dr. Quizem. You're certainly *looking*!

"100 Shares of Stock" (date unknown)

Summary: After Vern criticizes her business sense, Margie is pleased when she's offered a good price for her shares of stock in Amalgamated Chemical. Meanwhile, a rival is trying to unseat Mr. Honeywell as board chairman of that company, and offers her an attractive price to sell. When her shares of stock become crucial to the vote, Vern struggles to get his daughter to sign them over.

Note: This is an adaptation of the TV episode "Stock Control," aired on March 26, 1953.

"Freddie's Uncle" (date unknown)

Summary: With Vern heading out of town, Freddie tries to impress his visiting Uncle Maurice by pretending that the Albright apartment is his own, with Margie his maid and Mrs. Odetts his housekeeper. The plan unravels when Vern returns home unexpectedly, having been involved in a fender bender with Maurice at the airport, and then is told to win over the visitor as a prospective Honeywell and Todd client.

Notes: Charles Farrell gets a big laugh when Vern says, "I'm a pretty remarkable person," and then adds, "I once heard Charlie Farrell use that line in a picture called *Seventh Heaven*." According to this script, Freddie's usual abode is "a single room on Third Avenue."

"Foreign Legion" (date unknown)

Summary: Freddie buys a new car just as Vern finds $250 missing from his desk, and Margie's dad accuses him of theft. The missing money turns up, and Margie insists that her father apologize to Freddie. Unimpressed with Vern's half-hearted apology, Freddie pretends to join the French Foreign Legion, a trick that misfires when he unknowingly signs real enlistment papers.

Notes: Written by Jack Harvey and Lee Karson. George Neise plays Pierre, while Hans Conried is credited with the role of Congressman Cyrus Klingendinger. Freddie's wisecrack about Los Angeles smog gets a big laugh from the studio audience of locals.

"Little Moose" (date unknown)

Summary: Vern is eagerly anticipating a visit from the son of an old college chum, "Big Moose" Magruder, whom he believes will make a suitable companion for Margie. Instead of the strong, handsome, fun-loving type Vern expects, the young man who turns up is a "jerky genius" who makes Freddie look good by comparison. Wanting to discourage her father's interference in her dating life, Margie pretends to be seriously interested in him as a suitor.

    Quote: MARGIE (when Freddie shows up with his jacket padded to look more muscular): Dad, is it possible to get mumps in the shoulders?

"Vern's Birthday" (date unknown)

Summary: Honeywell and Todd's tiresome client Mrs. Purvis is in town, and Vern asks Margie to show her the sights. Busy with her plans for Vern's surprise birthday party, Margie fails to keep the appointment with the client. When Mr. Honeywell spills the beans about the party plans, Vern decides he should bawl his daughter out for standing Mrs. Purvis up, so that Margie won't suspect he knows about the surprise.

    Notes: Written by Lee Karson. Lois Corbet is heard as Mrs. Purvis, while Frank Nelson enacts the role of a furniture salesman.

"Vern Plays Cards at Home" (date unknown)

Summary: Margie and Connie want Vern to play bridge at home, instead of going to his club every night. Inviting some new neighbors to the apartment for a game, Margie outsmarts herself when she's stuck babysitting their bratty son.

    Quote: MARGIE (talking about the chatterbox Mrs. Motley): I bet her husband's afraid to take her to the beach. Her tongue might get sunburned.

"Vern Buys a Racehorse" (date unknown)

Summary: Vern and Mr. Honeywell pool their money to buy a racehorse, Bubbles LaTour. Seeing the check stubs for his purchases, Margie concludes that he's being a sugar daddy to the burlesque dancer of the same name. The confusion worsens when she confronts the dancer in the presence of her jealous husband, a wrestler.

    Notes: Bubbles' husband, known as Gorgeous John, is a riff on the popular real-life wrestler Gorgeous George. This is one of the only extant episodes to feature the character of Roberta Townsend, voiced here by Doris Singleton.

"Does Margie Marry Freddie?" (date unknown)

Summary: Freddie's uncle, whose name is also Freddie Wilson, is planning a second honeymoon at Niagara Falls. When Vern sees a telegram confirming the reservation, he believes it's Margie who's going to get married, and tries to persuade her she can't leave him, as he is "old and feeble." Catching on to his ruse, Margie ups the ante by pretending she and Freddie are already married, and borrows the janitor's baby to show Vern his "grandson."

    Notes: This episode finds Mrs. Odetts spying on the Albright apartment through her own window, which would have been an impossibility given the setup as shown on TV.

"Spending Spree" (date unknown)

Summary: Margie and Mrs. Odetts' winning sweepstakes ticket nets them a cool $1500 each. Margie is intent on collecting a bet with Vern, in which he promised to double her money if it was still untouched in her bank account at the end of the month. With the deadline fast approaching, Vern enlists the help of a slick salesman, Swifty Smith, to make Margie loosen her purse strings.

Note: This episode survives in an incomplete version captured from an Armed Forces Radio Service re-broadcast to military personnel.

Missing Episodes from Newspaper Listings

Although most of the radio *Margie* episodes are not known to be in existence today, basic synopses for a portion of them can be gleaned from newspaper listings of that era (see bibliography). Network publicists sent out teasers describing each week's episode, and some radio stations placed ads in local papers publicizing the shows to be heard that evening. Occasionally episode titles were included as well. Program logs and/or advertisements from newspapers were used to compile this list:

1952–53 Season

February 8, 1953. "[Margie] encounters a gambler monickered 'Trigger Mortis.'"
March 1, 1953. "Charity begins at home."
March 15, 1953. "Charles Farrell and Gale Storm step out bright and early to celebrate St. Patrick's Day."
March 22, 1953. "[Margie] seeks date with matinee idol."
April 5, 1953. "Insurance." "Margie believes her father has gone broke and takes steps to save money…"
April 12, 1953. "Father sends parrot as peace offering."
May 17, 1953. "Margie tries to prove her father is no judge of character."
June 21, 1953. "'Father's Day.' Margie takes a job that causes trouble at home when all she's really trying to do is earn money for a gift to give Vern…"

1953–54 Season

Beginning in the fall of 1953, *My Little Margie* was heard Sunday nights on CBS stations, and on MBS (Mutual) stations the following Thursday. Both air dates are listed for these episodes.

September 27 and October 1, 1953. "When … Margie learns she is to inherit a boat … home becomes a madhouse as frantic preparations are made for a long trip. Margie … suffers a letdown on learning it's a miniature ship sealed in a bottle."
October 4 and 8, 1953. "'Criss Cross.' New neighbors bring trying moments…. [Margie and Vern] make a date with their fellow tenants and two feuds come to light."
October 11 and 15, 1953. "Being a press agent is a new role" for Margie, whose father "has a new girl friend who wants to be a 'cover girl.' Margie … gets the lady on a lurid confession show—from which the storm develops."
October 18 and 22, 1953. "'Who's Crazy?' Margie manages to wind up as her father's date … in a hilarious doublecross."
October 25 and 29, 1953. "'Science Friction.' Vern … buys a spaceship [and] the results are almost catastrophic. It takes quick thinking by Margie … to bring things back to earth…"
November 1 and 5, 1953. "Shopping for a gift for her dad gets very complicated for

[Margie] when the jewelry store in which she's shopping is held up. Margie ... is arrested in the confusion that follows..."

November 8 and 12, 1953. "'The Hypochondriac.' Phony illnesses seem to Margie ... to be good stepping stones to business success. Just why, she can't explain—except via intuition. However, one false step leads to another and then to romance..."

November 15 and 19, 1953. "'Vern's Politics.' Vern ... is off and running—for mayor ... with Margie hot on the campaign trail."

November 29 and December 3, 1953. "'High Finance.' [Margie] rocks the stock market ... to get even with finance moguls she erroneously thinks caused her father ... to be fired."

December 6 and 10, 1953. "'Who's Margie?' [Vern] hires a girl to pretend she's Margie ... to save her from an unfortunate romance."

December 13 and 17, 1953. "When Vern Albright applies for the presidency of his company, he doesn't count on complications arising from the fact that he is unmarried."

December 27 and 31, 1953. "Margie has special plans for celebrating the advent of 1954."

January 3 and 7, 1954. "Margie Sings." "A Carnegie Hall debut for [Margie] results in complications never heard of ... despite her dad's protests..."

January 10 and 14, 1954. "'Margie's Engagement.' [Margie undergoes] a pretended courtship with a sailor in order to push Daddy Vern into popping the question himself."

January 17 and 21, 1954. "'The Stamp.' Margie mistakes a $3000 stamp for a three-center and sets the stage for fun."

January 21 and 28, 1954. "'The Auction.' When daddy buys a pistol ... it can cause many zany events ... [T]he comedy starts when Margie finds the gun—and shoots the works."

January 31 and February 4, 1954. "'The Bullfight.' A trip to Mexico with Vern going out on a limb..."

February 7 and 11, 1954. "'The Neighbors.' [Margie and her father] go out to find an apartment for a client but get themselves in the middle when the client finds one himself."

March 7 and 11, 1954. "'Vern Returns to High School.' Papa, the athletic hero, returns to the high school scene of his triumphs ... [I]t can provide some unusual comedy situations."

March 14 and 18, 1954. "A trip to the opera is in store for Margie ... when Vern's girl friend has a visitor from the South, and to make an impression, they go..."

March 21 and 25, 1954. "Margie plays a trick on her father when she discovers a man of identical appearance."

April 4 and 8, 1954. "...settling a quarrel..."

May 2 and 6, 1954. "Margie and her father take a boat trip to Paris and father meets up with a French golddigger on the way across."

May 9 and 13, 1954. "Margie and her dad take a hunting trip to Kentucky."

May 16 and 20, 1954. Margie "develops a special salad dressing and goes into business."

May 23 and 27, 1954. Margie "sets out to prove that there is no such thing as a bad boy."

May 30 and June 3, 1954. "Daddy and Margie spend Memorial Day on the farm."

June 20 and 24, 1954. "Margie plots a Father's Day surprise for her dad ... while he shares with her his recollections of her baby days..."

June 27 and July 1, 1954. "Margie and ... her father find themselves in trouble with their respective amours..."

July 11 and 15, 1954. "Margie gets job as maid to promote romance."

July 25 and 29, 1954. "Father tries to match Margie with the son of a college chum."

August 15 and 19, 1954. "Margie and her father entertain a wealthy bachelor."

August 29 and September 2, 1954. "Margie puts on a benefit show for a boys' club, reluctantly aided by ... her father..."

1954–55 Season

Air dates given below are for CBS' Sunday night broadcast. Rebroadcasts by MBS during this season could not be confirmed.

September 5, 1954. "Margie and ... her father go out West to visit their cousin, Cactus Kate..."

October 10, 1954. "Vern starts out to give a surprise birthday party for Freddie and it turns out to be a real surprise when everyone sings 'Happy Birthday' in jail."

October 24, 1954. "Father takes to his bed to prevent Margie from marrying."

October 31, 1954. "[This episode] concerns Margie's sudden desire to become a policewoman and her father's hair-breadth escape from under the wheels of the juggernaut of justice." According to the network press release, this was Margie's 100th radio broadcast.

November 14, 1954. "Hollywood columnist Sheilah Graham ... interviews Vern, Margie, Freddie and Mrs. Odetts ... to find out why they are adventuring in Hollywoodland."

November 21, 1954. "After attending six Thanksgiving dinners, Vern and Margie Albright still find themselves hungry for turkey. Their solution is symbolic of the day, a thanks to God for what they have."

December 5, 1954. "Margie Albright and her father Vern decide they need the expert help of Charlie Farrell to run a winter sports resort."

December 19, 1954. "Margie's handling of Honeywell's nephew saves Santa Claus."

December 26, 1954. "With a song in her heart ... Margie manages to involve Peter Potter, host of CBS Radio's *Juke Box Jury*, in a plot to prove to her father she has musical talent..."

January 2, 1955. "The New Year begins with a blank for ... Margie, but she recovers from her amnesia with the aid of a mink coat."

January 9, 1955. "A mechanical brain almost outwits [Margie] until Margie decides to polish up her gray matter."

January 16, 1955. "Margie and Vern have a reunion that begins mellow but ends stormy."

February 13, 1955. "Margie tries her hand at amateur matchmaking."

May 1, 1955. "Margie fiddles while her father Vern burns..."

May 22, 1955. "Are men or women better drivers?"

June 19, 1955. "The key witness to Mrs. Odetts' disappearance is a parrot.... The usually talkative bird decides silence is golden, while Margie and her father search for clues to their friend's whereabouts."

ADDITIONAL AIR DATES

The following air dates were confirmed by newspaper listings, but lacked story details:

February 15, 1953; February 22, 1953; March 29, 1953; April 19, 1953; April 26, 1953; May 3, 1953; May 10, 1953; May 24, 1953; May 31, 1953; June 7, 1953; June 14, 1953; February

18, 1954; March 4, 1954; March 28, 1954; April 11, 1954; April 18, 1954; April 25, 1954; June 6, 1954; June 13, 1954 ; August 1, 1954; August 8, 1954; August 22, 1954; September 12, 1954; September 19, 1954; September 26, 1954; October 3, 1954; October 17, 1954; January 23, 1955; January 30, 1955; February 6, 1955; March 6, 1955; March 13, 1955; March 20, 1955; March 27, 1955; April 3, 1955; April 10, 1955; April 17, 1955; April 24, 1955; May 8, 1955; May 15, 1955; May 29, 1955; June 5, 1955; June 26, 1955

Radio Guest Appearances

Hollywood Theater. "News Story." February 10, 1945.

The Casebook of Gregory Hood. "Fifth Avenue." Mutual, May 5, 1947. Gale guest stars in this radio drama about a San Francisco–based antiques expert who encounters crime as he travels the world in search of collectibles.

Lux Radio Theatre. "It Happened on Fifth Avenue." CBS, May 19, 1947. Gale, Don DeFore, Charlie Ruggles and Victor Moore recreate their movie roles in this one-hour radio adaptation of the popular film. Director William Keighley is the host. The story moves lickety-split in order to compress the film scenario into a much shorter running time, but it is a faithful retelling.

Your Movietown Radio Theatre. "Baby Doing Well." Syndicated, July 1947. Producer-Director-Host: Les Mitchell. Writer: Carey Shaw. Cast: Gale Storm (*Miss Evans*), Marvin Miller (*Pemberton Hollis*), Doris Kemper (*Mrs. Lucas*)

Pressed for money, a young woman enters a newspaper's beautiful-baby contest, submitting a 20-year-old photograph of herself. Miss Evans wins the contest and the $1000 prize, but she finds herself devising a series of ruses when the newspaper's owner, handsome Pemberton Hollis, wants more pictures of the prizewinner. She is able to stall him temporarily by claiming that her daughter has measles. When he persists, Miss Evans pulls out all the stops to keep the charade going, all the while feeling guilty and developing a fondness for Hollis.

Gale's character schemes almost as well as Margie Albright in this half-hour playlet. In a brief interview with host Les Mitchell before and after the performance, Gale talks about the premiere of her film *It Happened on Fifth Avenue*, reminisces about the role radio played in launching her career, and talks about the "series of short religious films" she and Lee hope to make together.

Screen Directors Playhouse. "Appointment for Love." NBC, August 26, 1949. Gale and Charles Boyer team in this adaptation of his 1941 romantic comedy. Boyer is cast as playwright Andre Cassil, who marries sensible, level-headed Dr. Jane Alexander (Gale, stepping into Margaret Sullavan's film role). When the newlyweds' careers and schedules conflict, Jane decides to take her own apartment in the same building, so that both can carry on their work. Andre must write his own third act that will bring him and his wife closer together. The episode is directed by William A. Seiter, who later helmed multiple episodes of *The Gale Storm Show: Oh! Susanna*. Featured players include Virginia Gregg, Jerry Hausner and Howard McNear.

Your Movietown Radio Theatre. "A Dime a Dozen." Syndicated, April 1950. Writer: Bud Lesser. Cast: Gale Storm (*Tina Berger*), Sarajane Wells (*Helen Wainwright*), Marion Richman (*Dagmar*), Ned LeFevre (*Jeff*), Terry O'Sullivan (*Gary Stewart*)

After inheriting money from an aunt, mousy home economics teacher Tina Berger goes to a modeling agency to be glamorized. Tina learns poise and how to dress, but just being more attractive doesn't satisfy her. She tells the agency's press agent Jeff that she wants to be an actress, and he proposes a bold scheme to make it happen.

Gale's leading man in this episode, actor Ned LeFevre, was one of the male contestants in the *Gateway to Hollywood* competition. LeFevre's movie career amounted to little, but he had sustained success as a radio performer.

World Day of Prayer. CBS, March 5, 1954. Sportscaster Red Barber hosted this 15-minute program, which also featured Gale and Dodgers pitcher Carl Erskine.

Juke Box Jury. KNX (Los Angeles), November 5, 1955. Host Peter Potter welcomes jurors Gale, Ken Murray and Mr. and Mrs. Edgar Bergen.

V

Recordings

Gale's singing talents were showcased in films starting in the early 1940s, but it wasn't until 1955 that she had the opportunity to release records. The architect of her success as a recording artist was Randy Wood (1917–2011), president of the up-and-coming Dot Records—with a little boost from his family. In the fall of 1954, his daughter Linda heard Gale sing on an episode of *The Colgate Comedy Hour* and called her to her father's attention.

"I made a college musical when I first started in pictures," Gale explained to columnist Lydia Lane (May 27, 1956), "but I never had any singing lessons. I was encouraged to train my voice, which I did for eight years. I studied classical music, but didn't use my voice except in one *My Little Margie* show." With that series coming to an end in the spring of 1955, Gale did not foresee doing another weekly television show, but was interested in continuing her career nonetheless. His company still young, Wood wasn't able to pay high fees at the outset, but worked out a percentage deal with Gale's husband Lee. *Variety* (July 27, 1955) reported that Gale would make her "wax bow" later that year on Dot Records, after finalizing a deal with Wood a few days earlier. Wood, who formed the company in 1953, began his musical career in Gallatin, Tennessee, about 30 miles outside Nashville. Owner of a small appliance store that also carried records, Wood established a mail-order business serving customers who wanted music that was hard to find elsewhere, especially rhythm-and-blues recordings. By 1950, the store had become Randy's Record Mart. The R&B records he sold were further promoted by a radio show he inaugurated at a Nashville station, heard widely in the region. Said Lawrence Welk, "Randy's radio show played what were called 'race records' in those days, and he knew what the huge black hits were."[1]

Aside from Wood's savvy customers, many music fans rarely heard R&B songs, as most white-owned pop music radio stations wouldn't play them. Soon Wood went from music retailer to music producer, forming Dot Records. Having one artist "cover" another's record was commonplace at the time; often any song that showed potential would be recorded by three or four artists. Wood quickly learned, after signing Pat Boone (born 1934), the commercial viability of having Caucasian artists cover songs originally written and/or performed by R&B artists. Boone's first hit was "Ain't That a Shame?" Wood followed suit with Gale, causing music historian Larry Birnbaum to tab her as "easily the best known of the white women who covered rhythm-and-blues songs" during that period.[2]

While Wood and his artists later attracted criticism for the practice of covering African-American artists this way, by those who saw it in retrospect as cultural appropriation, Boone demurred. He said,

> This revisionist idea has sprung up, somehow, that ... we were inhibiting the progress, instead of enhancing the progress, of the original artists. But in those early days, R&B music did not get played on pop radio.... People don't understand the necessary role the cover versions played. It was pop artists doing R&B music that focused the spotlight on the original artists and opened the door.[3]

Asked to explain the record industry success of a man once described as "a quiet fellow who can't play an instrument, can't sing worth a hang, and never was in show business before," Wood said, "I know what I like. It's the sound I'm interested in. I like nothing better than to go into a recording session and come out three hours later with something that a million people will pay a dollar for."[4] Looking back on 1956, UPI's Aline Mosby (February 12, 1957) called Randy Wood "the young genius of the year," noting Dot Records' reported $6 million gross. In less than four years, Wood's company had become such a power in the record industry that Paramount Pictures paid a multi-million-dollar fee to acquire it in early 1957. The deal made Dot Records a subsidiary of Paramount, but retained Wood at the helm of the record company, a post he maintained for the next ten years.

Gale's first single for Dot was "I Hear You Knockin'," covering a song previously recorded by blues artist Smiley Lewis. Gale said, "They warned me my first record wouldn't be a hit. I'd never done a song like that before. The record people selected the tune. I was scared. I decided to approach the number like playing a part. Then I could let my hair down and sing."[5] The result was an almost instantaneous hit. As one fan magazine put it, "The catchy lyrics, plus her vibrant reading of the tune, has pushed it to the top of the pop charts."[6] Other songs quickly followed, with "Teenage Prayer" and "Why Do Fools Fall in Love?" especially popular.

With "I Hear You Knockin'" quickly taking off, Wood came to California in November 1955, with conductor Billy Vaughn in tow, to record songs for Gale's first album. Said *Variety* (November 16, 1955), "Miss Storm's initial disking ... is already established as a hit and Dot is anxious to get a package out as quickly as possible." Author Serene Dominic said, "Producer Randy Wood set the commercial strategy of having Storm alternate between trying to woo the adults who appreciated a good Doris Day tune and suckering in the kids whose radios didn't make scheduled stops at black stations."[7]

Linda Wood, who had urged her father to sign her favorite TV star to a recording contract, commented, "I have some wonderful memories of going to Gale's recording sessions in Los Angeles with my dad and sitting close to her while she listened to the playbacks between takes. She always told me I was her lucky charm."[8]

On January 4, 1956, *Variety* columnist Mike Kaplan reported that three of Gale's singles had reached the Top 20 on national charts, with "I Hear You Knockin'" passing 1,000,000 in sales. "She's been on shellac only three months," the trade publication noted. "It's probably the most impressive disk debut yet." A few months later, Kaplan noted that all five of her Dot releases thus far had surpassed 400,000 in sales.

The popularity of her records received a boost in the fall of 1956 with the premiere of her second TV sitcom, *The Gale Storm Show: Oh! Susanna*. From the outset, the show had been designed to incorporate her musical gifts as well as her flair for comedy, and several of her singles were adapted as musical segments for the show. About a year later, August 24, 1957, syndicated columnist Erskine Johnson reported, "The 5,000,000 sales of Gale's Dot records in a year and a half, and her 'Dark Moon' hit, have given her the title of the nation's most popular feminine recording star. Last spring, in fact, she was for several months the only girl listed in the nation's top 25 singers."

"Dark Moon" was originally recorded by country singer Bonnie Guitar (born 1923), also a Dot artist. Initially, Gale demurred. "I didn't want to cover that song," Gale said, "because she'd already made such a good record of it. Randy told me, 'She wants you to.' I asked him to have Bonnie tell that to me herself, which she did."[9] Eventually, as one report put it, "Now Miss Guitar has been given a boost in her career by Miss Storm, and each has a hit record."[10]

Gale's time as a pop singer was short. The time she spent on her singing, and in the company of Wood, was causing problems at home with husband Lee. "I am sorry I spoiled her recording career," Lee said many years later. "I was the heavy; there's no doubt about that. I was seeing things that weren't there."[11]

Five years later, she made a brief musical comeback. *Daily Variety* (August 1, 1962) reported that Gale had formed her own "indie diskery," Confideo Records, with its first release to feature her singing "Cottage for Sale" and "One Way or Another." Milt Rogers served as arranger-conductor. Gale's final album release, *I Don't Want to Walk Without You,* came in 1966, using previously unreleased songs from her Dot sessions. In 1994, the compact disc release *Dark Moon: The Best of Gale Storm* introduced a new generation to her music.

Also released in the mid–1990s was her spoken-word recording *Poems from the Heart,* which featured Gale reciting favorite selections from the writings of Edgar Guest, Rudyard Kipling and Emily Dickinson, as well as passages from the Bible.

Albums

Gale Storm (Dot, 1956, DLP-3011)

Songs: "I Hear You Knockin," "My Happiness," "Brazil," "Tired," "Goody Goody," "That's My Desire," "Memories Are Made of This," "You Can't Be True, Dear," "Sweet Georgia Brown," "Teenage Prayer," "Music, Music, Music," "The Three Bells," (The Jimmy Brown Song).

Liner Notes: "Shortly before embarking on the *Margie* series Gale began taking voice lessons, displaying a beautiful lyric soprano. She can handle serious music as expertly as she manages a pop tune and with the same enthusiasm."

Sentimental Me (Dot, 1956, DLP-3017)

Songs: "I'm in the Mood for Love," "Pennies from Heaven," "I Cried for You," "Anytime," "If I Had You," "Don't Take Your Love from Me," "More Than You Know," "Smoke Gets in Your Eyes," "I'll Hold You in My Heart," "Back in Your Own Back Yard," "Hold On," "Sentimental Me."

Liner Notes: "Whether you sing in the shower, behind the wheel of your car, or in a recording studio, you're bound to have your favorite song. And they are your favorites because you usually associate them with some particular experience or person in your life. So I'm sure you'll understand the satisfaction and pleasure I've had in recording these songs which have a special significance for me..."—Gale

Gale's Great Hits (Dot, 1958, DLP-3098)

Songs: "Dark Moon," "Ivory Tower," "Now Is the Hour," "On Treasure Island," "Why Do Fools Fall in Love?," "I Walk Alone," "I Hear You Knockin'," "Never Leave Me," "Lucky Lips," "Tell Me Why," "Orange Blossoms," "My Heart Belongs to You."

Liner Notes: "Gale is a very accomplished actress. This ability to play a role, act a part, seems invaluable in helping her interpret various kinds of songs…. Gale can go from a rock'n'roller to a sophisticated ballad to a simple folk tune without a bit of trouble, and without any loss of believability."

Note: This album was also released by Dot under the title "Gale Storm Hits," with the same stock number and the same contents.

Softly and Tenderly (Dot, DLP-3197)

Songs: "Softly and Tenderly," "Wonderful Words of Life," "In the Garden," "Fairest Lord Jesus," "Let the Lower Lights Be Burning," "Sweet Hour of Prayer," "What a Friend We Have in Jesus," "In the Sweet Bye and Bye," "Higher Ground," "The Old Rugged Cross," "Take My Hand, Precious Lord," "God Will Take Care of You."

Liner Notes: "In *Softly and Tenderly* the microphone, which sometimes goes deeper than the camera, has caught an artist of consummate skill at an act of inner piety, a housewife kneeling in her apron."

Gale Storm Sings (Dot, DLP-3209)

Songs: "Happiness Left Yesterday," "Oh, Lonely Crowd," "You," "South of the Border," "Love by the Jukebox Light," "Soon I'll Wed My Love," "Winter Warm," "I'm in the Mood for Love," "My Reverie," "Angry," "Love Theme from *A Farewell to Arms*," "I Get That Feeling."

Liner Notes: "Here is a collection of 12 songs previously released as single records, all of which have played their way into many thousands of homes."

I Don't Want to Walk Without You (Hamilton, 1966, HLP-171)

Songs: "I Don't Want to Walk Without You," "The Majesty of Love," "Hungry Eyes," "Now I Lay Me Down to Sleep," "Crying in the Chapel," "Top of the Moon," "I Wanna Be Loved," "Go 'Way from My Window," "Don't Play That Melody," "To Nancy."

Gale Storm Collectibles (MCA, 1982)

Songs: "I Hear You Knockin'," "Ivory Tower," "Now Is the Hour," "On Treasure Island," "Why Do Fools Fall in Love?," "Dark Moon," "Lucky Lips," "Memories Are Made of This," "Tell Me Why," "Teenage Prayer."

Dark Moon: The Best of Gale Storm (Varèse Vintage, 1994)

Songs: "I Hear You Knocking," "Never Leave Me," "Memories Are Made of This," "Teenage Prayer," "For Someone," "Why Do Fools Fall in Love?," "Ivory Tower," "Sweet Georgia Brown," "Making Believe," "Now Is the Hour (Maori Farewell Song)," "Oh, Lonely Crowd," "On Treasure Island," "Tell Me Why," "If I Had You," "Lucky Lips," "Dark Moon," High School Play," "Love by the Jukebox Light."

Singles

Most of Gale's singles were released by Dot in both 45 rpm and 78 rpm versions, as was customary in the mid–50s. London Records released Gale's discs in the United Kingdom, on the London American Recordings label. In Canada, they were issued on the Reo label.

I Hear You Knocking / Never Leave Me (Dot, 45-15412)
Memories Are Made of This / Teenage Prayer (Dot, 45-15436)
Why Do Fools Fall in Love? / I Walk Alone (45-15448)
   Variety, February 1, 1956: "'I'll Walk Alone' is a good blues ballad which Miss Storm belts to the hilt. Reverse is an uptempo entry handled with a rolling beat. It could be the big one."
Ivory Tower / I Ain't Gonna Worry (Dot, 45-15448)
   Variety, April 11, 1956: "Although Cathy Carr's version of 'Ivory Tower' has the lead, Gale Storm's cover for Dot is due to pick up a lot of action. It's a strong production of a good tune."
Tell Me Why / Don't Be That Way (Dot, 45-15474)
Now Is the Hour / A Heart Without a Sweetheart (Dot, 45-15492)
My Heart Belongs to You / Orange Blossoms (Dot, 45-15515)
Lucky Lips / On Treasure Island (Dot, 45-15539)
Dark Moon / A Little Too Late (Dot, 45-15558)
   Billboard, April 6, 1957: "Gale Storm's vocal [on *Dark Moon*] has plenty of charm.... Gale Storm sings a swingy melody ['A Little Too Late'] with style ... with a happy beat and a chorus to showcase the thrush."
   Variety, April 3, 1957: "Miss Storm and vocal chorus build [*Dark Moon*] into a strong spinning bet. She switches to a breezy, rockin' groove for 'A Little Too Late.' It's due for a fair response from the spinners."
Love by the Jukebox Light / On My Mind Again (Dot, 45-15606)
Winter Warm / Go 'Way from My Window (Dot, 45-15666)
   Billboard, November 18, 1957: "A pleasant ballad about the niceties of being by the fire on a wintry night. Better than average material ... and fairly cuddly thrushing make it a contender." ("Winter Warm") ... "A salable effort by Miss Storm on a blues-patterned song. Strong, folk-flavored material has appeal." ("Go 'Way from My Window")
Happiness Left Yesterday / Oh, Lonely Crowd (Dot, 1958, Dot 45-15861)
   Allan Gilbert, Jr., *Northwest Arkansas Times* (Fayetteville, AK), November 21, 1958: "Miss Storm has a pair of vehicles that are well suited to her particular talents, sad, blue and cohesive."
I Get That Feeling / A Farewell to Arms (Dot, 45-15691)
You / Angry (Dot, 45-15734)
   Billboard, March 31, 1958: "Very strong cover of a tune ['You'] introduced by the Aquatones ... a warm vocal by the thrush ... a potent contender.... [Regarding 'Angry':] Smooth chirping on a pretty rockaballad [*sic*]."
South of the Border / Soon I'll Wed My Love (Dot, 45-15783)
Oh Lonely Crowd / Happiness Left Yesterday (Dot, 45-15861)
I Hear You Knocking / Ivory Tower (Dot, 45-16031; reissue 45-119)

I Need You So / On Treasure Island (Dot, 45-16057)
He Is There / Please Help Me, I'm Falling (Dot, 45-16111)
Dark Moon / Memories Are Made of This (Dot, 45-120)
One Way or Another / A Cottage for Sale (Confideo, 45-100)

Appendix A: Soundies and Telescriptions

Soundies

For a brief period in the 1940s, the jukeboxes popular in restaurants, clubs and other entertainment venues were supplemented by a type that added visuals to sound. In 1940, businessman James Roosevelt (son of President Franklin D. Roosevelt) entered into a partnership with the Mills Novelty Company, successful manufacturer of standard jukeboxes, to form Globe-Mills Productions. The company produced both the movie jukebox itself, known as the Panoram, and the film reels played within it.

A small item in *Motion Picture Daily* (January 29, 1941) announced that Gale, along with vocalist Martha Tilton, had "been signed by Cameo Productions, Inc., to appear in subjects for the Roosevelt-Mills Soundies machines." *Billboard* (May 10, 1941) reported that producer Sam Coslow had completed shooting on a new batch of 20 Soundies, under the direction of Josef Berne, with performers including Gale, Dorothy Dandridge, Mary Healy and Dick Hogan. As authors Maurice Terenzio, Scott MacGillivray and Ted Okuda pointed out, "Audiences greeted the little musicals with keen interest. The concept of seeing as well as hearing popular performers had great novelty value for audiences of the day."[1] Though movie audiences had already seen Gale in a few films, the video jukeboxes showed her singing songs not heard in her movies.

A 1941 newspaper item from Alaska invited readers to experience a newly installed Panoram as part of a "modern cocktail lounge." Owners of the establishment explained, "The Mills Panoram is a coin machine, operating automatically upon the insertion of a dime. It goes into action in a split second. The entire reel of several musical numbers plays without re-winding or waiting."[2] As another correspondent put it, "If you were seated in your favorite tavern or amusement spot in the home town, had your girl friend or the wife with you, and wanted to see a floor show, you'd put your coins in the slot near the table—and 30 minutes of Hollywood headliners would entertain your party ... a real, living floor show, which if your hi-de-ho host at the tavern had to pay for in cold cash, would cost him plenty; and anyway how could he get a floor show outside of Hollywood like the one on the Panoram screen?"[3] Unlike a standard jukebox, the Soundies could be played only as a set, in the order they were spliced into film.

In January 1942, R.C.M. Productions took an ad thanking the performers, including

Gale, who had appeared in Soundies during the previous year. Credited talent behind the cameras were executive producer Sam Coslow, associate producers Arthur Dreifuss and Neil McGuire, production manager Herman Webber and directors Josef Berne and Reginald LeBorg.

According to author Robert J. Lentz, the heyday of Soundies lasted only about two years. By 1943, he wrote, "their popularity began to wane." Factors affecting their popularity, aside from the war which "simply dominated everything else," included a wartime shortage of the raw materials needed to construct, as well as a musicians' union ruling that banned members from working in them between the summer of 1942 and late 1943.[4]

After their original use in jukeboxes, Soundies were made available on 16mm films sold to consumers. Some 40 years after they were made, audiences had a chance to appreciate them anew with Active Home Video's 1987 release of a compilation videotape.

Listed below are Soundies which featured Gale Storm.

I Know Somebody Who Loves You. February 10, 1941. Gale Storm, the Fashionaires, Bobby Sherwood and His Orchestra.

"Gale Storm, cute songstress, is the feature in this toy store setting, cooing ... with the aid of a novelty musical quartet.... Easy on the ears and eyes." *Billboard*, June 20, 1942

Penthouse Serenade. May 5, 1941. Gale Storm, Johnny Downs, The David Rose Orchestra.

Let's Get Away from It All. May 10, 1941. Gale Storm, Johnny Downs.

"Scene is a travel bureau, with some of the travel posters coming to life as attractive dancing girls." *Billboard*, February 17, 1945

Merry-Go-Roundup. December 15, 1941. Gale Storm, the Doro Brothers and Mary, The Palladium Handicap Girls, Bob Crosby and His Orchestra.

"[A] clever dude ranch short. Lyrics are amusing and the action is interesting. Fans will go for Miss Storm's looks and the trio's smooth harmony." *Billboard*, January 3, 1942

He Plays Gin Rummy. January 19, 1942. Gale Storm, Iris Dawn, Ted Fio Rito and His Orchestra.

Glamour Girl. December 14, 1943. Gale Storm, Ivan Scott and His Orchestra.

"Song is about a farm lass who doesn't want to be a glamour girl, with flashes showing her as a model, debutante, actress, etc." *Billboard*, January 29, 1944

I'm a Shy Guy. December 17, 1943. Gale Storm, Ray Shultis, Ivan Scott and His Orchestra.

"[T]he saga of a yokel who can't overcome his timidity. Action takes place in a park." *Billboard*, February 19, 1944

Telescriptions

A few years after Soundies had all but vanished from the scene, a similar product came into use, primarily to meet the needs of local television programmers.

In the early 1950s, while network programs covered numerous hours of the broadcast day, most TV stations also produced a significant amount of local, live programming. At that time, there were few shows available on film for daily reruns, and most stations had on-air personalities who hosted shows. Finding enough guests and acts to fill all that airtime could be a challenge, especially in smaller markets. Stepping in to fill that void was a company known as Snader Telescriptions, making short films that were intended to be folded into local TV shows, or plug gaps in the daily schedule.

The company's advertisement in *Sponsor* (January 29, 1951), proclaiming the short films "Top Hollywood Talent for Local TV Budgets," explained, "Each act is complete in itself and runs approximately 3½ minutes. Opening and close of each act is designed for easy integration into any length program, in combination with live announcer or master of ceremonies ... and smooth interlacing of live or filmed commercials." The company had around 400 Telescription shorts available in its catalogue. Aside from Gale, popular vocalists represented included Peggy Lee, Nat "King" Cole, Count Basie and His Orchestra and Tex Ritter. Corporate infighting led to difficulties for the company by 1952.

The following are Gale's short musical films for television:

Between the Devil and the Deep Blue Sea. #2802.
Almost Like Being in Love. #2803.
Are You from Dixie. #2805.
Honeysuckle Rose. #10008.
Swinging on a Star. #10011.

Appendix B: Gale Storm in Comics

In 1954, the television popularity of *My Little Margie*, and its sizable audience of younger viewers, led to the creation of a comic book series based on the show. Charlton Comics published the first issue in July 1954 and it was successful enough to last more than ten years (54 issues as well as two spinoff books).

Frequency varied over the book's ten-year span, with issues initially appearing at six-week intervals, but later issued bi-monthly, and sometimes quarterly. Most issues consisted of 36 pages, with an occasional jumbo-sized issue of 100 pages. Early issues cost ten cents; the price later rose to 12 cents.

Gale and Charles Farrell's likenesses were used as the basis for the lead characters in the comic. Some of the TV show's regular features were retained, such as Vern's stock phrase, "That's my little Margie!"

Not surprisingly, the comic book's stories were not entirely faithful to the characters and settings as established in TV episodes. Margie's boyfriend Freddie was carried over from the TV show, but on the printed page his name was spelled Freddy. Likewise, Vern was called "Verne" in the comic books. In issue #2 (August 1954), Mr. Honeywell is given a wife, though he was always a longtime bachelor on TV. While TV viewers knew that Margie and Vern lived in a New York high-rise, the comic book versions of the characters had a home that seemed to be firmly planted in a typical suburban neighborhood. Freddy and Mr. Honeywell were the most frequently seen supporting characters; Mrs. Odetts made a couple of appearances.

Various stories find Margie inheriting a boxer (and replacing his roadwork with dancing), being chosen as a baseball team mascot, and conspiring to trade in her car for a better model. Some were even a bit too unbelievable for the television show, as when Vern wants to hire a new secretary and Margie sends him Freddy in drag.

Among the artists who contributed were Chic Stone (1923–2000), better-known for his later work on the *Fantastic Four* and *Archie* comics, and, in later issues, Jon D'Agostino (1929–2010).

Gale's photograph, in character as Margie, appeared on the covers of most early issues, with Charles Farrell's seen frequently as well. The photos were typically headshots taken from studio publicity, usually incorporated into pen-and-ink action scenes. Gale's picture appeared for the last time in issue #16 (July 1957), although her likeness continued to be used throughout the comic's life.

In August 1955, Charlton released the first issue of *Margie's Boyfriends*, a spinoff.

The offshoot lasted 11 issues before being retitled *Freddy*; under that title, another 36 issues were published, keeping the spinoff alive through 1965. By the time of the spinoff, Freddy had black hair and no longer bore any resemblance to Don Hayden's TV character.

A shorter-lived spinoff, *My Little Margie's Fashions* (February-November 1959), grew out of a feature seen regularly in the original *Margie* books, in which she was depicted wearing outfits taken from sketches sent in by readers.

The original *My Little Margie* comic series lasted far longer than the television show's prime time run. The final issue, #54, was released in November 1964, with cover art that showed Margie Albright succumbing to "Beatlemania" and swooning over the likenesses of John, Paul, George and Ringo. The story inside found Margie getting a Beatles-inspired haircut, only to find when she attended a party that her friends had done likewise. Evidently Margie had eclectic taste in music, as another story in the same issue, "The Music Kick," shows us that she is also a fan of a hootenanny band, The Four Sniffles and a Drip.

Gale's photograph or likeness appeared in several other comic publications. Dell issued a one-shot comic titled *Oh! Susanna* (June-August 1960), based on the sitcom. Part of the publisher's "Dell TV Comedy" series, it followed earlier installments adapted from *Leave It to Beaver* and *The Real McCoys*. In the lead story "The Sea Horse," Susanna and Nugey come back from an afternoon at the racetrack the proud owners of their own horse. They promptly name the nag Huxley and stow him away in their *Ocean Queen* cabin, with havoc soon to follow. The likenesses of Gale, ZaSu Pitts (Nugey), and Roy Roberts (Captain Huxley) are used throughout.

Avon Publications released a comic book adaptation of *The Underworld Story*, using Gale's likeness, at the time of the film's release in 1950. Fawcett's *Motion Picture Comics* devoted its September 1951 issue to a retelling of Gale's film *The Texas Rangers*, with her likeness used to depict her character, Helen Fenton.

Real West Romances, volume 1, #5 (Crestwood, January 1950) has a cover photo of Gale and Audie Murphy in *The Kid from Texas*. Marvel's *Suspense*, issue #2 (February 1950), features a still from Gale's film *Abandoned* on the cover, showing her and Dennis O'Keefe. The stories inside are unrelated to the film.

Appendix C:
The Films of Lee Bonnell

Gale's first husband, like her a winner of the December 1939 *Gateway to Hollywood* competition, was actor Lee Bonnell (1918–1986). Like Gale, he was awarded a new stage name as part of his prize; his was to be Terry Belmont. However, he succeeded in ditching this moniker early in his Hollywood career, and once he began advancing in importance, he was allowed to appear as Lee Bonnell.

Both Lee and Gale reported for work at the RKO lot in January 1940, as stipulated in their contracts as featured players. Although Bonnell actually enjoyed a longer stay at RKO than his wife, and spent more time before the cameras there, his experience, like hers, was somewhat frustrating. RKO frequently used him in bit parts, and never entrusted him with a substantial role in a high quality film. Lee spent much of his RKO career acting in wartime dramas, eventually serving (on-screen, at least) in virtually every branch of the Armed Services. He was also used in low-budget Westerns, supporting stars like Tim Holt.

For his first year or two under contract, RKO executives appeared to view Lee as an up-and-coming leading man. In June 1941, *Motion Picture Daily* reported that his contract with the studio had been extended. According to *Showmen's Trade Review* (June 14, 1941), the extension, which came while Lee was shooting *Look Who's Laughing*, was "for a full year at a substantial boost in salary." The vote of confidence made him feel able to take on the responsibilities of marriage, and he and Gale were wed that fall.

In a *Motion Picture Herald* article (August 1, 1942), RKO vice-president Charles W. Koerner described the studio's plans to build up younger actors seen as having strong potential. According to Koerner, "the promising players now under contract" included Walter Reed, Jane Randolph, Joan Barclay—and Lee Bonnell. By that time, however, Bonnell's enlistment in the Coast Guard would be the beginning of a lengthy hiatus from acting. After the war, he continued to pursue his goals as an actor, but found that any momentum he had gained was largely lost.

Bonnell was ostensibly given a second chance at RKO in 1946, after his military discharge. *Showmen's Trade Review* (January 25, 1946) reported, "RKO has welcomed home a group of actors, who have to their credit a distinguished ... record of war service behind them." Henry Fonda, Robert Ryan and Tim Holt were among the veterans who returned to acting chores at the studio, as was Lee, whose first new role was in *Step by Step*. A studio press release listed him as among "the 25 young players now getting intensive training" with RKO's dramatic coach Lillian Albertson and vocal instructor Bob Keith. Others in Lee's class included Jane Greer, Martha Hyer and Steve Brodie.

However, before the year was out, as columnist Bob Thomas reported (November 1, 1946), "Some actors are not getting the break they deserve when they return from the service. For instance, RKO took back ... Robert Smith, Robert Manning, Lee Bonnell and Robert Anderson, then dropped their options without a chance to prove themselves." Indeed, of Bonnell's postwar roles at RKO, only *Criminal Court* and *San Quentin* (both 1946) were sizable enough to attract notice.

Of his attempts at a comeback after the war, syndicated columnist Louella O. Parsons (September 9, 1947) wrote, "There isn't a nicer guy in town than Lee Bonnell, husband of Gale Storm, but he's never gotten the break he deserved." Noting his cast-

RKO publicity shot promoting Lee's return to the studio after his wartime service.

ing in a strong featured role for Monogram's *Jiggs and Maggie in Society,* Parsons commented, "I hope it's just the beginning of a fine new career for him." But her good wishes for him went unfulfilled. Freelancing after his release from RKO, he landed only a few roles.

In the late 1940s, Lee and Gale hoped to make a religious-themed motion picture of their own. They acquired the rights to the life story of an Oklahoma City minister acclaimed for his work with juvenile delinquents, intending to make a film they would call *Hand on My Shoulder*. According to *See & Hear* (December 1951–January 1952), Lee later served as board president of Church Film Libraries, Inc., a nonprofit corporation formed with representatives from nine religious denominations "to prevent overlapping in the distribution of 16mm films to churches in the Western United States."

By the early 1950s, Lee recognized that his acting career was not meant to be, and made the transition to a successful life in the business world.

Too Many Girls (RKO, 1940). Director: George Abbott. Cast: Lucille Ball, Richard Carlson, Ann Miller. This college musical, based on the Broadway hit that introduced Desi Arnaz to American audiences, features Lee in a bit part.

Stranger on the Third Floor (RKO, 1940). Director: Boris Ingster. Cast: Peter Lorre, John McGuire, Margaret Tallichet. A young newspaperman, guilt-ridden because his testimony helped convict a man of murder, finds the tables turned when he himself is suspected of killing his neighbor. Unbilled, Lee has a couple of lines near the beginning of the film as a reporter working the courthouse beat.

Men Against the Sky (RKO, 1940). Director: Leslie Goodwins. Cast: Richard Dix, Kent Taylor, Wendy Barrie, Edmund Lowe. Still billed as Terry Belmont, Lee appears at the bottom of the featured cast in this drama about the dangers of developing a new type of aircraft. He has only a few lines of dialogue, but is prominently seen in the film's last ten minutes, playing a test pilot who has the task of testing the McLean Company's latest ship. Director Leslie Goodwins gives Lee multiple close-ups at the throttle as he finds out the hard way that the plane's landing gear is malfunctioning.

Let's Make Music (RKO, 1941). Director: Leslie Goodwins. Cast: Bob Crosby, Jean Rogers, Elisabeth Risdon. Lee appears unbilled as a hotel clerk.

The Saint in Palm Springs (RKO, 1941). Director: Jack Hively. Cast: George Sanders, Wendy Barrie, Paul Guilfoyle. This sixth entry in the B movie series finds Simon Templar solving a mystery involving rare stamps valued at $200,000. Lee is unbilled for his brief appearance as bad guy Tommy, who poses as a bartender so he can serve Simon a drink that comes with a knockout pill.

Footlight Fever (RKO, 1941). Director: Irving Reis. Cast: Alan Mowbray, Donald MacBride, Elisabeth Risdon. In his first substantial role at RKO, Lee plays John Carter. *Variety* (March 26, 1941) considered the film trite and predictable: "There's not an unexpected moment in it." The reviewer took note of Lee's performance, commenting, "Bonnell is not overly the matinee idol type but gives a sincere and able interpretation."

Lady Scarface (RKO, 1941). Director: Frank Woodruff. Cast: Dennis O'Keefe, Judith Anderson, Frances Neal. We hear about Lee's character before we see him in this film, which casts Anderson as Slade, the title gangster. George Atkins is one of her lesser associates, deemed appropriate for a minor job because of his physical appearance; he's "the kid who looks like he's fresh out of college. Sweet and innocent," or as Slade dubs him, "Fancy Pants." After Atkins' assignment at a hotel goes wrong, he and the woman posing as his wife make a hasty getaway, with the police in hot pursuit.

Parachute Battalion (RKO, 1941). Director: Leslie Goodwins. Cast: Robert Preston, Nancy Kelly, Edmond O'Brien. A varied group of Army Air Corps members arrives at Fort Benning, Georgia, for training. Lee is billed in the closing credits for his role as a private in the battalion, but has very little to do.

Father Takes a Wife (RKO, 1941). Director: Jack Hively. Cast: Adolphe Menjou, Gloria Swanson, John Howard. The lives of a shipping magnate and his family are disrupted by his midlife marriage to an actress. Lee's small role as a hotel desk clerk is made even more inconspicuous by the staging of the scene: He has his back to the camera throughout.

Unexpected Uncle (RKO, 1941). Director: Peter Godfrey. Cast: Anne Shirley, James Craig, Charles Coburn. Coburn plays the title role in this romantic comedy about the bumpy relationship between a shop girl and a businessman-playboy. Lee has a blink-and-you'll-miss it role as a masher.

The Gay Falcon (RKO, 1941). Director: Irving Reis. Cast: George Sanders, Wendy Barrie, Allen Jenkins. According to IMDb, Lee plays "Hysterical Woman's Brother," but he's not readily visible. *Variety* (September 17, 1941) credited director Reis with "a sure moneymaker" that "has made the most of the suspenseful moments and comedy situations."

Look Who's Laughing (RKO, 1941). Director: Allan Dwan. Cast: Edgar Bergen and Charlie McCarthy, Fibber McGee and Molly (Jim and Marion Jordan), Lucille Ball. RKO gave movie audiences the chance to see several favorite characters from popular radio comedies in this film. Lucille Ball plays Julie Patterson, Bergen's secretary. Bergen is apparently oblivious to Julie's love for him, so she has accepted a marriage proposal from Bergen's business manager, "young financial genius" Jerry Woods (played by Bonnell). Seen in the film's opening minutes, Lee is absent from much of its midsection, as Bergen and McCarthy become involved in the efforts to build an airplane factory in the McGees' town of Wistful Vista. Julie and Jerry's planned wedding is disrupted by Bergen, but in the end both men win the hand of a lovely lady. Lee and Harold Peary, as Throckmorton P. Gildersleeve, have the film's largest supporting roles, but are billed only in the closing credits.

Wedded Blitz (RKO, 1942). Cast: Leon Errol, Marion Martin. A comedy two-reeler (18 minutes) casts Errol as a movie character actor whose neighbors think his wife is seeing other men when he comes home night after night in various costumes.

Land of the Open Range (RKO, 1942). Director: Edward Killy. Cast: Tim Holt, Ray Whitley, Janet Waldo. Deputy Sheriff Holt's community is thrown into disarray when a crooked rancher's will leaves his property open to a land rush that gives preference to criminals. Lee has a featured role as Stuart, a surveyor whose work mapping one section of land tips off the good guys to a scheme that will put all the landowners at the mercy of a greedy lawyer. A scene in which Lee witnesses a break-in and safecracking lets him show that Gale isn't the only one in the family with horsemanship skills. *Film Daily* (December 12, 1941) called this "the type of western the patrons want."

The Mayor of 44th Street (RKO, 1942). Director: Alfred E. Green. Cast: George Murphy, Anne Shirley, William Gargan. In what RKO publicists called "a merry moving romance of Broadway's shakedown racketeers," Lee is billed with the supporting cast in the opening credits. Despite the billing, his role in the finished film (as a nightclub headwaiter) is quite small; his only audible line (to bandleader Freddy Martin) is, "Mr. Kirby and his party'd like to see you."

Army Surgeon (RKO, 1942). Director: A. Edward Sutherland. Cast: James Ellison, Jane Wyatt, Kent Taylor. In this World War I drama, a doctor and a pilot are rivals for the attention of a dedicated nurse, toiling at a makeshift hospital near the front lines. Lee, billed in the opening titles, has a small but noticeable role as Ramsey, an injured soldier trapped along with the lead characters when the hospital is bombed.

The Navy Comes Through (RKO, 1942). Director: A. Edward Sutherland. Cast: Pat O'Brien, George Murphy, Jane Wyatt. Ninth-billed Lee, in his last film before enlisting in the Coast Guard, is a member of the Navy gunnery crew commanded by O'Brien, whose other members include Max Baer, Jackie Cooper and Desi Arnaz. Mostly visible in the background of group shots, Lee's most prominent line finds him saying angrily, "Why don't you get your gear out of the bunkroom?" after the men conclude (wrongly, of course) that Murphy's character is a coward.

Despite the limited opportunities afforded to Lee onscreen, *Film Daily* (October 15, 1942) included his name in a list of "supporting players [who] turn in impressive work." According to a studio press release, he was also one of the players injured during the shooting of action scenes, suffering "cuts and bruises on arms and legs when he was washed down ... hatch by water. Mike Lally pulled him to safety as hold filled with water."[1]

Sagebrush Law (RKO, 1943). Director: Sam Nelson. Cast: Tim Holt, Cliff Edwards, Joan Barclay. Lee is unbilled for his small role in this film, his second time supporting Holt.

Step by Step (RKO, 1946). Director: Phil Rosen. Cast: Lawrence Tierney, Anne Jeffreys, Lowell Gilmore. A secretary and an ex-Marine, becoming entangled with Nazi sympathizers, are forced to go on the run when he is falsely suspected of murder. Lee was unbilled, playing a role so minor that he's difficult to spot.

Sister Kenny (RKO, 1946). Director: Dudley Nichols. Cast: Rosalind Russell, Alexander Knox, Dean Jagger. Russell received a Best Actress Oscar nomination for her starring role in this biopic about an Australian nurse who pioneered a new method for treating polio. According to IMDb, Lee plays a reporter in the film, but he isn't readily visible, and isn't one of the actors given dialogue in the scene where Sister Kenny is interviewed upon her arrival in San Francisco.

Criminal Court (RKO, 1946). Director: Robert Wise. Cast: Tom Conway, Martha O'Driscoll, June Clayworth. Flamboyant defense attorney Steven Barnes, whose courtroom dramatics are worthy of Perry Mason, defends his girlfriend, singer Georgia Gale, after she is charged with murder. Lee, eleventh-billed in the closing credits, has a small role as Barnes' loyal assistant Gil Lambert, whose job comes with a few surprises—such as when the lawyer suddenly whips out a gun in court to make a point. Just when things are looking bleak at Georgia's trial (Lee's character comments, "It's the toughest jury I ever saw"), Gil makes an offhand remark that just happens to trigger his boss' memory of an incriminating admission made by the real killer.

San Quentin (RKO, 1946). Director: Gordon M. Douglas. Cast: Lawrence Tierney, Barton MacLane, Marian Carr. Tierney plays ex-convict Jim Roland, member of the Inmates' Welfare League, an organization that tries to set prisoners on the straight and narrow. Lee has one of his better featured roles as Joe Carzoni, who like Roland went from San Quentin to serving his country in World War II. When Roland is wrongly implicated in a crime, it's Joe, now employed at a Fresno garage, who comes to his aid, offering his pal the use of what he calls "the best insurance I know," a .38 pistol he calls "Tillie." Lee is directed here by Gordon Douglas, who later helmed Gale's *Between Midnight and Dawn* (1950). *Variety* (December 4, 1946) named Bonnell one of several supporting players seen in "neat smaller roles."

The Last Nazi. *Film Daily* (October 1, 1947) reported that Lee was "set for a top spot in the Carl Krueger production *The Last Nazi*, which starts shooting at Enterprise next month with Richard G. Hubler directing." *Daily Variety* reported on October 8 that filming was underway. In December, the same publication reported that Lee and leading lady Marta Mitrovich were headed to Washington, D.C., making personal appearances when the finished film was "screened for government toppers." This is likely the same film as *Nuremberg*, listed in the American Film Institute Catalog as a 1961 release running 75 minutes. According to AFI, the cast included Bonnell, Mitrovich and Roy Bennett.

Jiggs and Maggie in Society (Monogram, 1947). Director: Eddie [Edward F.] Cline. Cast: Joe Yule, Renie Riano, Tim Ryan. This second film in a series based on the "Bringing Up Father" comic strip offers Lee a strong supporting role as a smoothie who claims to have traced Maggie's family tree, and urges her to host a party for the socially prominent. *Showmen's Trade Review* (February 14, 1948) noted, "As a shady character, Lee Bonnell turns in a good performance."

Smart Woman (Allied Artists, 1948). Director: Edward A. Blatt. Cast: Brian Aherne, Constance Bennett, Barry Sullivan. Bennett plays defense attorney Paula Rogers in this courtroom drama with romantic aspects. Lee is seen briefly in two scenes as her secretary Joe, whose duties include acting as gatekeeper while she's "in conference" with her son, and bringing her a bag lunch (saying apologetically, "They forgot to toast the bread"). He wears his glasses onscreen, befitting his role as a studious, businesslike office assistant.

The Checkered Coat (1948). Director: Edward L. Cahn. Cast: Tom Conway, Noreen Nash, Hurd Hatfield. *Daily Variety* (July 19, 1948) rated the film as "entertaining double bill material" that "rolls along at a fast clip with plenty of action, fair dialogue and three cold-blooded murders for those whose taste runs to that." Lee has a featured role as Dr. Pryor.

Showmen's Trade Review (June 1, 1946) reported that Lee had been cast in RKO's short musical film *Follow That Music,* starring Gene Krupa, but he is nowhere to be seen in the finished two-reeler.

Lee appears opposite Gale, playing her husband, in the short films *Rim of the Wheel* (1951) and *How to Go Places* (1954). Both are described in the Short Subjects section under II. The Films.

Chapter Notes

Preface

1. Joe Morhaim, "Breezing Right Along," *TV Guide*, June 29, 1957.
2. Gale Storm, comments from panel discussion, "From 'My Little Margie' to 'Murphy Brown': Images of Women on Television," Museum of Broadcast Communications, Chicago, Illinois, September 26, 1993. DVD courtesy of Cary O'Dell, Library of Congress.

I. Biography

1. "Busy Gale Storm Has to Control Her Impulse to Work Too Hard," *Asbury Park* (NJ) *Press*, June 1, 1957.
2. "Services Sept. 13 for Edna Cottle McKenzie," *Williamson County* (TX) *Sun*, October 22, 1970.
3. Harriet Van Horne, "Van Horne on TV," *El Paso* (TX) *Herald-Post*, November 3, 1957.
4. Sharon Divine, personal interview. All other quotes from Sharon Divine in this section are from this interview.
5. David Wharton, *The Soul of a Small Texas Town: Photographs, Memories, and History from McDade* (Norman: University of Oklahoma Press, 2000), p. 137.
6. "S.A. Cottle Attends Brother's Funeral," *Cameron* (TX) *Herald*, September 20, 1923.
7. "About Seton," www.seton.net/about-seton/setons-history-and-heritage/ accessed February 12, 2017.
8. Gale Storm, with Bill Libby, *I Ain't Down Yet: The Autobiography of My Little Margie* (Boston, Little, Brown, 1981), p. 15.
9. Jesse L. Lasky, with Don Weldon, *I Blow My Own Horn* (Garden City, NY: Doubleday, 1957), p. 250.
10. Gale Storm, interview, tribute held in her honor at South Shores Church, Dana Point, California, May 25, 2005. DVD courtesy of the Rev. Robert Perry.
11. "Sister of Local on Radio Sunday," *Aransas* (TX) *Press*, October 26, 1939.
12. Harry Niemeyer, "One-Woman Stock Company: Varied Roles Have Aided Gale Storm's Film Career," *St. Louis* (MO) *Post-Dispatch*, May 20, 1945.
13. *This Is Your Life*, NBC, April 20, 1955.
14. Nancy Anderson, "Gale Storm Enjoying Her Switch to Stage," *Abilene* (TX) *Reporter-News*, April 20, 1973.
15. "Boy and Girl and Hollywood," *Amarillo* (TX) *Daily News*, January 2, 1940.
16. Niemeyer, "One-Woman Stock Company."
17. "Jesse Lasky Coming to Texas in Search of New Film Talent," *Amarillo* (TX) *Globe*, August 2, 1939.
18. "The Diaries of Two Girls on a Trip to the Yukon," *Look*, September 9, 1941.
19. Gale Storm, "Teen-Age Marriages Do Pay Off," *TV-Radio Mirror*, February 1959.
20. Gale Storm, personal interview.
21. "Storm Named Gale Brewing for Welk on TV This Fall," *Columbus* (NE) *Daily Telegram*, August 24, 1957.
22. Gale Storm, personal interview.
23. Jean Lewis, "Dreams Do Come True," *TV Picture Life*, April 1957.
24. Niemeyer, "One-Girl Stock Company."
25. Lewis, "Dreams Do Come True."
26. Aline Mosby, "News-Notes from Hollywood," *Humboldt Standard* (Eureka, CA), October 4, 1952.
27. "In Today's News," *Boston* (MA) *Traveler*, September 6, 1952.
28. "Gale Storm Tells Why She Has Lasted," *TV Guide*, June 29, 1957.
29. Bob Foster, "TV-Radio," *San Mateo* (CA) *Times*, April 30, 1954.
30. Bob Thomas, "Star Has Rigid Schedule," *Biloxi* (MO) *Daily Herald*, September 30, 1953.
31. Donald Freeman, "TV-Radio," *San Diego* (CA) *Union*, July 5, 1953.
32. Vernon Scott, "Strapless Gown Sweeps Actress into Office," *Lubbock* (TX) *Evening, Journal*, April 10, 1953.
33. "Gale Storm Counts Her TV Blessings," *Galveston* (TX) *Daily News*, January 25, 1955.
34. Gale Storm, with Bill Libby, *I Ain't Down Yet: The Autobiography of My Little Margie* (Boston: Little, Brown, 1981), p. 77.
35. Linda Wood, personal interview.
36. Valerie J. Nelson, "Randy Wood, 1917–2011, Dot Records Founder, Industry Pioneer," *Los Angeles Times*, April 14, 2011.
37. "Nickel Juke Box Goes Hi-10c-Fi," *Blytheville* (AR) *Courier-News*, September 4, 1956.
38. "Busy Gale Storm Has to Control Her Impulse to Work Too Hard," *Ashbury Park* (NJ) *Press*, June 1, 1957.
39. Bud Goode, "Oh! Susanna—Oh, Baby!" *TV-Radio Mirror*, December 1956.
40. "Gale Storm Is Recovering from Second-Seriesitis," *Petersburg* (VA) *Progress-Index*, May 18, 1958.

41. Ken Prescott, personal interview. All other quotes from Prescott in this section are from this interview.
42. Ron Baker, personal interview. All other quotes from Baker in this section are from this interview.
43. "Gale Storm: Out of the Shadows," *TV Star Parade*, March 1965.
44. Dora Albert, "Catching Up with Gale Storm," *Modern Screen*, October 1972.
45. Vernon Scott, "Little Margie to Return to Screen," *Lima* (OH) *News*, April 15, 1969.
46. John Gruen, "Dinner Theaters Are Booming. Are They the Way 'Broadway' Will Survive?" *New York Times*, October 21, 1973.
47. Leslie Raddatz, "Where Are They Now?" *TV Guide*, January 27, 1973.
48. Dora Albert, "Catching Up with Gale Storm."
49. John Neville, "Storm Known as Gale," *Dallas* (TX) *Morning News*, May 16, 1971.
50. Jack Sheridan, "Gale Storm Debut Slated on Tuesday," *Lubbock* (TX) *Avalanche-Journal*, October 31, 1971.
51. Dora Albert, "Catching Up with Gale Storm."
52. Marilyn Beck, "Alcoholism Kept Storm Out of Business," *Kenosha* (WI) *News*, November 3, 1979.
53. Dennis Wholey and Robert Bauman, *The Courage to Change: Hope and Help for Alcoholics and Their Families, Personal Conversations with Dennis Wholey* (Boston: Houghton Mifflin, 1984), p. 213.
54. "Gale Storm's Toughest Part Was Pretending Sobriety," *Santa Ana-Orange County* (CA) *Register*, August 4, 1983.
55. Dan Valentine, "Nothing Serious," *Salt Lake Tribune* (Salt Lake City, UT), July 8, 1976.
56. Fran Erwin, "Pioneer Broadcasts Honor a Tornado of Talent," *Van Nuys* (CA) *Valley News*, March 24, 1977.
57. Gale Storm, personal interview.
58. "People," *Dallas* (TX) *Morning News*, January 6, 1980.
59. Beck, "Alcoholism Kept Storm."
60. Dennis McLellan, "A Star with a Place in the Sun: Gale Storm Is Looking Ahead to a Marriage and New Film Roles," *Los Angeles Times*, April 14, 1988.
61. Alan Eichler, personal interview.
62. Angela M. Williams, "Paul Masterson, Former Executive for ABC Network," *Santa Ana—Orange County* (CA) *Register*, May 14, 1996.
63. Dennis McLellan, "A Star with a Place."
64. Debora Masterson, personal interview. All other quotes from Debora Masterson in this section are from this interview.
65. Brendan Harrigan, personal interview. All other quotes from Brendan Harrigan in this section are from this interview.
66. Gale Storm, comments from panel discussion, "From 'My Little Margie' to 'Murphy Brown': Images of Women on Television," Museum of Broadcast Communications, Chicago, Illinois, September 26, 1993. DVD courtesy of Cary O'Dell, Library of Congress.
67. Cary O'Dell, personal interview.
68. Walt Belcher, "That Old White Magic," *Tampa* (FL) *Tribune*, August 1, 1995.
69. Todd Everett, liner notes, *Dark Moon: The Best of Gale Storm* (Varèse Vintage, 1994).
70. Gale Storm, personal interview.
71. Susanna Harrigan, personal interview. All other quotes from Susanna Harrigan in this section are from this interview.
72. The Rev. Robert Perry, personal interview. All other quotes from the Reverend Perry are from this interview.
73. Erin Harrigan, personal interview. All other quotes from Erin Harrigan in this section are from this interview.
74. Leigh Munsil, "TV Actress, Singer Gale Storm Finishes Full Life in O.C.," *Orange County* (CA) *Register*, July 29, 2009.
75. Gale Storm, personal interview.
76. Leigh Munsil, "Late Actress Gale Storm Loved O.C.," *Orange County* (CA) *Register*, July 3, 2009.

II. The Films

1. "Drama in Tourist Camp Unfolds in Palace Photoplay," *Muscatine* (IA) *Journal and News*, September 28, 1940.
2. Roy Rogers and Dale Evans Rogers, *Happy Trails: Our Life Story* (Simon and Schuster, 1994), p. 114.
3. Frederick C. Othman, "Hollywood Treating Margie Hart Terrible; She Even Has to Wear Clothes, and Would Leave Movies If It Weren't for Her Mules," *Lubbock* (TX) *Morning Avalanche*, May 15, 1942.
4. "Starlet Reaches Screen via Famous Talent Test," *Laredo* (TX) *Times*, March 5, 1944.
5. Robbin Coons, "Hollywood: How To Break the Caste System," *Big Spring* (TX) *Daily Herald*, September 25, 1944.
6. Edwin Schallert, "Quickie Princess Comes Into Own," *Los Angeles Times*, August 25, 1946.
7. Pericles Alexander, "Dallas Reunion for Stars and Studio Boss," *Dallas* (TX) *Morning News*, April 15, 1947.
8. "Screen Kisses Dull, Gale Storm Asserts." *Pacific Stars and Stripes*, May 13, 1949.
9. "Dirty Work Wins Star Soap Oscar," *Salt Lake* (UT) *Tribune*, January 15, 1950.
10. Carol Lee, "Audie Murphy and Gale Storm Bringing Back 'Billy the Kid,'" *Austin* (TX) *American-Statesman*, September 25, 1949.
11. Joe Collura, "Bundle of Energy: Gale Storm," *Films of the Golden Age*, #19, Winter 1999/2000.
12. "Audie Murphy Film Opens in Three Theaters Today," *Long Beach* (CA) *Press-Telegram*, November 16, 1950.
13. Collura, "Bundle of Energy."
14. *Ibid.*

III. Television

1. Sheilah Graham, "Prosperity via TV," *San Antonio* (TX) *Express*, May 31, 1953.
2. Dan Jenkins, "The Man Who Bet on Television," *TV Guide*, June 11, 1955.
3. "More Television Films Made in Hollywood Than Theater Movies, *Neosho* (MO) *Sunday News*, June 7, 1953.
4. Richard Gehman, "The Storm Behind 'My Little Margie,'" *Cosmopolitan*, December 1953.
5. Donald Freeman, "TV-Radio," *San Diego* (CA) *Union*, July 5, 1953.
6. "Film Maker: Roland Daniel Reed." *Broadcasting/Telecasting*, August 9, 1954.
7. Aline Mosby, "News-Notes from Hollywood," *Humboldt Standard* (Eureka, CA), October 4, 1952.
8. Dick Kleiner, "Gale Storm's Daughter Named for 'Susanna,'" *Burlington* (NC) *Daily Times-News*, May 17, 1957.

9. Nancy Anderson, "Gale Storm Enjoying Her Switch to Stage," *Abilene* (TX) *Reporter-News*, April 20, 1973.
10. Gale Storm, personal interview.
11. Milton R. Bass, "The Lively Arts," *Berkshire* (MA) *Evening Eagle*, February 19, 1953.
12. "TV Actor Divorced by Wife for Being Rude," *Logansport* (IN) *Press*, February 19, 1955.
13. "Cut-Ups Nuisance on TV Audience Shows," *Lowell* (MA) *Sun*, December 21, 1952.
14. Walter Ames, "Little Margie, Dad Quit Swank Abode," *Los Angeles Times*, September 5, 1954.
15. Gale Storm, comments from panel discussion, "From 'My Little Margie' to 'Murphy Brown': Images of Women on Television," Museum of Broadcast Communications, Chicago, Illinois, September 26, 1993. DVD courtesy of Cary O'Dell, Library of Congress.
16. Guy V. Thayer, Jr., "The Case for Hollywood," *Broadcasting/Telecasting*, January 11, 1954.
17. Pinky Herman, "Television—Radio," *Motion Picture Daily*, June 16, 1953.
18. James Bacon, "Gale Is Both Normal and Successful, Which Is Quite a Shock to Hollywood," *Cedar Rapids* (IA) *Gazette*, July 1, 1956.
19. Bob Thomas, "'My Little Margie' Nears End of Trail as Video Program," *Freeport* (IL) *Journal-Standard*, April 30, 1955.
20. Bob Foster, "Cab Calloway Hits with Unusual Disc," *San Mateo* (CA) *Times*, February 7, 1956.
21. Vernon Scott, "Gale to Change Name for New Show," *Galveston* (TX) *News*, April 10, 1956.
22. "Charting a New Course," *TV Guide*, October 1956.
23. "It's Gale Who Keeps Zasu [sic] Laughing," *Miami* (FL) *Herald*, February 15, 1959.
24. Ellis Walker, "Miss Storm Blows a Fresh Wind into 'Susanna' Script," *San Rafael* (CA) *Daily Independent-Journal*, October 6, 1956.
25. Bob Foster, "Gale Storm Has a Winner in New Show," *San Mateo* (CA) *Times*, September 17, 1956.
26. Gabe Gabriel, "'Oh, Susanna' Doesn't Hit on All Cylinders," *Chicago Heights* (IL) *Star*, October 12, 1956.
27. Jack O'Brian, "Slow Starting Series May Wiggle into Favor," *Hayward* (CA) *Daily Review*, January 24, 1958.
28. "Charting a New Course."
29. Dave Kaufman, "On All Channels," *Daily Variety*, May 11, 1956.
30. Walter Ames, "Gale Weathers a New Storm; Show Goes another Year," *Los Angeles Times*, May 20, 1957.
31. Steven H. Scheuer, "New Year Starts for Oh! Susanna," *Hutchinson* (KS) *News*, September 13, 1957.
32. Gale Storm, personal interview.
33. "Getting Back on Course," *TV Guide*, June 6, 1959.
34. "'Gale Storm Show' Begins Sailing Again," *Jefferson City* (MO) *Daily Capital News*, October 3, 1959.
35. "Show's Star Has Yen for 'Real' Travel," *Twin Falls* (ID) *Times-News*, June 9, 1961.
36. Vernon Scott, *Huntington* (PA) *Daily News*, October 10, 1958.
37. Erskine Johnson, "In Hollywood," *Lowell* (MA) *Sun*, April 11, 1954.

IV. Radio

1. Fredrick Tucker, *Verna Felton* (Albany, GA: BearManor Media, 2010), p. 435.
2. Wayne Oliver, "Charlie Farrell Considers Himself an Innkeeper," *Corpus Christi* (TX) *Caller-Times*, June 6, 1954.
3. "Producers Bare Fangs on 'Margie' 'Cat Women' Skit; Ask $1,200,000 Damages." *Variety*, December 9, 1953.
4. "Television Programs," *Athens* (OH) *Messenger*, June 29, 1955.

V. Recordings

1. Valerie J. Nelson, "Randy Wood, 1917–2011, Dot Records Founder, Industry Pioneer," *Los Angeles Times*, April 14, 2011.
2. Larry Birnbaum, *Before Elvis: The Prehistory of Rock 'n' Roll* (Lanham, MD: Rowman & Littlefield, 2013), p. 363.
3. Karen Schoemer, "More Mr. Nice Guy," *American Heritage*, February/March 2006.
4. "A Success Story Can Be Recorded," *Tucson* (AZ) *Daily Citizen*, January 19, 1956.
5. Aline Mosby, "Hit Record May Mean New Career for Gale," *Albuquerque* (NM) *Tribune*, January 19, 1956.
6. "Musical Success Is A 'Knockin' for Gale (My Lil' Margie) Storm," *Hit Parader*, February 1956.
7. Serene Dominic, *Burt Bacharach Song by Song: The Ultimate Burt Bacharach Reference for Fans, Serious Record Collectors, and Music Critics* (New York: Schirmer Books, 2003), p. 26.
8. Linda Wood, personal interview.
9. Todd Everett, liner notes, *Dark Moon: The Best of Gale Storm* (Varèse Vintage, 1994).
10. "Gale Storm Helps Record," *Sandusky* [OH] *Register*, June 11, 1957.
11. Gale Storm with Bill Libby, *I Ain't Down Yet: The Autobiography of My Little Margie* (Indianapolis, IN: Bobbs-Merrill, 1981), p. 144.

Appendix A

1. Terenzio, Maurice, Scott MacGillivray and Ted Okuda, *The Soundies Distributing Corporation of America: A History and Filmography of Their 'Jukebox' Musical Films of the 1940s* (Jefferson, NC: McFarland, 1991), p. 10.
2. "Sky Lounge Introduces New Panoram," *Fairbanks* (AK) *Daily News-Miner*, October 25, 1941.
3. Prescott Chaplin, "Jitterbugs, Attention! Soundies Bring Swing Bands to Eye as Well as to Ear," *Hammond* (IN) *Times*, October 15, 1940.
4. Lentz, Robert J. *Gloria Grahame, Bad Girl of Film Noir: The Complete Career* (Jefferson, NC: McFarland, 2011).

Appendix C

1. "New RKO-Radio War Drama Opens Tomorrow at Keith's," *Syracuse* (NY) *Herald-Journal*, December 2, 1942.

Bibliography

Birnbaum, Larry. *Before Elvis: The Prehistory of Rock 'n' Roll*. Lanham, MD: Scarecrow Press, 2013.
Cox, Jim. *The Great Radio Sitcoms*. Jefferson, NC: McFarland, 2012.
_____. *Radio Crime Fighters: More Than 300 Programs from the Golden Age*. Jefferson, NC: McFarland, 2002.
Dominic, Serene. *Burt Bacharach, Song by Song: The Ultimate Burt Bacharach Reference for Fans, Serious Record Collectors, and Music Critics*. New York: Schirmer Books, 2003.
Irvin, Richard. *Spinning Laughter: Profiles of 101 Proposed Comedy Spin-offs and Sequels That Never Became a Series*. Albany, GA: BearManor Media, 2016.
Lasky, Jesse L., with Don Weldon. *I Blow My Own Horn*. Garden City, NY: Doubleday, 1957.
Lentz, Robert J. *Gloria Grahame, Bad Girl of Film Noir: The Complete Career*. Jefferson, NC: McFarland, 2011.
Macfarlane, Malcolm, and Ken Crossland. *Perry Como: A Biography and Complete Career Record*. Jefferson, NC: McFarland, 2009.
Magers, Boyd, and Michael G. Fitzgerald. *Westerns Women: Interviews with 50 Leading Ladies of Movie and Television Westerns from the 1930s to the 1960s*. Jefferson, NC: McFarland, 2004.
Maltin, Leonard, ed., et al. *Leonard Maltin's Classic Movie Guide*. 3rd ed. New York: Plume, 2015.
Miller, Don. *B Movies*. New York: Ballantine Books, 1988.
Miller, James. *Flowers in the Dustbin: The Rise of Rock and Roll, 1947–1977*. New York: Simon & Schuster, 1991.
Nash, Jay Robert, and Stanley Ralph Ross. *The Motion Picture Guide*. New York: Cinebooks, 1987.
Okuda, Ted. *The Monogram Checklist: The Films of Monogram Pictures Corporation, 1931–1952*. Jefferson, NC: McFarland, 1987.
Storm, Gale, with Bill Libby. *I Ain't Down Yet: The Autobiography of My Little Margie*. Indianapolis: Bobbs-Merrill, 1981.
Stumpf, Charles. *ZaSu Pitts: The Life and Career*. Jefferson, NC: McFarland, 2010.
Terenzio, Maurice, Scott MacGillivray, and Ted Okuda. *The Soundies Distributing Corporation of America: A History and Filmography of Their 'Jukebox' Musical Films of the 1940s*. Jefferson, NC: McFarland, 1991.
Terrace, Vincent. *Encyclopedia of Television Pilots, 1937–2012*. Jefferson, NC: McFarland, 2013.
Tucker, David C. *The Women Who Made Television Funny: Ten Stars of 1950s Sitcoms*. Jefferson, NC: McFarland, 2007.
Tucker, Fredrick. *Verna Felton*. Albany, GA: BearManor Media, 2010.
Ward, Richard Lewis. *A History of the Hal Roach Studios*. Carbondale: Southern Illinois University Press, 2005.
Wharton, David. *The Soul of a Small Texas Town: Photographs, Memories, and History from McDade*. Norman: University of Oklahoma Press, 2000.
White, Betty. *Here We Go Again: My Life in Television*. New York: Scribner's, 1995.
Wholey, Dennis, and Robert Bauman. *The Courage to Change: Hope and Help for Alcoholics and Their Families, Personal Conversations with Dennis Wholey*. Boston: Houghton Mifflin, 1984.

Interviews

Baker, Ron. Telephone, February 9, 2017.
Divine, Sharon. Email, February 23, 2017.
Eichler, Alan. Telephone, April 14, 2017.
Frankham, David. Email, March 24, 2017.
Harrigan, Brendan. Telephone and email. March 17 and 22, 2017.
Harrigan, Erin. Telephone, April 28, 2017.
Harrigan, Susanna. Telephone, February 7 and 21, 2017.
O'Dell, Cary. Email, June 19, 21, 2017.
Perry, the Rev. Robert. Telephone, February 13, 2017.
Prescott, Ken. Telephone. January 31, 2017.
Storm, Gale. Telephone, January 19 and 24, 2006.
Wood, Linda. Email, March 28, 2017.

Newspapers

Abilene (TX) *Reporter-News*
Albuquerque (NM) *Tribune*
Aransas (TX) *Press*
Ashbury Park (NJ) *Press*
Athens (OH) *Messenger*
Austin (TX) *American-Statesman*
Berkshire (MA) *Evening Eagle*
Big Spring (TX) *Daily Herald*
Biloxi (MO) *Daily Herald*
Blytheville (AR) *Courier-News*

Boston (MA) Traveler
Burlington (NC) Daily Times-News
Brownwood (TX) Bulletin
Cameron (TX) Herald
Cedar Rapids (IA) Gazette
Chicago Heights (IL) Star
Columbus (NE) Daily Telegram
Corpus Christi (TX) Caller-Times
Dallas (TX) Morning News
Fairbanks (AK) Daily News-Miner
Freeport (IL) Journal-Standard
Janesville (WI) Daily Gazette
Jefferson City (MO) Daily Capital News
Galveston (TX) News
Hammond (IN) Times
Hayward (CA) Daily Review
Humboldt Standard (Eureka, CA)
Huntington (PA) Daily News
Hutchinson (KS) News
Kenosha (WI) News
Laredo (TX) Times
Logansport (IN) Press
Long Beach (CA) Press-Telegram
Los Angeles Times
Lowell (MA) Sun
Lubbock (TX) Avalanche-Journal
Madison (WI) State Journal
Miami (FL) Herald
Muscatine (IA) Journal and News
Neosho (MO) Sunday News

New York Times
Orange County (CA) Register
Petersburg (VA) Progress-Index
Portsmouth (OH) Times
Salt Lake (UT) Tribune
San Antonio (TX) Express and News
San Antonio (TX) Light
San Diego (CA) Union
San Mateo (CA) Times
San Rafael (CA) Daily Independent-Journal
Sandusky [OH] *Register*
Syracuse (NY) Herald-Journal
Tampa (FL) Tribune
Tipton (IN) Tribune
Tucson (AZ) Daily Citizen
Twin Falls (ID) Times-News
Van Nuys (CA) Valley News
Williamson County (TX) Sun

Websites

www.afi.com/members/catalog
www.ancestry.com
www.ctva.biz
www.digitaldeliftp.com
www.galestorm.tv
www.imdb.com
www.newspaperarchive.com
www.radiogoldindex.com

Index

Numbers in ***bold italics*** indicate pages with illustrations

Aaker, Lee 150
Abandoned 17, 94–97, ***95***, 237
Abbott, Bud 205
The Abbott and Costello Show 117, 162
Ackerman, Harry 205
Adam's Rib 117
Adamson, Harold 187
The Adventures of Cosmo Jones 69
The Adventures of Ozzie and Harriet 204
The Adventures of Rin Tin Tin 140, 150
Agar, John 112, 188, ***189***
Al Jennings of Oklahoma 60, 104, 107–109, ***108***, 134
Albert, Eddie ***91***, 92
Albertson, Jack 203
Albertson, Lillian 239
All-Star Party for "Dutch" Reagan 209
Allen, Gracie 1
Allen, Ray 204
Allen, Steve 28, 163, 208
Allied Artists Pictures 15, 89, 94, 95
Allwyn, Astrid 44
"Almost Like Being in Love" 235
Altman, Robert 203
The Amazing Colossal Man 172
America's Junior Miss Pageant 208
Amsterdam, Morey ***174***
Anderson, Betty Ann 13
Anderson, Judith 240
Anderson, Mary 104
Andrews, Julie 94
Andrews, Stanley 109
The Andy Griffith Show 186
"Angry" 230

Apple, Louis 73
"April Showers" 203
Archer, John 9, 44, 171, 211
Arden, Eve 101
Are These Our Parents? 79
"Are You from Dixie" 235
Armed Forces Radio and Television Service 215
Arms, Russell 184
Arnaz, Desi 239, 241
Asner, Ed 209
Audley, Eleanor 199

Babille, Edward J. 133
Bacall, Lauren 30
Baccaloni, Salvatore 192
Backus, Jim 21, 179
Bacon, Irving 160
Bad Men of Missouri 53
Baer, Parley 100
Baker, Graham 11, 39
Baker, Ron 26, 28, 33, 34, 35
Baldwin, Robert 49
Ball, Lucille 1, 12, 15, 26, 240
Barclay, Jane 238
The Barefoot Contessa 106
Barnes, Binnie 92
Barton, Charles 166
Basie, Count 235
Baskett, James 71
Bates, Florence 123, 137
Baxter, Alan 53
Baxter, Cash 28
Beaudine, William 64–65
Becker 33
Beery, Carol Ann *see* Hayden, Carol Ann Beery
Before Dawn 117
Bekassy, Stephen 145
Bellamy, Ralph 115
Belle of the Bowery see Sunbonnet Sue

Bennett, Constance 242
Bennett, Marjorie 146, 198
Benny, Jack 207; *see also The Jack Benny Program*
Bergen, Edgar 240
Bergerac, Jacques 191
Bergman, Ingrid 30
Berle, Milton 207
Bernerd, Jeffrey 78
Besser, Joe 162
Best, Willie 118, 127, 128, 135, 160
Between Midnight and Dawn 45, 105–107, ***106***, 140, 242
"Between the Devil and the Deep Blue Sea" 235
The Beverly Hillbillies 131, 165
Bewitched 165
The Big Record 207
Big Town 106
The Bigelow-Sanford Theatre 205, 206
Billy the Kid 99
"Bing, Bang, Bong" 176
Bishop, William 111, 181
Bissell, Whit 176
Blacker, Dolores 188
Blazing Saddles 92
Bliss, Lela 117, 126, 170
Blood and Sand 179
"Blues in the Night" 197
Blyth, Ann 96
The Bob Hope Show 206
Bonanza 194
Bonnell, Everett Leroy *see* Bonnell, Lee
Bonnell, Lee 3, 10, 12, 16, 20–***21***, 23–24, 26, 28–29, ***31***, 113, 121, 206, 208, 211, 228, 238–243, ***239***
Bonnell, Paul William 16, ***25***, 28, 35, 181

251

Bonnell, Peter Wade 15, 16, **25**, 28, 89, 181
Bonnell, Phillip Lee 15, 27, 28, 35, 36, 96, 150
Bonnell, Susanna *see* Harrigan, Susanna Bonnell
Bonnell Productions 16
Boone, Pat 179, 226–227; *see also The Pat Boone Chevy Showroom*
Borg, Veda Ann 71
Borland, Barlowe 39
Borland, Mary 80, 81
Boswell, Connee 86
Bouchey, Willis 199
Bowman, Ralph *see* Archer, John
Bradley, Bart *see* Braverman, Bart
"Brannigan's Bat" 212
Braverman, Bart 201
"Break It to Me Gently" 196
Breaking Up the Act 32
Bregman, Buddy 188, 196
Brendel, El 130
Brennan, Walter 101
Bretherton, Howard 67
Brissac, Virginia 82
Brodie, Steve 239
Broidy, Steve 94
Brooke, Hillary 117, 139
Brophy, Edward 87
Brown, Charles D. **84**
Brown, George Carleton 20, 143
Brown, James 140
Brown, Johnny Mack 80, 94
Buchanan, Edgar 190
Bullock, Jim 136
Bunny O'Hare 65
Burke's Law 26, 27, 208
Burnett, Carol 208
Burr, Raymond 96

Cactus Flower 28, 30
Caesar, Sid 165–166; *see also Caesar's Hour*
Caesar's Hour 24–25
Cameron, Rod 5, **18**, 30, 93–94, 112
Campus Rhythm 60, 73–75
Candido, Candy 66, 75
Cantor, Eddie 207
Captain Midnight 178
Captain Video 144
Card, Kathryn 127, 164
Carosone, Renato 194
Carradine, John 71
Carraher, Bob 122
Carter, Ben 86
Carver, Lynne 58
The Casebook of Gregory Hood 224
Castle, Nick 170, 174, 180, 184, 186, 194

Cat-Women of the Moon 214
CBS: On the Air—A Celebration of 50 Years 209
Celebrity Bowling 208–209
Celebrity Playhouse 207
Champion, John C. 94
Chandler, Chick 67
Chandler, Jeff 96–97
Chapman, Ben 151
The Charles Farrell Show 23
Charlton Comics 236–237
The Checkered Coat 242–243
Cheshire, Harry 151
Chester, Hal E. 104
Chico and the Man 203
Christian Broadcasting Network 121
Church Film Libraries, Inc. 239
Cimarron City 111
City of Missing Girls 43–46, **45**, 171
Claxton, William F. 113
Cleveland, George **84**, 85
Clifford, Carmen 190, 191
Clifton, Elmer 44
"Cloak and Dagger" 207
Cole, Nat King 235
The Colgate Comedy Hour 22, 205, 206, 226
College Sweetheart see *Campus Rhythm*
Colonna, Jerry 197
Columbia Pictures 17
Confideo Records 228
Connors, Chuck 171
Conried, Hans 206, 215, 217, 219
Coogan, Jackie 205, 206
Cookson, Peter 82
Cooper, Jackie **76**, 77, 241
Corbet, Lois 185, 220
Corio, Ann 60
Cortez, Stanley 104
Coslow, Sam 233
Cosmo Jones in Crime Smasher see *The Crime Smasher*
Cosmopolitan 142
Costello, Lou 205
Cottle, Joel Braxton 7
Cottle, Lois Miriam 6, 7–**8**, 30
Cottle, Minnie Lee Greenhaw 6–9, **8**, 10, 13, 30, 206
Cottle, Minnie Marjorie *see* Divine, Minnie Marjorie Cottle
Cottle, S.A. 7
Cottle, Sarah Turner 6
Cottle, Stephen 6
Cottle, Walter William **6**–7, 9
Cottle, W.E. 6
Cottle, Wilbur Walter 6, 8
Cottle, William Zebulon 7
Cottletown 6
The Court Jester 159
Courtland, Jerome 111

Cowan, Jerome 82
Cowan, Lester 20
Craig, Alec **38**, 39
Crane, Richard 144
Cranston, Joe 181
Crawford, Joan 9
Creature from the Black Lagoon 151
The Creature Walks Among Us 159
The Crime Smasher 67–69, **68**
Criminal Court 239, 242
Cromwell, Richard **68**
Crosby, Gary 215
Coslow, Sam 234
Cummings, Bob 204, 207
Curtain Call at Cactus Creek 100–102, **101**

D'Agostino, Jon 236
Dandridge, Dorothy 233
"Dark Moon" 6, 178, 228, 230
Dark Moon: The Best of Gale Storm 229
Dark Victory 80
"Darling, Je Vous Aime Beaucoup" 200
Darnell, Linda 9
Darro, Frankie **50**, 51
da Silva, Howard 104
Dateline: Disneyland 206
Daughter of Dr. Jekyll 125
Davidson, John **210**
Davis, Bette 80
Davis, Joan 101, 119, 179; *see also I Married Joan; The Joan Davis Show*
Davis, Rufe 47
Deacon, Richard 164
Dear Phoebe 165
Death Valley Days 109
De Carlo, Yvonne 67
December Bride 167, 213
DeFore, Don 16, 18, **88**, 90, 203–204
Del Ruth, Roy 15, 89–90
DeMille, Cecil B. 44
Dennis the Menace 109
Derman, Lou 3, 167
Desilu Productions 27, 204
Detective Kitty O'Day 82
Dickinson, Emily 228
Dimsdale, Howard 101
The Dinah Shore Chevy Show 207–208
Divine, C.C. 9
Divine, Minnie Marjorie Cottle 7–**8**, 13, 27, 30
Divine, Sharon 7, 9, 13, 27, 36, 116–117
The Donna Reed Show 167
Donny and Marie 209
Dot Records 22–23, 90, 176, 193, 227–231

Douglas, Gordon 242
Douglas, Mike 208
Downs, Johnny 14, 55–56, 75, 234
Drake, Christian 177
Dreifuss, Arthur 234
The Dude Goes West 90–93, *91*, 101
Dumke, Ralph 144, 193
Dumont, Margaret 66–67
Duncan, Kenne 65
Durocher, Leo 162
Duryea, Dan 103, 104, *108*
D'Usseau, Arnaud 42

East Side Kids 61–63
Easton, Robert 131
Eaton, Evelyn 77, 78
The Ed Sullivan Show 5
Edwards, Blake 94
Edwards, Ralph 5
Eichler, Alan 31
Ellenstein, Robert 207
Elliott, Scott 142
Emmy Awards 165, 208
Endfield, Cy 10
Evans, Ray 176
Eythe, William 17

Fairfax, James *164*, 165, 167, 168
Family Theater 212
"Far Away Places" 199
"Farewell to Arms" 186
Farrell, Charles 19, 21, 30, 115–116, 123, *124*, 134, 157, 162, 205, 206, 213–214, 217, 219, 236
Farrell, Deborah Ann 141
Father Goose 75
Father Knows Best 121
Father Takes a Wife 240
Fauntelle, Dian 126, 145, 159
Faylen, Frank 51
Fee, Melinda O. 45
Feld, Fritz 130, 205
Felton, Verna 213–214
Ferre, Cliff 152
"Feudin' and Fightin'" 180
Fidler, Jimmie 13
Fighting Mike McCall see *Stampede*
The File on Thelma Jordon 117
Finian's Rainbow 27
Fio Rito, Ted 66
Fisher, Doris 183
"Follow That Music" 243
Fonda, Henry 238
Footlight Fever 240
Forbidden Planet 192
Ford, Francis 113
Ford, John 113
Ford Theater 207
Foreign Agent 63–65
Foreign Correspondent 117

Forever Yours 15, 79–81
Forty Carats 29
Fox, Frank, Jr. 20, 31, 114, 143
Frankham, David 186
Frawley, William 196
Freberg, Stan 163
Freckles 56
Freckles Comes Home 13, *14*, 55–57, 75, 160
Freddy 237
Freedman, Bill 165
Freeman, Kathleen 33
Freeman, Mona *116*
Fulton, Ian 39
Funiculi, Funiculà" 170

Gale Storm (album) 228
The Gale Storm Appreciation Society 33
Gale Storm Collectibles 229
Gale Storm Hits see *Gale's Great Hits*
Gale Storm Show: A-OK, O'Shea 3, 27, 204
Gale Storm Show: Oh! Susanna 1–3, 5, 20, 23–26, *24, 25*, 33, 43, 124, 154, 157, 163–203, *164, 174, 189*, 224, 227, 237
Gale Storm Sings 229
Gale's Great Hits 191, 229
"Galway Way" 174
Gambling Daughters 47–49, 63
Garrett, Betty 32
The Garry Moore Show 208
Gateway to Hollywood 9–10, 12, 44, 211
The Gay Falcon 240
Gaynor, Janet 114
Geer, Will 100
The George Burns and Gracie Allen Show 121, 198
Gering, Walter 69
G.I. Honeymoon 2, 15, 81–83
Gilbert, Billy 153
Gilligan's Island 89
Givot, George 128
"Glamour Girl" 243
Globe-Mills Productions 230
"Go 'Way from My Window" 230
Godfrey, Arthur 119
Gombell, Minna 85
Goodwins, Leslie 240
Gorcey, Leo 63
Gottlieb, Alex 30, 165, 166, 167, 191, 194
Gould, Dave 67
Graham, Frank 69
Gramercy Ghost 17
Grand Prize 28
Granlund, Nils T. 65
Grant, Cary 90
Grayson, Kathryn 64
The Great Gildersleeve 213

Green Acres 92, 126
Greene, John L. 165
Greene, Lorne 194
Greenhaw, Albert Alton 6
Greenhaw, Parlee Huff 6
Greer, Jane 239
Griffin, Merv 208
Guilfoyle, Paul *41*
Guitar, Bonnie 228

"Hackie" 212
Hadley, Nancy 177
Hal Roach Studios 43, 114, 119, 153, 165, 193–194
Hal Roach: Hollywood's King of Laughter 210
Hale, Alan, Jr. 89
Hall, Huntz 63
Hall, Thurston 143
Halop, Billy 39
Hamilton, Margaret 185
Hand on My Shoulder 16, 239
Happy Gilmore 35
Harding, Ann 15, 89
Hardwicke, Sir Cedric 39
Harrigan, Brendan 32, 35
Harrigan, Erin 35
Harrigan, Joseph 31
Harrigan, Susanna Bonnell 10, 23–24, 28, 31, 34, 35–36, 181
Hart, Margie 59–60
Hawaii Five-O 130
Hayden, Carol Ann Beery 117–118
Hayden, Don 92, 113, 117–118, 127, 128, 132, 214, 237
Hayden, Harry 92, 117, 127
Hayes, George "Gabby" 54
"He Plays Gin Rummy" 234
"Heat Wave" 5, 191
Helene Curtis Industries 167
Hendrix, Wanda 116
Henry, Bill *72*
Henry, Gloria 109, 134
Here's Hollywood 208
Hey, Jeannie! 166
Hill, Craig 143
His Girl Friday 117
Hitchcock, Patricia 148
Hoffmann, Gertrude W. 117, 118, 122, 130, 136
Hogan, Dick *41*, 42, 230, 233
Holland, Edna M. 85
Hollywood Half-Hour 205, 206
Hollywood Premiere Theatre 203
Hollywood Theater 224
Holt, Tim 238
Homans, Robert 54
Home for Christmas 208
"Honeysuckle Rose" 235
"Hot Welcome" 206
Hour Magazine 209
House Un-American Activities Committee 104

How to Go Places 113, 243
Hubbard, John 129
Hughes, Gordon T. 213
Hughes, Thomas 39
Hussey, Ruth 112
Hutchinson, Josephine 39
Hyer, Martha 239

I Ain't Down Yet: The Autobiography of My Little Margie 2, 31
"I Cried for You" 181
I Don't Want to Walk Without You 229
"I Hear You Knockin'" 3, 6, 23, 207, 227
"I Just Can't Get Enough of You" 188
"I Know Somebody Who Loves You" 234
I Love Lucy 19, 118, 123, 126, 127, 151, 164, 196
"I Love Paris" 177
I Married a Monster from Outer Space 125
I Married Joan 21, 33, 119, 121, 179
I Want You 117
I Was a Teenage Werewolf 176
Ice Station Zebra 130
"If You Were the Only Boy in the World" 201
Iglesias, Eugene 154
I'll Bet 208
"I'll Walk Alone" 230
"I'm a Shy Guy" 234
Inescort, Frieda 104
International Television Corporation 167
"It Had to Be You" 187
It Happened on 5th Avenue 5, 15, 35, 87–90, **88**, 91, 203
It's a Great Life 111, 181
It's a Wonderful Life 87
"I've Got a Feeling" 186
"Ivory Tower" 191, 230

The Jack Benny Program 213
James, Jesse 52–53; see also *Jesse James at Bay*
James, Sheila 123
James Schwartz Productions 18–19
Jenkins, Dan 180
Jenks, Frank 82
Jennings, Al 108; see also *Al Jennings of Oklahoma*
Jergens, Adele 205, 206
Jesse James at Bay 47, 51–53, 58, 108, 110
Jiggs and Maggie in Society 239, 242
The Joan Davis Show 213
The Joey Bishop Show 177

The John Davidson Show 209, **210**
John Deere Company 43
"Johnny, Where Are You?" 207
Jones, Marcia Mae 51
Jordan, Louis 86
Judge, Arline 82
Judge Roy Bean 190
Juke Box Jury 225
Jungle Siren 60
"Just in Time" 207

Kane, Joseph 112
Kansas City Confidential 83
Karloff, Boris 193–194, 207
Karlson, Phil 82–83, 87, 111
Karlstein, Phil see Karlson, Phil
Karson, Lee 23, 29, 164, 166, 204–205, 214, 215, 217, 218, 220
Katzman, Sam 61
Kay, Edward (Eddie) 65, 83
Kaye, Danny 159
Kearns, Joseph 161
Keith, Bob 243
Kelly, Jack 152
Kelso, Edmond 51, 56, 70
Kennedy, Edgar **68**
Keyes, Evelyn 32
The Kid from Texas 97–100, **98**, 237
"The Kiddie Story Story" 212
King, Walter Woolf 63
King of the Zombies 70
Kinon, Richard 197
Kipling, Rudyard 228
A Kiss Before Dying 65
Kjellin, Alf 130
Klatzkin, Leon 182
Knotts, Don 92
Koerner, Charles W. 238
Kolb, Clarence 117, 118, 132, 133, 134, 140, 157
Kopell, Bernie 209
Krieger, Howard 203
Kuehl, Sheila James see James, Sheila

Lady Scarface 240
Land of the Open Range 241
Lang, Charles **41**
Langan, Glenn 172
Lansing, Joi 172
Laramie 94, 139
Lasky, Jesse L. 9–10, 207, 211
Lassie 157
Latell, Lyle 65
Lauder, Harry 170
Laurel and Hardy 153, 194
Lawman 180
Lawrence, Carol 87
Lebedeff, Ivan 60, 64
Lebieg, Earl 190

LeBorg, Reginald 234
Lee, Gypsy Rose 208
Lee, Lila 179
Lee, Peggy 235
Leeds, Peter 159
LeFevre, Ned 225
Lembeck, Harvey 208
Lentz, Robert J. 234
L'Estrange, Dick 144
"Let's Get Away from It All" 234
Let's Go Collegiate 13, 49–51, **50**, 74, 128, 155, 177
Let's Make Music 240
Lever Brothers Company 167
Lewis, Smiley 227
The Life of Riley 116
"A Life on the Ocean Wave" 188
"Lisbon Antigua (In Old Lisbon)" 191
Litel, John 78, 111
Little Men 39
"A Little Too Late" 230
Livingston, Jay 176
Livingston, Robert 47
Lockhart, June 28
Longfellow, Henry Wadsworth 6
Look 13
"Look for the Rainbow" 85
Look Who's Laughing 12, 238
Lord, Del 86
Lorillard Tobacco Company 167
Lorre, Peter 170
Louis, Jean 111
The Love Boat 31, 197, 209
"Love by the Jukebox Light" 179
Love That Jill 165
"Lovebirds" 184
Lowe, Ellen 47
Lowery, Robert 60, 66, 75, 135, 140
Luke, Keye 51, 155, 177, 184
Lupino, Ida 44
Lure of the Islands 5, 13, 59–61, 64
Lux Radio Theatre 224
Lydon, James (Jimmy) **38**, 39, 169, 171
Lynn, Betty 186

MacLane, Barton 92
MacMurray, Fred 197
Main Street to Broadway 20
The Major and the Minor 73
The Male Animal 12
Malone, Dorothy 191
Man from Cheyenne **57**–59
Mann, Edward Beverly 94
Marcus Welby, M.D. 194
Margie 117
Margie's Boyfriends 236–237

Margie's Little Margie 204–205
Markey, Melinda 118
Marshall, Herbert 81, 104
Marx, Neyle 77
Mary Poppins 39
MASH 203
Masterson, Debora 32, 33
Masterson, Paul 32, 33
Masterson's Madhouse 32
Maverick 152
Maxey, Paul 51, 129, 169
The Mayor of 44th Street 241
McCoy, Homer 142, 148
McDade Pottery 7
McGuire, Neil 234
Meader, George 132, 133
"Mechanic on Duty" 205
Meet Millie 194
Megowan, Don 159
Melton, Sid 167–168
"Memories Are Made of This" 186, 191
Men Against the Sky 12, 239
"Merry-Go-Roundup" 234
The Mike Douglas Show 208
Miller, Dick 190
The Mills Brothers 66
The Milton Berle Show 207
"Mimi from Tahiti" 66
Missionary to Walker's Garage 113
Mr. and Mrs. Detective 18, 203–204
Mitchell, Les 224
Mitchell, Shirley 214
Mitrovich, Marta 242
Monogram Pictures 2, 13–14, 50, 69, 80–81, 85, 89
Montgomery, George **110**, 111
Moore, Alvy 126, 144
Moore, Gar 104
Moore, Victor **17**, **88**
Moran, Patsy 64
Moran, Polly **38**, 39
Moreland, Mantan 51, 56, 70–71, 86
Morison, Patricia **76**, 78
Motion Picture Comics 237
The Movie Game 208
Mowbray, Alan 85
Mrs. Mike 165
Mrs. Wiggs of the Cabbage Patch 85
Mulhall, Jack 65
Murder, She Wrote 32–33, 209–210
Murphy, Audie 5, **98**, 99, 237
Murphy, Ralph 85
Murray, Forbes 47
Murray, Jan 207
Murray, John Fenton 165, 182
Murrow, Edward R. 208
Museum of Broadcast Communications 33

Mustin, Burt 187
Mutiny on the Bounty 165
Mutual Broadcasting System 212, 214, 221
My Cousin Rachel 165
"My First Husband" 94
My Hero 119
"My Isle of Golden Dreams" 179
My Little Margie (comic book) 236–237
My Little Margie (radio) 20, 212–224, **213**
My Little Margie (TV) 1–3, 5, 12, 19–22, 30, 33, 45, 60, 106, 112, 114–162, **120**, **124**, 164, 165, 166, 172, 184, 193, 206, 213, 236
My Little Margie's Fashions 237
My Three Sons 196
Mystery and Mrs. see *Mr. and Mrs. Detective*

Nader, George 130, 134, 143
Nagel, Conrad 80
"The Name of My True Love" 182
Nashville 203
National Velvet 41
The Navy Comes Through 12, 241
The NBC Comedy Hour 3, 23, 162–163
Nearly Eighteen 71–73, **72**, 74
Neil, Robert see Elliott, Scott
Nelson, Frank 216, 219, 220
Nelson, Gene 196, 206
Nelson, Miriam 203
The Nestlé Company 23, 165
Neumann, Kurt 99, 100
Newman, Joe 97
Newmar, Julie 204
Nichols, Robert (Bob) 127
Nigh, William 78
A Night at the Opera 63
Night of the Lepus 113
No Hard Feelings 29
"Nobody's Sweetheart" 203
Nolan, Jeanette 97
North, Sheree 32
Not of This Earth 190
Not Wanted 44
"Now I Lay Me Down to Sleep" 181

Oakland, Ben 184
O'Brien, Edmond 106
O'Brien, Pat 241
O'Connor, Donald 30, **101**
O'Dell, Cary 33
Official Films 121
"Oh, Brother" 86
O'Keefe, Dennis **95**, 97, 237
"On Moonlight Bay" 175

"On the Sunny Side of the Street" 86
One Crowded Night 12, 40–42, **41**
O'Shea, Michael 104, 212
Oswald, Gerd 65
Our Gang 114, 153
Our Miss Brooks 33, 101, 121, 123
"Out of the Wilderness" 212
Over Easy 209

Pace, Roger 144, 158
Pacific Pioneer Broadcasters 30
Paige, Mabel 143
Panoram 233
Pantomime Quiz 18, 205, 206
Parachute Battalion 240
Parker, Cecilia 49
Parker, Fess 151
Parker, Jean 82
Parks, Bert 208
Parnell, Emory 128, 155
Parsons, Lindsley 13–14, 50, 87
Parsons, Louella O. 239
Pascal, Milton 165
The Pat Boone Chevy Showroom 207
Payne, Sally 53, 54, 58
Peary, Harold 241
Pendleton, Gaylord **41**
"Pennies from Heaven" 185
"Penthouse Serenade" 234
The People's Choice 129
Perry, the Rev. Robert 34, 35
The Perry Como Show 206, 207
Perry Mason 99
Person to Person 160, 208
"Petticoat Army" 66
Petticoat Junction 190
Philip Morris 20, 118, 122, 126, 213, 214
Phyllis 187
Piazza, Ben 12
Picerni, Paul 151, 172, 187
Pitts, ZaSu 23, 33, **164**, 168, 184, 194, 237
Playhouse 90 184
Plaza Suite 28
Poems from the Heart 228
Porter, Cole 177
Power, Tyrone 53
Powers, Dr. B.O. 13
Prescott, Ken 26
Price, Vincent 101, 205
The Professor's Gamble see *Gambling Daughters*
Pryor, Roger 49, 63
"The Puppeteers" 206

Qualen, John 167, 198, 201
Queen for a Day 154

Racket Squad 119
Raff, Robert 136

A Rainy Day in Newark 28
"Rainy Night in Rio" 182
Raleigh Hills Hospital 30–31
Ramar of the Jungle 165
Rambeau, Marjorie *95*, 96
Randall, Meg 97
Randolph, Jane 238
Rawlinson, Herbert 65
Ray, Johnnie 125
Ray, Nicholas 87
Raye, Martha 26, 190
Raymond, Gene 205
Reagan, Ronald 206, 209
The Red Badge of Courage 99
Red River Valley 5, 58
Reed, Roland 121; *see also* Roland Reed TV Productions
Reed, Walter 238
Regan, Phil *84*, 85, 86, 87, 205
Revenge of the Zombies 33, 60, 69–71, 75
Revere, Anne *41*
Reynolds, Marjorie 116
Rhine, Larry 165, 174
Rhythm Parade 65–67, 75, 86
Rice, Craig 104
Riddle, Nelson 191
The Rifleman 171
Rim of the Wheel 112–113, 243
Ritter, Tex 235
RKO-Radio Pictures 10–12, 14, 40, 42, 43, 238–239
Roach, Hal, Jr. 2, *19*, 23, 114, 118, 119, 163, 164, 165, 167
Roach, Hal, Sr. 129, 210
"Roamin' in the Gloamin'" 170
Robbins, Gale 106
Robby the Robot 192
Robert Montgomery Presents 22, 206–207
Roberts, Allan 183
Roberts, Roy 23, *24*, 124, 137, 148, 154, 156, 165, 168, 186, 237
Robot Monster 130
Rocky Jones, Space Ranger 118, 144
Rodd, Marcia 32
Rogers, Roy 5, 12, 52–54, *57*, 58–59, 208
Roland Reed TV Productions 115; *see also* Reed, Roland
Romano, Tony 172
Roosevelt, Franklin D. 81
Roosevelt, James 233
Rope 42
Rosenbloom, Maxie *62*
Rosener, George 45
Rowan, Roy 216
Rudie, Evelyn 184
Ruggles, Charles 16, *17*, 89
Russell, Bob 184
Russell, John 180
Russell, Rosalind 241
Ryan, Robert 238

Saddlemates 46–47
Sagebrush Law 241
The Saint in Palm Springs 240
St. John's Methodist Church 8, 13
Sais, Marin 47
Salerno, Nicola 194
San Jacinto High School 9
San Quentin 239, 242
Sargent, Epes 188
"School Days" 85
Scott Paper Company 119, 121, 138
Screen Directors Playhouse 224
Seabrook, Edward E. 142, 148
Sedan, Rolfe 198
Seiter, William A. 224
Sekely, Steve 70
Selander, Lesley 94
Sentimental Me 228
Seton Infirmary 7
Seventh Heaven 219
Seward, Billie 41–42
The Shaggy Dog 197
The Shakiest Gun in the West 92
Shannon, Harry *41*, *103*, 185
Shayne, Robert 203
Sheena, Queen of the Jungle 177
Sheldon, Sidney 47
Shelton, John 64
Shepodd, Jon 157
Shermet, Hazel 174
ShirleyMania 210
Shore, Dinah 207, 208; *see also The Dinah Shore Chevy Show*
Show Business 15
Shower of Stars 207
Showtime Productions 204
Shuken, Phil 166
"Since You Came Along" 50
Singleton, Doris 220
Sister Kenny 241–242
Skadden, Helen 8
Skadden, Lewis Z. 8–9
"Sleep" 190
Smart Alecks 61–63
Smart Woman 242
"Smiles for Sale" 73
Smith, C. Aubrey 81
Smith, Charles 155
Smith, John 139
Smith, Queenie 133
Snader Telescriptions 235
Softly and Tenderly 229
"Some Rain Must Fall" 183
The Song of Hiawatha 6
Song of the South 71
Sons of the Pioneers 53–54
"Soon I'll Wed My Love" 188
Sothern, Ann 49
Soundies 3, 13, 90, 233–234

"South of the Border" 188
South Pacific 28
South Shores Church 5–6, 31, 34, 35
"The Spinning Wheel" 16
Stampede 92–94
Steele, Bob 47
Step by Step 238, 241
"The Stephen Foster Story" 212
Sterling, Jan 32
The Steve Allen Show 208; *see also* Allen, Steve
Stevens, Mark **106**
Stevenson, Robert 39
Stone, Chic 236
Stranger on the Third Floor 239
Stratton, Gil, Jr. 214
Stratton Porter, Jeannette 56
Strudwick, Shepperd 100
The Stu Erwin Show 114, 118, 123
Styne, Stanley 188
The Subject Was Roses 203
Sullivan, Ed 162; *see also The Ed Sullivan Show*
Sul-Te-Wan, Madame 70
Summerville, Slim 43
Sunbonnet Sue 5, 15, 83–85, *84*, 87
Sunset Blvd. 44
Suspense (comic book) 237
"Sweet Sixteen" 50
Swing Parade of 1946 85–87
"Swinging on a Star" 235
Swiss Family Robinson 39

"Tahiti Sweetie" 5, 60
Talbot, Lyle 71
Talbott, Gloria 125
Talman, William 99–100
Talton, Alix 126
The Tammy Grimes Show 165
"Taps for the Japs" 64
Tarloff, Frank 75
Tashlin, Frank 16–17
Taylor, Dub 112
Taylor, Ferris *41*
Teichmann, Howard 28
Telescriptions 5, 234–235
Temple, Shirley 210
Templeton, William B. 182
Tewes, Lauren 209
The Texas Rangers 104, 109–111, **110**, 237
Thayer, Guy V., Jr. 47, 118, 119–120
"There Is a Tavern in the Town" 173
They Shall Have Faith see *Forever Yours*
Thiesen, Earl 13
"This Is Mary Clayton" 73
This Is Your Life 5, 206, 207
The Three Mesquiteers 47

Tight Spot 83
Tinling, James 69
Tiomkin, Dimitri 80
Todd, Thelma 165
Tom Brown's School Days 5, 10–12, 37–39, **38**, 40, 169
"Tomorrow Is Forever" 22, 206
Tomorrow the World 42
Tomorrow with Tom Snyder 209
The Tonight Show 208
Too Many Girls 12, 239
Topper 143
"Torero" 194
Towne, Gene 11, 39
The Traveling Saleswoman 101
Treen, Mary 87
Turnabout 129
Turner, Lana 15
TV Guide 155, 175, 180

Uncle Joe 42–43, 56, 165
The Underworld Story 89, 102–105, **101**, 108, 237
The Unexpected 206
Universal Pictures 17, 95, 97
The Unsinkable Molly Brown 28, 31
"The Unsung Hero" 212
The Untouchables 151

Valentino, Rudolph 179
"The Valiant Lady" 212
Vallin, Rick **72**
Vance, Vivian 27
Van Enger, Charles 99

Van Zandt, Philip 45
Vaughn, Billy 193, 227
Vega$ 201
The Veil 194
Verdugo, Elena 194
Verne, Kaaren 170
"Vieni Sue"
Vigran, Herb 45

Waikiki Wedding 190
The Waltons 130
The War of the Worlds 117
Warner, H.B. 44, 211
Warner-Lambert Pharmaceutical Company 167
Warren, Charles Marquis 112
Waterfront 118
Watt, Nathaniel (Nate) 128, 133
Webb, James R. 53
Webb, Richard 178
Wedded Blitz 241
Welk, Lawrence 23, 24–25, 165–166, 226–227
Wharton, David 7
What Ever Happened to Baby Jane? 146
What's My Line? 206, 207
Where Are Your Children? 75–79, **76**, **77**, 111
Whirlybirds 143
White, Betty 33
Whitney, Eve 203
Wildcat 26–27
Williams, Guinn "Big Boy" 60, 109

Wilson, Don 185
Win, Lose or Draw 209
Windom, William 207
Windsor, Marie 63
Winninger, Charles 164
"Winter Warm" 184, 208, 230
Winters, Jonathan 162
Wish You Were Here 22
The Wizard of Oz 185
Woman of the North Country 17, **18**, 111–112, 145
The Women Who Made Television Funny 1
Wood, Linda 22, 226–227
Wood, Randy 22–23, 26, 206, 226–228
World Day of Prayer 225
"Would You Like to Take a Walk?" 179
Wright, Will 214
Wyatt, Jane 33

Yarbrough, Jean 43, 51
Yates, Hal 116–117, 133, 151
"You" 187, 230
You Don't Say 208
"You Make Me Feel So Young" 207
Your Hit Parade 184
Your Movietown Radio Theatre 224

Zahner, Jimmy **77**
Zulu 104

www.ingramcontent.com/pod-product-compliance
Lightning Source LLC
Chambersburg PA
CBHW081547300426
44116CB00015B/2788